CHRISTIAN ETHICS.

By Dr. ADOLF WUTTKE,
LATE PROFESSOR OF THEOLOGY AT HALLE.

WITH A SPECIAL PREFACE.

By Dr. RIEHM,
EDITOR OF THE "STUDIEN UND KRITIKEN."

TRANSLATED BY

JOHN P. LACROIX.

VOLUME I.—HISTORY OF ETHICS.

NEW YORK:
NELSON & PHILLIPS.
CINCINNATI: HITCHCOCK & WALDEN.

1876.

LETTER OF AUTHORIZATION.

DECLARATION.

WE, the representatives of the family of the late Dr. Adolf *Wuttke*, Professor of Theology at Halle on the Saale, have thankfully accepted the proposition of Professor JOHN P. LACROIX to translate into English the deceased author's *Christliche Sittenlehre* (Wiegandt & Grieben, Berlin, 1864–5), and we gladly second the wish of the esteemed translator by expressly and formally authorizing him, on our part, to publish the work in the English language.

MRS. PROFESSOR WUTTKE,

DR. EDUARD RIEHM,
  (as Guardian of the children).

HALLE, *March* 8, 1872.

NOTE OF TRANSLATOR.

In my labor upon this translation I have aimed at the truest practical reproduction, sentence by sentence, of the thoughts of the author. This method I deliberately preferred, rather than incur the risk of impairing the clearness of thought by entirely recasting the forms of speech. In a few cases I have employed unusual compounds, rather than resort to paraphrases or to an undue multiplication of subordinate clauses. On the whole, I am persuaded that those who are best acquainted with the difficulties of the original will be most indulgent toward the style of the version. This first volume, although only the Introduction to the entire work, is yet a complete whole in itself, viz., a survey of the whole current of the ethical thought of humanity from the earliest dawn of scientific reflection down to the latest results in Christian theology.

The motives that led me to undertake the translation have been various. Esteemed teachers exhorted me thereto, as soon as notices of the work began to appear. German scholars spoke to me enthusiastically of its unparalleled excellence. My chief motive, however, has been a compound of gratitude and hope,—gratitude to the devout thinker whose work had been, to me, the medium of so much spiritual good,—and a hope of helping others to the same good. For, in fact, no other human production has lifted, for me, so many vails from shadowy places in Revelation and Providence; none has worked so effectually in definitively directing my mind and heart toward that Light which stands, serene and ever-brightening, over against the comfortless spectacle of the successive and rapid extinguishment of every effort at social reform which does not kindle its torch at the central Source of all light. And no labor

that I have ever performed has been attended with such a joyous consciousness that the very toil itself was self-rewarding.

As to the specific merits of the work, I am happy to refer the reader to the considerate words of the distinguished theologian of Halle, Dr. Riehm, in the special preface which he has prepared for this translation. I could also, were it desirable, fill many pages with words of highest praise from the most respectable and the most diverse sources. And the praise is bestowed not only upon its scientific worth, but largely also upon the spirit of its author. All critics accord in testifying that we have to do here with a man singularly endowed with keenness of philosophic insight and with devoutness of Christian faith.

Whether, however, there is need here in America—where there is so strong a proclivity to run away after every glittering theological or social novelty, and where there are so many evidences that the general consciousness both of preachers and of people is not thoroughly enough grounded upon the central truths of the Gospel—of a work such as this (a work which, in so masterly a manner, brings the whole moral life into vital relation to its only possible Source, and which sweeps away so thoroughly every social or religious theory which does not stand the touch-stone of plain Bible-truth), it is for others to judge. We have been led to augur favorably, however, both from our own studies in the field and also from the expressed views of many of our most progressive teachers of ethics, viz., that there is a loud call for something more solidly philosophical and more thoroughly evangelical than is afforded by our common text-books on Moral Science;* and we feel pretty confident that few who once drink of the fresh thought-stream here opened will be disposed to dissent from the well-known utterance† of Dr. Hengstenberg, that Wuttke's *Ethics* ought to have its place in every pastor's library.

J. P. L.

* See Dr. Warren's *Introduction* to Vol. II.
† See *Evangelische Kirchenzeitung*, (Berlin), Sept. 4, 1861.

SPECIAL PREFACE TO THIS TRANSLATION.*

THE author of the work which here appears in English, Dr. Carl Friedrich *Adolf Wuttke*, has won for himself a distinguished place in the evangelical Church and theology of Germany. A few items as to his life and activity, and as to the spirit and character of his endeavors, may serve to call attention to a work which is widely circulated and much read throughout Germany.

Born in Breslau, November 10, 1819, in humble life, the young Wuttke obtained his preparatory education under circumstances of great difficulty and self-denial. In 1840 he entered the University of Breslau in view of studying theology, but he found very little satisfaction in the theology that was there taught. The superficial Rationalism which then prevailed in Breslau violently repelled him, and drove him at once and forever to a position of antagonism to this stand-point. As neither his religious nor his scientific wants found satisfaction in his theological teachers, he endeavored to satisfy the latter, at least, by turning his attention primarily and chiefly to philosophy. To this end he possessed dialectic talents of unusual excellence, and he received from the celebrated and, then, fully mature *Braniss* fruitful inspiration. His academic career he began in 1848, in Breslau, as Doctor and *privat-docent* of philosophy. His preferred field was the Philosophy of Religion. This led him to thorough studies in the history of religions. A fruit of his studies he has embodied in his "*History of Heathenism* in respect to religion, knowledge, art,

---

* *Dr. Riehm*, who has kindly furnished me this general preface, and to whom I am indebted for many valuable suggestions in regard to my undertaking, is one of the professors of theology at Halle, and also editor-in-chief of the *Studien und Kritiken.*—TR.

Morals and Politics, (Breslau, 1852–53),—a work which established his reputation as a scholar. Utilizing his extensive acquaintance with the historical material, his chief endeavor was to give here a faithful objective presentation of the subject-matter, and to avoid doing it violence by forcing it into harmony with preconceived theories,—and his success was so great as to obtain for him the warm recognition, among others, of that master of Indian antiquities, Dr. A. *Weber* of Berlin. At the same time, however, he was also able to present the religioso-historical matter in a clear synoptical order, and to elucidate it from higher religioso-philosophical stand-points.

The more he pursued his studies in the history and philosophy of religions, so much the more fully and renewedly he became convinced that the highest and the only soul-satisfying knowledge of the truth is to be found only by merging one's self into the Holy Scriptures and into the therein-witnessed revelations of the living God; hence he felt himself more and more attracted back to the field of theology. In 1853 he obtained the degree of Licentiate in Theology, and changed his field of instruction from philosophy to that of theology; having been called to Berlin, in November, 1854, to an extraordinary professorship of theology, he found an enlarged and appreciative sphere for the exercise of his gifts.— In virtue of his firm and independent nature—partly inborn and partly developed in the severe school of experience—he felt also a pressing need of a firmly-based construction of his theological views, and of a clear, distinct, and unambiguous expression of the same. This need was in part met by the Lutheran form of doctrine. It is true, he saw very clearly the defects and imperfections which a scientific construction and demonstration of this doctrinal formula bring to light; taking into consideration, however, its essential features, he found in it the purest and truest didactic presentation of evangelical truth.* To preserve this form of the truth in its main features,

---

* As a German Protestant, Dr. Wuttke had practically only two choices in his Church-relations, namely, between the Lutheran Church and the Reformed or Calvinistic Church. The so-called "United" Church of Prussia has little more than a legal existence, the individual societies having mostly remained essentially Lutheran or Reformed, as before the union.—TR.

and by his own deeper study of the Scriptures as well as by earnest systematic thought so to raise it to a new scientific construction that it should express the truth of the Bible in a still richer degree, and that in its form and demonstration it should answer the requirements made upon it by the present stand-point of theology and philosophy, and that it might be raised to a more full development also in fields wherein it had as yet attained only to an imperfect and very inadequate expression,—such was the life-task to which Dr. Wuttke felt himself, with ever-deepening conviction, called by God. And this life-task he endeavored, in the greatest conscientiousness and in the most unwearied and exhausting labor, to fulfill. And the animating spring of his labor was the consciousness so repeatedly expressed by him, that theology *is intrusted with the preservation of sacred treasures.* Fidelity in preserving the intrusted truth-treasure,—such is the animating spirit of his theologico-scientific labor; and with this fidelity are connected the limits and imperfections of the same. In this fidelity he was earnestly resolute, even in the face of the coryphei of theological and philosophical speculation, in rejecting all views and thought-constructions which seemed to him foreign to the spirit of the Holy Scriptures, however much they might seem to be characterized by profundity or by loftiness of thought, and however much they might bedazzle by brilliant ingenuity and by their artful application to Biblical ideas. This fidelity made him a decided opponent of all efforts which he regarded as bent on seeking an accommodation between faith and unbelief. In this fidelity he deliberately consented to sacrifice the favor and approbation of the majority of his contemporaries; and he neglected no opportunity, where he felt the duty of championing the pure evangelical truth and of assailing perversions and misrepresentations of the same, manfully and with open visor to enter the lists, and to fight it out with keen weapons and without respect of persons. It is true he has, in his earnestness, not always awarded due honor to the views of the *ideally*-inclined theologians, nor to the results of historical and critical Scripture-examination. For his own person, however, he was, in this work, never concerned, nor for the interests of any party, but solely and simply for Christian truth and for the kingdom of God.

In this sense and spirit he exercised his office of theological teacher in Berlin. One can well imagine how glad the late Dr. Hengstenberg was to have found in him so able a co-laborer, and also that he became warmly and intimately attached to his younger colleague.* But also the other members of the Berlin faculty, though in part of different churchly and theological tendencies, fully appreciated his scientific ability and his faithful and fruitful academic activity; and they expressed their esteem publicly by conferring upon him, in 1860, the doctorate of theology.

In the autumn of 1861 he accepted a call to an ordinary professorship of systematic theology in our university at Halle. Although, as the representative of a strictly churchly theology, he stood here somewhat isolated, still the positive evangelical tendency (a tendency based on faith in the revelations and redemptive acts of God as witnessed in the Scriptures) of the other members of the faculty (and among them the universally known and revered Dr. *Tholuck*) afforded a broad and firm basis for a richly productive official co-operation. Highly esteemed by his colleagues for his straight-forwardness, reliableness, punctuality, and conscientious fidelity in all his official duties, he exercised, here, his calling as teacher in a circle of hearers, at first relatively narrow, but which soon grew visibly larger, especially in the case of his lectures on Christian ethics; and he had the joy of seeing the seed, he had sown, spring up and bear fruit in many youthful hearts,—until on the 12th of April, 1870, after a brief sickness, it pleased the Lord whom he served to permit him, unexpectedly early, to pass from faith to sight.

Along-side of his more specific professional activity, Dr. Wuttke was always ready to serve the church by special addresses, in ecclesiastical and other assemblies, on weighty questions of the day. Quite a number of these addresses have been published in Hengstenberg's "Evangelical Church Journal." To one of them, which was delivered in 1858, at a church-diet at Hamburg, is due the preparation of his widely-popular and excellent work, "The German Popular

* Dr. Wuttke, however, was free from the ultra-confessionalism of Hengstenberg; he even favored the "Union." See *Neue evangelische Kirchenzeitung* of May 7, 1870.—TR.

Superstition of the Present," which appeared in 1860 in its first, and in 1869 in a new and enlarged second, edition. This work combines laborious selection with a lucid grouping of the abundant material, and is inspired by a vital interest for the health of the German national life and for the healing of its defects by the divine power of the Gospel.

For the judgment and appreciation of some portions of the work here presented to the public, it will not be out of place to observe that the author took a lively and active part also in the political life of the nation. As early as during the revolutionary storm of 1848 he defended for a while, as editor of a conservative journal in Königsberg, the cause of legal order and of the government. And during his activity among us,—though in other respects living in the greatest seclusion,—he frequently appeared publicly, in political meetings in Halle and in other towns of the province of Saxony, as the spokesman of the constitutional party; and once he took part also in the labors of the national diet, to which the confidence of his fellow-citizens had called him.

The work here given to the English-reading public, *Christian Ethics*, which appeared in 1861–'62 in its first, and in 1864–'65 in its second, revised and enlarged, edition, is Dr. Wuttke's only considerable *theological* work. He has here entered upon a field, the cultivation of which, his special life-task as above indicated, must have pressed upon him with very great urgency. Upon no other field had the scientific treatment of the theology he represented, remained to such a degree imperfect and unsatisfactory. Although Christian ethics, after the precedent of *Danæus* on the Calvinistic side, had been raised by Calixtus to the dignity of an independent theological science, nevertheless the prevalent one-sidedly dogmatic interest hindered and prevented its thorough development. And when finally, since the last decade of the last century, a more lively scientific interest was turned to the subject, then, unfortunately, Christian ethics became involved in an almost slavish dependence upon the philosophical systems of a *Kant*, a *Fichte*, a *Fries*, a *Hegel*, and a *Herbart*, as they successively rose and followed each other. From this cramping pupilage, ethics was indeed emancipated by the Reconstructor of the collective body of German theology,

Schleiermacher, and also radically renovated from the basis of the *specifically Christianly-ethical principle.* But in Schleiermacher, as well as in *Rothe*, Christian ethics appeared rather in the garb of theologico-philosophical speculation; it was not based directly upon the Holy Scriptures; on the contrary, these highly deserving men endeavored to be just to the positive Biblical basis of evangelical Protestantism by undertaking to reconstruct the contents of the Holy Scriptures directly out of the Christian consciousness; in a word, these ethical systems stood in no manner of close connection with ecclesiastical dogmatics. On the other hand, *Harless* had produced an ethics based directly upon, and derived from, the Scriptures; but in his method he had disdained the learned structure and the dialectical procedure of modern science. *Wuttke* was the *first* theologian who made the attempt, upon the foundation* of the Lutheran dogmatical ground-views as enriched and vitalized by personal self-immersion in the study of the Scriptures, to carry out, by means of the dialectical method, (which theology had assumed at the time of the supremacy of philosophy), a strictly scientific, organic structure of Christian ethics, which should embody in itself the fruits of precedent labors upon this field, and also polemically elucidate its relation to the various other ethical systems. In this work, however, he makes no other use of this dialectical method than simply to purify theological ethics from all elements foreign or hostile to the Biblico-ecclesiastical ground-thoughts, and to bring these ground-thoughts to more complete expression by process of inner self-development. Hence the great majority of churchly-minded theologians could, with great reason, welcome in Wuttke the, until then, lacking scientific standard-bearer upon the field of

---

* That in the construction of his ethical system, Dr. Wuttke did not allow the Lutheran symbols to construe the Bible, but on the contrary measured them *by* the Bible, and freely criticized them where found defective, we have both his own reiterated avowal (as where, § 80, he declares it his purpose to write, not an ethics of this or that Church, but a Christian Ethics; and where, in his preface, p. 4, he declares the governing principles of his labors to be "honest loyalty to the Gospel"); and also his actual contrasting of the Lutheran and the Reformed ground-views (see § 37), and his ample admission that the Lutheran view *needs* to be complemented.—Tr.

ethics; and consequently his work met with an astonishingly rapid circulation and a thankful reception. But also those who—as the writer of this preface *—stand in many respects upon the ground of other theological convictions, and who do not fully agree with many views and judgments expressed in the work, have every reason highly to prize this system of Ethics, and for the following reasons: because of its firm Biblical foundation,—because of its sharp and clear vindication and presentation of the ethical ground-thoughts of the Holy Scriptures against, and in the face of, various wide-spread errors and prevalent thought-currents of the day,— because of its thoroughly carried-out aim, in connection with all the rigor of a scientific method, to present in broad and clear light the sublime directness and simplicity of the truth of the Gospel,—because of the richness of the subject-matter which it presents, and—to mention especially one single feature—because of the exceedingly valuable, and hitherto almost entirely lacking, history both of the science of ethics and also of the ethical consciousness itself.

I doubt not, therefore, that this work will meet with a hearty welcome also in America and in England, and that too in theological circles which, while not sharing the special ecclesiastical views of the author, will yet not fail worthily to appreciate his conscientious fidelity to Scripture-truth and the scientific significancy of his labors; and I feel confident that the work will prove serviceable in the promotion of a healthy and practically-fruitful theological knowledge.

Dr. Eduard Riehm,
Professor, in ordinary, of Theology at Halle.

Halle, March 14th, 1872.

* I am indebted to Dr. P. Schaff for the following: " Dr. Riehm is a liberal Unionist of the critical school of Hupfeld, his predecessor."—Tr.

AUTHOR'S PREFACE

TO THE FIRST EDITION.

———◆•◆———

THE theology of the nineteenth century has aimed at giving special prominence to the ethical phase of Christianity; and yet, strangely enough, the scientific treatment of Christian ethics has shown, as compared to the other branches of theology, a far inferior productiveness, and in fact a degree of barrenness. This phenomenon is not explainable from any precedent over-fruitfulness, nor from any unquestioning satisfaction with any already-attained relatively-definitive perfection of the science, nor from the imposing pre-eminence of any exceptionally great author; on the contrary, every competent theologian knows perfectly well that no other branch of theology is so far from having reached any, even relatively, settled completeness and generally-accepted form and contents, as precisely the science of ethics. Even the very idea, contents, and boundaries of ethics, are as yet in many respects so unsettled that the different presentations of the science have often only very remote resemblances to each other;

and there are some recent theologians who look upon the ethical field as something like an ownerless primeval forest wherein they are at liberty to roam at simple discretion and to give free scope to all sorts of pet speculations. We would of course not wish to shut the field of theology against philosophical thought; on the contrary, we regard its scientific completion as possible only on condition of its permeation with mature philosophical thought-labor. In view, however, of the not only manifold, but also (in very deep-reaching and essential ground-principles) self-contradicting philosophical systems of the time, we could not advise Theology—that guardian of sacred treasures—to cast itself away, in characterless self-forgetfulness, into the arms of the first transiently-shining philosophical system, and to seek its glory only in a pliable self-conformity to the rapidly-passing Protean forms of the philosophies of the day. Remarkable indeed, though not precisely very praiseworthy, is the metamorphic capability of those theologians who have kept pace in their theology with the entire history of philosophy from Kant down to Hegel, and have furnished the public at each decade with an entirely different form of theology. It is not scientific truthfulness to attempt violently to force together irreconcilable elements; and it is high time that the day were past when men presume to introduce Spinozistic and other kindred Hegelian

conceptions into Christian ethics as its own contents proper. We fully recognize the high services of precisely the latest forms of philosophy, for the science of ethics; but we must guard against allowing theological ethics, as conscious of its divinely revealed contents, and as basing itself upon the holy Scriptures, to be cramped and thrown into the background by these philosophical systems. Precisely the most recent developments in this field justify us in entertaining, at this point, a prudent distrust. The manner in which some have introduced philosophical, or a so-called " theological, speculation " into the field of Christian ethics, reminds one only too much of the feats of the suitors of Penelope in the house of Ulysses, who presume to cast their footstools at the head of the returning master, and yet prove incapable even of bending the bow of the hero, to say nothing of shooting through the twelvefold target.

What we attempt in the present work is neither speculative ethics nor yet Biblical ethics in the sense of a purely exegetico-historical science, but, in fact, a system of theological ethics based on the substance and spirit of the Bible, and constructed into a scientific form, not by the help of a philosophy foreign to that spirit, but by the inner self-development of the spirit itself. Whether we have properly comprehended this spirit, and whether we have faithfully *learned* from the general

2

history of science, including also philosophy, others
will have to judge; this much, however, we know,
that we have endeavored to acquire such learning
only in honest loyalty to the Gospel. And the fact
that we have omitted to employ many technical
forms that have been imposed upon this science by
ingenious authors, will, we hope, be regarded, by
those who have grown familiar with said forms, as at
least an indication of a sincere endeavor on our part
to avoid breaking the impression of simple evangelical truth by any element foreign to the spirit of
the Scriptures, however much it may enjoy the pres-
tige of profundity, and however artfully it may have
been fitted upon Christian ideas.

BERLIN, *Dec.* 31, 1860.

AUTHOR'S PREFACE

TO THE SECOND EDITION.

------·------

WITHIN a surprisingly brief period a new edition of this System of Ethics has become necessary.

To many critics of the work we feel ourselves thankfully indebted; of others, however, we regret to have to say that, instead of scientific earnestness, they have manifested only passionate hostility. It is true, we have gone at our work with honesty and plainness of speech, and have touched somewhat ungently upon certain sore places in the more recent forms of theology; and the tone of ill-will in which the opposers have indulged would seem to indicate that the right spot has been probed; and we are in fact cheerfully ready to be subjected to the most searching criticism. There is an immense difference, however, between actual confutation and unworthy abuse. Some critics have charged this work with being an "*attentat*" against the "inalienable" con-

quests of modern science; this sounds almost as badly as when, in times past, a certain class of theologians spoke of "*attentats*" against the teachings of the Church and against the symbolical books. There is, in fact, in the field of contemporary unbelief both an "orthodoxy" which does not stand a whit behind the intolerance of former and much-despised ages in its hereticating of dissenters, and an authority-faith in the so-called "heroes" of contemporary science, which exalts the pretentions of the said science to infallibility in exact proportion as it is zealous against a real faith in the Scriptures, and tramples their claims into the dust. Just such a deference to writers who let only *their own* light shine, (a light kindled not at the divine light, but only at the faintly-shining wisdom of the anti-Christian world,) still weighs down like an Alp upon the theology of the present day, and especially upon ethics; and to do battle against a spiritual despotism of this character, must be to take a step in the direction of true progress. Incredulity constitutes, in fact, in our day no slight recommendation; will the public, therefore, not let us enjoy the advantage of a little incredulity as to the Apostolical calling

of certain recent authors who have forced the Pantheism of Spinoza into the doctrines of Christianity? We are not unaware, however, that only that one can hope for favor and popularity with the multitude of to-day, who makes amends for his faith in the living Christ by strewing incense upon the altars of the divinities of recent literature,—who fuses together the Apostolical doctrines with the unquestioningly infallible-assumed "results of modern culture," —in a word, who selects the golden middle-way between simple evangelical faith and God-denying unbelief: the tints just now in vogue are indefinite and indesignable. We frankly confess that, in scientific respects, we can less readily come to an understanding with this nondescript olla-podrida theology than with those who make a clean sweep of Christianity at once. Upon firm earth one can walk erect, in water one can swim; but in a miry marsh, which mingles earth and water together, one can neither walk nor swim. We must submit to let those who imagine that they stand or swim upon the heights of "modern" culture look disdainfully down upon us, and reproach us with not being abreast with the times; let them do that to which they are called;

we, however, have a sure prophetic word, and we think we do well to give heed to it as to a light that shines in a dark place, until the day dawn and the morning-star arise in the hearts of all, [2 Peter i, 19]; and we feel confident that in so doing we have chosen the "good part, which will not be taken from us" when the specious fruits of the un-Christian culture of the day shall be swept away, without leaving a trace, by the streams of still newer progress. To those to whom appreciation for recent science is synonymous with an unconditional homage to every pretentiously-rising system, we must be content to appear as non-appreciative; meantime, however, may we not suggest that these gentlemen would do well to come to an understanding among themselves as to precisely *which* of the more recent and violently inter-contradictory systems represents the real progress proper, and as to *how long* it will do so, before we be peremptorily required to disregard the exhortation of the Holy One, to "hold that fast which thou hast, that no man take thy crown" [Rev. iii, 11]. We regard it as the first scientific duty of a true truth-seeker not to suffer himself to be captivated by the flickering glare of great names

and by the sham-gold of pretended latest discoveries, and not to let himself be intoxicated and carried away by the indiscriminate applause of the multitude. We greatly rejoice to see that precisely the most recent productions upon the field of ethics (Harless, Schmid, Palmer) give proof of evangelical soundness, and we shall anxiously await to see whether the rapidly-erring and deteriorating "theology of progress" will not, in its turn, enter upon this field,—whether Rothe, who (encouraged and urged on by the well-calculated applause of this party) shows as yet no signs of hesitation to do service in the ranks of the sympathizers with Strauss and Renan, will not make up his mind to turn to the service of sound words, or whether in the interest of an erroneous system he will drive even still deeper the wounds which he has already inflicted upon evangelical faith,—to which at bottom his heart belongs.

Halle, *August,* 1864.

CONTENTS.

CONTENTS.

CHRISTIAN ETHICS.

------◆◆◆◆◆------

INTRODUCTION.

I. IDEA OF ETHICS, AND THE POSITION OF THIS SCIENCE IN THE FIELD OF SCIENCE IN GENERAL.

SECTION I.

ETHICS, as belonging to the sphere both of philosophy and of theology, is the science of the *moral*, and hence *Christian* ethics is the science of Christian morals. But the moral lies in the sphere of the freedom of rational creatures, as in contrast to mere nature-objects. Man, as a rational being, has the end of his life, not as one realizing itself in him spontaneously and with unconditional necessity, but, on the contrary, he has it primarily only ideally, in his rational consciousness, so that he cannot attain to it by a mere unconscious letting himself alone, but only by a personally and freely-willed life-activity; but also, for that very reason, he can fail of it by his own fault;—and the essence of this life-development of man, as relating to the realizing of his rational life-purpose, is the *moral;* that is, when normal, the morally-*good*, and when guiltily-perverted, the morally-*evil.*

So much merely preliminarily; the more complete demonstration can be given only further on. The sphere of freedom is that of the moral; whatever is moral is essentially free, and whatever is free is moral. There is, indeed, an immorally-

incurred unfreedom, but even this unfreedom is essentially different from the unfreedom of nature. He who, in contradiction to the Christian as well as to the universally-human consciousness, denies moral freedom in general, and places even man's moral activity into the sphere of unconditional necessity, may indeed give a *description* of the seemingly-moral, but he cannot place upon man a moral *requirement;* in the presence of the "must" the "should" disappears. Such a denier would at least have to regard the contradictory and almost universal consciousness of freedom as also posited by unconditional necessity —thus surrendering all right to assail the same. We may therefore here preliminarily presuppose it as the utterance of the general human consciousness when not perverted by one-sided theories, that the moral lies neither in the sphere of cognition nor of natural necessity, but in the sphere of the freedom of the rational will. Where there is no freedom of will, there we speak neither of the morally-good nor of the morally-evil. Moral willing, however, is not of a blind, fortuitous, but of a rational, character; that is, it wills a rational something, something willed by God, and that too in a rational manner—or, indeed, it wills it *not;* but also this non-willing, that is, the morally-evil, relates, though negatively, to a rational end.

In the Scriptures, the ethical phase of Christian doctrine is designated as "the knowledge of God's will in all wisdom and spiritual understanding" (Col. i, 9); that is, of that which God "requires" of us (Deut. x, 12; comp. Phil. iv, 8). Of other definitions of ethics we will mention but the more important. Unquestionably all such are to be rejected as express merely an outward collection of single moral thoughts, as, *e. g.*, "an ordered digest of rules by which man, and, more specifically, a Christian, is to shape his life;" this would not be a science, but only a collection of material for a science; moreover, rules are only one phase of the moral thought, for rules must have a basis, an end, and an inner logical unity, all of which lies outside of this definition. Many writers designate ethics as the *description* of a morally normal development. But, properly speaking, only that can be described which is real; not, however, that which simply *ought*, but is not *necessitated*, to become real. Even the describing of the person of Christ as the ideal of the moral, gives only a part of Christian ethics, inasmuch as Christ could

not, in his actual life, represent *all* the phases of the moral. And besides, ethics has not merely to do with the morally-normal, but it has also to treat of sin and the contest with it as an actual power; and, moreover, it has not merely to describe, but also to prove and to establish.

The majority of theological moralists present at once the definition of *Christian* ethics; but this more restricted notion cannot be understood without the more comprehensive notion of ethics in general. The declaration (Harless and others) that ethics is the theoretical presentation of the Christianly-normal life-course, or the development-history of man as redeemed by Christ, is both too narrow and too broad at the same time: too narrow, inasmuch as ethics must unquestionably speak also of the *non*-normal life-course, and that, too, not merely incidentally and introductorily, but as of one of its essential elements; and too broad, because, in fact, many things belong to such a life-course which belong *not* to the sphere of the moral, but to the objective workings of divine grace upon the moral subject. Such a definition is rather that of the order of Christian salvation, which, however, is not wholly embraced in the notion of the moral. It is true, Christian ethics must take into consideration the workings of divine grace, but only, however, as its presupposition; the becoming seized upon by the influence of divine grace *leads*, indeed, to morality, but lies not itself in the moral sphere. According to *Schleiermacher*, Christian ethics is " the presentation of communion with God as conditioned by communion with Christ, the Redeemer, in so far as this communion with God is the motive of all the actions of the Christian, or the description of that manner of action which springs from the domination of the Christianly-determined self-consciousness;"* this, however, is two mutually complementing definitions, each of which expresses by itself only one phase of ethics.

As to the name applied to the science, the German expression "Sittenlehre," usual since the time of Mosheim, is ambiguous, being capable of being understood as the doctrine of customs instead of the doctrine of the moral. The term *ethics* is the most ancient, as dating from Aristotle himself; ἦθος, radically related to ἔθος, from the root ἔζω, " to set " and " to sit," signifies in Homer the seat, the dwelling-place, the home, and hence, at

* *Christl. Sitte*, pp. 32, 33.

a later period, that which has become the fixed definite home of the spirit—that wherein the spirit feels itself at home as in its own peculiar element, and hence *manner*, primarily in the sense of habit; that is, a manner of action as having become second nature. In this sense the word ἦθη occurs also in the New Testament (1 Cor. xv, 33.) But the signification of the word advances, further, to that of the moral proper, as objective-grown custom, which presents itself to the individual with the authority of law; ἦθος is therefore a spiritual power to which the individual subordinates himself, as in contradistinction to the rude lawlessness of man as uncultured and savage, and which, in so far as it is no longer a power foreign and opposed to man, appears as *character.** The Romans used generally, for this idea, the term *mores*, and hence Cicero and Seneca speak of a *philosophia moralis*. In Germany this science was formerly called "Moral"—*theologia s. philosophia moralis*—and frequently also *theologia s. philosophia practica*. But after the word "Moral" had been appropriated by the advocates of deistic illumin-ism, and degraded into the most spiritless superficiality, the term became involved in such prejudicial associations that later writers preferred to avoid it, and resorted again to the German term used by Mosheim, or to the one originally used by Aristotle.

SECTION II.

As a *philosophical* science, ethics forms a part of the philosophy of the spirit,—has as presuppositions speculative theology and psychology, and stands in the closest relation to the science of history as the objective realization of the moral life. As standing within the science of spirit, it presents, as in contrast to *knowledge*, the *active* phase of the rational spirit-life, whereby man, as having come to rational self-con-sciousness, makes into reality that which exists in him primarily only as an idea,—makes his spiritually-rational nature as existing objectively to him into a nature freely-willed and posited by himself.

* Aristot., *Eth. Nic.*, i, 13.

All philosophy has to do essentially with three objects: the thoughts of God, of nature, and of the human spirit. Ethics, as belonging to the third sphere, has, co-ordinate to itself within this sphere, the science of *psychology* as treating of the nature of the individual mind and of its development, and the science of *history* as portraying the development of the collective spirit; it is in some sense the unity of the two; it is psychology, in that it presents, in fact, the highest form of the soul-life, the rationally-free life; and it is history, in that it embraces man not as isolated, but as an organic member of the whole, and considers his activity as directed toward the rational shaping of collective humanity. Ethics gives to history its rational goal; and all morality has the perfect shaping of universal history as its ultimate end. A real understanding of history is not possible without ethics; universal history is the realization of the moral—the good and also the evil—within humanity; hence history, the actual contents of which lie of course outside of the sphere of purely philosophical knowledge, is an important teacher of morality—teaching by example in sacred history, and by caution and warning in profane.

The position here assigned to philosophical ethics takes the definition of that science in its widest sense, and embraces also *right* and *art*. While the view which merges morality essentially into either right or art is very one-sided and a mistaking of the nature of the moral in general, it would not be less erroneous entirely to shut out the moral from these two spheres, and to place it simply *along-side* of them; the moral is rather, as the *superior* element, *above* them, and right and art have truth only in so far as they are special realization-forms of the moral; there is, in truth, no immoral right and no immoral beauty, although by sinful man the wrong is often regarded as right, and the un-beautiful as beautiful.

Schleiermacher, in his Philosophical Ethics, gives a definition of philosophical ethics, based on the views of Fichte and Schelling, which entirely differs from the usual one. In assuming two chief sciences, that of nature and that of reason, whereof each may be treated either empirically or speculatively, according as the reality or the essence of the object is more directly taken into view, he obtains four sciences in all. The empirical science of nature is natural history; the speculative science of nature is

physics; the empirical science of reason is history; the speculative science of reason is ethics. Hence ethics "is the knowledge of the essence of reason," and stands in the same relation
to history as speculation to experience, and is hence essentially
the philosophy of history. Under such conditions it would be
more correct to call ethics the philosophy of the *spirit;* but
Schleiermacher evades this, no less manifest than necessary,
consequence; logic and psychology belong, according to him,
not to ethics, for psychology corresponds to natural history, and
hence is "the empirical knowledge of the activity of the spiritual;" and logic belongs, empirically-treated, to psychology, and,
speculatively-treated, to physics.* Though, by means of this
strange conception of logic and psychology, the immeasurable
sphere of ethics as fixed by the first definition is somewhat reduced, still there yet remains for it a very unusually wide field,
and it embraces, with the exception of physics, the whole of
philosophical theology and of the philosophy of history; and
as natural history and physics have like extent of field, differing
only in point of view taken, so the fields of empirical history
and of ethics are also co-extensive, and ethics is nothing other
than the speculative consideration of history. "History is the
example-book of ethics, and ethics is the form-book of history;"
but history is, when so viewed, every thing which is not mere
nature; and as, in the highest instance, nature and reason are essentially identical, nature being reason, and reason nature, hence
"in the highest view of the matter ethics is physics and physics
ethics," whereas in a lower view of the matter ethics is conditioned, as to contents and form, by physics, and physics by ethics.
It is evident at once that according to these definitions ethics is
something entirely other than what is usually understood thereby in the scientific world; and it involves not a little courage
to undertake to justify the applying of the term ethics to this
extensive field. This scientifically-unjustifiable extension of the
field of ethics has occasioned much confusion; and Rothe's
"Theological Ethics" suffers also from this lack of limitation,
whereas Schleiermacher himself carefully avoided applying to
theological ethics this philosophical conception, which in fact
sprang more from an ingenious thought-play than from an inner
consequential development of the ground-principle. Indeed,

* *System der Ethik*, edited by Schweizer, 1835, §§ 55, *sqq.*, 60, 61, 87.

even in his philosophical ethics, Schleiermacher very soon introduces a much narrower notion, without any logical justification
thereto in his system. Thus ethics is, presently, made to appear as "the scientific presentation of human *action*," which
manifestly cannot be regarded as identical with the notion of
the "speculative knowledge of the essence of reason." But also
this new declaration is much too indefinite; it is not action in
general, but *moral* action, that belongs to ethics. Should we
thus find this narrower definition too comprehensive still, then
we are relieved by the declaration that ethics is the "speculative knowledge of the collective activity of reason upon nature,"
and are at once thrown into a field so narrow as to be obliged
to exclude from ethics a very essential, nay, the most essential,
part of this science. For all morality is not embraced in an
activity of reason upon *nature;* in however wide a sense "nature" be taken, still it always stands over against reason as of a
different character,—is that which, in empirical respects, constitutes the field of natural science, natural history, etc. The
moral cultivation of the heart—humility, truthfulness, the moral
disposition in general, the whole sphere of the purely spiritual
life—belongs not *at all* to this activity upon nature. On the
other hand, this definition is also much too comprehensive, inasmuch as there may be also an extra-moral and an immoral
interpenetration of reason and nature, and an immoral activity
of reason upon nature; but should it be said that this, now
would not be the true moral reason, then this would vir
tually imply that the moral is to be sought elsewhere than in
this activity of reason upon nature,—would place it in reason as
such. As, in the view of Schleiermacher, ethics is only the
speculative reverse-side of history, hence he requires, consequentially enough, that it be presented essentially historically. "The
style of ethics is the historical; for only where manifestation
and law are given as the same is the view taken a scientific one.
Hence the style can be neither imperative nor consultative. The
form of ethics is the development of a theoretical view. The
formula of the 'should' is entirely inadmissible, as this formula
rests upon an antagonism to the law, whereas it is the part of
science to present this antagonism as a mere *appearance*." This
position, (harmonizing with the view expressed in his "Discourses on Religion,") which, from the stand-point of Panthe-

istic determinism, is quite consequential, we simply mention in passing, in order to explain, in some manner, this position of ethics in Schleiermacher. Even as the other speculative science, namely, physics, does not present what should be, but what really is and must be, so also Pantheistic ethics has to do only with the "is" and the "must be," but not with the "should;" *all* reality is here rational; all disagreement with the law is mere appearance; there exists nothing else than what *must* be; hence ethics has simply to present for the reason-life the laws, even as physics, for the nature-life, and is just as certain of the agreement of reality with these laws as astronomy is certain of the occurrence of a calculated eclipse of the moon. On the contrary, so soon as by the admission of moral will-freedom, even the *possibility* of an antagonism of moral reality to the moral law is conceded, ethics presents itself at once with the *should;* for the moral law has unconditional validity, whether man really fulfills it or not. Ethics is only in so far purely historical as perfect morality is also personal reality; hence *Christian* ethics bears, indeed, essentially *also* a historical character, because Christ is, for it, the moral ideal;—for others, however, it bears the form of the "should." Pantheistic ethics makes collective humanity the real expression of the moral idea,—makes humanity its Christ. And that Schleiermacher's philosophical ethics is by no means free of a Pantheistic character, is undeniable.

Hegel conceives of ethics as one of the phases of the Philosophy of the Spirit, and more specifically as the sphere of the *objective* spirit in contradistinction to that of the subjective, which embraces anthropology, the phenomenology of the spirit, and psychology. The spirit, as having come to itself and become free, realizes itself, in that, as free rational will, it posits itself outwardly,—forms for itself a world corresponding to itself, which is the expression of the spirit. This objective reality of the free spirit, which becomes for the individual subject an objective power whereby the subject is determined in his freedom, and which consequently is to be recognized by the individual, is, as of a universal character, *for* the individual, law. Hence this will of objective rationality is *right,* which becomes for the individual, *duty.* But in that right does not remain a merely objective power, but makes itself immanent in the individual subject, so that the individual will becomes an expres-

sion of the general will, and right finds in the subject free recognition—becomes subjective disposition—so the notion of right transforms itself into that of *morality*, which in its turn—by not remaining merely subjective, but by forming for itself in the spheres of the family, of civil society, and of the state, a complete rational reality, wherein the free spirit finds its self-created and perfectly self-answering home—exalts itself to *customariness.** Hegel styles this development of the objective spirit, not ethics—to which he surely had a higher right than Schleiermacher for his much more comprehensive notion, (inasmuch as the ethical is the highest phase of this development,) —but the *philosophy of right.* The entire contents of this philosophy of right fall indeed into the sphere of ethics in the wider sense of the term, though the entire contents of Christian ethics do not fall into the sphere of this philosophy of right. Ethics has, according to the Christian view, not *merely* to create an objective world of rationality, but also to make the moral personality itself a perfect expression of rationality; hence many things which Hegel treats of in the philosophy of the *subjective* spirit belong to ethics; and this is doubtless the principal reason why Hegel (much more cautious and less arbitrary in his notions and their definitions than Schleiermacher) designates the science of the objective spirit, not ethics, but the doctrine of right.

SECTION III.

As a *theological* science ethics forms a part of systematic theology, in which it stands in closest connection with dogmatics, and has dogmatics as its immediate presupposition. The two sciences belong together in organic unity, and cannot be entirely separated from each other. Dogmatics presents the essence, the contents, and the object of the religious consciousness; ethics presents this consciousness as a power determining the human *will.* Dogmatics embraces the good as *reality*, that is, as it, through God, is, or becomes, or, by the fault of moral creatures, is

---

* *Philosophie des Geistes*, § 481, *sqq.* ; *Rechtsphilosophie*, p. 22, *sqq.*

not; ethics, on the contrary, embraces this good as a *task* for the free, and hence moral, activity of man; that is, as, on the basis of the religious consciousness, it *should become* in reality. Dogmatics presents reality, in the sphere of the divine and religious, *for* man, as an object of the religious consciousness; on the contrary, ethics presents the religious consciousness as a power creating a spiritual reality; that is, it presents a reality as *going out from* man as a religious subject. Hence dogmatics bears predominantly an *objective* character—relates to *knowledge;* and ethics predominantly a *subjective* character—relates to *willing.*

Theoretical theology—in contradistinction to practical theology, which presents the ecclesiastico-pastoral application of the subject-matter given in theoretical theology—is partly historical and partly systematic. Ethics has indeed a historical foundation, and stands in constant relation to history, but in itself it is no more history than is dogmatics; exegesis and Church history furnish only the material for ethics. The separating of ethics from dogmatics, with which it was formerly, and up to the time of Danæus and Calixtus, intimately involved, is difficult, and, in fact, not without violence, entirely practicable; both sciences reach over into each other like two intersecting circles, and have, under all circumstances, *some* territory in common; the general foundations of ethics are based in the corresponding thoughts of dogmatics.

The usual and quite natural statement, that dogmatics shows what we should *believe,* and ethics what we should *do,* is only proximatively correct, and is inadequate; for also the moral laws and maxims are an object of faith; and "what we *should* believe" bears, even in the correct expression itself, the character of a moral requirement. Believing, itself, is of a moral character; ethics cannot confine itself to the mere outward action, but must have to do also with the inward, with the disposition. According to Harless, dogmatics presents the essence of the objective ground of salvation, and of the objective mediation of salvation, whereas ethics presents the subjective realization of the life-goal

as established by Christ; dogmatics presents the objective sal-
vation-power as determining the Christian; ethics presents the
personal life-movement of the Christian toward his highest life-
goal; ethics gives answer to the question, What thinkest thou
of Christ? dogmatics to the question, What thinkest thou of
the right manner of the Christian's life in the world? This
declaration limits the two sciences quite too much: dogmatics
must in fact speak also of man and of the order of salvation;
and ethics must speak also of the objective law and of sin.
According to Schleiermacher's theological ethics, ethics presents the Christian self-consciousness in its relative motion, while
dogmatics presents the same in its relative rest; dogmatics answers the question, What must *be*, because the religious heart-
state *is?* ethics the question, What must *become* out of the
religious self-consciousness and through the same, because the
religious self-consciousness *is?* This antithesis is not entirely
to the point, for, on the one hand, dogmatics treats not merely
of what is, but also of what becomes, as, *e. g.*, in the doctrines
of regeneration and of eschatology; as, on the other hand, ethics
treats not only of what becomes, but necessarily also of what
morally is, as well normally as abnormally. Virtue is not a
mere becoming, but an *ens*, as Schleiermacher himself admits;
the good when attained, certainly does not for that reason cease
to be an object of ethics. The antithesis of motion and rest is
in this sphere utterly unapt. Schleiermacher presents the matter also thus: the dogmatical propositions are those which
express the relation of man to God as an interest, namely, as,
under its manifold modifications, it passes over into *conceptions;*
whereas the ethical propositions express the same thing, but as
an inner impetus, ὁρμή, an impulse, which goes out into a cycle
of actions. But also this is not quite correct; for also ethics
expresses a relation of man to God in conceptions or thoughts,
which do not *per se* include in themselves an inner impetus, as,
e. g., in the questions as to the moral essence of man, as to the
moral idea *per se,* and in the entire doctrine of goods.

The difficulty in defining the difference lies less in the general
antithesis than rather in those points where both sciences must
treat of the same topics. The doctrines of the moral essence of
man, of the divine law, of sin, of sanctification, of the Church,
belong strictly to dogmatics; but ethics must necessarily treat

also of all these things, so that it might after all seem advisable, in order to avoid repetitions, to unite both into one science again, as was formerly the case, and as has been done recently by Nitzsch, and in part also by Sartorius. But the separate treatment of ethics rests in fact, aside from weighty practical reasons, upon a wide-reaching inner difference; and those points which fall within the scope of *both* sciences, are nevertheless treated, in each, from a different stand-point, and in a very different manner. Both of them present a life of the spirit—of God or of man—but dogmatics views this life as an objective fact, while ethics views it as a task for the free activity of the rational subject; hence dogmatics has essentially an objective and real character, while ethics has a subjective and ideal one. Dogmatics has constantly to do with an object transcending the individual, with God, with Christ, with man in general; ethics has to do primarily always with the individual moral *person*; and with the totality only in so far as it rests upon the moral action of the individual personality. What dogmatics teaches relates not to me as this single person, but as a human being in general; what ethics teaches concerns me precisely as a person. Dogmatics treats of sin *per se*, as an objective something and as an historical fact; ethics treats of the same as a personal malady and as guilt. Dogmatics treats of the kingdom of God as an objective organism; ethics treats of the same in so far as the moral subject is an organic member thereof. Dogmatics treats of sanctification as a manifestation-form of the kingdom of God; ethics treats of the same as a subjective life-manifestation of the person. "The kingdom of God comes indeed without our prayer"—that is dogmatical; "but we ask in this prayer that it come also to us"—this is ethical. Dogmatics sketches the physical chart of the kingdom of God; ethics sketches the ways and dwelling-places therein. The object of dogmatics is absolutely independent of the freedom of the individual subject—is either eternal or an historical fact—is in nowise within the power of man; the object of ethics is, in its reality, absolutely dependent on the free resolution of the subject—is *per se* a pure idea, the realization of which is a requirement upon the free activity of man.—Dogmatics presents that which *is*, or *was*, or *will be;* ethics presents that which *should* be or should *not* be; hence dogmatics presents always an unconditionally-secured result,

either of an accomplished or of a destined movement; ethics,
however, presents a task, the accomplishing of which is conditioned on the free assent of man. The contents of dogmatics
relate essentially to knowledge and faith; those of ethics to
volition. Dogmatics wills that man accept the truth; ethics
wills that he do it. Hence man's relation to dogmatics is rather
passive—womanly; and to ethics rather active—manly. In the
sphere of dogmatics there is a revelation of the divine *for* man;
in that of ethics a revelation of the divine *through* man, who
has received this element into himself. In dogmatics the movement of the divine goes out from the divine middle-point toward
the created periphery; in ethics, on the contrary, it goes back
from the periphery toward God as the middle-point. In dogmatics God is conceived of as the ground, as the point of
departure; in ethics as the goal of the life-movement; in dogmatics man's relation is more epic; in ethics more dramatic.
Dogmatics is predominantly ontological and historical; ethics
is predominantly teleological. Both sciences treat of man and
his activity—dogmatics, however, in so far as man is an object
for God; ethics, in so far as God is an aimed-at object for man.
Dogmatics is related to ethics, as psychology to pedagogy, as
physiology to dietetics, as botany to horticulture, as animal
sensation to motion.*

From all this it is apparent that ethics has dogmatics necessarily as its presupposition—that it is the second and not the
first. Ethics is faith as having become a subjective life-power
—faith in so far as it is an operative force. The popular instruction in the Scriptures implies, throughout, this relative
position of dogmatics and ethics, in that it presents the moral
command after the subject-matter of faith, and bases it thereon;
thus already in the Mosaic legislation (Exod. xx, 2, *sqq.*), and
thus again in most of the New Testament epistles. (Comp. also
Matt. vii, 21, 24, *sqq.;* John xiii, 17; xv, 1, *sqq.;* 1 Cor. xiii, 2;
Col. i, 4–10; 2 Tim. iii, 14, *sqq.;* Titus i, 1; James i, 22, *sqq.;*
ii, 14, *sqq.;* 1 John ii, 4.)

Deviating entirely from this view, *Rothe* places ethics in a
wholly different field from dogmatics. In his view ethics belongs to speculative, and dogmatics to historical, theology; they
do not stand *along-side* of each other, do not run parallel to each

* Comp. Palmer: *Moral,* 1864, p. 21, *sqq.*

other, but belong to entirely different forms of theology. The difference of the two sciences lies not in their respective objects, for these objects are in fact essentially the same, but in the manner of their scientific treatment. Dogmatics is the science of dogmas, that is, of the ecclesiastically-authorized articles of faith, and hence has an empirically-given historical object, and is therefore essentially historical, and not at all speculative; speculative theology is, on the contrary, the presupposition of dogmatics. But ethics has nothing whatever to do with ecclesiastical doctrines, but must be treated purely speculatively, and is, as a speculative science, a presupposition of dogmatics. The theology of the evangelical Church has had from the very beginning, in the introduction of moral theology, no intention of creating a second science *along-side* of dogmatics, but has tended, though without being clearly conscious of it, toward a speculative theology; and this science would *necessarily* lead out beyond the hitherto-observed ecclesiastical rut—would progressively metamorphose the dogmas.* This view, constituting one of the many eccentricities of the Rothean theology, is utterly without sufficient ground. It is entirely arbitrary to place speculative theology *along-side* of dogmatics, and to declare ethics as belonging exclusively to the former. *Both* sciences admit of being treated purely theologically *or* purely speculatively, though indeed *all* their contents cannot be embraced speculatively; and with the same right whereby the speculative doctrine of God and of the world is excluded from dogmatics, may also the speculative portions of ethics be excluded from this science, and ethics be, then, declared as a purely empirical science. A large portion of ethics proper lies without the scope of a purely speculative treatment, as is in fact sufficiently evinced by the third part of Rothe's ethics. It may indeed be questioned whether speculation is admissible at all in theology; if it is, however, once admitted, then it is quite as much in place in dogmatics as in ethics—as indeed not an insignificant portion of the Rothean ethics is nothing other than speculative dogmatics; and there is no manner of justification for degrading dogmatics, as in contrast to the historical development of the science, into a merely dogmatico-historical *statement* of the doctrines of the Church.

* *Ethik*, i, 88, *sqq.* All references to Rothe are to the first edition of his *Ethik.*

And in that Rothe regards the dogmatical field as not at all bordering upon the ethical, he obtains full liberty to extend immeasurably the boundaries of ethics, so that this science thus receives a compass elsewhere unparalleled, even in Schleier macher's philosophical system. Not merely does Rothe preface his ethics with a thorough presentation of the whole of speculative theology by way of introduction (in which connection he reaches far over, and not any too aptly, into the field of natural philosophy), but also he receives into ethics itself many entirely foreign subjects, *e. g.*, eschatology. Moreover, also the facts of redemption through Christ are presupposed in this ethics, as a Christian one, not however as furnished by dogmatics, but by the immediate religious consciousness. Under such circumstances it seems more than arbitrary to declare the scientific presentation of this consciousness, *not* as the scientific presupposition, but as a sequence of ethics.

II. SCIENTIFIC TREATMENT OF ETHICS.

SECTION IV.

OF the three possible methods of presenting ethics, the empirical, the philosophical, and the theological, the first and most ancient is to be regarded as the mere fore-court to the science itself. And *philosophical* ethics, as resting upon the inner necessity of rational thinking, can never, even when it is inspired by a Christian spirit, entirely assume the place of *theological* ethics, and displace the latter as a lower stage of the science; rather can it only be the scientific presupposition and support of the same, without, however, taking up into itself its actual collective contents; for theological ethics bears in its foundation and essence predominantly an historical character —has for its source the historical revelation, and for

its essential contents the (not philosophically necessary) thoughts of the actual existence of sin and of
the collective history of salvation, whereof the central point is the historical Christ (who is at the same
time the perfect ideal of the moral), and it treats also
of the circumstances of humanity and of individual
man, as having become real within the scope of Christian history, which also, as the results of free action,
are not to be regarded as philosophically necessary.

A merely empirical ethics, furnishing only a series of observations and rules, as with the Chinese, the Indians, the older
Grecian sages, and also to a large extent inside of the scope of
Christian history, is only a collection of material for scientific
ethics, but not ethics itself. In the sphere of science we have
to do only with the antithesis of philosophical and theological
ethics, in the place of which, however, we may not, as Schleiermacher does,* substitute the antithesis of Christian and philosophical ethics. Over against Christian ethics stands, not
philosophical, but non-Christian ethics; also a philosophical
ethics may be Christian, and a Christian ethics philosophical;
a believing Christian will in fact never otherwise philosophize
than in a Christian spirit.

The antithesis between philosophical and theological ethics
is in itself simple and clear; for philosophical ethics, only that
is valid which is developed from the *per se* necessary thought,
with inner necessity; it presents the moral as a pure revelation
of reason; theological ethics, on the contrary, conceives it as a
revelation of faith in the personal God and in the historical
Christ—as an expression of obedience to the revealed will of
God; hence between the two methods of presentation there is
in fact not merely an antithesis of method and source, but also
of compass. Theological ethics, embracing also the sphere of
the historical facts of free will-determination, transcends the
limits of philosophical ethics. The two could only then be perfectly co-extensive when the sphere of moral freedom should be
merged into that of unconditional necessity; that is, when the

* *Christl. Sitte*, p. 24.

rational ground and presupposition of the ethical itself should be denied.—The ethical thoughts which relate to the realized free acts of man and of Christ can be treated of in philosophical ethics only hypothetically, so that philosophy shall apply the results obtained in the sphere of pure thought to the, not philosophically, but historico-empirically ascertained conditions; that is, not as pure but, in some sense, as mixed philosophy. But if also the historical facts of Christianity are to be taken up into philosophical ethics, as Palmer assumes,* then its difference from theological ethics is at least, not to be placed in the fact that the latter bases itself upon Scripture; for indeed philosophy cannot come at these facts otherwise than from the Scriptures, and is then in fact no longer purely philosophical.

While purely philosophical ethics can develop only the *general* moral ideas, but not their application to definite historically-arisen relations, on the other hand, a purely theological ethics, as absolutely excluding all philosophical treatment, is defective, at least, in scientific respects. Theological ethics *can* appropriate to itself philosophy, and it is all the more scientific the more it does this; but it cannot take philosophy as its exclusive ground and source without ceasing to be theological. Hence theological ethics is, in respect to *extent* of contents and to the *means* at its disposal, richer than purely philosophical ethics. The highest perfection of *Christian* ethics is a vital union of the philosophical and the theological manner of treatment, namely, in that the ideas given in the moral reason itself are treated and speculatively developed as such, and receive from Christian revelation their religious confirmation; while, on the other hand, the actual truths lying in the sphere of the free activity of man himself are taken up from revelation and from historical experience. Such a presentation of ethics preserves its Christianly-theological character by the fact that, in view of the constantly-renewed alternation of philosophical systems, and of their not unfrequently weighty and essential mutual contradictions, it does not make the validity of the firmly-established truths of revelation dependent on their agreement with a particular philosophical system, but, on the contrary, makes the acceptance of philosophical thoughts and of their sequences dependent on their harmonizing with the certain truths of revelation. If this

* *Moral*, p. 19.

relation is otherwise understood, then it is in fact no longer a theological, but a philosophical, system.

This antithesis between philosophical and theological ethics is entirely rejected by *Rothe*, in that he presents a theological ethics which is essentially speculative, and in that he definitely distinguishes *theological* speculation from philosophical, and requires of theological ethics that it *must*, as a science, be also speculative, whereas dogmatics cannot in the nature of things be such. Every speculation begins with a *proto-datum*,—philosophical speculation with the self-consciousness. But this self-consciousness is not mere self-consciousness, but is at the same time in some manner a determined one, is also a *God*-consciousness; the *religious* subject recognizes his self-consciousness not as an absolutely pure one, but as always at the same time affected by an objective determinateness, namely, the religious. Man is never otherwise conscious of himself than as being conscious at the same time also of his relation to God. This point may, says Rothe, be in itself controverted, but in the sphere of piety, that is, in the *theological* sphere, it is not controverted: "we deny to no one the right to question the reality of piety itself, but with impiety we have, as a matter of principle, nothing to do; there *can* be a system of theology only on the presupposition of piety; for all who are impious our system of speculation has no validity, and, as related to them, we must continue in error." According to this, there are two kinds of speculation, a religious and a philosophical; the latter has its point of departure in simple self-consciousness, the former in the *pious* self-consciousness; philosophical speculation conceives the "All" through the idea of the *ego*, theological speculation through the idea of God, but both are *à priori;* hence theological speculation is *theosophy;* it begins with the idea of God, with which idea philosophical speculation ends; the evidence is the same in both. Speculative theology must be essentially different for every peculiar form of piety, inasmuch as the starting-point, namely, the peculiarly-determined pious consciousness, is different. Hence there is also a peculiarly *Christianly*-speculative theology, and likewise for every Church a special one, and hence also a special *evangelico*-Christian theology; and this special speculative theology has in fact validity only for this particular Church—is for the others without significancy. This theolog

ical speculation, however, is not in any way bound by the dogmas of the Church in which it originates, but is independent of them—knows itself as co-etaneous with them; nay, it *must* in its every nature be *heterodox;* its purpose is in fact to develop the consciousness of the Church still further, and to reconstruct the existing dogmatical definitions. In the circle of theological sciences speculation occupies the first and highest place. The difference between theological and philosophical *ethics* becomes, now, perfectly plain. Both are speculative; but philosophical ethics proceeds from the moral consciousness purely as such; whereas theological ethics proceeds from the same as it exists in the Christian individual belonging to a particular Christian Church, that is, as a peculiarly-determined religious consciousness, and from the historically-given ideal of morality in the person of Christ.

This view appears to us entirely erroneous. We cannot possibly admit any other than a purely philosophical speculation, at least as of a scientific character. In the first place it is incorrect, in point of fact, that philosophical speculation always proceeds from self-consciousness as in contradistinction to theological speculation, which is made to proceed from the God-consciousness. Spinoza starts directly from the idea of God, and his philosophy will surely not be called a theological speculation; in like manner also Schelling. Hegel begins with the idea of pure being; and this is certainly also not identical with self-consciousness.—Theological speculation, Rothe holds, differs only in its beginning, from philosophical, in that this beginning is, in it, somewhat more determined and more rich in contents, namely, as being already a religiously-determined self-consciousness. This is the view of Schleiermacher, who also proceeds from the religiously-determined self-consciousness; however, Schleiermacher does not undertake to base thereon a system of speculation, but simply a theological description of the pious conditions of the soul, and to argue toward their presuppositions, which in fact cannot, in any sense, be called speculation. Rothe—herein less consequential than Schleiermacher—goes beyond him in two respects: first, in that he carries the religious determinateness, the self-consciousness, even into the confessional phase; and, secondly, in that he undertakes to make this purely empirical fact the foundation of a system of specu-

lation. The original self-consciousness upon which Rothe bases
speculative theology, and more specifically ethics, is not merely
religiously determined in general (as, *e. g.*, with Schleiermacher,
a feeling of absolute dependence), but also Christianly-relig-
iously, nay, even evangelically-Christianly, etc., and only on the
basis of such a quite specific determinedness is, in his view, a
theological speculation possible. This, however, is, properly
speaking, not a theological speculation, but a Christian, a Protestant, a Lutheran, or a Reformed speculation, and has in fact
validity only for this special ecclesiastical circle; others, belonging to another Church, *may* construct their own peculiar speculations—with the speculations of others they have no concern,
nor others with theirs; and yet all this is assumed to be not
merely science, but in fact speculative science. We can find in
it, however, only arbitrary assumption, and can recognize such
products neither as speculative nor as scientific, neither as Christian nor as evangelical. In the first place, a real science, and
hence above all a true speculation, cannot rest upon a merely
fortuitous ground, but only upon an absolutely certain one. A
speculation which concerns itself not as to whether its starting-
point, its foundation, is certain and true, is manifestly worthless.
Now the pretended theological speculation of Rothe bases itself
upon an entirely fortuitously-determined religious consciousness,
without inquiring as to its legitimacy, and then speculates thereupon unsuspectingly, further. Again, as the starting-point of
this speculation is of a fortuitously-determined character, hence
it can never have any validity save for the definite and limited
circle of persons who in fact chance to recognize this starting-
point,—has, in fact, no general significancy, as indeed Rothe himself expressly admits; and hence there is absolutely no possibility
of harmony between the speculative theologians of different
Churches; they must simply let each other alone, and deliver
themselves in monologues; and he who speculates from the
Protestant consciousness must renounce all hope that a Roman
Catholic Christian may understand him, and in any degree enter
into his line of thought—for he cannot do so. But this is a
positive contradiction not merely to all speculation, but in fact
to all science; nay, to the very nature of truth in general, and
to morality itself. Truth—and every science claims to be its
expression—can *never* be particular, but necessarily claims *uni-*

versal validity; every real science purposes to convince all men
who are rational and at all capable of scientific thought; hence
to renounce all hope of convincing other men, for the reason
that they chance to find themselves otherwise confessionally-
determined, would be positively immoral. No real science in
general is at liberty to construct itself upon a fortuitously-given
basis, and to regard other equally fortuitous bases as equally
valid and unassailable. I cannot, without treason to the truth,
speculate evangelically-Christianly *simply* because I find myself
in my earlier religious self-consciousness evangelically-Christianly determined, but only for the reason that, for convincing
grounds, I have recognized this evangelically-Christian consciousness as *per se* true, as *universally valid* truth, and which therefore excludes, as erroneous, every contradictory view. And for
the simple reason that the truth, in its very idea and essence,
can and may *never* be merely subjective, but *must* have objective
and universal validity, and because *all* men *should* come to a
knowledge of the truth (1 Tim. ii, 4), I absolutely *dare* not construct a system of speculation which, on principle, excludes the
hope of persuading other persons of different confessions, which
purposes to have for such no convincing power, and does not
regard them as called equally with me to recognize the truth,
which as truth must be absolutely valid for them also. Without
a firm and absolutely verified basis there can be no science. A
speculation upon a chance, fortuitous basis is idle play without
purpose and without worth. There would, in fact, be as many
mutually-excluding and equally-entitled speculations as there
are such chance presuppositions; and what would be the significancy of a science which aims not at convincing those in
error, but only at furnishing an interesting entertainment for
the already convinced? If the assumed foundation is not to be
itself an object of a preliminary scientific examination, then in
fact any and every one would be fully entitled to say: I find
myself not merely so or so religiously, but also so or so *morally*,
determined,—I find in my moral self-consciousness this particular desire and this particular aversion, and on the basis of this
determinedness I propose to construct a system of speculative
ethics! The distinction between philosophical and theological
speculation in Rothe's sense would in fact be simply the distinction between science and unscientific arbitrariness. We

fully admit that only a moral spirit can truly speculate upon the moral, and only a Christianly-pious spirit upon religion; but *that* a person is moral or pious is only an individual fact, but not a scientific basis of a system,—is a moral presupposition, but not a material principle of the speculation itself; piety is only the subjective condition, the impulse *toward* and the power *for* speculation, but not the scientific foundation thereof.—The strange contradiction, that this speculation, though proceeding from a determined ecclesiastical consciousness as the unassailable and unquestionable basis, yet at the same time claims to be entitled to pass out *beyond* the ecclesiastical consciousness, and even sets up heterodoxy as one of its requirements (a requirement which Rothe himself meets in a high degree), we need not here further elucidate.

Rothe presents theological speculation as co-etaneous, *alongside* of philosophical. Now, however, if, as he expressly affirms, philosophical speculation in proceeding in its development necessarily arrives at the idea of God, and there ends, that is, precisely at the point where theological speculation begins, then, in fact, speculation may, from this idea of God as obtained in a purely scientific manner, simply advance further, so that consequently we now have a theological speculation resting not upon a fortuitous and empirical presupposition, but upon a scientific result,—to which the one assumed by Rothe bears only a relation of premature over-haste. The entire distinction between theological and philosophical speculation, we must consequently declare as scientifically unfounded; and we cannot, with Rothe, look upon the difference between philosophical and theological ethics as the difference between a speculation without presuppositions and a speculation with presuppositions, but only as the difference between a speculative and a non-speculative ethics, or an ethics resting essentially on history. Purely philosophical ethics knows nothing of Christ, of redemption, nor even of sin as a reality, and hence cannot possibly answer the full idea of a Christian ethics, although it may and should, in that which it is competent to embrace, be of a very Christian character; and as the entire moral life of the Christian rests upon redemption and spiritual regeneration, hence there is not a single point in this life, where a purely philosophical ethics could suffice. Hence the view of Schleiermacher, that Christian and philosophical

ethics are of exactly of the same compass, we must regard as incorrect.* In his Philosophical Ethics he himself expressly declares that the notion of *evil* has no place in it, but is only obtained from the experience of real life; but in Christian ethics this notion is an essentially co-determining element of the whole.†

Theological and philosophical ethics do not mutually exclude each other, but stand in intimate connection, and may go hand in hand; we must admit both of them, each in its own field, and each with the task of combining the other as much as possible in itself. But for each of the two manners of treatment, we must lay claim to universal validity. Whether we have recognized a truth philosophically or theologically, we regard this much as settled, that it is a truth not merely for *us* Protestant or Roman Christians, but for all men who seek truth at all; and those who do not admit it, we can regard only as in error. This is not intolerance, but simple fidelity to the truth; every truth is, in this sense, intolerant,—claims the right to be accepted of all men.

Ethics is frequently so treated that philosophical ethics, as *pure*, precedes, and Christian ethics as *applied* ethics, follows. This is not correct; Christian ethics is not a mere application of philosophical, but has, in so far as it rests on history, an essentially other character, and other ground-thoughts peculiar to itself.—We purpose here to present a System of *Christian* ethics, which, for the reason that it is to embrace all the phases of the Christianly-moral, must be essentially *theological;* but in the inner organizing and in the developing of the ground-thoughts, philosophical considerations must furnish the deeper scientific foundation.

III. HISTORY OF ETHICS AND OF THE MORAL CONSCIOUSNESS IN GENERAL.

SECTION V.

CHRISTIAN ethics cannot be understood without its history, nor the latter without the history of the systems lying anterior to and outside of Christianity.

---

* *Christl. Sitte, Beil*, p. 4.   † *Ibid.*, pp. 35, 36.

But the history of ethics presupposes a knowledge of the historical development of the moral consciousness in general, whereof ethics proper is simply the scientific fruit.

The mistakes committed in a large portion of the field of more recent ethics, spring largely from non-attention to the history of this science; and yet no other theological science has so long and rich a history, and so many relations to the history of the human mind anterior to and outside of Christianity, as, in fact, this very one; Greek philosophy has had, upon the development of Christian ethics, a wide-reaching influence. But the history of ethics cannot be separated from the history of the moral spirit in general, out of which ethics sprang, and of which it is simply the scientific form; also the moral consciousness itself has a history, the knowledge of which is of much higher importance than that of the history of mere ethics. Not every moral consciousness has produced an ethical system, for only the more gifted nations have risen to science at all, and ethics is one of the most difficult; but the moral consciousness of a people, even though not developed into a scientific form, is to be looked upon as the historical basis for another higher and ultimately scientific national consciousness. Even as botany considers the germination and foliation no less than the blossoms and fruit,—as the history of religious doctrines presupposes the history of the religious life, as the history of philosophy presupposes and develops further the history of civilization,—so also the history of ethics cannot be given without, at the same time, taking into consideration the history of the moral consciousness itself; the ethical thoughts of Plato and Aristotle are not to be understood merely from themselves, but largely only in the light of the moral spirit of the Greeks in general.

The history of ethics itself, though frequently touched upon, has not as yet been sufficiently presented. The most complete work is that of *Stäudlin:* "History of the Ethics of Jesus," 1799–1823, 4 vols., of which the work, "History of Christian Morals since the Revival of the Sciences," which appeared as early as 1808, is to be regarded as a continuation; and to it is to be added the same author's "History of Moral Philosophy," 1822 (and, as a short compendium, the "History of Philosoph-

ical, Hebrew, and Christian Ethics," 1816). The rich body of matter scattered through these works, is much diluted and not always reliable, and is constructed into no vital unity. The superficial Rationalistic stand-point precludes a proper understanding whether of philosophical or of theological ethics. It is stated as a high merit of the ethics of Jesus, that, in it, are combined the "better elements of the Platonic and Stoic systems;" the portraiture of the "wise Teacher" of morals, Jesus, is about as insipid as well possible. Rousseau's "excellent" moral discussions are lauded to the skies, while Luther is treated as a person of narrow prejudice; the doctrine of the inspiration of the Scriptures is repeatedly declared as dangerous to morality. The "History of Moral Philosophy" and several minor treatises on the history of special ethical subjects (the oath, marriage, the conscience) are very superficial and inaccurate.

De Wette wrote a "Christian Ethics," 1819; (more briefly presented in his "Compendium of Christian Ethics," 1833, in which the history of ethics constitutes far more than half of the whole book; the first work, because of the negligent printing, is almost useless for unprofessional persons, and is very dependent on Stäudlin, even to his typographical errors, though in particular parts surpassing him).—(Meiner's "History of Ethics," 1800, utterly worthless. Marheineke's "History of Christian Ethics," etc., 1806,—only a fragment.) E. Feuerlein's "Ethics of Christianity in its Historical Chief-Forms," 1855, furnishes only unequal and often unclear or inadequate outlines; the same author published a "Philosophical Ethics in its Historical Chief-Forms," 1856–59. *Neander's* "History of Christian Ethics," 1864, enters also upon Greek ethics, though here from a somewhat antiquated stand-point, and is somewhat ununiform, breaking off the historical development by an unhappy classification, and furnishing rather single points than a connected presentation.

A.—MORAL CONSCIOUSNESS AND ETHICS OF HEATHEN NATIONS.

SECTION VI

The most of historical heathen nations have indeed collections of ethical life-rules, based almost always

upon religion, but before the golden age of Greek philosophy they had no ethics proper.—The ground-character of all heathen ethical consciousness and of heathen ethics is, that the starting-point and the goal of the moral is not an infinite spirit, but either the impersonal nature-entity, or a merely individually-personal being. The starting-point is not the infinite God, and the goal is not the perfection of the moral personality in a kingdom of God as resting upon the moral perfection of the individual person, and in the communion of the person with the infinite personality of God, but it is always merely a limited something,—either a merely earthly civic perfection with the rejection of a trans-mundane goal (the Chinese), or the giving-up of personal existence altogether (the Indians), or a merely individual perfection irrespective of the idea of a kingdom of God embracing the individual personality as a vital member (the Egyptians, Persians, Greeks, and Germans).—There is throughout a lack of the knowledge of true moral *freedom;* either it is rejected on principle, or it is ascribed only to a few specially-gifted ones, while the rest of mankind are, as barbarians, incapable of any moral freedom and perfection. Hence there is, further, a general lack of a knowledge of *humanity* as called, in its totality, to the accomplishing of a moral task. It is uniformly only *one* people, or an aristocratic class of a people, that is morally active; the slave is incapable of true morality. But where humanity itself is regarded as called to morality—with the Buddhists—there the moral task is an essentially negating one,—is directed to the annihilating of personal existence. There is throughout a lack of the knowledge of the moral *depravity* of the natural man, and hence of the

necessity of a spiritual new-birth; morality is not so much a struggle, as rather a simple development. There is indeed a consciousness of immoral conditions of humanity, yea, of a natural unaptness for the good; but these conditions are almost always attributed to mere civic and individual degeneracy, and this unaptness is confined to barbarians and slaves. And the idea of the *highest good* is embraced either merely negatively, or is referred to earthly weal, or is left entirely in doubt,—at best is sought in merely individual perfection.

The heathen moral consciousness can be understood, evidently, only in the light of the religious consciousness upon which it always rests. That, of the majority of heathen nations, we possess only loosely-connected moral precepts and observations, moral adages and practical life-rules, but not ethical systems proper, is no obstacle to our knowledge of their moral consciousness, inasmuch as systems always bear in fact traces of the subjective character of their authors, whereas, the popular collections in question, based, for the most part, on divine authority, are an objective unclouded expression of the consciousness dominant in a people.

It is the essence of heathenism to possess the idea of God only under some form of limitation, to conceive of God as a being in some degree limited;* and to this corresponds also the moral consciousness. Where God is conceived of as an unspiritual *nature-being*, there morality bears essentially the character of un-freedom, as it were of impersonality,—is either a mechanical adapting of self to universal nature, an absolutely goal-less passive subordinating of self to the ever-uniform unchangeable order of the world (*China*), or a subordinating of the personal human spirit to the divine being conceived of as nature, with which the free personality is in essential contradiction (*India*). Where God, however, is conceived of as a limited individual *spirit*, and then consequentially as plurality, there the personal human spirit stands not in perfect moral dependence upon Him,

* See the author's *Gesch. d. Heidentums*, i, § 11 *sqq.*

but is relatively co-ordinate with Him,—has not God's will as its unconditional law; the foundation of the moral becomes predominantly subjective and unsettled; the self-love and the self-seeking pride of the strong subject appears as the legitimate chief-motive of the moral life (*West-Asia* and *Europe*).

With the prevalence of such views the *goal* of moral effort, the *highest good*, can also be embraced only as a limited something. Among the naturalistic nations, the Chinese and the Indians, this goal has no positive contents at all, for the personal spirit as placed under the dominion of an impersonal nature-power cannot aim to attain to any thing positive which did not already exist; its goal can only be the greatest possible self-denial of the personal spirit as over against nature. In *China* the moral spirit can attain to nothing which has not already always existed by nature and hence with necessity; it behooves not to create a spiritual, moral kingdom, but *to uphold* the eternal kingdom of necessarily-determined *order* as already existing by nature *without* any personal act,—to subordinate to, and keep in passive harmony with, it, one's own worthless individual existence.—In India, with the Brahmins as well as with the Buddhists, where the consciousness of the personal spirit has awakened to a much higher validity, moral effort assumes a truly tragic character, in that the total, violent contradiction of the personal spirit to the personality-overwhelming divine nature-entity comes to consciousness. The ultimate goal of the moral spirit is here not only not a positive entity, nor indeed even the upholding of an eternally-uniform world-order, but the *passing away* of personal existence into the general indeterminate nature-existence; the highest good is complete *self-annihilation* through moral effort.—With the Occidental Indo-Germanic nations the personal spirit is indeed no longer merged into the impersonal nature-existence, for the divine is itself conceived of as personality. But because of the merely limited individuality of the divine,—which rises to the height of an infinite personal spirit only in the last results of philosophy, *not* recognized by the masses of the people,—the certainty of the moral goal falls away also. The personal spirit looks not to cease to be, to vanish in the mechanical whirl-din of the great world-machine, as in China, nor to melt away into the incomprehensible and ineffable proto-Brahma or *nirvana* as in India, on the contrary,

it looks to attain to a positive result, but it finds therefor no
assured, firm footing; and, as in this life the moral hero sinks
tragically under the envious disfavor of the gods or of fate, so
also is the lot he has earned in the next world of an entirely
doubtful character; Achilles would fain exchange his lot in the
lower world for the position of a servant upon earth, and Socrates is not fully confident whether for his philosophical virtue
he will attain to the enjoyment of converse with the great dead.
At best, doubting hope looks only to a merely individual well-
being, and the idea of a real kingdom of God, which has its
roots in the earthly life of moral man, and its crown in a trans-
mundane perfection, and of which the essence is the *history of
humanity*, remains unknown even to the most highly enlightened heathendom.

The moral *freedom* of the person is indeed actually denied
only by a few of the more consequential philosophers of India,
but yet it is nowhere recognized in its full truth. With the
Chinese, it is smothered under the weight of all-dictating State-
law; with the Brahminic Indians a radical Pantheism admits
only for the less-clearly and less-logically thinking classes of the
masses, a very limited form of freedom; but to the more educated consciousness all initiatorily-active freedom appears as illegitimate, as *per se* sinful, or, more consequentially still, as mere
appearance. Impersonal Brahma is the solely real existence,
and all individuality is but an absolutely dependent, immediate
manifestation-form of this One, utterly devoid of free self-
determination.—The Greek even in the highest philosophy, far
beyond the limits of the national consciousness, concedes free
moral self-determination not to man as man, but only to the
free Greek; the barbarian has only a half-humanity, is utterly
incapable of true virtue, and is not called to free service under
the moral idea, but only to an unfree service under the free
Greek. Even Aristotle knows nothing of a general morality
for all men.

One of the most hampering limits of heathen morality, is its
total lack of the idea of *humanity*. The religion of the *Buddhists*,—the sole one which transcends the limits of nationality,
and even in many respects approximates Christian views,—has
indeed conceived the thought of humanity as equally called in
all its representatives to truth and morality, and has sent out

missions beyond its national boundaries, but it has done this only because, religiously and morally, it bears a predominantly negating character; in the consciousness of the nullity of all being, fall away also, as null, the limits between nations; but this morality aims not to *build up* a spiritual kingdom of moral reality, but, on the contrary, to *liberate* the moral spirit from all reality as being *per se* null,—even from its own personal existence.

The consciousness of a guiltily-incurred moral *depravity* of unredeemed humanity, which gives to Christian morality a so deeply earnest back-ground, finds in heathendom but faint and even delusory echoes. To the Chinese all reality is *good;* the sea of life is mirror-smooth, at worst, is but superficially disturbed by light waves which the shortest calm suffices to settle again. To the Indian all existence is equally good and equally evil,— equally good, in that all reality is the divine existence itself,— equally evil, in that it is at the same time an untrue and an illegitimate self-alienation of the solely-existing Brahma, or, with the Buddhists, an expression of absolute nullity. The guilt lies not on man, but on God and on existence in general; man suffers from the untruthfulness of reality, but has not himself guiltily occasioned it.—The *Persian* conceives of evil in the world much more earnestly and with higher moral truthfulness. Humanity is really morally corrupted, and is so because of a moral guilt, because of a fall from the good; and man has the task of morally *battling* against the evil and for the good. But this fall lies *yon-side* of human action and of human guilt,—lies in the sphere of the divine itself. Not the rational creature, not man, has guiltily fallen, but a god; the divine is itself hostilely dualistic,—the good god is from the beginning opposed by the guilty evil one, and the real world—not merely the moral one, but also nature—is the work of *two* mutually morally-opposing divine creative powers. In this—no longer naturalistic, but *moral*—dualism there lies a much higher truth than in the Indian doctrine of unity, according to which the distinction of the world from God is explained away into a mere appearance, into a self-deception, either of Brahma, or, and more consequentially, of man; and man has, in the Persian view, a much higher *personal* moral task. But in that this view throws the weight of the guilt from man and upon the divinity, the moral struggle

lacks, after all, its true ground and truth.—With the *Greek* even this (in its principal nerve paralyzed) earnestness of the Persian is thrown into the shade by the, in other respects, higher theory of an inner harmony of existence. That which in the Christian world-view is the moral *goal*, is conceived here as the essence indestructibly inherent in reality, so that the moral activity has only to develop the *per se* essentially faultless germ of the spiritual essence of man, in order to attain to the highest good. Of a positive struggle against a potent reality of evil in man, even the most enlightened philosophers have no consciousness; and whatever reality of such an evil in existence forces itself upon the sound feelings and judgment, is sought for, by the intensified self-complacence of the most highly-cultivated Greeks, not in the moral essence proper of man, but yon-side of man in the world of the gods, which world appears itself in the morally better-feeling poets as morally tarnished, as an object of just censure,—or yon-side of the god-world in irrationally dominating fate,—or in the extra-Greek world of mankind, which, as barbarous, is also involved in moral degradation.—By far the highest view of the moral and of guilt, appears among the ancient *Germanic* nations, the world-view of whom was indeed more fully developed only in Christian times, and not unaffected by Christian influences.

SECTION VII.

The obscured and only very partially developed moral consciousness of *savage* nations lies outside of the field of history;[*] the more tender consciousness of the half-civilized nations, especially of the *Peruvians* and *Mexicans*—the former of whom especially developed *social* morality to a degree of one-sided maturity,[†]—appears rather as potent custom than as a clearly self-conscious consciousness. The very definitely and detailedly developed moral consciousness of the *Chinese*, as expressed in numerous and in part sacred-esteemed writings, is devoid of higher ideas,

[*] *Gesch. des Heident.*, i, p. 40 *sqq.*, p. 163 *sqq.*
[†] Ibid., 251 *sqq.*, 303 *sqq.*

and is rather merely soberly empirical, purely political, and directed predominantly only to outward purposes. The essence of this morality is an effortless
conformance to an eternally-changeless world-order,
a remaining in the just middle-course; there is no
consciousness of a forfeited perfection of the human
race, nor of a perfection yet morally to be attained
to. There is pre-supposed the unclouded goodness of
human nature, the entire agreement of the ideal and
of reality. There is no call for a sanctifying of an
unholy reality,—there needs only that the individual
existence of man be modeled upon pure human pat-
terns, and conformed to never entirely erroneous, and
always uniform common custom. The bright point
in Chinese morality is *obedience*, in the family and in
the State; its ground-character is passive persistence
in the constantly homogeneous, goal-less movement of
the universe,—a steady pulse-beat the significance of
which lies not in the goal, but in the movement itself.

The Chinese, whose religious views constitute a barren and
tame, but clear and consequential Naturalism, have special interest for moral life-rules; the ancient books of their religion,
the *Kings*, which were collected and digested by *Confucius* in
the sixth century before Christ, contain in the main simply a
very detailed system of morals; so also nearly all their later religious, philosophical, and historical writings.

The life of the All bears every-where, even in its spiritual
phase, a nature-character; there is no history with a spiritual
goal to be attained to by moral activity, but only a nature-
course with a constantly uniform character manifesting itself in
constant, unvaried repetition; morality looks not forward, but
simply backward to that which has been and will always remain
as it is, and all reformatory action upon an occasionally somewhat deteriorated present is but a *mere* return to the previous
better. Instead of progress the goal of moral effort is uniformly
simply a conserving, or a return to the past. There is no ideal

yet to be reached, but the ideal has already always existed, and has never suffered but slight becloudings; humanity is already perfect from the very beginning, *without* history and without development; morality never looks to the creating of something which has not already been,—at best aims only at remedying a slight but never deeply seated disorder. Good is not that which in the nature of things *ought* first to become, but that which already *is* from the beginning; the highest good is not a goal and end, but it is that itself which eternally is; man has and enjoys it as already given from the start; it is the Paradise into which he is placed by nature herself, and which he has never really lost,—at the worst, only a few thorns and thistles have insinuated themselves into it, which however can only render the Paradisaical life of the "Celestial Kingdom" only a little more incommodious for man, but not by any means banish him out of it, and in fact are very readily to be got rid of. The stream of world-history flows on of itself without the co-operation of man; man has simply to yield himself to it, to adapt himself unresistingly to the eternally-unvarying order of the world, to join himself, as a passively revolved wheel, into the constantly uniform-moving clock-work. Hence morality has no high goal, but requires only repose and order, and a passive submission to the minutely-tutorial civil law and to the equally valid laws of custom; there is no violent struggle, but only a quiet persisting and laboring. The highest symbol of morality is the natural sky, with its eternally-unvarying orderly revolution. As the real world is the mutual interpenetration of the two primitive principles, heaven and earth, and the equilibrium and *mean* between the two, so consists also morality in the preserving of equilibrium, in the observing of the *just mean;* the middle way is always the best. Hence ethics is by no means rigid and severe,—aims not at high reality-transcending ideals, is of a mild gentle nature, sober, practical, temperate, without high inspiration; it requires of man scarcely any thing which could be difficult to him, or which would involve much self-denial; he is not required to divest himself of his natural character, but has only to observe *measure* in all things. Man, that is, of course, only the Chinaman, is consequently already capacitated by nature to fulfill perfectly *all* the requirements of morality, and there are in fact also absolutely perfect, sinless

men. Virtue is of *easy* practice, for it is the natural expression of the soul-life, and has not to contend against any evil rooted in the heart, and it meets in fact with no actual hostility to itself in the world; it awakens not displeasure, but always love, esteem, and honor; for mankind is in fact generally and, as a whole, good; actual evil is always a mere exception; the gate is wide, and the way is broad which leads to life, and many are those who walk upon it.

As being a mere expression of general, natural world-order, morality stands in direct connection with the course of nature. The observance of the just mean preserves equilibrium in the All, and every disturbance of this equilibrium by sin re-echoes through the whole, and effects, directly, disturbances in nature, especially when the offending one is the vicegerent of heaven, the emperor,—who is called by his very office to the presenting of a moral ideal, of a pattern of virtue. Drought, famine, inundations, pestilence, and the like, are not so much positively inflicted punishments of a personally-ruling God, as rather direct natural consequences of the sins of the emperor, and of the people as imitating him. Instead of an *historical* connection and an *historical* working of sin upon coming generations, as in the Christian world-theory, there is here a *natural* connection and a *natural* working of sin upon contemporary nature and the contemporary generation. This naturalistic parallel to the Christian doctrine of inherited sin, has a deeply earnest significancy. Man in his moral activity has to do not merely with himself, but with the totality of the universe; by sinning, he disturbs the order and the harmony of existence in general; every sin is an outrage against the All, and consequently also against the highest manifestation thereof, namely, the Middle Kingdom; all sins are crimes, all are hurtful to the public weal; in the Chinese view nature suffers by sin; in the Christian, history.

The focus of the moral life is the *family;* in it manifests itself directly the divine life,—which consists in the antithesis of the male or active and of the female or passive, in heaven-force and earth-material, and in the union of the two. The family life is a living worship of God, and the family duties are the highest, and have the unconditional precedence of all others; to the obedience of children to parents all other obedience must give way. What heaven is for the world, that the father is for

the children, and reverence toward parents is a religious virtue. Hence marriage is a moral duty from which no virtuous man can excuse himself; the celibate interrupts the ranks of the family and commits an outrage on his ancestors.

But the full realization of morality appears in the *state*, which is simply the all-sidedly developed family. The emperor, as the son and vicegerent of heaven not governing arbitrarily but by eternally valid heavenly laws, is the father and teacher of the people,—not merely protecting right, but also, as a pattern of virtue, guiding and conserving the morality of the people. In China every thing is the State, and the State is everything; it is the great ocean into which all the streams of the spirit-life ultimate, and morality itself stands absolutely under the guardianship of the State. Not as man, but only as a citizen of the State and a member of the family, has the Chinaman a moral life; all morality is accomplished by obedience to the laws of the State; and between civil and moral law there is no distinction.

SECTION VIII.

The *Indians*, the Brahminic as also the Buddhistic, conceived morality, on the basis of their consequentially developed Pantheism, essentially *negatively*. All finite reality, and above all, that of the human personality, is null, untrue, and illegitimate,—either because, with the Brahmins, it is only the self-estranged divinity, or because, with the Buddhists, the essence of all existence in general is nihility; hence the ground-character of morality is self-denial, world-renunciation,—a passive endurance instead of creative activity. The moral goal, the highest good, is not a personal possession, but a surrendering of personality to the impersonal divine essence or to nihility. There is no realizing and no shaping of a moral kingdom based on personality, nor even a preserving of existing reality, but a dissolving of the same. All reality, in so far as it is a finite formation,

is evil,—not, however, through the guilt of man, but
in virtue of its very essence from the beginning; and
there is no other redemption than its annihilation.
But while, in the purely Pantheistic doctrine of the
Brahmins, the thought of the development of the
world out of God recognizes in fact in existence a
divine and hence relatively *good* substratum, and regards mankind as emanated from God, as participant
in this divine substance in different degrees, according as they stand at different distances from the divine
proto-fountain,—the *distinctions* of *caste*,—on the other
hand, the doctrine of the *Buddhists* annihilates, together with the divine proto-Brahma, also these con-
centric circles around the ungodded middle-point,
and requires equal, absolutely world-renouncing morality of *all* men, even irrespective of the limits of
nationality, and changes the positive self-torture,
which appears among the Brahmins as the acme of
pious morality, into a quietistic, self-denying patience
resting upon hopeless grief at the nihility of all
existence.

The Brahminic Indians have, in their books of law, ancient
and rich collections of moral doctrines. Almost equally esteemed
with the Vedas, and attributed to a divine origin, is the book
of the Laws of *Manu*, the parts of which belong to very different ages, though the most recent belong certainly anterior to
the fourth century before Christ; the moral precepts proper are
as yet unseparated from the religious and civil. Also the Vedas
and the later philosophical and legal writings contain much
moral matter.

Basing himself, in contrast to the nature-dualism of the Chinese, upon the unity of the universe as divine, the Brahmin
regards the real world merely as a, neither necessary nor strictly
legitimate, but rather mere dream-like self-alienation of primitive Brahma, which is destined, after an essentially purposeless

continuance, to be absorbed back into its source. Hence morality has no positive aim, but rather simply looks to an escaping
from individual existence, a dissolving of personality into the
impersonal. The continuance of personality through metemp-
sychosis is punishment, not reward. Existing reality is not, as
in China, good as such, but, as separate existence, is evil, and
is good only in its general divine substance; only the latter, but
not the former, may be held fast to. The moral subject is not
man as such; there is in fact no unitary humanity, but only different, narrower or wider, circles around the divine middle-
point, classes of men differing essentially by nature both spiritually and morally, and of whom the lowest stand even below
many brutes, and are absolutely incapable of the moral life; to
teach to these latter the Vedas or the Laws, is a crime worthy
of the deepest damnation. Only the three highest castes are
capable of a knowledge of the truth, and hence also of morality.
But also with these the moral duties and capacities are very
different, and the Indian speaks not of the moral duties of *man*,
but always only of the duties of the *castes*. The *vaiçja's* highest
good is riches; his virtue, industrious acquiring; the *xatrija's*
highest good is power, and his highest virtue, courage; and
only the *Brahmin* is capable of the highest morality; but this
morality directs itself, not transformingly and productively,
upon reality, but only, disdainingly and renouncingly, away
from the same,—not, however, in order to virtualize a free, self-
conscious personality as over against nature, but in order to
merge back the personal spirit, as illegitimate, into the impersonal essence of the universe. The highest virtue is renunciation, not indeed merely of sensuous enjoyment, of earthly weal,
but of one's own self-conscious personality; and the acme of
this morality is, consequently, self-annihilation as sought through
persistent self-torture, to the end that Brahma alone may exist.
The highest good of the true man, that is, of the Brahmin, is to
become at one with Brahma, not in the sense of a moral life-
communion of the personal spirit with a personal God, but as
a dissolving of the *per se* illegitimate personal spirit into the
general, the impersonal. That which is in the present state the
sum and substance of all wisdom, namely, to know that "I am
Brahma," attains to full truth by the dissolving of the ego into
Brahma; the goal of morality is, "Brahma alone is, not I;"

and as man, even now, while in deepest sleep,—wherein he knows nothing of the world and of himself,—is nearer to divinity than when in his waking hours, so the goal of virtue is the total falling to sleep of the personal spirit, the exhaling of the dew-drop that trembles on the lotus-leaf. The holding fast to personality is the essence of all evil. Nothing can nor should permanently endure but the divine essence alone, which tolerates nothing other than itself, and for which all reality of the world is, at best, only a dream-phantom, a transient hallucination;— even in the eyes of the deeper instructed of men, the world in general is only a false imagination of the foolish, and does not really exist *at all*. The Chinese aim, in morality, simply to conserve the already-existing; the higher nations aim at transforming it into a more spiritual reality; the Indians aim at dissolving it into nonentity. The West-Asiatic nations see the truth in the future, and long, hopefully, and through moral effort, for a better reality than is offered by the present; the Indians look sadly into the present, with indifference into the future, and with satisfaction only into the past, when as yet nothing else existed but unitary Brahma, and into *that* future which simply returns to the condition of this past. The Chinese work for the present; the higher nations, for the future; the Indians work not at all, but simply endure and perish; they aim not at implanting the free moral spirit into reality, but at tearing it away from the same,—not at transfiguring reality by the spirit, but at emancipating the spirit from the same. Indian morality is less a creative working than a sacrificing, and hence is essentially identical with the practice of religion, of which the highest phase is *self-mortification*—aiming at a total annihilation of personal existence. The way which the world has traveled out from primitive Brahma, this way it must travel back again; nature herself accomplishes this by *death ;* man accomplishes it by morally-pious self-annihilation. That which is with nature the natural goal, is with man a moral end. Even as Brahma developed himself out of his pure transparent unity into the world of plurality, so must man fold himself back out of his isolated existence again into unity; man, the highest fruit of mundane existence, must gather himself out of the dispersion of Brahma in the world, back into unity,—must give up his separate existence. Man must die away, not indeed to sin, or merely to

sensuousness, but to himself,—must cease to be a real personality, must renounce every feeling, every volition, every thought, which contains any thing whatever other than Brahma alone. The fearful self-tortures of the Indians are not penance for sins, but the highest virtue-exercises of saints. A vital consciousness of guilt, the Indian is utterly devoid of; the evil of existence is not his own, is not the fault of man in general. Whatever is and transpires, is directly Brahma's act. It is true, evil inheres by nature in all existence, but it is not to be imputed to man, and there is no other redemption from the same than the destruction of the finite, even of one's own being. The entire scope of morality bears a negating character; the truly knowing one needs not merely not to do any positive works, but he avoids them from principle, because they belong simply to the realm of folly.

For man, even in so far as he is an *object* of the moral activity, the Indian has no concern; he has a higher love for nature, which stands nearer related to the nature-divinity, and constitutes the narrowest circle around the divine center-point. In nature he beholds his mother, and he loves it reverently as the most direct and most unclouded revelation of Brahma. The same Indian who can heartlessly see a *pariah* famish without so much as stretching out to him a helping hand, reverently avoids, as a severe sin, the breaking of a grass-blade, or the swallowing of a gnat; a Brahmin allows himself not, without ground, to break even an earth-clod.—Marriage and the family-life in general can only be a transition-stage for the, as yet, morally immature. The Brahmin who has risen to true knowledge must leave father and mother, wife and child, and, dead to the world and to himself, live henceforth only in solitary contemplation of Brahma,—standing for years, in the forest, upon the same spot, emotionless as a tree-trunk, and seeking or accepting only the scantiest food; every thing finite must have become absolutely indifferent to him, until, vegetating on like a plant, and fading away, he attains to the long-sought death. For society and politics, only those who belong to the inferior castes can have any further interest,—for the Brahmin himself these things have no attraction, and, higher than the warrior-hero and than the zealously-ruling prince, is he who exchanges a crown for the life of the hermit.

5

More remarkable still is the moral consciousness of the *Buddhists*, whose world-historical and influential religion—an off-shoot of the Brahminic—was founded by the Indian prince *Sakya-Muni* in the sixth century before Christ,—the sole heathen religion which sent out missions beyond the national limits,—so that within a few centuries it extended itself throughout all middle, southern, and eastern Asia, as far as into Japan. The sacred books of the Buddhists are chiefly of moral contents, for here religion passes over almost entirely into morality.

While in Brahminism the ground and essence of all existence is the one absolutely indeterminate and un-positive proto-Brahma, Buddhism goes a step further, and declares this indeterminate, empty substratum to be *nonentity* itself. All things are sprung of nonentity; hence nonentity is the contents of all being,—hence all reality is *per se* null, and finds its truth only in that it returns to nothing. As the beginning, so is also the *end* of all being, and hence also that of man and of his moral efforts, *nonentity*. Every thing is vain, in heaven and upon earth; heaven and earth themselves are vain, and upon the ruins of a crumbling world sits, eternally enthroned, empty Naught. The *moral* element of this atheistical religion lies in the fact that the Buddhist is really and truly in earnest with the comfortless thought, and,—in striking contrast to the lustful, pleasure-seeking atheism of modern times,—presents to man the God-forsaken world as in fact really such, and forbids to him all enjoyment of the same,—that he has no joy in it, but makes deep *grief* at all existence the foundation of all morality. The Buddhist is fully conscious of what it signifies to place nature above spirit, to seek God only in nature and in the world in general. Not being able to rise to the conception of a personal God, he disdains the impersonal nature-God, and chooses rather to live without God in the world,—only, however, as one who has *no* hope at all. Buddhism in its pure form is a religion of despair, and its ethics answers to this character, and is essentially different from the Brahminic. Here no divine proto-Brahma unfolds himself into a world; and hence the different castes of mankind have no longer any essential meaning; no one man stands, by nature, nearer to the divinity than another, but all men are equal; there is no plant-like branching-out of a divine proto-germ, but only a homogeneous sea of equally-

worthless sand-grains. With the Brahmin moral freedom is
essentially trammeled, and in fact, consequentially regarded,
annihilated, by the fact that Brahma alone works all and in all;
but for the Buddhist no such limitation exists. No divinity
forcibly interferes with human action. Moral effort, however,
has no reality, as a highest good, for its *goal;* the ultimate goal
is annihilation; and this thought is here much more deeply and
sadly embraced than with the Brahmins. While with the Brahmins, man and the entire world sink back into the divine
essence, with the Buddhists they fall into utter annihilation;
and the goal of all life and effort is a traceless extinguishment—
nirvana. The Buddhist *strives* not; he only patiently *endures*
the pain of inner nothingness, that falls to the lot of all living
existence. The entire history of the world is but one grand
tragedy; in deep pain worries on all that lives, until it succumbs
to death, and the consciousness of this pain is the beginning
and the end of all wisdom. In comparison with this acme of
all wisdom, namely, the knowledge of the four-fold misery inherent in the world, that is, birth, old age, disease, and death,
all other questions lose their importance. *All reality is vain
and irrational;* this is the basis of all morality. Hence, man
should break loose from all love to real existence,—should renounce all earthly pleasure; the only feeling that beseems the
sage is that of *pain* and *compassion.* For a positive moral acting, aiming at the production of a reality, there is here no place;
man strives only to urge his way out of this world of pain, for
misery is the essence of the world, and all moral wisdom consists in the greatest possible breaking away from all liking for
the same. In the God-void world, man feels homeless,—finds
therein no rest and no satisfaction; his future is annihilation;
his present, the renouncing of all joy. The world-renunciation
of the Brahmin is rather active and manly, for by the throwing
off of his finite existence he returns into Brahma. The world-
renunciation of the Buddhist is rather passive and womanly,—
does not rise to positive self-torture and to real self-destruction;
on the contrary, the Buddhist waits, still and patient,—supports
the misery of life in unmurmuring pain, until his existence falls
away; the characteristic of this world-theory is a quiet, gentle
grief, for the thought of the empty nothingness of all things
cannot inspire to manly action; and the pain of existence should

not be additionally heightened by voluntary act. Man is simply to disdain the world,—not because he compares it with a better sinless one, but because evil and misery are inseparable from it. Separated from all the world, and as a homeless wanderer, or as a hermit in forest or desert, the pious man should live in beggar-garb, devoid of adornment, utterly possessionless, entirely isolated, indifferent to joy and grief, and dead to all emotions. Marriage, as productive of new existence, is *per se* of evil, and is absolutely forbidden to the saint; the family bonds have no significancy for him, and sensuous enjoyment is in his eyes a pure folly. The most ancient and pure doctrine of Buddhism requires such renunciation of *all* men, and it is only a deteriorated form of later times that conceded that *all* did not need to lead this *spiritual* life, but that a portion of the people might content themselves with an inferior severity.

Buddhistic ethics contains but few positive precepts; almost all of them are negative; virtue consists essentially in omitting; "thou shalt *not*," is the almost unvarying beginning of the precepts; all of them aim simply at preventing the spirit from taking delight in existence,—forbid worldly pleasure, but do not create a moral reality; and, as relating to other living creatures, beast as well as man, they guard against all multiplication of the already so widely-prevalent misery. Hence there goes here, hand in hand, with the intensest world-despising, the greatest gentleness toward all living beings; no creature may be tormented, nor even slaughtered; in order to alleviate the pain of another creature, man should rather himself endure it. Hence the Buddhists have been, in fact, the gentlest of heathen nations; but their gentleness is not so much an expression of active love as rather merely of compassion,—is simply a non-interfering, a sparing, but not a positive helping. The dumb, patient enduring of pain, a complete indifference to joy and sorrow, is not the heroic pride of a deeply self-conscious personality, but the womanly, submissive patience of a heart broken with pain.

SECTION IX.

The moral consciousness of the *Egyptians* and of the Semitic nations, especially of the *Assyrians* and *Babylonians*, is, as yet, only very imperfectly and par-

tially known, so that a very definite characterizing of it is not yet possible. So much appears to be reliably ascertained, that among these nations (which constitute the transition from naturalistic East-Asia to the Occidental nations among whom the divine is conceived of as a personal spirit) both the moral bases and the essence of the moral subject and of the moral task, are conceived in a higher and more spiritual manner than was the case among the earlier nations, —in a manner which brings personality to a greater validity. The Pantheistico-naturalistic character of the religious and moral world-theory is overcome, and a morally dualistic one struggles more definitely into the fore-ground. Morality passes over from the mere preserving and persisting of the Chinese, and from the self-renouncing of the Indians, into a *struggle* against *evil*, as super-humanly originated, though not exclusively dominant, and as in fact ultimately to be overcome.

Egypt stands on the dividing-line between the naturalistic and the personally-spiritual world-theory; the divine is indeed primarily and originally, as yet, a pure nature-power, but it struggles up into spiritual personality, and such a personality is recognized also in man; among the Semitic nations this consciousness comes into the fore-ground more prominently still. The presupposition of the moral is no longer the perfect and uniform goodness of existence, as with the Chinese, nor the essential evilness of the same, as with the Indians, but an inner *moral antagonism* of existence. Over against the personal-*become* good divinities, stands evil as a divine entity different from them, and which is primarily less spiritual, and expressive rather of mere nature-character; and man in his moral struggle stands in the midst of this antagonism,—has to determine himself *for* the divine good, and *against* the not less divine evil. Thus, in virtue of the contest of the antagonism dominant in the world, the moral subject becomes more nearly independent

and free, than among the purely naturalistic nations; his moral
task becomes, by far, more earnest and arduous,—calls far more
emphatically for personal self-determination. Hence these nations have produced grander world-historical characters than
the earlier ones,—have become world-historically *militant* nations. And the goal of the militant struggle is the ultimate
victory of the good over the evil *by* the personal spirit, which is
also itself *not* destined to be dissolved back into a general impersonal nature-existence, but, triumphing over mere nature,
preserves its own personality.

But this breaking-forth of the rational spirit and of its moral
task into greater distinctness, manifests itself otherwise among
the Egyptians than among the Semitic nations. It is among
the Egyptians that the personal nature of the moral spirit comes
first to full self-consciousness. The spirit is a something *other*
than nature and higher than it,—is not destined to servitude
under it, but to personal, free moral self-determination and to
personal immortality, over against death-dominated nature.
But this antithesis of the moral personal spirit to nature does
not as yet rise, in the earthly life, to complete victory. Even as
Osiris succumbs to the evil divinity, Typhon, so must man ultimately succumb in the struggle with unspiritual nature,—only,
however, in order to attain in the yon-side to the full enjoyment
of spiritual personality. The morning-twilight of the freedom
of the rational spirit dawns in Egypt, but it is not as yet day.
It is only through struggle, through suffering and dying, that
the spirit becomes free,—in the world of the gods as well as in
the world of man. Osiris becomes a true ruler only in the next
world, and so with man also; only out of death spring forth life
and victory. Also over the Egyptian's moral life a dusky vail
is thrown, a melancholy breath poured out,—as with the Indians, though relieved by a brighter hope. To the Indian all
moral life is but a rapidly passing meteor, vanishing away without trace; to the Egyptian it is a conflict, painful indeed, but
resulting in an ultimate permanent victory of the moral person.
Man *has* not as yet complete freedom and complete personal
validity, but he *will* have them after death if he only struggles
manfully here below; and he is conscious of entire personal responsibility for his life and his fortune after death. His per-
sonally-moral life falls not a prey to a universally-dominating

nature-necessity, but to the personal decision of the first personal
victor (Osiris) over nature and over death. By Osiris, the
king of the yon-side world, where alone true life first begins,
man's moral life is judged—weighed in the scales of righteousness. In personal communion with Osiris, the just man lives,
happy thenceforth. Osiris, the highest representative of spiritual divinity, the forerunner and pledge of immortality, the first-
born among those who have died and are now living after death,
is also the highest representative of Egyptian morality, the
ground-character of which is, a persistent battling for righteousness. The ostrich-feather, the symbol of truth and righteousness, is one of the highest badges of honor.—But it is only in
the next world that true righteousness is realized; here upon
earth rule as yet, invincibly, the powers of evil. Hence the
Egyptian, in contrast to the Chinese, turns all his love and his
interest to the yon-side life. The dwellings of the living were
for the most part paltry huts; the dwellings of the dead are
monuments of the highest art and of an unparalleled zeal for
labor; the tombs hewn out the rocks, and the pyramids intended
for the sepulchers of kings, belong among the wonders of the
ancient world, and bid defiance to the ravages of time. The
present life is, as with the Indians, lightly esteemed, not, however, because of the nullity of all existence in general, but because it is contrasted with a higher life, which, as the highest
good, is a richly promising moral goal. Reminders of death
attend the Egyptian wherever he turns, and the mummies and
the images of the dead were an eloquent *memento mori* even at
his most convivial banquets. "The Egyptians," says Diodorus
(i, 51), "regard the time of this life with very little esteem; the
dwellings of life they designate as inns, but the graves as everlasting mansions."

The heathen *Semitic* nations, especially the Assyrians and
Babylonians, base themselves, in religion and morality, entirely
on the ground of the subjective spirit, of the individual personality. The general unity of naturalism they have given up, but
they have not as yet risen to that of the infinite spirit. The
spirit appears only in the multiplicity of single forms; hence
these nations never appear in history as a unity, but always as
a plurality. In religion as well as in morality there is manifested
the reckless independence of the (now, for the first time, vigor-

ously and mightily self-conscious) subjective spirit, from any
and all unconditional objective authority, whether of nature or
of spirit,—an untamedness and intractableness of the strong individual will, daring deeds, but also a violent wildness of the
unbent will and of the passions,—a highly excited turmoil without goal or purpose.　Man, as a personal individual, comes into
the fore-ground as possessed of paramount rights.　Morality is
devoid of any certain basis and rule; the strong individual will
breaks through all barriers.　It is the era of great heroes, and
of great tyrants and God-despisers,—from *Nimrod* who began
to be a mighty one upon earth, a mighty hunter before Jehovah
(Gen. x, 8), to *Nebuchadnezzar*, who daringly exalted himself
against God.　The moral consciousness, as bewildered by an
over-intense self-consciousness, manifests predominantly a defiance on the part of this strongly egotistical subject against all
objective power, even against God; cruelty and coarse sensuousness characterize even the rites of religion, and hence much
more also the moral life.　Nineveh and Babylon attained, in
ante-Christian times, to the culminating-point of the godless,
pleasure-seeking, luxurious life.　Religion and morality stand
here in the most violent contrast to those of India; the rude,
the violent, the tumultuous, tolerates no law, no regulated order.

SECTION X.

To a higher stand-point, though not to a higher
development thereof, than the earlier nations, rise the
merely transitorily world-historical *Persians*.　The
violent dualism of two mutually *morally*-opposed personal gods, calls also morality to an earnest moral
struggle against ante-mundane, god-sprung evil; the
moral personality comes much more emphatically into
the fore-ground than ever before; the moral task becomes more difficult, but it has the certain promise
of ultimate victory over evil, not merely in a yon-side
life, but within the scope of history itself.　Morality
has here, for the first time in heathendom, a *positive*
goal inside of the field of history, namely, the realiz-

ing of a kingdom of the good upon earth; and the Persians are the sole heathen people who make a definite *prophecy* the foundation of their religiously-moral striving. Hence the essence of Persian morality consists in a definitely hope-inspired conscious struggle against evil as potent in the world, as well as in, and upon, man himself, and which, both in its guilty origin and in its effects, appears as a not natural but moral and utterly illegitimate corruption,—in a progressive *purification* of man from every thing which springs from all-invading and all-infecting evil,—in a word, in struggling against the world of Angramainyus. Man stands forth with his moral will, legitimated and victorious, over against a potently ruling *divinity*.

The Persians, whose world-historical significancy proper extends from Cyrus to Alexander the Great, have not been able within this short period to develop their religiously-moral consciousness into a scientifically matured form. The chief source for the same—the *Avesta*—is far inferior in contents and development of thought to the so-rich and deeply-suggestive sacred writings of the Indians; and yet the moral view, as a whole, is a higher one. The real world, in which man has morally to work, is here no longer the immediate divine essence itself, but it has come into existence essentially by a personal, divine act. The spirit, in its personal reality, is no longer a mere momentary phenomenon upon the alone-eternal nature-ground, as in China and India, nor is it fettered and hemmed by nature, as over-potent in this life, as is the case in Egypt; but it is already the higher creative power *over* nature, although not as yet a perfectly free and omnipotent Creator. Hence the world, in its relation to the moral spirit, is no longer a foreign and heterogeneous element, but as a spirit product, is unhostile and even congenial to the spirit; man begins to feel at home in the world, and hence he places no longer the goal of his moral striving merely in the yon-side, but he conceives it as to-be-attained-to

within the field of history. This goal of moral effort is, however, not to be reached by a mere simple, natural development of man, but by a constant and earnest struggle against positively extant evil. Evil is no longer, as with the Buddhists and, in part already, with the Brahmins, the substance of the world,—inheres not in the *essence* of existence as inseparable therefrom, but has in fact *become*, through the moral fault of the personal spirit,—is a guilty *fall* from the originally good. This is a thought more strongly approximative of the Christian world-theory than we have as yet met with in our development of the history of the moral consciousness. Wherever evil is regarded as naturally necessary, there the vitality of the morally evil is paralyzed; the Chinese entertain not this view, simply because they conceive of evil in general only very superficially; the Indians conceive of it far more profoundly and earnestly, but they recognize not the moral root of the same; the Persians regard *all* evil as springing exclusively from personal act. This act, however, is not an historical one, but a pre-historical one; not a human act, but a divine one. The unitary divinity *per se*, however, cannot do evil, as is attributed to the Indian Brahma, but the good God, *Ahura-Mazda*, remains free of all evil; it is another no less personal god, that by free self-determination, chose the evil and now thrusts *his* world into the world of Ahura-Mazda, and is involved in all real evil whose proto-source he is, —namely, *Angra-mainyus*, that is, "the evilly disposed," the author of death, of falsehood, of all impurity, and of all hurtful creatures,—the spirit which constantly denies the good.

Although, according to this, man has thrown off the guilt of evil reality from himself upon the world of the gods, still he conceives of his moral nature and life-task, in regard to this evil, more highly than did the earlier nations. Man, as created good by the good god, is placed, with complete personal freedom, in the midst of the *moral* antagonism of the world, and has now actually to accomplish in his own person the moral task of coming constantly into closer communion with Ahura-Mazda, and to contend against Angra-mainyus and all his works. Morality is a *struggle*, and rests not upon mere natural feelings and impulses, but upon the distinct consciousness of the holy *will* of the good god,—upon the *Word* expressly revealed to men. By this view, morality is made to throw off all

nature-character, and is placed in the purely spiritual sphere, and at the same time the subjective caprice of the Semitic nations is overcome, and, for the moral, an objective law obtained, a law that is to be received purely spiritually. The revealed holy Word is the mightiest weapon against Angra-mainyus.— This moral struggle is a much more vigorous one than in Egypt, for it is joyously and hopefully conscious of final victory, even within the sphere of history. The Egyptian regards his god— who is at the same time his moral example—as defeated for the present world, and driven to the future world; the Persian feels himself called even here to a courageous co-militancy with Ahura-Mazda, who persistently struggles against evil, and does *not* succumb to it, not even in the present world. The Persian regards himself as a co-worker with God, and does not mournfully long for the next world; for his moral effort, he has a high object, namely, to combat against a god and the evil creation of that god,—also a high goal, namely, the redemption of a world from evil,—and also a high confidence in victory, for there will ultimately come the Rescuer, Çaoschyanç, that is, the Helper, who will accomplish the victory. It is not by mere chance that the Persians—who usually showed themselves hostile to foreign religions, and especially to all sensuous idolatry— manifested constantly a high regard for the *Jews*, in whose higher idea of God they met in fact with a somewhat related element.

In correspondence to its religious presupposition, Persian morality bears primarily a *negating* character, though in a wholly different manner than among the Indians. While the system of the latter is directed against existence, and especially against the personal nature of man, Persian morality on the contrary directs itself, with the most complete consciousness of the validity of the personality, negatingly against every thing which belongs to the world of Angra-mainyus. *Self-purification* from every thing which stands really, or even merely symbolically, in relation with evil, death, or corruption,—the killing of poisonous and hurtful animals, and the like, are not merely moral requirements, but even acts of worship, and the Avesta gives, on these points, very precise and detailed directions.

But also the positive phase of the moral life is much more highly developed in the moral consciousness of the Persians than in that of the earlier nations. The Persians acquired

among their contemporaries the reputation of high moral earnestness as in contrast to the luxuriousness of the Semitic nations. They were, in their prime, a very vivacious and vigorously active people; indolence springs of Angra-mainyus; labor, especially agriculture, internal improvements, etc., are required by the good god, and are sacred duties; this is somewhat as it is in Chinese morality, but from a different reason; the Chinese labor for the present, the Persians for the future.—The moral relation to other men is here kindly and noble; a high esteem for the personality, in every respect, forms the basis of social virtue. Honesty, strict truthfulness, and a high feeling of personal honor, distinguish Persian morality very widely from East-Asiatic. It is a morality of vigor and manliness.

Where evil is no longer regarded as a merely abstract something, as a quality of existence in general, but as a concrete guilt reality, not a mere neutrum, but as borne by personality, there only can the moral struggle against the same be really earnest. The Chinaman labors quietly and busily in mechanical persistence; the Indian patiently endures; the Egyptian mourns, and longs to pass out of this world; the Shemite riots and enjoys; but the Persian battles with a manfully-moral earnestness. The defective phase of his moral consciousness is essentially this, that he throws evil off from himself upon the sphere of the gods,—that he has not recognized the evil of his own heart.

SECTION XI.

The moral consciousness of the *Greeks* is very different from that of the Persians; though rising above it, it yet seems to throw the approximation to the Christian view, that lay in the Persian consciousness, farther again into the back-ground. The heathen mind could not remain stationary at Persian dualism; the Greeks endeavor to bring about a reconciliation of the antagonism of the universe, by throwing this antagonism into the past, and by regarding the present as an expression of the *harmony* of existence as effected at the very beginning of history by a victory

of the personal spirit over the nature-powers that opposed it; the dualism of hostile antagonism gives
place to a dualism of *love*. No evil god and no
nature-power hostile to the personal spirit, offer ob-
struction to the moral activity. Morality is not a
struggle, but a progressive development of man as
per se good and pure; by following his own inwardly
harmonious nature, by *enjoying* the intrinsically beautiful existence of the world, and by exalting sensuous enjoyment by means of spiritual culture, and by
equally developing all the phases both of his sensuous
and of his spiritual life, man arrives at the harmonious perfection of his personality,—at the highest goal
of moral effort. The *beautiful* is *per se* the good; in
enjoying and creating the beautiful, man is moral.
The *battle* is not against a world of evil that is to be
destroyed, nor in championship of a moral idea that
is to be realized; but its end is simply to develop the
full personality of the hero. The Greek battles for
the sake of battling; the battle is even enjoyment, is
heroic play. The Greek ideal is the vigorous, youthful personality,—in the world of gods, the youthful
Apollo, in the world of heroes, *Achilles*, until, at the
close of Grecian history, it assumes a world-historical
form in *Alexander the Great*. But the entire ideal
element inheres in the person of the hero; a *permanent* moral world-historical reality, the Greeks could
not create; they lacked the positively world-historical
purpose; Alexander's world-conquering deeds aimed
at, and were able to effect, only an exaltation of the
person of the hero, and necessarily ended in anarchy
at his death, and the Greeks became an easy prey to
that nation which aimed with iron-persistency at the
positive purpose of a unitary historical reality, and

absolutely subordinated the person to the same. The
moral idea is, with the Greeks, more an object of
artistic enjoyment than of moral realization. For the
positive basis of the higher moral life, the *family*,
their moral consciousness is extremely defective, and
the idea of *man* as man, has not as yet come to consciousness; only the Hellene, but not the barbarian,
is regarded as a truly moral personality. Slavery is
the indispensable foundation of the free state.

The precedent antagonism of existence, which comes to consciousness in all heathen religions,—primarily as an antithesis
of nature and spirit, which rises with the Persians to a moral
character,—is, with the Greeks, not indeed entirely overcome
(heathenism in fact never rises beyond it), but in fact reduced
to harmony, a harmony, however, which, as viewed from a Christian stand-point, must be regarded as delusive. The consciousness of this antagonism comes to expression in myths concerning
ancient combats between the spiritual gods and Titanic nature-
powers; the gods came off victorious, and the present world
expresses the peaceful reconciliation of the earlier antagonisms;
every-where, both in the world of gods and of men, spirit and
nature are in harmonious union; there is nowhere mere spirit,
and nowhere mere nature. What appears as a hostile power
over the personal spirit, was already vanquished *anterior* to
human history; no inimical, evil god disturbs the beautiful
harmony of existence; the Titans have been thrust into Tar-
tarus. The foundation of Greek morality is therefore joy in
existence,—love as enjoyment; man has not to sacrifice his existence and his wishes, but only to heighten the former, and to
fulfill the latter, in so far as they express the character of harmony, of the beautiful; he has not, as with the Indians, to
renounce the world, but on the contrary to enjoy it, as bearing
every-where the stamp of the beautiful, and to remain in genial
peace therewith,—has not, as the Persian, to battle against its
reality as permeated with evil, but simply to pluck from it the
fruits of happiness. Greek morality is the morality of him who
is complacently self-satisfied, without any severe inner struggle.

The Hellene has, in his consciousness of the harmony of ex-

istence, on the one hand a powerful stimulus to virtue; he endeavors to preserve this harmony, and hence is in general amiable, frank, and honorable; to a certain degree he shows also magnanimity toward his enemies,—respects the moral personality; but, on the other hand, he has in this consciousness also the tendency to make *light* with the moral; he believes himself already to have attained to the good, and not to need to undergo a severe struggle for its possession,—believes himself to have already, in his natural proclivities, also the right. Hence he is inclined to take life unseriously; even unnatural lusts pass for allowed, if they only appear under the form of the beautiful. The beauty of the manner beautifies the sin, and the worship of Aphrodite lends to sensuality itself a religious sanction. Greek effeminacy and luxuriousness—despised only by the Spartans—became even a by-word among the Romans; and even the dark passions of hate and revenge found in the Greek consciousness little condemnation; no Greek took offense at the barbarous mistreatment of the hero Hector. The most virtuous citizens were not respected, but banished; sycophants were honored, and the friends of truth hated or killed.

A high sense for beauty raises indeed the moral consciousness to a high and harmonious conception of moral beauty, and the poets sketch moral ideals with master-hand; but these ideals are more for esthetic enjoyment than for moral imitation. Even morality becomes to the Hellene a matter of mere spectacle, and in no heathen nation is the contrast between the ideal and the real life so great, as in that one which conceived the ideal the highest. For the practical life the requirements of the moral consciousness were other than for poetry; the same people which admired female ideals, such as Penelope, Antigone, and Electra, as presented in song and upon the stage, placed womanhood and marriage, and the family-life in general, much lower in real life than did the Chinese or the ancient Germans; and it was not merely in the censured license of the frivolous world, but also in the moral views of the most highly cultured, that talented concubines (especially after the example of Aspasia, notorious for her connection with Pericles, and also honored by Socrates) stood higher than house-wives proper, and became the real representatives of female culture, and ideals of female grace. Sparta, by its legislation, overthrew on principle the proper life

of the family; the penal laws against bachelors which finally became a necessity, furnish proof, how popular this anti-family legislation was.* Solon found it necessary in the interest of the State to protect by penal enactments the merest natural duties of the marriage-state, at least within the bounds of a minimum requirement;†—so great was already in his day the general disinclination to wedlock, which, though forming the foundation of all true morality, was regarded in the Golden Age of Greece as little better than a necessary evil. The bringing about of abortion and the exposing of new-born children, was a right of parents, which was not only protected by laws, but even defended by the most esteemed philosophers. The perverseness not only of frivolous practice, but of the general moral consciousness, is manifested most strikingly in the prevalence of unnatural vice, as apologized for even by philosophers themselves; and the dark picture of St. Paul not merely of Greek morality itself, but also of the moral consciousness of the Greeks (Rom. i, 21 sqq.), is perfectly corroborated by historical reality. In certain efforts of recent date to clarify the Christian world-view by the help of the "classical" one, these facts ought not to be left out of sight. The heathen Germans stand in this respect very much higher than the Greeks.

However fully the moral consciousness of the worth and dignity of the personality is developed, still the dignity of true manhood is conceded only to the free Hellenes, who constituted by far the smallest number of the Greek population. (In Attica at its highest prosperity there were 400,000 slaves, in Corinth 460,000). The barbarian and the slave have no right to the full dignity of personality. Freedom without slavery is, in the eyes of a Greek, an absurdity. The generally prevalent mild treatment of their slaves was more an expression of natural kindheartedness and of personal interest than of conceded right; the Spartan slave-massacres were the expression of an undisputed right of the State and of the free citizens; even Plato and Aristotle are unable to conceive of a State and of political freedom without the personal unfreedom of slavery. The so-called notion of "humanitarianism" limits the practice of this virtue to the possessors of slaves; and the higher the right and the might of the free citizens are placed, so much the more complete and

* Plato: *Symp.*, p. 192. † Plutarch: *Solon*, c. 20.

striking becomes also the rightlessness of the slaves. That slaves are but domestic animals possessed of intelligence was a general maxim, recognized even by philosophers.

Though the reality of the moral consciousness and of the moral life of the Greek is in many respects far below that of other heathen nations, still the moral idea that underlies this reality is a higher one. That which, in the Christian world-view, forms the presupposition of all truly moral life, namely, the *reconciliation* of the contradiction and of the antagonism in the world of reality, the higher right and the higher power of the personal spirit over unfree nature, this is recognized by the Greeks, though indeed with heathen perversions, in a higher manner than is the case among the earlier heathen nations. Only man as redeemed by the historical redemption-act from the power of his sinful naturalness, and as now for the first having risen to a truly *free* moral personality, is capable, according to the Christian view, of accomplishing true morality;—also the Hellene makes the reconciliation of the antagonism, the actual harmony of human nature and of existence in general, the presupposition of morality, and conceives this reconciliation as one that falls indeed before human history, but yet is accomplished by the free act of the personal spirit; whereas with the earlier nations (where the consciousness of the inner antagonism and contradiction is also recognized) the right of the personal spirit is either rejected, or else thrown for its realization into the far future, either into the life after death, or at least toward the close of the world's history. It is true, this thought of a reconciliation is made possible only by the fact that the consciousness of moral guilt is kept away from the antagonism that is to be reconciled, and that this antagonism is conceived rather as of a primitive cosmical character, and moreover that not man but the personal gods enter into the sphere thereof, and, battling, overcome,—so that there is left for man nothing further than the enjoyable repetition of the same in artistic *play;* the Olympic games are a commemoration of the battles of the Titans; and, accordingly, the entire moral life becomes to the Greek an artistic play;—nevertheless the ground-thought is still of high significancy,—the thought that only man as having *become free* through the reconciliation of the antagonism of real existence is capable of morality. But that the carrying-out of

this thought is weakened down on all sides, that the Greek does not in his moral consciousness rise out of his esthetic play to full earnestness of life, this is in fact simply the heathen character of this consciousness. And even in the fact that to the Hellene, morality appears *so easy*, there lies a presentiment of the true thought, that to the morally emancipated man the moral law appears no longer as a *yoke* or burden, but is, on the contrary, the direct, unforced, bliss-inspired and blissful life-outgush of sanctified human nature. To no nation of heathendom does morality become so light a task as to the Hellenes. The Hellene knows no moral code of laws compelling the moral subject to *obedience*, with objective authority; and even the moralizing philosophers themselves, in striking contrast to the Chinese, the Indians, and even the Persians, tarry almost exclusively in the sphere of general thoughts, and give only seldom definite precepts for the details of life. The moral subject bears the law within himself, and bows himself under no foreign objective law. And this is in fact but a heathen perversion of the *per se* true thought, that with the spiritually-regenerated the law of God is written in their hearts,—that to them his yoke is easy and his burden light. As the Chinese and Persian consciousness shows some resemblance to that of the Hebrews, so the Greek consciousness has analogies to the Christian, especially as the latter is presented by that Apostle who labored among the Greeks. That with the Greeks the analogical thought rests upon an untrue foundation, and worked hurtfully in its carrying-out,—that it led to sinful presumption, and created a morality actually inferior in many respects to that of the Chinese, the Indians and Persians,—this evinces not the fallaciousness of the thought *per se*, but only the perversity of the natural man, who turns all the truth attainable by him into the service of sin, and thus confirms the weighty utterance that only he "whom the *Son* makes free is free indeed." He who is inwardly unfree, and yet imagines himself free, is morally in greater danger than he who is unfree and also knows himself as such. The Greek appears morally more responsible and more guilty than the other heathen, because he has a higher knowledge; and the Apostle's moral sentence upon the heathen [Rom. i, 18 *sqq.*] falls upon the Greeks with much greater force than upon the other heathen.

SECTION XII.

To a philosophical form,[*] the moral consciousness of the Greeks rose, with some distinctness, for the first, through *Socrates ;* before him we find little more than a practical morality expressed in disconnected moral maxims, without further proof or development. Socrates, who speculated less on metaphysical questions than simply on the *good*, not only bases the moral upon philosophical knowledge, but finds in fact in this knowledge the essence and the highest degree of the moral. To know is the highest virtue, and out of this virtue follow directly and with inner necessity all the others; a contradiction between knowledge and volition is inconceivable; practically, morality manifests itself in the subordinating of the irrational desires to rational knowledge, and especially in obedience to civil laws. Unconscious of the might of evil in the natural man, Socrates conceives the moral essentially only as measured by a rational calculating of outward fitness to ends. His significancy for moral philosophy lies in his calling attention to rational knowledge as the source of the moral, and to the no longer arbitrarily subjectively-determined good as the end of rational effort.

The Greeks occupy themselves very early with the nature of the moral; the most ancient so-called Wise Men are, for the most part, moralists. It was very long, however, before the Greeks reduced their isolatedly-presented, and rather empirically-based, moral maxims to any sort of unity and order. Philosophy proper occupied itself primarily with purely metaphysical questions, and the moral views expressed were, with the earlier philosophers, for the most part, a mere supplement of

[*] Wehrenpfennig: *Verschiedenheit d. eth. Princ. b. d. Hellenen*, 1856.

observations and life-rules but loosely connected with their speculations proper.

Socrates was the first who, as it was said, called philosophy from heaven to the sphere of the earth; it is with him essentially moral, and, from merely metaphysical speculations, he turns away with a certain displeasure; even in his consideration of the idea of God, greater prominence is given to the moral phase of the divine activity. With him the knowledge of the *good* is the chief end of philosophy; but, for the simple reason that here ethics springs exclusively from philosophy, the element of knowledge far outweighs in it the element of the heart. The ethics of Socrates is a coldly rational calculating; it has not, as has Christian ethics, an historical basis and presupposition, but is invented purely *à priori*. Man is by nature thoroughly good, —is, in his freedom, not simply at first as yet undecided, but he has by nature a decided tendency to the good, just as reason has a natural affinity for the truth. Evil is by no means to be explained from mere volition, but only from error. The human understanding can err, and the act resulting from error is the evil; without error there would be no evil, and it is absolutely impossible that man should not also will that which he has recognized as good. It needs, therefore, only that men be brought to a knowledge of the good, and then they will also act virtuously. The motive to the moral is not love, but knowledge; to instruct is to make better; the philosopher is also the virtuous man, and *only* the philosopher can practice true virtue; the ignorant man is also immoral. Self-knowledge—the γνῶθι σεαυτόν—is the presupposition of all morality,—not, however, in the sense familiar to Christians, of a knowledge of the heart as inclined to sin, but only in the sense of a knowledge of the logical nature of the thinking spirit; in his dialogues, Socrates does not think of bringing men to a knowledge of their moral guilt,—he simply aims to convince them as to how little they as yet *know*. Hence ethics is with him a one-sided doctrine of knowledge. There is properly-speaking only *one* virtue, and this is *wisdom*, that is, knowledge; and all other virtues are only different forms of this one virtue.*

* Aristotle: *Eth. Nic.*, vi, 13; iii, 6, 7; *Eth. Eud.*, i, 5; vii, 13; *Magn. Mor.*, i, 1, 9; ii, 6; Xen.: *Mem.*, i, 1, 16; iii, 9, 4, 5; iv, 6, 6; Plato: *Lach.*, p. 194 *sqq.*; *Apol.*, p. 26; Diog. L., ii, 31.

Practically, wisdom manifests itself mainly in *self-mastery*, that is, in governing by knowledge all appetites, dispositions, feelings, and passions. Man must always remain master of himself,—must in all circumstances, however different, always act strictly according to his knowledge and in harmony with himself,—must not let himself be led by unconscious desires; and, inasmuch as a man's knowledge cannot be taken from him, and as the changeable movements of feeling are under the control of knowledge, hence man has in this faculty of knowledge also complete *happiness*, and the wise man is necessarily also happy; and this happiness depends exclusively on himself. Therein consists the freedom of the sage.—Knowledge, virtue, and happiness are consequently not essentially different from each other, —are simply different phases of the same thing. In that Socrates essentially identifies the good with knowledge, he raises it above the arbitrary caprice of the individual subject, seeing that truth is not dependent on the good pleasure of said subject. Thus the good has a validity independently of the individual, and all rational men must recognize the same thing as good. Hence the moral idea has attained to contents of a general and necessary character; and Socrates recognizes the objective significancy of the same, in that he ascribes right wisdom to God alone.*

These general thoughts form the scientific basis of the subsequent currents of philosophy. Socrates himself does not rise beyond them and enter into details. Whenever the question is as to giving to these general thoughts more definite contents, he refers to the laws of the State, in the fulfilling of which man fulfills the requirements of morality. Hence his morality is merely Greek civic virtue,—has no higher ideal contents. To obey the laws of the State is the sum of all duties; a δίκαιος is the same as a νόμιμος. To do good to one's friends, and evil to one's enemies, is a moral requirement,† though indeed to suffer wrong is better than to do it,—the doing of evil to one's enemies being in fact not a wrong, but a legitimate retaliation.‡

In general the tendency of Socrates is toward a dry, prosaic utilitarianism. His moral views, in so far as they are not idealized by Plato, are devoid of all ideal enthusiasm. And in his

* Plato: *Apol.*, p. 23.   † Xen.: *Mem.*, ii, 6, 35.
‡ Plato: *Rep.*, i, p. 335; *Crito*, p. 49.

own moral life he by no means rises beyond ordinary Greek morality; and it required all the superficiality of modern deistic "illuminism," to undertake to place Socrates as a moral ideal by the side of Christ. In Plato's *Symposium*, Socrates surpasses all the others in drinking, and even outquaffs the whole company without getting intoxicated himself; and yet even this Platonic Socrates is already considerably idealized. In Xenophon[*] he goes with a friend to a hetaera, who is sitting as a model for a painter, and instructs her in the art of enticing men. The manner in which it has been attempted to justify this, is not of the most happy. If, in such a case, Socrates knows of nothing better than to indulge in plays of dialectical skill, evidently his judgment of the matter itself is not very condemnatory. And in other respects his bearing toward lasciviousness,[†] gives evidence of deep erroneousness of moral consciousness even in the philosopher himself. Of moral and family love, Socrates has, so far as our knowledge of him goes, scarcely a presentiment. When his wife comes, with her child, into the prison, to take leave of her husband after his condemnation to death, Socrates simply turns to his friends, and says dryly, "Let some one, I pray you, take the woman away from here, to her house;" and she is led out by a slave; and in his last long farewell speech to the world, Socrates bestows upon wife and children not a single word. For his virtues, such as they were, he is worthy of praise, but still he manifestly does not rise *above* mere Greek virtue.

SECTION XIII.

From Socrates there sprang up several mutually-differing schools, the peculiarity and difference of which lie especially in their ethical views.—The *Cynics* (through Antisthenes) develop the doctrine of Socrates as to the ethical significancy of knowledge, into one-sided prominence in its practical application. Knowledge works directly the good; virtue, as resting exclusively on knowledge, is the highest goal of human life. It manifests itself essentially in the

[*] *Mem.*, iii, 11.   [†] *Ibid.*, i, 3, 14, 15.

struggle against irrational desires; desirelessness is
the highest virtue.— Over against the Cynics, the
Cyrenaics (through Aristippus) emphasize the other
phase of the wisdom-life, namely, *happiness*. Happiness is the highest good, and therefore the highest
goal of the moral; virtue is only a means to this end.
And happiness consists in the feeling of *pleasure*, in
enjoyment. Hence enjoyment is the goal of the moral
striving; in it alone man becomes free, because in it
the desires that press and disturb him come to quiet.

Both of these schools undertake to find an *objective* ground
for the moral; in fact, however, neither of them finds any thing
more than a strictly *subjective* one; the Cynics take their starting-point in subjective knowledge, and in the *will* as determined
thereby; the Cyrenaics, in *feeling*. Both schools are equally
one-sided developments of tendencies that existed in germ in
Socrates. If knowledge, virtue, and happiness are essentially
the same thing, then it is indifferent which of these phases is
made the starting-point,—whether it be said that virtue consists
in an unconditional obedience to knowledge, or in the striving
after happiness; and hence the Cynic is right when he asserts,
that in following knowledge we need not inquire as to the
sensation of pleasure or displeasure, for true happiness follows
from virtue of necessity; and if sensation should seem to contradict this, then it is simply to be despised as a false one. The
Cyrenaic is likewise consequential when he asserts, that in following the feeling of happiness we need not inquire as to philosophical knowledge, for as happiness follows from virtue of
necessity, hence in the feeling of pleasure we have certain proof
that we are practicing virtue, and hence also that we correctly
understand the good.

The *Cynics* give exclusive predominance to the rational tendency in Socrates; there is for the good in the widest sense of
the word no other decisive criterion than knowledge. And the
knowledge of the good and the manner of action that rests exclusively upon this knowledge, are the sole thing which has real
worth for man. Only the good in this sense is beautiful, and

only evil is deformed; whatever else is pleasant for the senses or feelings is entirely worthless; and even all knowledge that does not relate to the good is useless. True freedom consists in perfect indifference to whatever lies outside of the individual spirit. All evil rests upon error,—has its source in false impressions and ideas, but not at all in the heart. The wise man is, in virtue of his knowledge, free from all evil.—The independence of the personal spirit is here most one-sidedly conceived of, as a contemptuous turning-away from all objective reality,—as an over-confident trusting in one's (evidently very immature and fortuitous) subjective knowledge, as a complete self-isolation of the persistently opinionated subject. Hence there result an absolute indifference to all outer existence, even to all historical reality and to social custom, a throwing off of all reverence for the objective reality of the spirit as developing itself in history. However much of truth may lie in the ground-thought of Cynicism, still its practical development on the basis of its defective presuppositions leads almost necessarily to a caricature,—to an unbridled insolence of the immature spirit, giving birth to such phenomena as that of Diogenes. There is manifested in this school the pride of easily-satisfied self-righteousness, the haughty self-isolation of the subject as breaking loose from all objective realization of the rational spirit.

The *Cyrenaics* pushed to its extreme the other phase. A happiness which I do not feel as pleasure, is none at all. If virtue makes happy, then I must at once also feel it. Hence that which is truly good, must at once evince itself as such in the sphere of the sensibilities; and, conversely, that which impresses me pleasurably must be good, otherwise there would be another form of happiness than that produced by virtue. Hence between one pleasure and another there can be no essential moral difference; consequently the feeling of pleasure or of displeasure is a perfectly safe guide in the sphere of the moral. Hence the chief point in practical wisdom is, to procure for one's self the feeling of pleasure; from this principle the inquiry must first take its start. By observation, for example, I find that temperateness is a virtue, because intemperateness occasions suffering. Hence true wisdom as founded on this basis consists in the rational governing of the *measure* of each particular pleasure, and not in the knowledge of any general principles; such prin-

ciples, other than the one just given, do not exist, but each enjoyment is governed by its own particular measure, which is discovered for the most part simply through experience.

SECTION XIV.

Plato gives to Greek ethics a deeply suggestive scientific basis and form. The world is an expression of the divine ideas, a thing of beauty. That which answers to the divine idea, namely, the god like, is good. Man has the task, in virtue of his rational spirituality, to realize the good, consciously and with freedom; the essence of virtue is, pleasure in the good as being the truly beautiful,—love. As expressing in itself the harmony of the soul, virtue is also the condition of true happiness; not the direct pleasure-feeling, however, but rational knowledge, decides as to the good, and such knowledge works the same directly. Hence virtue is neither indifferent to pleasure, nor does it consist therein, but it produces it. However, all virtue, because of the imperfection essentially inherent in existence, remains ever imperfect in the earthly life; the corporeal nature of man itself is a hinderance.—Virtue is in its essence *unitary*, but because of its relation to the manifold soul-powers and life-manifestations, it manifests itself fourfoldly, as *wisdom, manliness, temperateness,* and *justness,* of which the first is the fundamental one, and dominates the others.—Morality, however, is not a something belonging merely to the individual person, but has its full reality only in the moral community-life, the *State,* which rests not so much on the family and on moral society, as rather constitutes, itself, the exclusive form of the moral society-life, and in fact itself produces the family and all other moral forms of

communion, out of itself, and dominates them with
unconditional authority. The absolutism of the State
swallows up into itself every right of the moral personality and of the family, and it is not as man, nor
as a member of the family, but solely as citizen, that
the individual is capable of realizing true morality.
But also only an inferior number are capacitated
thereto; and therefore these few who are capable of
true wisdom are called, by this very fact, to the unlimited governing of the others. The moral task is
consequently not a general one for humanity,—is
not the same for all, and is in its full truth not
possible for all.

Plato, far surpassing Socrates in spiritual profundity, developed with creative originality the thoughts which his master
had possessed rather only as mere presentiments, into a scheme
of profound speculation, very different from the popular moralizing of the son of Sophroniscus. His ethical thoughts, which
are not shaped into a rounded system, are expressed more especially in the following of his works: *Protagoras, Laches, Char-
mides, Euthyphron, Gorgias, Menon, Philebus, Politicus,* and in
his work which presents the realized moral organism, the
Republic or *State.*

In the thought of the rational spirit, which Plato conceives
more deeply than was ever done before, he obtains a much more
solid foundation for the moral than did the earlier philosophy.
The world is in its essence, not indeed created, but formed by
God, the absolute, rational spirit,—is the most perfect possible
expression of his thoughts, a copy of the divine eternal ideas.
The realization of an idea is the beautiful; hence the *cosmos* is
an object of beauty.* The rational immortal spirit of man—his
ideal phase—has the task of realizing the beautiful, the ideal,
and the highest end of human life is ideality, that is, it is, to
become like God; this God-likeness, which consists in justness
and in sincere piety, is the *good,* and the highest good is God.

---

* Especially in his *Timaeus.*

himself.* This thought of God-likeness, however, Plato does not further develop, nor indeed could he do so, seeing that the God-idea itself, as embraced from a heathen stand-point, was too unclear. The idea of the good is here not derived from the idea of God, but conversely it is undertaken to determine the idea of God from the idea of the good, as being fundamental and *per se* certain. Evidently we have not to do here with the Christian thought of God-likeness. The thought of a divine command falls back behind the thought of the idea of the good as innate in reason itself. This mode of viewing the matter lies in the nature of the case, seeing that in fact there could be here no question of any other revelation of the divine will. The good which is conceived merely in a general and rather indefinite manner as the inner harmony and order or beauty of the soul, as the untrammeled domination of reason, and hence rather under a formal than a material aspect,† is *per se* a something divine and true, and as such to be aspired to; and the individual pleasure-feeling is not the measure of virtue, nor the good itself.‡ It is true, virtue alone renders truly happy, that is, works complete inner harmony of soul, and there is no happiness without virtue, for virtue itself is simply such a harmony or beauty of soul,§ and to do wrong is the greatest of all evils, greater than to suffer wrongs,‖ but happiness is not one and the same with every chance pleasure-feeling.¶ It is not this feeling, in its dependence on the accidentalities of outer circumstances and of the frame-of-mind, but only the idea of the good, that can be known and truly identified;** hence the pleasure-feeling cannot be the decisive criterion as to the good, and the good cannot be aspired to merely for the sake of the pleasure.—The knowledge of the idea of the *good*—which, like the consciousness of any and of every idea, is not the product of a reflective course of thought, that is, not derived knowledge, but on the contrary

* *Rep.*, pp. 500, 505 *sqq.*, 613 (Steph.); *Theæt.*, 176; *Menon*, p. 99; *Euthyphron*, p. 13.

† *Gorgias*, p. 504 *sqq.*; *Phileb.*, 64, 65.

‡ *Gorgias*, p. 495 *sqq.*; *Phaed.*, p. 237 *sqq.*

§ *Gorgias*, 470 *sqq.*, 504–509; *Menon*, p. 87 *sqq.*; *Rep.*, pp. 352, 444, 583, 585; *Phil.*, pp. 40, 64.

‖ *Gorgias*, pp. 469 *sqq.*, 477, 527.

¶ *Phil.*, p. 11 *sqq.*; *Gorgias*, p. 494 *sqq.*

** *Gorgias*, pp. 464, 500; *Menon*, p. 87 *sqq.*

a direct reason-knowledge, and the highest of all that can be known—is the foundation and presupposition of virtue; without knowledge there is no virtue; virtue is not a natural quality of man, but is learned and appropriated by learning.* And the knowledge of the good leads with inner necessity to the practicing of that which is recognized as good; evil rests essentially upon error, and is never committed with consciousness and intentionally;† herein Plato perfectly harmonizes with Socrates. The will has, over against knowledge, no discretion whatever, but is the direct and necessary expression thereof. The lower, sensuous desires can indeed withstand reason, but the will of the spirit itself cannot do so. That also the heart—the spiritual essence of man himself—may have a natural tendency to evil, Plato has not the least conscious suspicion. Nevertheless an obscure presentiment of the entrance of corruption into the universe does find expression in his notion, that the present enchainment of the spirit to a body is not an original and normal, but a guiltily-incurred state of things. In fact, according to Plato, the soul existed as a rational personality once before in a bodiless state, and only in consequence of a moral transgression was it joined to a trammeling corporeality, so that it is now, as it were, fettered in a cell or a dark cavern.‡ Also for still another reason, the good, though indeed the highest end, is yet never fully attainable in the earthly life. For inasmuch as the real world is not solely and purely the work of the absolute God-will, but, on the contrary, a product of two factors,—whereof the one is the formless proto-material which is in fact a relative nonentity ($\mu\dot{\eta}$ $\delta\nu$), and the other the ideal God-will,—and as the former, because not posited by God himself, does not perfectly yield to the formative working of God when impressing his ideas upon it (even as the impress of a seal never reflects perfectly clearly every feature of the same),—so the world is not an absolutely perfect one, but only the best possible one,—is not the pure and mere expression of the rational spirit, but there lingers in it a never entirely-overcomable irrational residuum,—an evil lying in the essence of the world itself, which though not sprung from the fault of moral creatures, is yet the

* *Menon*, p. 87 *sqq.*

† *Prot.*, pp. 345, 352 *sqq.*, 358; *Menon*, p. 95; *Gorg.*, p. 468.

‡ *Timaeus*, p. 41; *Phaedrus*, p. 246 *sqq.*; *Rep.*, p. 514 *sqq.*

ground and source of all moral guilt,—a proto-evil.* So also is
there in man himself a primitive antagonism never entirely
overcomable in the present life, namely, between reason and the
lower animal desires, which latter should in fact be morally
dominated by reason.† In Plato, therefore, there is lacking to
the moral consciousness that joyous confidence which character-
izes Christian morality. "Evil can never be annihilated, for
there must always be something over against the good; it cannot, however, have its seat among the gods, but it inheres in
mortal nature; therefore man should strive as soon as possible
to flee hence and to escape thither."‡ "True philosophers are
minded to strive after nothing other than to decease and be
dead, seeing that, so long as we still have the body, and our
soul is united with this evil [the body], we can never attain to
that whereafter we aspire;"§ and they lay not violent hands upon
themselves simply because they are placed by God in this life as
upon a watch, which they are not at liberty to abandon at will.‖

Hence morality consists primarily in this, that man turns
himself to the ideal, the spiritual, and away from the merely
sensuous. This is, however, only one phase of morality, the
ideal; the other phase is the real one. Even as God, in impressing his ideas upon matter, shaped the world into an object
of beauty, so must also man actively merge and imprint himself
into the actual world-existence, and shape it into beauty. Hence
virtuousness is delight in the beautiful. And the beautiful is
harmony, not merely sensuous but also spiritual. The essence
of virtue is, as this delight in the beautiful, love, or eros,—a
thought that is developed by Plato with very great emphasis
(especially in his Phaedrus, Lysis, and Symposium). This is,
however, by no means the Christian idea of love—that love in
which man knows himself at one with another in virtue of communion with God,—but it is a love to the manifestation, to the
beautiful. Not the divine per se is loved, but the concrete, and
even essentially sensuous manifestation. It is not a love of soul
to soul, but one that clings to the sensuous form. Hence it has
in Plato's state no significancy for the family. It is true, eros
exalts itself from the sensuous to the spiritual, to soul-beauty;¶

---

* Tim., p. 46 sqq., 54; Polit., 269; Rep., 611 sqq.; Phaedrus, 246 sqq.
† Rep., 436 sqq., 589; Gorg., 505.   ‡ Theaet., p. 176.
§ Phaedo, p. 63 sqq.   ‖ Ibid., p. 62.   ¶ Symp., 209 sqq.

the sensuous element, however, remains the basis, and does not
receive its worth simply from the spiritual. The beautiful is
per se, and in all of its manifestations, a revelation of the divine,
and the divine is accessible to us only under the form of the
beautiful; where beauty is, there is also the divine. This is the
characteristically Greek stand-point; beauty and grace excuse
all sin; even the frivolous is recognized as good, provided it is
only beautiful. The recognition of love under *every* form, even
under that of unnatural vice, is so characteristic of the Greek,
that even Plato attempts a philosophical justification thereof,
which is far from complimentary to Greek ethics.* In love, here,
predominates by no means self-denial, as is the case with Christian love, but simply pleasure; I love another not for his sake,
but for my own sake. This love knows nothing of a self-sacrificing suffering, but only a self-enjoying, at farthest only a suffering of longing and jealousy. It is true, mere sensuous love as
directed to merely fleshly enjoyment, is blamed;† but where a
higher spiritual love, not merely to the body but also to the
soul, exists, and in the beautiful the divine element is recognized, there sensuous love, even when it assumes the form of a
misuse of sex, finds its justification, and becomes a virtue, and
even a religious enthusiasm.‡ "Beautifully enacted, it is beautiful; otherwise, however, shameful."§ The very circumstance
that Plato speaks so repeatedly and so extensively and with
visible approval of this absolutely vicious love [Rom. i, 27],
while at the same time he scarcely touches upon the morally
close-related mere sexual love, and, in his long discourses on
eros, honors wedlock love with not a single word, and further
that he attempts to repress‖ the feeling that instinctively impresses itself upon him, that there is something shameful therein, by the help of strangely ingenious turns of thought and
disguises and enthusiastically poetical expressions, which cannot but make upon the modern reader a truly distressful
impression,—all this is a notable and significant index of the
moral bewilderment of the Greek spirit.

Plato's development of the idea of the moral is as follows:

* *Symp.*, p. 181 *sqq.*, 216 *sqq.*; *Phaedrus*, p. 250 *sqq.*
† *Gorg.*, p. 494; *Phaedrus*, p. 250; *Symp.*, p. 180 *sqq.*
‡ *Phaedrus*, p. 251 *sqq.*   § *Symp.*, p. 183.
‖ *Phaedrus*, p. 237 *sqq.*; comp. 230, 242; *Symp.*, p. 183.

Virtue, as essentially constituting a unity, appears primarily as *wisdom*, σοφία, consisting in a knowledge of the truth and of the good; upon wisdom as the chief virtue, depend all the other virtues. Now, in that wisdom brings to the consciousness what really is, and what is not, to be feared in our moral efforts and in our struggle against hostile powers, it develops our natural zeal in acting into the virtue of *manliness* or courage, ἀνδρεία. And in that it teaches us what is the inner harmony of the soul, and what is the proper subordination of sensuous and irrational desires to reason, it develops the virtue of *temperateness* or *prudence*, σωφροσύνη, which preserves the right inner order of the soul through the domination of reason over all lower life-forces and pleasure-desires; these lower desires are not crushed out, but simply kept within proper limits, and placed in the service of reason. In that wisdom guides to outward activity the harmony of the inner soul-life in its relation to other men, it develops the virtue of *justness*, which preserves harmony with and among men, in that it respects the rights of each individual; it presupposes the other three virtues, and indeed gives them their proper force and significancy.* To justness belongs also *piety* or holiness, ὁσιότης, which preserves man in his proper relation to the gods;—Plato uses here, constantly, the plural.† A more full development of the virtues Plato has not given; and the necessity of precisely the four ones actually given is based more on the nature of the State than on that of the moral person. A special treatise on duties is not given; and, in consideration of the notion that an inwardly harmonious and hence virtuous soul finds, of itself, the proper course in each particular conjuncture,‡ such a treatise appears indeed as superfluous. That morality is not conceived of as of a merely individual character, but, on the contrary, as realizing itself essentially in moral communion, is a great advance of the moral consciousness; but in that this thought is carried out in the most rigid one-sidedness, and, as it were, with a theoretical passionateness, and in that it lacks the proper historical and religious bases, Plato has arrived, in his enthusiastically and persistently pursued ideal of a State, at a positive caricature, which has brought upon the great philosopher, in the eyes of those

* *Protag.*, pp. 332, 349; *Rep.*, p. 428 *sqq.*, 442 *sqq.*, 591.
† *Euthyphron*, p. 6 *sqq.*; *Gorg.*, pp. 507, 522.　　‡ *Polit.*, pp. 294, 297.

who look upon the real world with practical sobriety, the appearance of ridiculousness, or at least the reproach of an utterly unpractical theorizing;* and it has often been undertaken to rescue the reputation of the great man by simply holding his state-theory as a mere ideal not in the least designed for realization. But both this reproach, and also this attempt at vindicating his honor, do injustice to the philosopher. Unquestionably his work on the *State* is the most mature and the most fully perfected of his writings,—one upon which he wrought with the highest and most enthusiastic preference. (His work on the *Laws* has greater reference to the real world, which as yet was very different from his ideal State, and expresses rather a preliminary expedient, until the true state finds a bold creator.) That his ideal of a state was not intended by him for realization, has no good evidence in its favor, and is on the whole incredible; on the contrary, it cannot be doubted but that Plato made repeated attempts, and with well-grounded hopes, at realizing his state-theory by the help of Dionysius the Younger in Syracuse;† and his own declarations as to the practicability of his state-theory confirm this.‡ From our own social views these theories differ very widely, it is true; but to a Greek, and especially to the state-institutions of the Doric tribes, which were regarded by Plato with great admiration, they were by no means foreign, and they have already in the laws of Sparta an actual prototype in very essential points. Precisely in its contrasts to the Christian view of moral communion, to the idea of the Christian Church and of the Christian state, the Platonic state is very instructive.

Not individual man, but the state, is the moral person proper, by which all the morality of the individuals is conditioned, produced, and sustained. Not the moral individual persons make the state, but the state makes the moral persons. Without the state, and outside of it, there is no morality proper, but only unculture. Hence the task of the state is to make its citizens into morally good persons,—to undertake the cure of souls.§ The state,—which in its inner constitution as a harmonious

---

* Made as early as by Aristophanes, and even by Aristotle: *Polit.* ii, 1-5, 12.

  † See K. F. Hermann: *Gesch. u. Syst. d. plat. Phil.*, 1839, i, 67.

  ‡ *Rep.*, p. 471 *sqq.;* 499, 502, 540; *Legg.*, 709.   § *Gorg.*, p. 464.

moral organism, answers to the three phases of the soul-life of man, and represents (1) reason or thought and knowledge, and (2) courage or zeal, $\theta\nu\mu\delta\varsigma$, and (3) sensuousness, in the three classes of society, namely, (1) the savans, who therefore rule, (2) the warriors, and (3) the producers, that is, the instructing, the protecting, and the providing classes,*—realizes inner harmony, and hence at the same time justness and happiness, in that it does not permit each individual to act and work at his personal discretion, and to select his own life-calling, but on the contrary in that it assigns to each his special and appropriate position in the whole,—a position which the individual must unquestioningly accept and fulfill, without intermeddling in any manner in any other form of activity. A rigorous separation of ranks and of professions by the state itself, is the unconditional presupposition of a healthy state-life. The rulers have the task of assigning the individuals to the particular classes, according to their capabilities.† The productive class, which corresponds to sensuous desire, has as its special virtue, temperateness or modesty, which it realizes by keeping itself within its proper bounds. Courage and wisdom belong to the two higher classes; these two are the gold and silver, while the productive class is but ignoble brass. The producer is not to concern himself with state matters, but simply to attend to handicraft and agriculture.‡ Slavery is presupposed as a mere matter of course; however, where practicable, only non-Greeks are to be sold as slaves.§

The rulers have wisdom as their essential virtue; there can never be in the state but a few of them, and it is best when there is but one, and this one a philosopher. The good of the whole requires the exclusive dominion of the best,—an absolute aristocracy or a monarchy.‖ And as wisdom can find the right course in each particular case, whereas laws must always be merely general, and often do not apply to particular conjunctures, hence the power of those who rule should not be cramped by many laws, but must have scope for free movement, and must decide in each particular case with entire discretion; and the wise ruler will often, without law and *against* the will of the

* *Rep.*, p. 369 *sqq.*, 412 *sqq.*, 435.

‡ *Polit.*, p. 289 *sqq.* ; *Rep.*, pp. 374, 397.

‖ *Polit.*, p. 292 *sqq.*, 297 ; *Rep.*, pp. 473, 540.

† *Ibid.*, pp. 412–415.

§ *Rep.*, p. 469.

citizens, and hence with force, realize the weal of the state, and force the citizens to let themselves be made happy.*

The truly free personality is conceded accordingly only to the sage, who is at the same time the ruler; all the other citizens of the state are, in their entire life, absolutely subject to the state, the spiritual essence of which finds its expression not so much in abstract law as in the perfected personality of the ruling sage. Though the members of the third class are left more free, still this is done only out of contempt; "even if shoe-cobblers are bad, still they bring little danger to the state."† The true citizen, the one possessing the virtue of wisdom and manliness, is under the absolute guidance of the state; the absolutism of the state is without limitation. The two higher classes, as the proper and complete representatives of the spiritual essence of the state, the sentinels of the same, are reared and educated, and determined in their collective life by the state. In their education first importance is given to music and gymnastics, in order that they may learn to love and practice harmony; the education of the future rulers—who can become rulers only at the age of fifty years, after having passed the test of severe trials—requires, additionally, special acquaintance with mathematics and philosophy.‡ To any other religious culture than that given by philosophy, Plato, who clearly saw the worthlessness of the popular religion, could not refer.§

The state as including in itself and guiding all morality, and as realizing justness, has all and every right; the individual citizen of the state has rights only in so far as the state concedes them to him; even to his life he has no right, so soon as he is no longer capable of benefiting the state; the physicians are charged with the duty of letting the incurably sick perish without help.‖ The state alone is entitled to property; private property is not to be allowed. The producing class labors not for itself, but solely for the state.¶ With this principle Plato supposes himself to have quenched at once all the sources of contention and disquiet. Even the art of poesy stands under the rigid censorship of the state; and dramatic poetry is not to be tolerated at all.** The appropriate meters to be used in

* *Polit.*, pp. 293–296; *Rep.*, pp. 473, 540.   † *Ibid.*, p. 421.
‡ *Ibid.*, p. 402 *sqq.*, 424, 519 *sqq.*, 535.   § *Ibid.*, p. 386 *sqq.*
‖ *Ibid.*, p. 405 *sqq.*, 409.   ¶ *Ibid.*, pp. 416, 464.   ** *Ibid.*, p. 391 *sqq.*, 568.

poetry are carefully prescribed, and of musical instruments only the cithara and the lyre are allowed.*

The *family* is not the foundation, but only a branch of the state, and merges itself into it. Personality has here no right of its own. No one consort belongs to the other, but both belong exclusively to the state. Wedlock proper is consequently inadmissible, on the contrary the citizen is obligated to the begetting of children in the interest of the state; in this connection personal love to the sex has no validity, but only civic duty. The citizen is not permitted to choose for himself the wife (who is conceded to him only temporarily), but the state gives her to him,—ostensibly by lot, but in reality the rulers are to "make use of falsehood and deception," and cunningly to guide the lot according to their own judgment, so as always to bring together the most suitable pairs. Men are under obligation to beget from their thirtieth to their fifty-fifth year; women to bear from their twentieth to their fortieth year. This of itself implies that there is to be no permanent marriage relation; on the contrary a change of wives is expressly required; no one is permitted to regard any woman as his own exclusive possession.† It is laid down as a principle for the free and active citizens proper, "that all the women should be in common to all the men, and that no woman should live solely with one man, and that also the children are to be in common, so that no father shall know the child begotten by him, and no child its own father."‡ Hence the children are, immediately after their birth, to be taken away from their mothers, and to be reared in common on the part of the state, and the greatest possible care is to be taken that the mother shall never again recognize her child. The children are nursed by the women in common and interchangeably; feeble and physically imperfect children are to be exposed.§ After the lapse of the determined period of life, the procreation with the persons specifically assigned by the state, and as having taken place at the order of the state, is to cease, and, from this time on, both the men and the women may form temporary connections with each other on the principle of elective affinity, with the one proviso that births must be prevented, or, where this cannot be done, the child must be left

---

* *Rep.*, pp. 398, 399.   † *Ibid.*, 449 *sqq.*
‡ *Ibid.*, 457.   § *Ibid.*, 457 *sqq.*

to perish without food.*—The woman is not a family-mother, but only a state-citizen, and she has political duties, in real and even magisterial state-offices, to fulfill. The women must perform the same work as the men,—must even take part, entirely nude, in the gymnastic exercises,—must march out in war, though in battle they are to occupy only the rear-ranks; for indeed between men and women there is no other difference than simply that the former beget, and the latter bear, and that the former are stronger than the latter.†

This family-undermining absolutism of the state has to do however, only with the first two classes, while the producing class are less affected by this care of the state for them, and may act with greater freedom. The great task toward which all moral community-life is directed, namely, to realize the idea of the body politic, by means of the moral freedom of the individual, Plato was unable to accomplish otherwise than by an unconditional and unquestioning non-permission of the free personal self-determination of the individual. Objective morality entirely swallows up the subjective. This is, however, not peculiar to the view of Plato, but is the Greek tendency in general. Plato manifests rather a decided progress toward the development of the free moral personality. While in the legislation of Sparta, somewhat as in that of the Chinese, the impersonal law held ruthless domination, and disallowed of the personal self-determination of the individual in very essential things, and while in the democracy of Athens the irrational caprice of the masses was the predominant power over the individual, in the Platonic state the personal spirit of the wisely taught and tested regent attains to domination. From the stand-point of heathen antiquity, which knows of no right of the person over against the state, but concedes the absolute right of the state over the individual, this is a progress; and that which appears therein as unnatural and as a harsh one-sidedness indicates not so much the untruthfulness of the consequential progress, as rather the untruthfulness of the fundamental view common to all the Greeks.

That the spirit of wisdom and power can be and is to be poured out upon all flesh [Joel iii, 1], and that there is no difference before God, but that all are equally called to be children

---

* Rep., 461. † Ibid., 451 sqq., 471, 540.

of the truth and of wisdom, this thought is unknown to entire heathendom, and therefore also to the greatest of heathen philosophers. Of a morality absolutely valid for all men and without exception, Plato knows nothing; without slavery, society does not appear to the Greek as possible; but the slave is not called to, nor capable of, free self-determination, and hence also not of true morality; and even of the free, only a relatively small number are accessible to true wisdom and virtue. Capability and incapability for the good are transmitted through natural generation from parents to children.* The reason for this dividing of humanity into a minority who represent reason, and into an irrational, passive multitude who require absolute guidance, lies not exclusively in the general Greek national consciousness, but also in the philosophical world-theory of Plato in general. The primitive dualism of existence manifests itself also in humanity. Even as the world is not an absolutely pure and perfect expression of the spirit, and as the rational spirit is not an absolute power, but has simply to shape a formless proto-material not created by it, and to impress itself upon it, without however being able entirely to master and spiritually transfigure it,—so also in humanity the men of the rational spirit, namely, the philosophers, stand over against the spiritually dependent and relatively unspiritual multitude, whose destination it is to be absolutely guided and shaped by the former.

SECTION XV.

The essential advance of the ethical view of Plato beyond earlier theories consists in this, that he emancipated the idea of the good from all dependence on the individual pleasure-feeling, that he conceived it as unconditionally valid and lying in God himself, and that consequently he regarded morality as God-likeness, as an image of God in man, and hence as a phase of the spiritual life constituting an essential part of rationality itself, and that in consequence thereof he conceived morality as a *per se* perfectly unitary life, and reduced the plurality of moral forms of action to

* *Rep.*, 459 *sqq.*, 546.

a single principle, namely wisdom.—But the characteristically heathen dualism, which (though reduced by him to its minimum) is yet not entirely overcome, rendered it impossible for him to rise to the full freedom of the personal spirit in God and in man, and hence to the full knowledge of the moral idea. The real personality is recognized neither in its rights and power, nor in its guilt. There remains in all existence, even in the most highly developed moral life, a never entirely overcomable residuum of an unfree, unspiritual, and morally spirit-trammeling matter, over which God himself is not absolutely master. But the limitation of the moral lies not in the guilt of the personal spirit, but in the unspiritual (and not by it entirely controllable) nature-ground of things. The possibility, and therefore also the requirements, of the moral are different for the different classes of men, but even the most free is not entirely free. The moral freedom of the freest, namely, the philosophers, is trammeled by the fetters of a corporeality not in harmony with the moral task, that of the rest of men by lack of knowledge and of moral capacity, and that of the free Greek citizens, additionally, by the power of the rulers as extending beyond the expressed laws, and that of the unfree Greek citizens, still additionally, by the weight of the entire mass that presses upon them from above. From this progressively and descendingly increasing unfreedom there is no redemption within the sphere of historical reality, but only yonside of history, through death.—Morality bears, neither in its progressive realization nor in its guilty perversion, the character of historicalness,—is in no respect a power essentially modificatory of universal history, and consciously aiming at such modification as its

end; and even the ideal state is and remains simply
the very limited activity-sphere of a special moral
virtuosity of the governing individual spirit, without
a higher world-historical purpose in relation to the
totality of humanity.—Also the moral consciousness
itself rises not entirely above the character of the
merely individual; the connection of the same with
the God-consciousness is only of a loose character,—
is not really based in the same.

The gain accruing to moral knowledge through the labors of
Plato is not to be lightly estimated. Light and order are given
to the previously dark and confused mass. There is henceforth
no more question of merely isolated and not deeper-grounded
moral rules, but morality has acquired a firmer basis,—has come
here for the first to serious self-examination. In fact, Plato occupies himself so predominantly with the foundation-laying
thoughts that he does not reach the task of carrying out a
special doctrine of virtue or duty. In these ground-thoughts
there are, in so far as is possible from a heathen stand-point,
some approximations to a Christianly-moral consciousness; and
they would have been more marked still, had the philosopher
only succeeded in severing the chain which still held the already
floating ship fast anchored to the soil of naturalism, namely, by
overcoming the thought of an unspiritual proto-material as
offering a hinderance to the personal God,—in a word, had he
succeeded in changing the μη ὀν which lies at the basis of the
real world, into an οὐκ ὀν. But neither Plato nor the heathen
spirit in general was able to do this. Even Aristotle was able
only silently to vail the, also to him, troublesome thought of
dualism, but not scientifically to master it. But wherever the
rational spirit is not absolutely the ground and life of every
thing, there also the full idea of morality is not possible; for
only the thought of the complete mastery of the spirit over
every thing unspiritual, and the confidence of untrammeled liberty, assure to morality foundation-ground and courage.

Though in the recognition of the limits of freedom there lies
an approximation to the Christian thought of the natural de-

pravity of the human race, yet there lies in it, on the other hand, also an all the greater departure from the same; for these limits are not placed in the sphere of moral guilt, and hence of moral freedom, but yon-side of morality in the sphere of a nature-substratum not to be overcome by the moral spirit. The hampering of morality has not sprung from an historical act, and hence is not to be overcome by an historical act. The consciousness of the moral imperfection of the world, which despite all the idealism of the Platonic world-view comes often to painful expression, leads not to the thought of a needed redemption. The sage emancipates himself, so far as, in view of the imperfection inherent in the essence of all existence, it is possible, from the limitations of his moral life, and he emancipates others only through philosophical instruction and through absolutistic state-guidance, but not through a sanctifying communion-grounding historical act.

In the idea of the state there lies indeed the presentiment, that morality, in its true character, is not a merely individual quality, but, on the contrary, has an historical significancy and task, but Plato does not rise beyond the mere presentiment; and when he is on the very point of passing beyond the limits of a merely individual morality, and into the sphere of an historical one, he hesitatingly checks his step and turns back. His State forms no link in history, and has no history as its goal. As it is not sprung of history, but only of the ingenious intellect of a theoretical philosopher, so it is designed to be nothing other than the platform upon which the geniality of the individual personality of the philosophic regent may find scope for itself. Neither people nor ruler are to be the representatives of an historical idea; on the contrary, the people is only the passive material for the formative hand of the state-artist, and the ruler only the executor of a philosophic theory. The state itself is to be only an individual organism along-side of many other state-organisms, likewise ruled by individual geniality. Hence it must also be only very small; even a thousand citizens suffice. The thought of regarding the state as a vital member in an historical collective organism, lies very far from Plato. Hence, though his state is a moral organic system, yet it has no world-historical character; it has neither behind it an historical presupposition, nor before itself an historical goal. That hu-

manity in general is a goal of the moral striving, that it may be brought together into a moral unity, that a state of peace among all nations is to be aimed at—of all this Plato has not the remotest presentiment; rather does war appear, even for his ideal state, as in accordance with order, and as a necessary matter of course; for in fact Greeks and non-Greeks are enemies by nature.* Let this state-ideal of the profoundest Greek philosopher, as presented without any trammeling from a resisting real world, be compared with the Old Testament theocratic state as brought to realization among a stubbornly resisting people, and which had, from the very beginning, a world-historical goal, and which kept in view, and had as the basis of its entire organization, the thought of the salvation, and hence also of the peace and unity, of entire humanity,—and the result will be very suggestive.

Most manifestly appears the weakness of Platonic ethics in its relation to the *religious* consciousness. The beautiful conception of the God-likeness of the moral man, Plato is not able to carry out; the founding of the moral upon the divine will is foreign to him, and must have been so, for the Greek knows nothing of a revelation of this will, and the philosopher could not invent one; he was only able to refer to the rational consciousness of man himself; but to raise this consciousness to a universally-extant and valid one Plato did not venture to hope, and hence he placed simply the authority and even the strong dictatorial power of the philosophers, in the stead of the authority of a divine revelation. Also his profoundly-conceived God-idea, which far surpassed all previous results of heathenism, Plato did not venture to carry out in its entire ethical significancy, and to make it consequentially the basis of the moral. It is true he is far removed from the folly of certain modern theories, which present morality as entirely independent of piety; he in fact makes piety a very essential element of all moral life, and derives even from the idea of a divine judgment after death, a very potent motive for morality;† still, piety is with him not the foundation of all the virtues, but only a single one of the same, and that too not the first one, but only a form of justness; and even such as it is he ventures not to refer it directly to the philosophically-recognized God-idea, but only to

* *Rep.*, p. 373, 469 *seq.*   † *Gorg.*, p. 523 *sqq.*

the *gods* of the popular religion. But as he himself exposes the immoral character of the Greek mythology with a noble indignation, and on that account, bitterly censures the so highly and universally-revered Homer, nay, even would have his poems, for moral reasons, banished from his ideal state,* it is consequently difficult to say how he could justify and require piety toward these gods. There remains here a wide-reaching and unbridged chasm in his ethical teachings.

SECTION XVI.

The completer of the Platonic philosophy, and of Greek philosophy in general, namely, *Aristotle*, who in many respects passed independently beyond Plato, and who was less idealistic than he, and more devoted to the study of sober reality, presented ethics for the first time as a special systematically carried-out science, —in connection with Physics on the one hand, and with Politics on the other. The greatest possible repression of the dualism of the primitive elements of existence, as still yet admitted by Plato, leads Aristotle not to a deriving of the moral idea from his more fully developed God-idea, but to a still more confident grounding of the same in the rational self-consciousness, which appears here less clogged than in Plato. A sound psychology affords for ethics a scientifically firm basis, but the repression of the Platonic antithesis of the ideal and of reality gives it a morally feebler character.

Of the three different presentations of Aristotelian ethics, only the *Ethica Nicomacheia* (that is, *ad Nicomachum*) is, in the eyes of the trustworthy results of criticism,† to be regarded as

---

* *Rep.*, p. 377 *sqq.*, 386 *sqq.*, 598 *sqq.*, 605.

† Spengel, in his *Abhandl. d. Kgl. Baierschen Akad.*, *philos.-philol. Klasse*, 1841, iii, 2; 1846, p. 171 *sqq.* Brandis: *Aristoteles*, 1851, i, p. 111 *sqq.*; ii, p. 1555 *sqq.*

a genuine work of Aristotle, though probably not prepared by himself for publication, but only sketched for personal use in his lectures; while the *Eudemic* ethics (Εὐδήμια) is very probably a work of Eudemus, a disciple of Aristotle, and is derived mostly from the first-mentioned work, with some original additions,—the so-called *large* ethics (μεγάλα) being a digest from both. In his *Politics*, which Aristotle separates from ethics, though as subordinate thereto, morality is contemplated in its complete realization in the state as the moral community-life. Hence this work is evidently to be reckoned to his Ethics, and to be regarded as its carrying-out.

Aristotle gives to ethics its name—which it has ever since borne—and a scientific form which served as a model for the entire Christian Middle Ages. His comprehensive *Ethica*, consisting of ten books, contains indeed many excellent thoughts, and, above all, gives evidence of a close observation of reality, and in this respect is by far more sober and less idealistic than Plato; as a system, however, it is still very defective, and contains chasms on very essential points. Only relatively few general thoughts are really scientifically developed; by far the larger part is treated rather empirically and aphoristically; Aristotle expressly renounces all attempts at scientific strictness of demonstration and development, for the reason that, in his view, the subject does not admit of this, but only of probability. Hence the form of presentation—in direct contrast to Plato's uniformly spirited and either scientifically or poetically inspired style,—sinks not unfrequently to dry common-sense observations, and lingers for the most part entirely within the sphere of the popular grasp.*

Aristotle does not rise to the full idea of the absolute God—an idea which is attained to only in the thought of creation—but he halts immediately before reaching it; he pushes, however, still further into the back-ground the primitive antithesis between God and the not truly real proto-material of things, which was already very much enfeebled in Plato, without, however, entirely overcoming it. He is loth to admit a primitive

---

* Compare Biese: *Philos. des Arist.*, 1838 *sqq.*, 2 vols.,—a studious presentation, though not sufficiently digested philosophically. Brandis: *Arist.*, 2 *Abth.*, 1857 (especially pp. 1335-1682): profound but too detailed. Trendelenburg: *Histor. Beitr. z. Phil*, ii, 1855, p. 352 *sqq.*

antithesis of being, but he also fails to pronounce the word which alone leads beyond it,—the word with which the Old Testament begins. The world is in his view not merely the best possible one, but it is the absolutely perfect expression of the will of the rational spirit. Hence he gets rid also of that notion of Plato, of an evil that pervades all real existence, and especially humanity. All reality is, on the contrary, good; also the corporeality of man is no longer an imprisonment inflicted for a previous guilt, but it is the normal organ of the soul. And of an historically-originated depravity, Aristotle has no notion whatever. It is true, the great mass of the populace are so qualified by nature that they have no inner tendency toward virtue, but are guided by sensuous impulses and fear (Eth. Nic., x, 10), but the better-gifted free-born man is by nature thoroughly good, and hence has in his own reason the pure fountain of moral knowledge. On this presupposition Aristotle can have perfectly free and confident scope on the basis of the subjective spirit; and notwithstanding that he conceives the idea of God as the rational absolute spirit, more profoundly than Plato, still he connects the study of nature and of the moral spirit much less closely with the God-idea than does Plato. From the very circumstance that he finds in the real world a much more pure expression of the divine thought than Plato, he is enabled to confide himself more unquestioningly to reality, to merge himself trustingly into the real world, to read in its traces the words of divine truth; and he has also much less need of the supernatural element, which, because of the God-opposed undivine substratum of the universe, was highly necessary in the system of Plato.

Hence in Aristotle morality is entirely rooted in the soil of the subject; it appears less as the holy will of God to man, than as the absolutely normal essence of the spiritual life, as called-for by the rational human spirit itself. While there was in Plato at least the foreshadowing of the truth, that the goal of the moral striving lies in God-likeness and in the pleasure of God in man, and hence bears an objective character, in Aristotle the subjective character comes decidedly into the fore-ground, namely, in the thought that this goal is the personal well-being of the moral subject. In Plato the highest and truest is and remains an object of the yon-side, an absolutely ideal somewhat

that is never perfectly presented in reality, and never entirely to be attained to,—in Aristotle all ideality becomes also real, and all that is true a quality of the this-side, and that, too, not as brought into reality from without, but as wrought-out from within. The real world is also in moral respects a perfect expression of the idea, and no longer a mere feeble impression thereof,—is the original, is an organism that potentially unfolds itself with its own inherent power. Hence we find no longer any longing and thirsting after a better and ideal world, no poetical contemplating, no painful consciousness that the spirit is fettered and bound in bands of unfreedom by an unspiritual substratum of the universe; with Aristotle life has no longer a tragical character; from his world-theory there spring no longer any dark and mysterious tragedies; his theory is a quieting, genial one; and with the falling away of the longings of unsatisfaction, falls away also poetry; the sober prose of the spirit as contenting itself with the world as it is, takes its place. And in this very contentedness there lies a greater antithesis to the Christian world-theory than is presented in the Platonic consciousness of an inner antagonism of existence. The rather mystical contemplativeness of Plato gives place to a calculatingly rationalistic view.

The psychological examination of the presuppositions of ethics, is much more largely and deeply carried out by Aristotle than by Plato, and constitutes the bright point in his philosophy; but that his ethics has, in fact, predominantly only a psychological character, and is rooted neither in religion nor in history, is its weak side. While Plato makes at least an effort to give to morality an ideal character transcending reality, the ethics of Aristotle rather confines itself with unquestioning satisfaction to the sphere of the reality of man, without even raising the query, whether this reality is in a state of normal purity, or on the contrary of deterioration; and it is characteristic of their respective views of the moral, that the thought of personal immortality which stands forth so prominently in Plato, and which gives to the moral striving its proper tone and consecration, retires in Aristotle into a very dubious back-ground. In fact, he directly declares it as absurd ($\check{\alpha}\tau o\pi o\nu$) to affirm, that no one is happy until after he has died (Eth. Nic., i, c. 11, 13); he knows only of a morality of the this-side. And he expressly

declares death as the greatest of all evils (φοβερώτατον ὁ θάνατος);
"for it is the end of every thing; and for the deceased there
appears to be no longer either any good or any evil" (Eth. Nic.,
iii, 9), and hence death robs man of the highest goods (iii, 12).

SECTION XVII.

All striving has a goal, and this goal is for the rational striving a *good*, and hence the highest goal is
the *highest good;* and this highest good is a perfect
felt *well-being*, which is not a merely passive state,
but a perfect active life of the rational spirit; and
hence it consists essentially in *virtue*, which in its
turn includes *per se* in itself the *feeling* of *happiness*.
—Virtue itself is either *thought-virtue* or *ethical virtue*, according as it relates to reason or to sensuousness. Thought-virtue is acquired by learning, ethical
virtue by practice. As the good consists in harmony,
and hence in a proper measure, hence the non-good
consists in a too-much or a too-little. Hence virtue
is always the observance of the proper *mean* between
two unvirtues. The presupposition of all moral action
is the perfect freedom of the will, a doctrine to which
Aristotle,—in opposition to the view of Socrates that
the knowledge of the right necessarily leads to its
practice,—holds distinctly fast.

The rational spirit is not a reposing or merely passively moved
entity, but an activity. The thinking spirit is at the same time
a volitionating, an acting, and a working spirit. All volitionating aims at something as an end, namely, in all cases, that
which appears to him, who volitionates, as a good. Hence the
good (τὸ ἀγαθόν) is primarily that whereon the striving is directed in view to its attainment. Now there are many and different
ends and goods, whereof some are related to others merely as
co-adjutant, as means to higher ends and goods. But if the
striving is a rational one, that is, a sure and consistent one, then
there must be a last end, a highest good, which is not a mere

means to another end, but which is aimed at for its own sake, and for the sake of which alone we aim at all other goods, and which is hence an absolutely perfect end, a τέλειον, which has its end, το τέλος, within itself. Honor, riches, knowledge, etc., are goods, though they are not sought for their own sake, but always for a higher purpose to which they are but the means,—are but the partial goods of one perfect good; and this good is the *perfection* of one's own existence and life, the *well-being*, εὐδαιμονία, that is, the vitality of the life as perfect in itself, and as being its own end,—ζωῆς τελείας ἐνέργεια. This well-being is not sought in the interest of another good, but for its own sake, and is hence the highest *good* (Nic., i, c. 1 *sqq.;* comp. Eud., i, 1). This "eudaemonia" is by no means one and the same with our notion of happiness, but includes the same in itself. Happiness is only the one, the subjective phase, namely, the happiness-feeling that is connected with this "eudaemonia," whereas the "eudaemonia" itself has essentially and primarily an objective significancy, namely, the being well-conditioned or blessed, the possession of the all-sidedly perfect life. Hence it is not without meaning when a special examination is entered upon as to whether the pleasure-feeling is included in the "eudaemonia" (Nic., i, c. 9).—The good is accordingly by no means a mere idea never entirely realizable in the this-side, as with Plato, but it is a full reality already in the present life,—finds this reality in the actual being and life of the sage; it is not a merely abstract general something, but a definite quality inherent in individual existence; not a yon-side something transcending all special goods, but one that is realized in the totality itself of these goods (Nic., i, 4). This totality, however, is not a mere sum, for were this the case the highest good might be increased by some newly added good, but it is a unitary whole, whereof the different goods are but the special forms (Nic., i, 5).

Well-being as a purely human good is not mere life, for life exists also with plants and animals, nor yet the mere sentient life, for this exists also with animals; but it is the *rationally-active* life, and hence the perfectly active life of the rational spirit,—is not mere being and determinatedness, but a self-determining, an ἐνέργεια,—is not merely a good, but *works* the good on and on (Nic., i, 6, 7). This implies of itself that the highest good, well-being, is not outside of or merely subsequent

to *virtue;* on the contrary, virtue itself constitutes a part of the essence of the highest good, which in fact consists in activity, though it is not *per se* the whole highest good; for to perfect well-being belongs also the happiness-feeling, the feeling of pleasure, which results upon the successful issuing of the virtuous activity. Hence this happiness-feeling is not a something independent of virtue, and existing outside of and along-side of it; on the contrary the virtuous life already contains happiness as its necessary constituent; for only he is virtuous who does the good *gladly,* who has joy in virtue. In so far, therefore, one may indeed say that the highest good consists in the practicing of virtue, and of all the virtues (Nic., i, 7–9). However, Aristotle admits that to perfect well-being belong also such goods as are not already directly given in virtue itself, such as are even independent thereof, as, *e. g.,* earthly affluence, good descent, beauty, health, a happy close of life, etc. (Nic., i, 9–11). With this very true concession to the natural consciousness as unprejudiced by any one-sided system, the consequentiality of Aristotle's ethical system is manifestly broken. For if there are real goods, and conditions of the highest good, which are independent of moral perfection, and if consequently the truly virtuous man may possibly be without the highest good, then there prevails no moral world-order, and morality is deprived of its assurance; and as it is a legitimate goal to strive for the highest good, hence it follows that man must strive after still other possessions *outside of* morality, and which do not depend thereon, and which he can consequently acquire only in extra-moral and hence immoral ways. But as Aristotle does not recognize any guilty corruption of human nature, hence the above concession involves him in an absolutely insolvable dilemma, in a violent contradiction with his own system. He prefers, however, to be in contradiction with himself, rather than, in the interests of his system, to deny manifest experience, to the true understanding of which he does not possess the key.

But wherein now consists virtue, and hence the most essential element of well-being? In man there is a two-phased life, sensuousness and reason, which are often in conflict with each other. Sensuousness, in so far as it is not purely vegetative, namely, the nutritive activity of the physical life, but sensuous desire, may be and should be governed by the reason. Virtue assumes

accordingly a twofold form; in the first place it relates to the proper condition of reason itself, and in the second place to the proper condition of the sensuous nature, as consisting in the subordination of the same to reason; in the first sense it is *thought-virtue*, in the second *ethical* virtue (αρετή διανοητική and ηθική). The former is mainly wisdom; the latter includes temperateness, liberality, etc. That the former belongs among the virtues, appears from this, that we praise it in a person as his merit (Nic., i, 13). The word ethical as applied here to virtue is taken in its narrower sense, as relating to practical habits. It is clear at a glance, that this division of the virtues is entirely inadequate, unless the one or the other class of virtues is taken in a wider sense than is strictly admissible. For there are purely spiritual virtues, *e. g.*, humility, truthfulness, fidelity, thankfulness, which are in no way connected with sensuousness, and are yet not intellectual or thought-virtues. But if we take wisdom, as in Plato, in the wide sense of an inner harmony of the rational soul in general, then very manifestly the ethical virtues which consist in the controlling of the sensuous nature, would not be co-ordinate but subordinate thereto.—The thought-virtue can be taught or learned, especially by abundance of life-experience; on the contrary, the ethical virtues are acquired by frequent repetitions of the same actions, that is, by habituation,—are essentially facilities in acting, acquired by practice. By nature we have no virtue, but only the possibility and capability thereof; and the capability becomes a real virtue only by practice and habit. Hence virtuous actions are primarily not the consequence, but the ground and presupposition of virtue. It is only by repeatedly acting virtuously that man *becomes* virtuous (Nic., ii, 1, 2). How it is possible to act virtuously before one has virtue, and what motive man can have to act virtuously before he is virtuous, Aristotle asks indeed, and he recognizes the difficulty of the question, but he does not solve it. The indication that we possess virtue is this, that in our virtuous acting we feel also delight. Virtue is neither a passion, such as anger, fear, love, hatred, etc., because the passions are natural movements not springing from our will, nor bearing as yet *per se* any moral character, nor is it a faculty, for this is given by nature, but it is a *facility* (ἕξις), that is, the moral manner of our bearing toward the passions; and indeed it is that particular facility

whereby man becomes a *good* man, and his work a good work (Nic., ii, 5).* This is of course as yet a very insignificant and purely formal definition. In order to give it some contents, Aristotle resorts to this course: In every matter there is only a single form of the right, but manifold forms of the wrong,—even as in regard to a mark there are many directions for shooting by it, but only one for hitting it, for which reason also the right is much more difficult to find and to do than is the unright. The unright in a manner of acting is either a defect or an excess; the right is the correct measure, and hence the mean between the two. Hence virtue is (and this is its complete definition) a freely-willed facility in observing the *middle-way* (μεσότης) as correctly determined for us by reason and by the judgment of the judicious (Nic., ii, 6; iii, 8; comp. Eud., ii, 3). [That in this connection only the *ethical* virtues are meant, appears from the entire context. But by this circumstance the general definition of virtue becomes again more unclear.] The middle-way is in all things the best. Virtue aims consequently not at a mean between good and evil, but at the best, and the best is the mean between too much and too little. Thus, bravery is the mean between cowardice and fool-hardiness; temperateness, the mean between dissoluteness and insensibility to pleasure-sensations; liberality the mean between prodigality and niggardliness; love of honor stands mid-way between unbounded ambitiousness of fame and an absolute indifference to the opinion of others; evenness of temper, between irascibility and stupidity, etc. (Nic., ii, 7). From this it follows that any two mutually-opposed faults stand to each other in a much more violent contrast, than does either of the two to the corresponding virtue (Nic., ii, 8).

It is very manifest that this merely quantitative distinguishing of good and evil does not touch the essence of morality at all, and in its practical application undermines all certainty of the moral judgment, which is thereby transferred from the sphere of the conscience into that of the calculating understanding. In this view evil is not qualitatively, that is, essentially, different from the good, but it differs only in number and degree; hence there is between the two no radical antithesis, but only a gradual transition; in fact the transition from one vice

* Comp. Trendelenburg: *Histor. Beitr.*, i, pp. 95, 174.

tu the opposite one passes necessarily through the corresponding
virtue. Aristotle himself becomes conscious of the defectiveness
of his definition of virtue; he concedes that there are also actions and tempers in regard to which the notion of the too-much
or too-little is not at all applicable, as, *e. g.*, delight in misfortune, envy, murder, theft, adultery, which are all *per se* and in
their essence wrong, and do not simply become so by rising to
a certain height; there can be, for example, no permissible degree of adultery, and so of the other cases (Nic., ii, 7). And if
notwithstanding this he is still unwilling to discard his definition of virtue, this only evinces the utter perplexity of the the-
orist; for by making this concession, his definition is completely
undermined, inasmuch as it is thereby implied that the difference between good and evil is not a quantitative but a qualita-
tive one. And the matter is made much worse still by the
express admission, that virtue is often not in the actual middle
between the two opposite-standing faults, but stands *nearer* to
the one extreme than to the other,—that bravery, *e. g.*, stands
nearer to fool-hardiness than to cowardice, liberality nearer to
prodigality than to niggardliness, etc., and that of two errors
the one is usually less hurtful than the other (Nic., ii, 8),—for
by this admission not only is the ground-principle entirely overthrown, but also all possibility of a certain judgment as to
morality is cut off. By what rule is one to find in the diagonal
the correct virtue-point, if this point is an eccentric one? Aristotle himself feels the great difficulty which results from charg-
ing the moral consciousness of the individual with the duty of
such a calculation; and he knows no better counsel to give than
that given by Circe to Ulysses in regard to his sailing between
Scylla and Charybdis, namely, to steer nearer the less dangerous
Scylla,—to go nearer the extreme that is less remote from the
mean virtue, than to the other, and to incur the risk of the less
fault of the two; and in order most easily to find the middle-
way, one must sometimes deviate (ἀποκλίνειν) on the side of excess, and sometimes on the side of defectiveness (Nic., ii, 9).
More patently than this, Aristotle could hardly possibly have
confessed the insufficiency of his definition of virtue.

Morality presupposes the freedom of the will; only that which
takes place from free self-determination is morally imputed to a
man, is praised or blamed. Virtue belongs exclusively to the

sphere of freedom; that is unfree which is either forced or which is done from ignorance; passionate movements of feeling, such as anger or sensuous desire, do not destroy the freedom of the will, for man can and should control them by reason; even in case of moral violence, by the excitement of fear, etc., the freedom of volition remains; involuntary is only the forced action which takes place with inner resistance (Nic., iii, 1–3; comp. Eud., ii, 6). From willingness as the more comprehensive notion, the *resolution* is, as the narrower, to be distinguished, namely, the will as deliberately directed to a definite and possible-regarded goal (Nic., iii, 4, 5). A resolution is free also in regard to the recognized good or evil. Every resolution is, it is true, directed to a good,—with the sage always to the truly good, but with others to that which to them *seems* to be good; from this it does not follow, however, that men always sin simply from *error*, and that where there is a real knowledge of the good, the resolution must necessarily be directed to this, as is taught by Socrates and Plato. Such a view is contradicted even by the general moral judgment both of individuals and of the State, which makes man, as soon as he has come to understanding, responsible for all the evil which he does, and imputes it to him as guilt. It is true, many do evil simply from the error of their moral judgment or from the worthlessness of their character, but both that error and this worthlessness are their own fault, and do not excuse them; in fact man can even purposely do what he has recognized as evil, namely, by inquiring not after the good, but only after the agreeable; and the opinion that no one does evil voluntarily and consciously, conflicts with undeniable experience and with the essence of will-freedom (Nic., iii, 6, 7; v, 12; vii, 2, 3). In this connection Aristotle makes the significant and almost surprising observation, that the character which has become evil by guilt can just as little be thrown off again at mere volition, as the person who has made himself sick by his own fault, can become well again at mere volition; once become evil or sick, it stands no longer within his discretion to cease to be so; a stone when once cast cannot be caught back from its flight; and so is it also with the character which has become evil. This thought might have led further; Aristotle, however, does not follow it out, and he leaves unanswered the closely related question, as to how,

then, a reformation in character is possible. Moreover, he does not concede to evil any other than an individual effect,—knows nothing of any natural solidarity of evil in self-propagating, morally-degenerated races. Every man, at least the free-born Greek, is, on the contrary, perfectly good by nature, and the sensuous nature with which every one is born has, in reason, its perfectly sufficient counterpoise.

SECTION XVIII.

In carrying out his system into details Aristotle treats first the *ethical* virtues, and as their chief representatives: courage, temperateness, liberality, magnanimity (from which the love of honor is, as of a lower quality, to be distinguished), the proper control of temper, and, as predominantly social virtues: amiability, truthfulness, readiness in good-natured wit, shame, but especially justness and, as closely-related therewith, fairness or equity. As intellectual or *thought-virtues* are examined, more largely, prudence and wisdom; and their significancy is more closely defined than in Socrates and Plato. As considered under another phase, namely, in respect to the degree of the moral power virtualizing itself in the doing of the good, the moral character is distinguished into *virtuousness* in the narrower sense, into *temperateness*, and into *heroic* or *divine* virtue.

The carrying-out of the ethical matter proper, though rich in suggestive thoughts and observations, is devoid of a general scientific development from *one* central principle; nor do we find as yet any strict organic classification. The Platonic division of the virtues (§ 14), though made the basis, is neither strictly observed nor further developed. Differing from Plato, Aristotle does not first discuss wisdom as the root of all the other virtues, but, on the contrary, *manliness* or *courage* (ἀνδρία) which stands mid-way between fool-hardy daring and coward-

ice. It relates not to all the evils that are to be assailed, but
essentially to death; and also not to every mortal danger, but
more especially to the most honorable of these dangers, danger
upon the battle-field, and besides also to mortal danger by sea
and in sickness (Nic., iii, 9–12). This limitation, though explainable from the warlike national character, is not based in
the moral idea; and for courage in the full sense of the word in
the face of *all* evils, Aristotle finds no place at all in his system
of virtue. The motive to courage is not the thought of an
eternal crown,—for death is for the virtuous man the most fearful of all evils, for precisely for him life has the greatest worth,
—but this motive is only a delight in duty and in the beautiful
(Nic., iii, 12).—The second virtue is *temperateness* or moderation (σωφροσύνη), which consists in the observance of the right
mean in regard to sensuous pleasure, even as, on the other
hand, courage relates to evil, that is, pain. The extending
of this virtue to other than the sensuous, and that too the lowest sensuous feelings of taste and of sensibility, is expressly
disallowed; and hence there remain moral phenomena, both
virtues and vices, which find no place whatever in the classes
of virtue admitted by Aristotle. As to the question, by what
rule the proper measure is to be judged, we are not answered;
virtue is simply placed in the middle between the immodera-
tion which surrenders itself passionately to sensuous pleasure,
and which sinks man to the brute, and an entire desirelessness or insensibility to sensuous pleasure, which, however,
only rarely or in fact strictly speaking never exists,—for
then man would be no longer human (Nic., iii, 13–15); in
which case the finding of the virtuous mean between the
two faults would be a rather difficult matter.—*Liberality* or
generosity, as the third virtue, is the observance of the middle-way in the use of property. It gives cheerfully, out of
delight in the beauty of the action, but only to such as deserve it; that it rests on love is not stated. As especially important, is extensively discussed, liberality for public and
generally useful ends, for theatrical entertainments, for popular diversions, for the feasting of the collective citizenship,
for the outfitting of war-ships, and for the keeping up of a
state of luxury in the interest of the dignity of the person,—
the virtue of μεγαλοπρέπεια (Nic., iv, 1–6). Of the moral dan-

gers of riches for the moral disposition itself, aside from the
two errors of prodigality and niggardliness, nothing is said;
on the contrary, riches is regarded as a high and much to be
desired good.—*Magnanimity* (μεγαλοψυχία) belongs only to
men of high gifts, and is, as opposed to empty pretense, on
the one hand, and to self-disparaging pusillanimousness, on
the other, the proper respecting of self, the moral pride of
the great man,—while the proper self-respect of the ordinary
person is not magnanimity, but only modesty; the former
virtue stands higher than the latter.   Only he can be magnanimous who is adorned with all the virtues, that is, the
truly great man; and he puts this virtue into practice, in that
he strives after true *honor*, that is, after the esteem of the
great and noble, as the highest of external goods, while he
disdains the honor and reproach which come from unimportant men.   But proper magnanimity is only possible when, with
the inner virtue-merit there is associated also an outwardly
happy and eminent condition, such as rich possessions, a high-
born family, power, etc., for this brings honor; hence the
magnanimous man will seek, though not primarily and chiefly, after these things, not so much for their own sake, as
simply for the honor associated with them.   In less great
souls the virtue of magnanimity gives place to the *love* of
honor which looks only to inferior degrees of honor, and
which holds the mean between immoderate ambition and
pusillanimity (Nic., iv, 7–10).—The virtue of *equanimity* or
gentleness, (πραότης) occupies the mean between irascibility
and phlegmatic insensibility, and hence consists in the proper
tempering of anger, and is practically of difficult observance.   Not to indulge in anger at all is stolidity, and not to
defend one's self against offenses is dishonorable and cow-
ardly.   It is advisable not to repress wrath, but to let it
come to expression; the indulging of vengeance stills wrath.
Aristotle regards revenge as a something entirely legitimate,
and simply warns against over-indulgence.   More specific
limitations of this dangerous virtue he regards as impracticable, holding that feeling decides this best in each particular
case, and that minor deviations from the right mean are here
not to be censured (Nic., iv, 11).

Without any strict logical connection, Aristotle now passes

to treat of the *social* virtues. Between the vices of a fawning seeking for approbation and a yielding to the wishes of every one, on the one hand, and an unsocial abruptness, on the other, stands the virtue of friendly and polite *amiability*, a virtue which (in distinction from personal love) relates not to definite loved persons, but to all with whom we come into association, and does not rest on love (Nic., iv, 12). Between vain-boastfulness and ironical self-disparagement, lies the virtue of *truthfulness* of discourse, especially in relation to the speaker himself, in other words, straightforwardness and honesty. But inasmuch as too strong self-praise is more offensive to others than self-disparagement, hence it is advisable to speak rather too humbly than too highly of one's self (Nic., iv, 13). A third social virtue relates to social intercourse and jesting, and is, in contrast to buffoonery and excessive irony, on the one hand, and sardonic moroseness on the other, cheerful facetiousness and gracious aptness in wit (εὐτραπελία) (Nic., iv, 14; comp. Eud., iii, 7). Aristotle speaks here merely incidentally of *shame*, that is, the fear of disgrace, which is indeed not *per se* a virtue, but only an instinct; it becomes a virtue only under special circumstances, namely, when a mature person has really done something of which he must feel ashamed, and also in youth, because here the passions are violent, and shame is a check against them. The morally matured man, however, is never to have occasion to feel ashamed, for he is not by any means to think of himself as being so constituted as to be capable of doing anything shameful (Nic., iv, 15). Of the true moral significancy of shame, which is so suggestively indicated in Gen. iii, 7, Aristotle has no conception.

The most important social virtue, the one which in fact includes all the others in so far as they relate to our conduct toward others, is *justness*, which consists in respecting the laws of the State and the rights of others, so that every man is treated as he deserves and as he has a right to claim. In a narrower sense justness relates only to the "mine" and the "thine," to property and earnings. The principle of the just mean is here of difficult application, as there is manifestly no immoral form of conduct which can contain too great an observance of the rights of others (Nic. v, 1–14.)

Related to justness, and belonging thereto in the wider sense of the word, is the subordinate virtue of equitableness or *fairness*. It accomplishes—in contrast to the rigid observance of the letter of the civil law—true justness outside of the requirements of the law, which can in fact only express the general, and cannot apply to every individual case; hence it is an improving and perfecting of the law, in that in the interest of justness one does not in certain cases insist on a right which the outward law concedes (Nic., v, 15). Against his own self man cannot, properly speaking, do injustice; even suicide, as being voluntary, is not an injustice to one's self, but only to the State.

In respect to the intellectual or *thought-virtues*, of which only prudence and wisdom are more especially treated (Nic., vi, 1–13), the thought of the middle-way is of course no longer applicable ; they do not themselves observe the just mean, rather is it they themselves that discover it. *Prudence* or sensibleness (φρόνησις, more than prudence as the word is usually taken, but also not synonymous with reasonableness, as Brandis would have it) is the spiritual facility of making in each particular case suitable practical decisions in regard to what is good or evil for the actor. *Wisdom* (σοφία) is of a higher character, and gives to prudence its right basis. It is the proper knowledge of the ultimate grounds of true knowledge, and the deriving of the same from these grounds, and hence refers to the immutable, whereas prudence has to do with the mutable and transitory ; wisdom relates to the universally valid ; prudence, to that which is befitting for the individual; and hence prudence is the specific practical application of wisdom, which latter expresses rather the moral idea *per se*. Hence prudence or sensibleness is the applying of moral wisdom in the ethical virtues. Wisdom and prudence do not constitute the whole of virtue itself, as Socrates affirms, but they are, as ὀρθός λογός, the necessary presupposition of all the other virtues.

Aristotle passes now to another manner of considering the moral bearing, namely, not, as thus far, in reference to its material quality, but in reference to the degree of moral energy therein virtualized. Over against the threefold gradation of the immoral that is to be distinguished in this respect,

namely, viciousness, incontinence, and brutality,—wherein
the moral consciousness and the moral will are either badly
constituted or feeble, or entirely wanting,—stands the threefold gradation of the moral, namely, *virtuousness* in the narrower sense, *continence*, and *heroic* or *divine* virtue; the latter
makes man entirely like the gods, but is attained to only seldom; but equally seldom is also the opposite extreme, brutality. Incontinence is a weakness of the moral will, for the
person knows that his desires are evil, nevertheless he follows
them, and hence sins (what Socrates declares as impossible)
consciously and from passionateness. On the contrary, he
who is continent or firm in character acts constantly in harmony with his rational insight. The feeble and hesitative
manner in which Aristotle attempts to answer the perplexing
questions which present themselves in this connection, indicates very clearly, how little knowledge he has of the perversity of a corrupted heart (Nic., vii, 1–7). While Socrates
covers the majority of sins with ignorance and error, and
thus palliates their guilt, Aristotle, who recognizes the manifold contradiction between knowledge and volition, goes so
far in the other direction, as to admit inborn faults and passions, and even inborn unnatural vices, and to find therein
a degree of excuse for the deviating of those who are thus
afflicted, from better knowledge; "the fact of having such
proclivities, lies outside of the sphere of the morally evil;"
and when man is dominated by such evil proclivities, it is only
in an improper sense that his conduct is to be called immoral
(Nic., vii, 6). How such an innateness of evil proclivities is
to be explained, we are not informed. The proclivity to *anger* especially is to be judged very mildly,—there lies in it
even something rational, as in contrast to the sensuous desires,
and at all events no presumption; and its justification lies in
its universal prevalence. In general it is excusable to follow
one's natural proclivities, and this all the more so the more
they are universal (Nic., vii, 7). The incontinent are not
properly speaking vicious, but only similar to the vicious,
and for the reason that in them there is no evil purpose
(Nic., vii, 9.)

After an extended consideration of friendship as a special
field of the moral activity, Aristotle concludes with an ex-

tensive discussion of *pleasure* (ἡδονή) and *well-being* (εὐδαιμονία) as results of virtuous conduct. Pleasure is not identical with the good,—is not the highest good, but many kinds of pleasure are goods, and hence to be aimed at, while others are not so. Pleasure is the result of a power-exertion in coming to its goal, and hence is an attendant of life-development *per se;* now, according as this power-exertion is good or evil, so is also the pleasure attending it, and only the pleasure which is connected with an exercise of virtue is true pleasure (Nic., x, 1–5). *Well-being* is not a mere condition, but is essentially life-activity, and indeed such a life-activity as is not a purposeless play, but a rational practicing of virtue. Now as cognition is the highest spiritual exertion of power, hence the acquiring of the knowledge of wisdom is coincident with the highest well-being; all other activity is less constant and permanent, less free and independent,—rests less upon itself and has its end less within itself. Hence the practically-acting life stands only in secondary importance, as in fact also the life and the happiness of the gods, or of God, consists not in such an outward-working activity, but only in reflection. In third importance stand the outward goods of fortune: health, riches, etc. Now, though such goods are indeed also necessary to well-being, still they are needed only in a moderate degree, and the sage can be happy even with relatively small goods of fortune; for he who develops and perfects the thinking spirit with great zeal is the most beloved of the gods, and is the happiest, for he is most like the gods (Nic., x, 6–9). Herein this ethical system returns to its starting-point, though we cannot say that this return results from a natural and organic development. Indeed, the fact that well-being is indicated as the highest good, at the outset of the ethical development, and that now it presents itself in the end as the result of the moral life-activity, would seem to present an excellently rounded development-course of the system; but Aristotle essentially disturbs this organic development of his thoughts by his preference (surprising, in view of his previous discussions) of the contemplative life to the outwardly-active life, and for the assumed reason that the former, as being the truly divine life, far transcends the latter; and when he is at the very point of making the transi-

tion from merely individual morality into the consideration
of the moral community-life,—which rests quite predominantly on the practically-working activity of all the individuals
and is primarily the result thereof,—he throws this activity
with a strange disdain into the background, behind the
purely intellectual activity of the unsocial individual spirit.
In this connection Plato is at least more consequential, in that
he by no means directs the philosopher to the merely contemplative life, but concedes to him political domination as his
peculiar right and his highest calling. It is evidently no
very virtue-encouraging thought, that the highest well-being
should be one-sidedly placed in an activity, for which only
the fewest virtues are requisite.

SECTION XIX.

The idea, already so strongly emphasized by Plato,
of a moral *community-life*, is developed by Aristotle
further still, and more judiciously, without his being
able, however, fully to divest it of the one-sidedness of
the general Graeco-heathen world-view. The idea of
humanity as a moral whole is entirely wanting to him
also ; individual morality has absolute predominance.
The *family* is indeed somewhat more highly conceived of than in Plato, because the reality of life is
more impartially observed, but yet it is not recognized as the basis of the moral whole, but only as a
subordinate manifestation-form of morality as bearing
upon the moral community-life. Wedlock-love and
family-love in general is only a special form of *friendship* as expressive of individual morality. Friendship, however, is not so much a duty as an expression
of the striving after individual well-being,—bears not
an objective but a subjective character.—But also
friendship forms neither the basis nor the transition to
a moral community-life ; the community-life, on the

contrary, is based directly upon the laws as expressive of the moral idea, and as constituting the *state*,
the task of which is, under the guidance of the morally higher-gifted, to tutor and direct the great multitude of the morally-immature, and to habituate them
to the good.

To the examination of *friendship* Aristotle devotes two entire books of his Ethics, in great detail.   Friendship is indeed virtue, but not a special virtue along-side of the others;
it is rather a special manifestation-form of virtue in general.
Its definition is more comprehensive than is usual in modern
times, and includes in itself love in general, but it is by no
means identical with the Christian idea of love; it has not
an objective and general, but only a subjective and individual significancy; it loves not for the sake of the loved one,
but for the happiness of the lover,—seeks primarily not the
weal of the other, but its own, loves not man as man, but
only this or that person according to individual election, to
the exclusion of others.   The idea of general love to man, as
a duty, is to Aristotle also as well as to the Greek in general,
utterly foreign.   The highest attainment consists in true
friendship to one or to a few chosen ones.   Toward the rest
of mankind there is shown only a very feeble and luke-warm
good-will, a justness and fairness which respect essentially
only particular rights,—humaneness in the usual sense of the
word.   Aristotle connects the examination of friendship directly and expressly with that of pleasure, and places it before the more particular development of the latter, and considers it also under such a phase as that it appears not so
much as duty as rather as a virtualization of the striving
after happiness.   Friendship seeks indeed also the weal of
the other, but first of all it seeks reciprocal love, and can exist only where it finds this; nevertheless, that friendship
which loves only for the sake of the pleasure and the benefit,
is not the true and lasting love, but only that which exists
between those who are good and resemblant in virtue, inasmuch as here the *per se* lasting good and the person himself
are loved; in the friend I love, at the same time, that which

is for myself a good; such true friendship, however, is seldom, and can never exist at the same time with many persons (Nic., viii, 1–7; ix, 4, 5). Friendship in the narrower
sense presupposes a certain moral similarity between its subjects; but in a wider sense it may also exist between the dis-
similar, especially where the one person has a spiritual pre-
eminence over the other, and where consequently the kind of
the love is with each party a different one. Under this cate-
gory belongs the love between husband and wife, parents
and children, and between the higher and the lower in rank.
The higher of two persons will, and ought to, be more loved
in this relation, than he himself loves, because loving is
measured by the worth of the beloved object (Nic., viii, 8, 9).
This feature is characteristic of the predominantly individual
and subjective character of love, in Aristotle's system. Even
parents and children stand to each other only in this individual relation,—they adapt the degree of their love according
to the individual worth of the other; the family has not an
objective character which is to be held sacred under all circumstances, and which is superior to all individual choice;
the degree of love diminishes with the increase of the worth
of the subject as compared with the worth of the object; and
for self-sacrificing maternal love, Aristotle, although he ob-
serves it, has no just appreciation.

Of *wedlock* and of sexual love, Aristotle speaks on the whole
only incidentally and very inadequately. Wedlock is the
most natural of all friendships, and has for its end not merely
the generation of children, but also the aiding and complementing of each other in all the relations of life (Nic., viii,
14; comp. Oecon., i, 3). The husband, as the stronger, has
the duty of protecting the wife and remaining faithful to
her (Oecon., i, 4), and the right to rule over her,—not absolutely, however, but only in the sphere belonging to him
(Nic., viii, 12). Children stand to their parents in a permanent debt-relation,—cannot divest themselves of their obligation to them, though the father may cast off his son (Nic.,
vii, 16). The obligation of children to fulfill the will of the
parents is not, however, unlimited, because other obligations
may modify it; the chief duty of children is to show rever-

ence to their parents, and when they need it, to assure them
sustenance (Nic., ix, 2).

In his further discussion of friendship Aristotle makes
many ingenious observations. Those to whom one has shown
benefits, one is accustomed to love more than those from
whom one has received benefits, because every one esteems
especially highly that which himself has done, whereas he
feels the debt-relation as in some sense disagreeable (Nic.,
ix, 7). It is true, Aristotle does not exactly praise this feeling, but he finds it very natural, and has for it no blame.
The truly good man loves himself perfectly, but this legitimate self-love is not an enjoyment-seeking selfishness, for he
loves in himself only the better part, and he promotes his
own weal, in that he loves and works the good; and even
when he makes sacrifices for others, he wins for himself the
higher good (Nic., ix, 9).

In conceiving of the essence of the family as a mere friendship, it is natural that Aristotle should not make it the basis
of the wider community-life, the State, but that he should
place it rather in the sphere of individual morality, and that
he should make the transition to the discussion of the state,
neither from friendship nor from the family, but rather derive the thought of the state immediately from the general
thought of morality, and transfer all the moral significancy
of the family to the thus self-based state. This transition
Aristotle makes thus: the teaching of virtue suffices not for
the great multitude to induce them to virtue, seeing that
they are guided almost exclusively by fear and not by knowledge. The multitude must be trained to virtue and constantly guided, and hence stand in need of laws; the training
of a father suffices not for this, because it lacks the necessary
authority and coercive power; only the rationally-governed
state has both of these, and is hence the necessary condition
of a more general realization of morality (Nic., x, 10).

Aristotle is too judicious an observer of reality, idealistic-
ally to expect all salvation from mere instruction, and not to
admit the moral unimpressibility of the great multitude; he
speaks thereof in the strongest expressions; "the great multitude obeys force rather than reason, and punishment rather
than morality;" "the majority abstain from evil not because

it is disgraceful, but because they fear punishment; guided
only by their passions they aim at nothing but sensuous pleasure, and shun nothing but the pains that are contrary thereto; but of the morally beautiful, and of the true joy therein
contained, they have not the least notion, seeing that they
have never tasted it" (Nic., x, 10); and this moral incapa
bility he expressly refers to the nature that is inborn in them,
and only a few happy ones are free of this innate imperfection; "this nature itself lies evidently not within our own
power, but is by some kind of divine causality conferred
on the truly happy."   To explain this broad difference of
natural endowment, he does not make the least attempt, and
in this he stands far below Plato, who derives the imperfection of human nature (which he also admitted, but conceived
of as universal), from a previous guilt in a life antecedent to
the earthly life.   Aristotle renounces also all hope of radically bettering the morally unreceptive multitude, as indeed
he knows of no possibility of doing it; he contents himself
with keeping them in check, and with placing them under
the discipline of an objective moral reality, the state, or at
least with accustoming them, by force and by potent custom,
to order and to obedience, and with restraining them from
the outbreaks of inborn passion; to be truly free in moral respects, however, is the exclusive privilege of the few who are
naturally-gifted.

   Aristotle recognizes thus the necessity of a moral community-life, which, as upheld by the pre-eminent moral spirit of
the few specially-endowed individuals, furnishes, itself, the
basis of the morality of individuals in general, and develops,
and guides, and keeps it in bounds.   This is a weighty
thought far transcending the shallowness of modern rationalistic liberalism, which recognizes no other objective form of
the moral community-life, than that which has grown up on
the broad basis of the morality of the great multitude,—a
merely abstract product without any power and effectiveness
of its own.   Aristotle regards it as absurd to base a moral
community-life upon the disposition and the spiritual sovereignty of the masses; he calls for the sovereignty of the
spiritual and moral heroes,—the exclusive authority of the
most highly gifted personalities; but he is, as yet, too deeply

involved in the peculiarities of the heathen world-view, to penetrate to the bottom of the defectiveness of human nature, as partially recognized by him, and to find the true solution of the enigma, and to divine the nature of the true remedy; he knows only man's outward phase, but not the depths of the human heart. He ventures not to entertain any doubt as to the moral nature of the state-sages and philosophers, and he knows no other redemption, than (as in contrast to the profound spiritual blindness and the moral stupidity of the masses) in an immeasurable exaltation of the insight and the moral strength of the state-leaders and the sages.—Aristotle sees, in the state, not a remedial institution actually realizing true morality, but only a police-organism acting outwardly, checking the evil, and restoring outward discipline. The state can only ameliorate, but not radically cure; true wisdom and morality are not imparted by it to those who are by nature incapable thereof. This view throws light upon the decided preference of Aristotle for a contemplative life, uninvolved in any political activity. The highest goods can fall to the lot only of the few; the fact is not, that many are called while but few are chosen, but that only a few are called and chosen; there prevails here an absolute predestination, not, however, from a monotheistic, but from a fatalistic ground.

SECTION XX.

The State is related to the individual citizens of the state and to the smaller social organisms—the household-life and the local community—as the absolutely determining and enlivening whole to the members,—is not so much the product as rather the ground of all morality. The threefold gradation of dependence in the household-life, and above all, the relation of *master* and *slave*, as resting upon a primitive nature-destination, is the presupposition of the state. Placing a higher worth upon the natural social relations than Plato, and confining himself more fully to his-

9

torical reality, Aristotle escapes the unpractical idealism of Plato, but also attains to less definite results,
and furnishes rather a criticism than a self-consistent
theory of the nature of the state. Emphasizing the
development of the individual citizen to free self-
determination more strongly than Plato, he modifies
the despotic absolutism of the latter, and presents as
the moral chief-task of the state the moral disciplining of the free citizens. But the state-idea attains to
a universally-human significancy neither in its outward nor its inward relation; humanity both in the .
barbarian and in the slave, is of an imperfect grade,
and capable of no moral emancipation.

Of the *Politics* of Aristotle we have to do only with the
more strictly ethical contents. He does not connect this
work directly with his Ethics, but treats of its subject-matter
from a more practical stand-point; hence he gives, on the
one hand, in his Ethics, the more general thoughts of the
doctrine of the state, and, on the other, he repeats in his
Politics some of the thoughts of his Ethics.

The state is the highest moral communion, and hence realizes the highest of all goods. Its type is the household-life;
its task is not merely to afford protection and help for the
life of the individuals, but essentially to found and promote
the true life, that is, the spiritually moral life, of the whole.
The state is not itself the product of the already developed
moral life of the individuals, but it is the presupposition
thereof; outside of the state there is no moral development;
only he who belongs to the state can be moral; the whole is
antecedent to the parts, and the rational man is a part of the
state; the state is the first, the citizen of the state the second;
outside of the state lives only the animal or God (Pol., i, 1, 2).
Hence the moral relation of the household-life is a presupposition of the state only in so far as it is a constituent element
of the same, but not in such a sense as to imply that it already existed before the state and independently of the same.

It is peculiarly characteristic that of the threefold foundation of the household-life, as stated by Aristotle, namely, the relation of man to wife, of father to children, and of master to slave, he treats of the first two only merely incidentally and briefly, but of the third chiefly, and very thoroughly. Aristotle furnishes for the first time, and in its entirety, a formal *theory* of *slavery*,—a phenomenon very significant for the history of ethics.

The opinion that slavery is not a something entirely natural, but is based only upon violence and arbitrary laws, Aristotle emphatically rejects. A household-life without possessions and without serving instruments is not conceivable, and hence also not without slaves, which are in fact living instruments and possessions. Even as the artist and artisan stand in need of instruments, so the housefather, of slaves, which are consequently absolutely his property, and subject to his discretion; this is a natural, and not a merely legal relation, strictly analogous to the relation of soul and body, —the former as the absolutely dominating, the latter as the absolutely dominated factor. And reality corresponds to the want. Men differ in fact from each other in such a manner that the ones, as being really rational, possess themselves, and represent the soul of humanity, whereas the others represent the body of humanity,—are corporeally strong, and adapted for bodily toil, but are spiritually unfree and ignoble, and, though distinguished by reason from the brute, are yet not governed by reason but by sensuous desires. These are destined by nature to be slaves, and it is well for them that, as the property of others, they are spiritually dominated (Pol., i, 3–5). And Aristotle expressly says that those who are destined by nature to slavery are the non-Greeks, the barbarians. Greek prisoners-of-war are slaves not indeed by nature, but by law, and hence legitimately.—What the significance of slavery is, appears clear from the fact that it is a characteristic of a slave that he may be injured with impunity (Nic., v, 8),—that the notion of justness holds good only between such persons as have rights, and hence not between master and slave; that the legitimate and uncensurable manner of ruling over slaves is the tyrannical, the end of which is simply the profit of the master (Nic., viii, 12; Pol.,

i, 8, 9), and that to a slave as such a relation of love or friendship can as little have place as to a horse or ox,—in which
connection, however, it is to be observed, that in so far as
the slave is also a human being a certain inferior form of love
is admissible. The slave has indeed also a degree of virtue,
for he is required to obey and to be modest and temperate,
but his morality differs from that of the master, not merely
in degree but in essence; while the master is capable of all
virtue, the slave is utterly incapable of the power of delib-
eration (το βουλευτικόν) and hence evidently of the thought-
virtues—prudence and wisdom (Pol., i, 9). The more humane
directions as to the treatment of slaves (Oecon., i, 5; of
questionable authenticity) are to be interpreted in the light
of these principles.

Aristotle subjects the Platonic state to a very keen and
sound criticism; the community of goods and of wives he
rejects, as both unnatural and morally corrupting, and even
impossible (Oecon., ii, 2 sqq.). Of his own views Aristotle
is more reticent than Plato, and he gives rather merely general thoughts than specific details. Only that one should
take active part in political life who possesses all civic virtue, and especially far-seeing insight; but such virtue can
exist only where there is leisure for its development, that is,
in such persons as are free from the necessity of laboring for
the common wants of life,—and hence not in day-laborers,
artisans, or farmers (Oecon., iii, 5; vii, 9). The soil must be
cultivated by slaves. Leisure stands higher than labor, and
is indeed *per se* happiness. A proper state-constitution must
have for its end the weal of all the free citizens constituting
the state; it may be equally well monarchic, or aristocratic,
or republican (the latter being that wherein all the truly free
citizens take part), and over against these stand as their perversions: tyranny, oligarchy, and democracy, all of which
look to the good, not of the whole, but only of individual
persons, or of classes in society (Oecon., iii, 6–8; iv, 1 sqq.).
It is best for the State when the best citizens bear rule; and
the best one is not to be bound by trammeling laws, but
stands free above the law, although in general Aristotle places
the validity of the law higher than Plato, and is not hopeful
of finding such "best" ones very frequently. The mass of

free citizens are indeed to have part in deliberating upon the laws and in promoting justice, but not in actually governing (Oecon., iii, 9 *sqq.*). Aristotle inclines most strongly to a monarchy limited by laws, and, in this, has his eye manifestly upon Alexander the Great.

The state provides for the public worship and for the moral culture of the citizens; hence it prescribes, in order to the obtaining of a vigorous population, the institution of *marriage*. Maidens are to marry at their eighteenth year, and men at about the age of thirty-seven, in order that the children may stand in a proper relation to the age of the parents, and in order that the differing duration of the productive period of the two sexes may stand in some degree of harmony, and the children be robust. The laws are to prescribe the manner of life of the woman while pregnant, and the physical and spiritual training of the children. In relation to the exposing of children, the maxim holds good, "that no physically imperfect (πεπηρωμένον) child is to be raised." Where, however, the traditional usages forbid the exposing of children, there the excessive increase of the population is to be prevented by forbidding the procreating of more than a legally fixed number, and the fetus is to be destroyed before the period of sensation and quickening (Oecon., vii, 15, 16). The education of the children stands, as a matter of high importance, under the care of the state; overseeing this education up to the seventh year, the state then actually undertakes it itself; for the citizens belong not to themselves, but to the state. The boys—and the question is only as to these—are to be instructed in grammar and drawing, because of the utility of these sciences, and in gymnastics in order to the development of courage, and in music in order to the employment of the leisure which becomes the free citizen (labor being confined to the slave), and in order to the awakening of the sense for harmony (Oecon., viii, 3-7).

Though Aristotle presents numerous forms of state-constitution as possible, and as good and appropriate according to existing circumstances, yet to the state of true human freedom he is not capable of rising. Even his most free and most democratic constitution rests absolutely on the basis of

slavery, and on the antithesis of the Greeks, as true men, to the slave-like barbarians. The education of the citizens is, in Aristotle, quite similar to the education of a cavalier in the age of Louis XIV. and XV. It is easy enough to be liberal-minded when all the labor falls to the lot of those who, as unfree, have no share in political life. The fact that a so-called anti-Christian "humanistic" culture of modern times regards the Greeks as the champions of true humanity, of humanitarianism in the broadest sense of the word, and their age and their world-theory as "the paradise of the human mind," from which we of modern times have to learn and receive true humanitarian notions,—is no striking evidence of great impartiality of view. Though Aristotle concedes to the different classes of citizens in the state a somewhat greater freedom and independency of development than Plato, in that he does not attribute all right exclusively to the absolutism of the state, still this recognition of a relatively free self-development does not by any means reach down to the laboring classes; the laborers are absolutely passive and for the most part personally rightless members of the state,—are but the immovably soil-bound roots of the tree whose richly-developed branches and leaves wave freely in the air above. The distinction and the classification of the ranks in society are not a *moral* ordinance, but a merely *natural* and hence unfree one,—rests not upon a moral self-subordination to a moral idea, but upon the compulsory necessity of extra-moral nature-differences,—springs not from a like moral dignity and task, but from the naturally different moral nature of the different classes of mankind. The slave and the laborer are *morally* entirely different and inferior beings, and have neither the task nor the capability of even comprehending the full moral idea, much less that of realizing it; this is the privilege of the higher classes of free citizens. A moral redemption of the great multitude from this ban of moral unfreedom and incapacity is an utterly foreign thought even to the philosopher; nay, he would feel called upon, should he conceive of even the possibility of such a redemption, to assail and prevent it with all his might, for with it would fall to the ground, for the Greek, not merely all reality of the state, but also all possibility of a social com-

munity-life. It is only among the rudest barbarians that he can conceive of a moral equality of the individuals; and the Christian idea of humanity, as moral, must have appeared to the Greek as well as to the Roman as a falling back into rude barbarism; and the war of life and death as carried on against Christianity by the otherwise so tolerant Romans, had, at bottom, not so much a religious as rather a social motive; it was the perfectly correct consciousness, that Christianity, although essentially a purely religiously-moral power, would inevitably radically undermine the foundation-principles of the heathen state, and shatter to pieces the entire absolutely slave-based social fabric. The thought of recognizing the slave and the barbarian as morally equal to the freeman, and as called to equal moral dignity and eternal glory, appeared to the Greek, no less than to the Roman, as a treason to human society, as a high crime against the solely possible foundations of a rational state. Beyond this world-theory Plato and Aristotle did not rise.

As in relation to those within the Greek state, so also in relation to the non-Greeks, is the thought of humanity, in Aristotle, radically defective. The non-Greeks belong only in a very loose sense to humanity at all,—are really but half-men, destined by nature to be dominated over by the Greeks, as born for ruling. War upon them is treated of by Aristotle, unhesitatingly, under the head of the legitimate occupations of life, and more specifically under that of the *chase:* "War is, in its very nature, a branch of industry; for the chase is a form of the industrial activity, which comes to application as well in relation to wild beasts, as also in relation to those men who are destined by nature to be ruled over (πεφυκότες ἄρχεσθαι) but are not willing thereto,—so that consequently such a war is a just one" (Oecon., i, 8). War is regarded by no means as an evil, but as a normal life-manifestation of the nations, as a necessary condition of the virtualizing of one of the most essential of the virtues. The relation of the moral community-life to the rest of mankind is consequently in no sense one which looks to the realizing of a moral communion, but is a purely negating and destructive one. Ethics proclaims not peace but war,—aims not at emancipating and redeeming, but at subjugating; non-Greek humanity is not

an object of moral influencing, but of violent subjugating.
The Greek knows no mission of the word, but only of the
sword.

SECTION XXI.

The form of Grecian and heathen ethics which attained in Aristotle to its highest perfection, is that of the
natural man as contented in and with himself; it lacks
the consciousness of the historical reality and of the
historical development of sin,—of the antagonism of
the reality of natural man, as sprung from an historical
act, to the moral idea, and of the earnestness of the
moral struggle against sin; instead thereof we find
the introduction of a proud distinction between a
multitude incapable by nature of true morality, and
an elect minority of free-born men capable of all
wisdom and virtue, and among the latter a lofty
virtue-pride of man as having attained without severe
inner struggle to an easily-won self-satisfaction. Humility is not a virtue of a free sage, but only of the
slave and plebeian, as born unto serving obedience.—
Morality rests only upon the knowledge (independent
of the religious consciousness) of the *per se* good, but
not upon love,—neither upon love to God nor upon
love to man; love is not the ground, but only a
co-ordinate manifestation-form of virtue. Hence
also the solely true moral community-life is only a
product of wise and rational calculation, but not
of love; and the primitive community-life of moral
love, namely, the family, is not the basis, but only
one phase of the state-life. The moral view of
Aristotle, and indeed of the Greeks in general, is
consequently not merely manifoldly different from
the Christian view, but indeed radically opposed
thereto.

It is very important clearly to realize this inner antithesis of Aristotelian and Christian ethics, and all the more so as Aristotle has had, even up to the latest times, a so great and so largely bewildering influence upon the shaping of Christian ethics. Though not wishing to undervalue the high scientific significancy of the Aristotelian system, we are yet not at liberty to find in it thoughts which are really foreign to it.

The Christian consciousness rests entirely upon the recognition of the general necessity of redemption, and indeed not simply in reference to a moral defectiveness inborn in man, but to one that has fallen to all men through historical guilt. Of this Aristotle knows nothing. When Brandis says : "The doctrine of hereditary sin would not have seemed foreign to him," inasmuch as he saw very clearly the corruption of human nature,* we think he is quite incorrect. It is true Aristotle ascribes to the great multitude, and above all to those who are born for service and labor, an inborn badness, and he describes it in the strongest colors and as a real insuperable incapacity for true virtue ; and it is under this head that falls the confirmatory utterance cited by Brandis, namely, that it is good, in the state, to be dependent, and not to be at liberty to do whatever one may please, "for the liberty to do what one pleases cannot hold in check the evil that is inborn in all men"(το ἐν ἑκάστῳ των ἀνθρώπων φαῦλον) (Pol., vi, 4). Were this to be taken in its full and unlimited sense, Aristotle would thereby come into contradiction with his other so definite and repeated declarations as to the perfect will-freedom of those who are capable of true virtue, and thus overturn his entire ethical system,—which rests absolutely on the presupposition of this freedom. The fact is, he is speaking here as a statesman and not as a moralist, and alludes therein to the great multitude of those who, though arriving at magisterial offices, are yet not philosophers nor truly free. Indeed, he expressly says that the truly good should not by any means be limited by laws, but stand absolutely *above* all law ;† and though he admits that such persons are very rare, yet he presupposes that there are actually

* *Arist.*, ii, p. 1682.

† *Polit.*, iii, 13 : κατὰ δὲ τοιούτων οὐκ ἐστι νόμος, αὐτοὶ γάρ εἰσι νόμος

some such. Now the fact that Aristotle unquestionably excepts the true philosophers as the elect few, from the otherwise all-prevalent moral corruption, does not offer any thing similar to the Christian doctrine of natural sinfulness, but indeed the very opposite,—is not, as the Christian doctrine, an expression of deep humility, but on the contrary, of unmeasured pride, as despisingly conscious of a superiority to the rest of mankind. To make exceptions to the general prevalence of sinfulness limits not merely the thought of this sinfulness, but entirely overthrows it; the virtue-merit of the few chosen ones—and these are of course always the philosophizing moralists themselves—stands forth all the more glaringly the deeper the rest of mankind are degraded. It affords no similarity to the Christian consciousness when, to the few philosophers, *that* character is attributed which Christianity ascribes exclusively to the God-man.

To what height the proud self-consciousness of the philosopher, as pretendedly perfect in his virtue, rises, some idea may be obtained from the following description of the virtue of magnanimity: "Magnanimous is he, who, being worthy of great things, esteems himself as in fact worthy of them. . . . The greatest of outward goods is honor; hence the magnanimous man has to act with propriety in respect to honor and dishonor. . . . As the magnanimous man is worthy of the greatest things, he must necessarily be a perfectly good one; to him belong whatever is great in every virtue; . . . hence it is difficult to be really magnanimous. . . . In great honors, and honors shown him by eminent men, the magnanimous man rejoices moderately, as at that which he deserves, or which even falls below his desert; for, for a perfect virtue there is no entirely sufficient honor. Nevertheless he accepts it, because there is no greater one for him. But the honor shown him by ordinary men, or for inferior things, he disdains, for they are not worthy of him." After having observed, that in order to true magnanimity also outward gifts of fortune are requisite, and that the magnanimous man thinks only very lightly of men and things, and regards only few things so highly as to expose himself to danger for them, Aristotle says of him further: "He is inclined to do good, but disdains to receive benefits, for the former is characteristic of the eminent, and the latter, of the

inferior; and he gives more liberally in return, for thereby he who was before a creditor is made a debtor. Also he gladly recollects those to whom he has done favors, but *not* those from whom he has received benefits! for the receiver of a benefit becomes subordinate to him who renders it, whereas *he* is fond of being superior to others; therefore he also hears mention, with pleasure, of the former (his own good deeds), but with displeasure of the latter (the received benefits); . . . he remains inactive and hesitating when no great honor or great work is involved; he does only a little, but that little is great and honor-bringing; . . . he acts boldly and openly, for he cherishes contempt for others; he speaks the truth, save when he speaks with irony; and he does this when he has to do with the great multitude; . . . he admires nothing, for nothing appears to him as great. . . . The movements of a magnanimous man are slow, his voice restrained and his pronunciation measured. For he who is interested in few things, is not in haste; and he who regards nothing as great, is not zealous." (Nic., iv, 8, 9). This portraiture of one who, as judged from a Christian stand-point, is but a courtly fool, is the virtue-ideal of Aristotle.

A very essential defect of Aristotelian ethics is the falling into the back-ground of the religious character of the moral; and in this respect it is far inferior to that of Plato. The moral stands out alone in entire self-sufficiency, not needing any other ground or basis than itself; the good is good without reference to God,—is good in and of itself, and is at the same time the motive of its own realization. That the moral is essentially God's will, that it brings man into life-communion with God, that man has an immediate moral life-relation to God, that piety is the ground and life of all virtue,—of all this we find in Aristotle but a few very faint and wavering hints. And this is especially surprising in view of the fact that the world-theory of Aristotle is, in other respects, by no means inimical to a close connecting of the moral with the religious, seeing that his God-idea is a very highly developed one, and that he derives all life of the world and of its contents absolutely from the proto-causality of the highest self-conscious reason, that is, the personal God. It is not so much the consequentiality of his philosophical system, as the feebleness of the religious con-

sciousness and life in Aristotle himself, that occasioned him to develop the religious phase of the moral so imperfectly; he does not reject this phase, he even alludes to it, but he does not develop it.

Morality in Aristotle lacks therefore its essential motive; for, in that he himself expressly and repeatedly declares, against Socrates, that from the knowledge of the good the willing of the same does not necessarily follow, but, on the contrary, a contradiction may occur between willing and knowing, he thereby indeed evidently shows that he has observed real life with greater impartiality than Socrates, but he has also thereby rendered impossible any clear understanding of the moral life. For if knowledge does not invariably result in willing, what then is the impelling power which calls forth willing, or the lack of which works non-willing? It is not love, for love appears not as directed toward the good *per se*, or toward God as the highest good, but only toward the individual manifestation, as individual friendship,—not as a motive to virtue, but as one particular virtue along-side of many others. The willing of the good springs not from love, but appears as something entirely independent and unbased, along-side of knowledge and along-side of love; and for the very reason that Aristotle knows not the moral power of love, he can discover for the civic virtue of the great multitude no other motive than fear.

SECTION XXII.

After the time of Aristotle, philosophy declined with accelerating rapidity, degenerating more and more into a shallow popular moralizing, loosely grouped around a few superficial foundation-thoughts, and consisting, for the most part, simply in unconnected observations on isolated topics. The decline of thought manifests itself in a constantly growing inappreciation of the objective significancy and validity of the moral idea, which latter assumes more and more an individually-subjective character, even in cases where it seemingly subordinates the subject to

itself, as in Stoicism,—or subordinates the same to
nature, as in Epicureanism,—and the decline reaches
its lowest point in the total doing away with all general and objective significancy of the moral idea, in
Skepticism.

The moral theories that rise after Aristotle are in no sense
vigorous and truly philosophical products of thought ; they
are but feeble out-shoots of the antecedent, more vigorous
spirit-life, without bloom and without fruit.   Moreover they
stand less closely connected with Plato and Aristotle than
with certain other tendencies of thought that sprang from
the influence of Socrates.   On the basis of the Cyrenaics
sprang up Epicureanism ; on that of the Cynics, Stoicism ;
while the last form of Greek philosophy, also in the sphere
of ethics, namely, Skepticism, may be regarded as a further
development of the tendency of the Sophists.
    By Socrates this much was gained, that the moral, rational
subject was recognized in his freedom and rights, that the
moral idea in general had come to consciousness.   With
Plato and Aristotle, however, this freedom and this idea are
not of a merely individual, subjective character, but they are
brought into relation to the living whole of rational reality.
A course of action is not good for the reason that I regard it
as such, but I must regard it as good because it is good *per
se ;* the moral has essentially a general and objective validity.
The later philosophy holds one-sidedly fast to the position
gained by Socrates,—makes of the subjective consciousness
the highest criterion of truth, even in moral things, and that
too in its individual, absolutely self-dependent character,
apart from any organic union with the rational whole.   The
good is good because I recognize it as such.   In this subjectivistic tendency, philosophy turns away from Aristotle and
falls into the channel rather of the earlier schools, but with a
still stronger emphasizing of the subject.   Hence also the interest for general and for natural philosophy grows less, and
attention is concentrated on the subjective, on morality, and
this consists now essentially in subjective *opinions ;* lacking
in fundamental ideas, it becomes feeble, lax, shallow ; it

comes into the hands of the masses, and, in this marsh-like
out-spreading, it becomes stagnant and spiritless ; in the
place of philosophical schools proper we find hostile *parties*,
as it were, confessional sects of the mass of the cultured, a
party spirit which supplies for these sects the place of their
already-vanished religion; every cultured person sought to
belong to some such philosophical sect, and he selected and
molded it according to his ôwn taste, and the choice itself
of the school became really simply a matter of taste.—The
original antithesis of Greek philosophy, as Materialism and
Spiritualism, as Ionic and Eleatic philosophy, which appeared
later as the antithesis of the Cyrenaics and the Cynics, repeats itself, especially in the sphere of ethics, as Epicureanism and Stoicism; the former regards the spirit as determined
by nature ; the latter, nature as determined by the spirit.

SECTION XXIII.

The doctrine of the *Epicureans*,—which was wide-
spread among the mass of the cultured, and which
subsequently became even the dominant spirit of the
age, but which still remained without any scientific
development, as, in fact, it was incapable of such,—is
the consequential unfolding of the individual pleasure-
principle, the theoretical expression of irreligion and
immorality. The subjective pleasure-feeling is the
highest criterion of truth and of the good ; the yielding to natural proclivities, even the sensuous, and the
greatest possible enjoyment of the present, are the
highest virtue,—prudent calculating for prolonged
pleasure, the highest wisdom,—anxious concern as to
a future retribution and a divine world-government,
the greatest folly ; our striving and thinking should
regard only this life.

Epicurus, (*ob.*271 B. C., see Diog. L., x, 1 *sqq.*), who stood
most closely related with the school of the Cyrenaics, obtained very soon for his doctrine—which has so much to

recommend itself to worldlings—a wide acceptance; and while the solid thinking of Aristotle became almost forgotten, this thought-sparing, self-styled philosophy continued to spread wider and wider,—formed, in fact, by far the most numerous of the sects, and sustained itself until long after the advent of Christ. The more superficial the wisdom, so much the greater the party that clings to it. This doctrine, as comprehended in a very few thoughts and forms of expression, soon became fixed and stationary and received no further development, but nevertheless an all the wider practical application. From the so wide-spread sect there have not come down to posterity even the names of self-styled philosophers of any great eminence, to say nothing of systems of thought.

Happiness is the highest good, and hence to strive after it the highest wisdom and morality; all cognition looks to it as its end. For man only that is true which he *feels*, which he becomes acquainted with through the senses, namely, concrete sensuous reality. Whatever transcends this is at least doubtful, and to fear the doubtful and supersensuous disturbs happiness. Fear of the gods and of a life after death must vanish away, for of them we have no knowledge. Sensuous feeling, and hence the individual pleasure-feeling, is the highest criterion of all truth, and hence also of the morally-true, the good. But we feel only the sensuous, the corporeal, hence only this is for us true and real. Individual being, and hence multiplicity, is the solely true existence,—and hence, first of all, the individual subject ; consequently to carry out the rights of the subject is the moral task. This task looks in no sense whatever to the realizing of a something transcendent to the individual,—of an idea; man is not to follow an all-prevalent law, but, on the contrary, his individual nature,—is not, in any sense whatever, to deny himself, but in fact to cling to and assert this his particular existence, such as it is. Man is not an upholder of a spiritual world, on the contrary, he is himself absolutely supported and guided by nature,—should merge himself harmoniously into nature, should therein feel himself *well*. This feeling of one's self-well is the chief end of life, and therefore the solely true measure of the good. Enjoyment

is the end; the yielding of one's self over to one's own naturalness, is the means.

Now, for this manner of life there was of course no great degree of wisdom requisite; nevertheless direct unconscious desire may lead astray, and hence it must be guided by considerateness. Man must consider in each separate case whether an immediately inviting pleasure is not connected with a subsequent greater pain, and in this case he must avoid it, or at least confine it within the necessary limits, and that simply in order to render the pleasure-feeling a lasting one. The pleasure of the soul is greater than that of the body, because it is more lasting, and hence it is more to be sought after; however, the difference is not essential, inasmuch as the soul itself is but a refined body. Higher than the pleasure which consists in the present gratifying of a natural impulse, is the pleasure of *being* satisfied, that is, when desire and the soul are in a state of comfortable repose; for this reason a certain degree of temperateness and moderation are among the conditions of happiness. Hence virtue is indeed an element of a wise life, not for its own sake, however, but as a means to a higher pleasure-enjoyment,—even as one takes medicine as a means to health. Right and wrong, to which the virtue of justness relates, are nothing *per se ;* right is only the contents of mutual compacts that are entered into for reciprocal benefit; their violation is the wrong. Where there are no compacts there is neither right nor wrong, and hence also no justness or righteousness. Moreover, only so far as it redounds to my utility, have I to practice justness; and the evil of unjustness is simply the damage I incur,—especially through judicial infliction. Friendship is of much value, wedlock-love properly of none at all. From offices of state the wise man keeps himself aloof; he acquires for himself wealth as far as practicable, and thus provides for his future.

An essential condition of happiness is the being free from all fear of spiritual powers—of the gods and their displeasure, of death and a retribution in the "yon-side." Gods there may indeed be, but as they are to be conceived of as in a state of bliss, hence they cannot possibly have any concern for the world and for men. Death does not fall within the

scope of feeling, and hence does not exist for us at all,—does not concern us in the least. So long as we have feeling, death does not exist, and when death does exist, then we have no feeling; hence it disturbs our happiness only when we foolishly harbor a fear of it. But, that with death, all is over with man, is a matter of course, as in fact the soul also is but a fortuitous combination of manifold atoms which, at death, again fall apart. In order to get rid of the tormenting superstition of a life after death, one needs but to study physics. The all-comprehending and dominating chief-condition of happiness is, therefore, *prudence*,—which in each particular case chooses and determines the proper measure and the proper means of pleasure. Man is, consequently, lord of his own fate, and herein consists his freedom; fortune, as mere chance, has but a minor share in our destiny. But that perfect happiness is not to be reached in the way recommended Epicurus knew very well, and he himself depicts the miseries of humanity in very dark colors; he does not, however, throw the blame for them upon man, but upon the imperfectness of the fortuitously-arisen universe itself; and, by this course, he does not fall out with his system, but in fact finds for it a fresh justification; the more numerous the miseries to which man, without his own fault, is exposed, so much the stronger stimulus, and so much the greater right has he, to strive after the enjoyment of life.

SECTION XXIV.

The subjectively-idealistic *Stoicism* which took its start from *Zeno*, teaches a morality of conflict,—of struggle on the part of the rational spirit (as being alone of worth, and as being absolutely a law unto itself) against sensuousness, of thought against pleasure, as belonging to a lower sphere. Virtue is the solely true good, and all other seeming goods are either indifferent or irrational. But this struggle rests simply on the thought of an unreconciled and irreconcilable antagonism of existence,—knows not the higher

thought of the inner unity of all veritable existence,—
rests on the pride of the subjective understanding and
of the absolutely self-legislating individual will, over
against all objective reality, even over against a moral
commonalty with laws binding on the individual subject. Stoicism leads, therefore, on the one hand, to
an unbounded virtue-pride, and on the other, to a
querulous despising of reality, also to a disregarding
of caprice-checking custom, nay, even to a suicidal
non-esteeming of one's own temporal life,—pretend-
ing to an inner peace, but really betraying evidence
of un-peace. Any moral significance, and any even
slight presentiment of absolute ethical truth, are to be
found only in the more general thoughts of the Stoics; but all the more dubious, arbitrary, nay, even perverted, is the particular application of these thoughts
to definite life-relations.

Stoicism stands on the one hand incomparably higher in
spiritual vigor and dignity than Epicureanism, and forms a
direct antagonism thereto, but, on the other hand, it passes
far beyond the truth in the direction of the opposite extreme,
and its one-sided unnaturalness manifests even more clearly
than Epicureanism the insufficiency of heathen principles for
arriving at true moral wisdom.—Zeno, a contemporary of
Epicurus, illustrated the teachings of his system (see Diog.
Laert. viii) by moral strictness of life, and by the commission of suicide at an advanced age; his writings are lost.
His school, which collected within itself the nobler class of
minds, and which, while less numerous than that of the Epicureans, yet exhibited far more spiritual activity than the
latter, continued to exist until the downfall of paganism,—
especially among the Romans, where, though much toned-
down and transformed, it was represented not only by the
rather eclectic Cicero, but also by *Seneca,** by *Epictetus*

* From him are extant numerous moral writings in popular rhetorical
style.

(toward the close of the first century A. D.),* and by *Marcus Aurelius Antoninus*.†

On the dualistic antithesis of matter and spirit rests the corresponding ethical antithesis between merely sensuously-natural objective existence and the rational spirit in the individual free subject. Not the mere nature-entity, but the spirit, is the true entity, and it is such in full, freely self-legislating self-sufficiency; its destination is to manifest itself as independent in relation to nature, and to base itself entirely upon itself. Not the passive, but the active entity is the solely true one,—not enjoyment but activity; it is only as active that the spirit is in its true reality, whereas, as merely enjoying, it sinks below spirituality. Man, as related to objective existence, is a self-poised absolutely freely self-determining being,—is, as a rational spirit, perfectly self-sufficient, needs nothing outside of himself in order to be a spirit, to be free, to be happy; he should not let himself be determined by any thing whatever external to himself. Whatever is to have worth for man, and hence is to form a part of, and to contribute to, his perfection and happiness, must proceed from and depend upon himself alone; every thing else, whatever it may be, concerns him not, is indifferent to him,—can, and may, neither hinder nor promote his perfection and happiness. It is in being self-dependent that the wise man is truly free.—The essence of man, in distinction from the brute, is not enjoying and feeling, but *thinking;* it is not in enjoying, but in thinking, that he is free, that he is a rational spirit; and the more he seeks to enjoy external objects and finds pleasure therein, so much the more is he dependent and unfree, so much the more is he irrational, and hence so much the less a true man. Thinking and not feeling is, therefore, the decisive criterion of the truth and of the good; hence there should be first judging and then acting. All rational, and hence moral, activity must rest on knowledge; to act

---

* His lectures, for the most part merely popular moral exhortations, are preserved in Arrian; besides these we have the *Enchiridion Epicteti*, Which has been much used even in Christian times.

† From him we have Τὰ εἰς ἑαυτὸν, (moral meditations)—disconnected, and, in many cases, merely suggested thoughts and life rules, with much repetition and without regular development.

from mere feeling is irrational; there is no virtue without knowledge. Philosophy itself is a practice of virtue, and knowledge is the first and highest virtue. Out of the knowledge of the good springs, of itself and from inner necessity, pleasure in the good and a striving after it, just as from a knowledge of the evil springs an abhorrence of the same. But these movements of the sensibilities are not the ground, but only the attendants of the moral activity; the ground thereof is knowledge alone. From erroneous knowledge, however, spring irrational sensibility-movements and strivings of the soul, that is, the passions, which are consequently to be regarded as a soul-disease. Now, though all evil springs from error, yet is man nevertheless responsible therefor, for the error itself is guiltily incurred. It is by the knowledge of the good, that is, by perfect consciousness, that volition is distinguished from impulse or instinct. The will aims at the truly-known good, impulse at the merely seemingly good. Knowledge, as an essential manifestation of rationality, is, like the latter itself, germinally innate in man, and hence it is in all men essentially the same; simply the further development and the particular application of the same is left to one's own judgment.

The essence and the fundamental thought of the good is *conformity to nature* (ὁμολογία, *convenientia*, τὸ κατὰ φύσιν, *convenienter naturæ vivere*). Nature is taken here, not as outer sensuous nature in contradistinction to the self-conscious spirit, but as the general order of the world, as the *natura rerum*, the inner conformity-to-law of the All, and, above all, the rational nature and conformity-to-law of one's own spiritual existence and life. Hence conformity to nature is agreement with one's self—the inner order and spiritual health of the life. Even the brute puts forth effort primarily not from pleasure and for pleasure, but for natural self-preservation and self-development. The true nature of man, however, is not the sensuous nature but the reason. To live right signifies, therefore, to live according to reason. Hence evil is a contradiction to the rational nature of man, and the direct opposite of the good,—differs from the good not merely quantitatively, but also qualitatively and essentially,—is the anti-natural and anti-rational.

Virtue is, therefore, in its very essence, a "being well;" hence it has a feeling of happiness as its immediate and necessary consequence, and thus it is itself *per se* the highest good. He who is truly virtuous is happy in the same manner as God; he who is vicious is necessarily wretched. Not this happiness-feeling, however, but the good as such, is the rational end of the moral activity; virtue is to be sought for its own sake without reference to the happiness-feeling; the pleasure-sensation is indeed the consequence, but not the end of moral action. There are, in fact, other pleasure-sensations than those which flow from virtue, and other pain-sensations than those which follow from vice; also external things, things not dependent on us and our free determination, such as health, riches, etc., may excite pleasure-sensations, and hence contribute to our external happiness. Now, if the end of our striving were not the good *per se*, but happiness, then our effort would be directed toward a something that is not fully within our power; but nothing can be truly good, and hence truly to be sought after, which is not dependent upon us and within the scope of our will. The pleasure which arises independently of us from external things may be agreeable, and hence these things may be useful, but real goods they are not. Hence the antithesis of the *honestum* (τὸ καθῆκον, τὸ καλόν) and the *utile*. Thus the happiness and perfection of the sage rests entirely upon himself; he is the free creator of his well-being; all that is really good depends solely upon himself; all that is not dependent upon him affects and disturbs him not. Every wise man is a rich man, a king.—As the good differs from the evil, not in degree but in essence, hence all the virtues are essentially equal to and homogeneous with each other; for a virtue inferior to another could be possible only by its being somewhat participant in evil; but this is impossible from its very idea. Hence whoever has *one* virtue has them all; and they are all intimately involved in each other. Likewise, all vices are essentially equal to each other, and, *e. g.*, to kill a cock needlessly is just as bad as to commit parricide.

From the Stoic notion of the self-based freedom of the sage, as well as from their view of the essence of virtue, it follows that there may be entirely perfect men, men who are

free of all error and of all immorality, fully possessed of all knowledge and virtue and happiness. That there really are such is taken for granted; and delineations of this self-acquired glory are given in the most glowing colors, and form a favorite topic of Stoic philosophy. On the other hand, we find not the least trace of the notion of a natural corruption of mankind; there is admitted (as was the case in Aristotle's system) simply a difference between the rude multitude little inclined to, and little capable of, the good, and the more happily-gifted ones,—the latter being of course the Stoics themselves; and it is given as an essential characteristic of a sage, never to repent of any thing.*—In consequence of the diametrical antagonism between good and evil, there is no mean moral sphere between the two, no sphere of moral indifference. There are indeed things that are *per se* indifferent to man, and which can hence *per se* neither increase nor diminish his worth and happiness, but their actual application is in each particular case either good or bad. In classifying the virtues, the Stoics, for the most part, follow Plato.

Zeno himself based the moral on religion; also some of his disciples understand by the "nature" with which man is to be in harmony, the divine contents and the divine conformity-to-law of nature, and hence that which harmonizes with the divine will; and they conceive of reason as a manifestation of the divine activity in things. But the later Stoics, for the most part, lost sight of this religious character of the moral, and presented it as quite independent of religion,—as a spiritual life-sphere resting strictly and independently upon itself. In Epictetus and Marcus Aurelius the religious element comes again more into the fore-ground; they recognize reverence for the gods, or for God, as a virtue and as a ground of the moral,—conceive of virtuousness as God-likeness, and viciousness as godlessness, and even attribute high worth to prayer, though here, of course, there is no trace of penitential prayer, but for the most part, only the spirit of the Pharisee's prayer : "God, I thank thee that I am not as other men."† It is in fact not impossible that in

---

* Cic.: *Pro Murœna*, 29.

† Arrian: *Dissert. Epict.*, iii, 24, 96 *sqq.* ; iv, 10, 14 *sqq.*, (ed. Schweigh.); M. Aurel. Ant.: εἰς ἑαυτὸν, ix, 40.

the more religious tendency of later Stoicism there is a degree of influence from Christianity.

This view of the moral produced in fact among the Stoics an earnest moral striving, though without enthusiasm or heart, and only in the manner of a cold logical calculating. Feeling amounts to nothing at all; of the potency of love there is not a trace; thought passes directly over into action, and feeling merely accompanies the act as a something entirely indifferent. The love of neighbor is regarded only as a mode of action, but not as an affair of the heart. The sage ought indeed to help the wretched according to his means and according to their worthiness, but to feel *compassion*, or even to act as if one felt it, would be unworthy of a wise man; for the truly wise man is above all suffering; and the wretched suffer only from lack of knowledge, because they regard external things, which are not within their own control, as real goods.* The friendliness to man which is so earnestly recommended by the Stoics flows not from love, and their patience under received injustice springs only from contemptuous pride. Hence, while, on the one hand, wrath, revenge, envy, slander, etc., are condemned as unworthy of the sage, partly because every passive feeling-movement is immoral, and in part because the sage is too proud to allow himself to be disturbed by the acts and manners of others,—yet, on the other hand, it is held as an unworthy weakness to *forgive* others for their injustice, for that would be equivalent to declaring the injustice as indifferent, and to lightly esteeming justice.† The Christian principle, "Forgive and ye shall be forgiven," has no force for a Stoic, because he believes himself never to be in circumstances to need forgiveness.

The morality of the Stoics is a constant *contest* of the spirit against sensuous nature and against the unspiritual and irrational in the objective world in general; but as this contest is directed against a primordial and never entirely-overcomeable antagonism in existence itself, and hence can never lead

---

* Epict.: *Enchir.*, 16; M. Anton., v, 36; vii, 43; Diog. L., vii, 123; Cicero: *Pro Murœna*, c. 29; Seneca: *De clementia*, ii, 5, 6.

† Stobæus: *Ecloga ethica*, ii, 7, p. 190 (Heeren); Diog. L., vii, 123; Cic.: *Pro Mur.*, 29.

to an objective victory, it assumes consequently not so much an actively outward-working character, as rather that of a passive resistance against irrational reality. The sage does not undertake to produce a real world of the moral spirit; on the contrary, he retreats within himself in proud contempt of the actual world; only himself, but not the outer world, can he make perfect;—the real struggle is carried on not by a victory-confident assaulting of immoral reality, but by a contemptuous turning away from the same,—by an indifference to pleasure and pain, the depicting of which is given again and again in endless reiteration. This blunt, indifferent enduring of pain is not the fruit of a pious faith in a divine world-government or of love toward mankind, but it is the proud defiance of the absolutely self-relying subject as against a world imbued with a primitive and essential irrationality. This indifference toward all that excites the sensibilities restrains indeed the Stoic from Epicurean sensuality, but is very far from leading to a true resistance of one's self; the sensuous is only despised, but not positively assailed. Stoic ethics requires no severe self-denial, no fasting, no renunciation of sensual enjoyment; it only requires that one be moderate and that one place no value on the enjoyment; but after all, this restraint was, for the most part, but a mere flourishing of rhetoric;—Seneca accepted, with the greatest suavity, riches upon riches, which his pupil Nero conferred upon him.

The lightly esteeming of the non-spiritual extends also to the physical life. The Stoics indeed regard the instinct of self-preservation as a fundamental impulse of human nature, and as a strictly normal expression of the law which requires harmony with one's self and with nature, but it is not inconsistent therewith that they should regard life itself as an object of indifference—seeing that it is not within man's own control. Death must not be feared, but must—as a power not within our control—be despised; and in so far as it is a nature-law, and one that liberates us from a painful bodily life, it is to be regarded even with pleasure. The thought of immortality is, in this connection, regarded merely as a possibility; if the life of the soul continues on, then the wise man is happy; but if it ceases, then ceases for him also all pain; in neither case is there the least ground for fear.—But

the Stoic goes still further. The wise man is a free lord over himself; but in death he is overcome by an external power. It does not become the sage, therefore, to let the close of his life depend merely on any such extraneous power; it is but a virtualization of his own self-dependent freedom, that he should close his life when it pleases *himself*, that is, when he has satisfactory reasons therefor. To the Stoic, *suicide* is, under certain circumstances, not only allowed, but even a duty, a heroic virtue. Among the circumstances that justify suicide, irrespective of self-sacrifice for country or friends, are the following: great distress, poverty, incurable disease, physical maiming, and other oppressive afflictions, deprivation of liberty, and in general, any essential hinderance to living freely and in conformity to reason, such as infirmity from age; all these are divine hints that it is time to take one's voluntary departure; "The door is open,"—is a saying which the Stoic fondly reiterates as an expression of his perfect liberty, even in regard to the ending of his life.* Suicide is defended with great zeal, and almost with enthusiasm, by *Seneca*, on the ground that it is an assertion of the true self-dependence and freedom of man; for this reason man may and should proceed to suicide even when the above freedom-hindering evils are merely in threatening prospect, inasmuch as, if he does not, he may in the end be hindered from the accomplishment of this self-liberation. Only a *single* way leads into life, but thousands lead out of it. No one is wretched save through his own fault; for if misfortune falls upon him, he is at liberty to depart; life keeps none back. The wise man lives only so long as life pleases him; the lancing of an artery opens to him the way to freedom. Death is, after all, unavoidable, why then adjourn it till the evil day? The foulest death is better than the cleanest slavery; the prudent man seeks the easiest death; yet if it cannot be otherwise, he does not shun even a painful suicide.†
—And the practice corresponded to the theory. Zeno himself is said to have hanged himself at an advanced age, because he had broken one of his fingers; his disciple Cleanthes

* Diog. L., vii, 130; Arrian, i, 9, 20; i, 24, 20; i, 25, 18 *sqq.*; ii, 1, 20; M. Anton.,v, 29; Cic.: *De Finibus*, iii, 18.
† *Epist.* ii, 5 (17); vi, 6 (58); viii, 1 (70); *De ira*, iii, 15, (ed. Fickert).

starved himself to death because his gums became sore. The frequent suicides among the Roman Stoics are a matter of notoriety.—This doctrine and this practice are often regarded as in conflict with the general view of the Stoics, which, in fact, denies that pain is a real evil. The inconsistency is only apparent, and contains, at all events, a very true confession. If man has no higher consolation against the miseries of existence than the pride of the self-centered, self-satisfied individual spirit, then it is simply mere truthfulness when he confesses that he is not equal to the misery of real life,—that he has not the moral power entirely to overcome it by morality, and to say with joy, "We glory also in tribulations." The Stoic knows nothing of an almighty father-love of God, and less still of any personal guilt; he lacks the entire basis upon which the courage of a Christian heart can even grow stronger amid all the buffetings of life; he rises only to a defiance of the miseries of reality; but this defiance, seeing that it is not exalted to moral courage by the pious confidence of a God-thirsting heart, is not equal to the task of humbly bowing itself under suffering, but only to that of destroying itself in bitter accusation against the moral order of the world, and in the consciousness that the real world is not worthy longer to contain such a sage.

Stoic morality is of a purely individual character, aims only at virtualizing the free self-dependence and self-sufficiency of the individual subject. For an objective reality of the moral thought, and for a moral community-life, the Stoic has no appreciation, and hence also none for the naturally-moral basis of society, namely, *marriage*,—which, in fact, as requiring self-submission to an objective moral reality, appears as a trammeling fetter for the individual subject; and it is doubtless only from the striving after the maintenance of the complete self-sufficiency of the wise subject in the face of all objective moral reality, that are to be explained the strangely perverted views of the sexual relations that prevailed among the Stoics. By them marriage itself was lightly esteemed, and, while passionate love and lustfulness were condemned, sexual communion outside of marriage was expressly defended against all criticism;* and of Zeno and Chrysippus, it is made out with a

* Epict.: *Enchir.* 33.

good degree of certainty, that they required community of wives among the wise, and that they declared allowable, sexual communion between nearest blood-relatives (even between parents and children), and also whoredom, self-pollution and ped erasty.* It must not be forgotten that in these opinions—with the exception of incest, which is readily explainable from their one-sided, calculating spirit,—the Stoics had the moral consciousness of the Greeks on their side, and that for their community of wives they were countenanced by the teachings of Plato.—Also in other respects their moral relations to other men are neither frank nor pure. The lofty contempt which the sage indulges in toward all non-sages, disengages him also from many moral duties toward them; thus he is not under obligation always to tell them the *truth;* falsehood is allowable not only in war, to the enemy, but also in many other cases,— especially in view of attaining an advantage.†

The morality of the Stoic is the pride of the natural man who is conscious of being a moral creature, but who has no suspicion of a morality higher than and transcending the individual subject, nor of a personal moral depravity. His oft-repeated high-sounding descriptions of self-complacency make any thing but an agreeable impression. This pride restrains him, it is true, from many unworthy acts; in consequence, however, of his total lack of an objective standard, it did not guard him from grave moral errors, nor from an almost fanatical hate against a higher world-theory, which, at a later period, offered itself to him in Christianity; and Marcus Aurelius was not in the least deterred by his so high-sounding discourses on kindness, tolerance, and charity, from letting loose a fearful persecution upon the Christians,—in whose martyr-courage he could discover only criminal obstinacy.—Though Stoic ethics was distinguished from the essentially-related ethics of the Cynics by the fact that it discarded the unspiritual and unrefined form of the latter, and that it respected the spiritual under every phase, and hence also in art, and placed a high estimate upon the worthy appearance of the body and upon cleanliness, nevertheless at bottom it does not really transcend

* Diog. L., vii, 13, 33, 131, 188; Sext. Emp.: Ὑποτυπώσεις, iii, 24.
† Stob.: *Ecl. eth.,* ii, 7, p. 230 (Heeren).

the same. It does not rise beyond the mere formal notion of the moral as a conformity to nature; the material constructions to be put upon the contents of the moral idea are left to the subjective discretion of the individual; and though it really stands higher than Epicurean ethics, still it did not spiritually vanquish the same. Instead of an absolutely and objectively valid moral idea, and of the expression of a divine will, we find only man's subjective knowledge of his own nature; the contents of the moral law, the Stoic discovers only by the observation of his own personal peculiarities; and the possibility that this self of his might be a morally perverted one he does not even remotely suspect.

SECTION XXV.

Epicureanism and Stoicism are two diametrically opposed but also mutually requiring and complementing phases of the Greek spirit; both are equally one-sided, both are equally remote from the Christian ethical idea;—both refer all moral truth back to the individual subject. In the place of Christian morality, the Epicureans offer joyous voluptuousness; the Stoics offer the high-minded pride of complete self-righteousness; neither party feels the least need of redemption, of divine grace; for the Epicureans regard the *per se* sinful as right, while the Stoics imagine themselves to have overcome the same through their *per se* pure individual will.

Epicurean ethics emphasizes the nature-phase in man; Stoic the spirit-phase; the former teaches an unresisting, voluptuous giving-over of self to sensuous nature, the latter an earnest but only partially successful resisting of the same; the former is absolutely indifferent as to moral knowledge,—natural instinct supplies the place of knowledge; the latter manifests a busy seeking after knowledge, and esteems it as a virtue; the former is a crude realism,—in all essential features a materialistic naturalism; the latter is a one-sided idealism,—in all essential

features a ploddingly-calculating spiritualism; the former bears a feminine character,—is passive, yielding, lax; the latter bears a masculine character,—is active, earnest, rigorous; the former suited better the effeminate Ionic tribe and the Orient, the latter rather the stern Doric tribe and the Romans.

The Epicurean seemingly gives sway to the universal, namely, to nature, to which the individual subordinates himself; in reality, however, the individual subject is set free from the bonds of the universal, of the spiritual, of rationality; the Stoic also seemingly subordinates the individual subject to a general thought, namely, the moral idea; in reality, however, also here the universal is made to yield to the individual subject; in the place of a general moral idea we find, strictly speaking, only the calculating opinion of the individual; it is the self-will of the subject in the face of the spiritual objective world, namely, history, that asserts itself as rational freedom. According to both systems, therefore, the truth is found only within the subject; nature and existence in general have value for the Epicurean only in so far as they can be enjoyed, that is, in so far as they are *for* the individual subject,—in every other respect existence is indifferent; in the eyes of the Stoic, existence is truth only in so far as it appears *in* the subject; the sage is the embodiment of the moral order of the universe, which, apart from him, exists but very imperfectly. In both systems the higher thought of Plato, namely, that, by the moral, the real harmony of existence, the harmony between nature and spirit, is realized, is one-sidedly perverted; the Epicurean effects this harmony only by sacrificing the rationally-personal spirit to nature, the Stoic by sacrificing nature to the individual personal spirit; it is no longer a harmonizing, but a giving up, of one of the two phases of existence.

Though Stoic ethics is in many respects graver and more worthy of man than Epicurean, nevertheless both systems are equally remote from the Christian view. The Epicurean does not recognize the spiritual personality as the highest factor; the Stoic does not recognize the rights of objective reality; but Christianity recognizes both as absolutely belonging to each other. In both systems, the natural man, the individual subject, thrusts himself in his fortuitous reality into the foreground, as having the highest claims; in both the subject is of

himself perfectly competent to attain to all perfection,—has no need, in this work, either of God or of history; neither has even the faintest presentiment of the moral significancy of history, of humanity as a unity.   In both, therefore, there is absolutely no humility of moral self-denial, but either a mere lustful devotion to world-enjoyment, or a haughty contempt of the external world,—and hence in neither of them is there the least felt need of redemption; the sole redemption from the burden, not of guilt but of an evil world of reality, is, suicide with the Stoic, and sensuous intoxication with the Epicurean. In neither system is there manifest the least approximation to the Christian principle,—no progress beyond Plato and Aristotle, but rather simply the moral consciousness of heathenism in its incipient dissolution,—which is consummated in Skepticism.

SECTION XXVI.

The subjectivism that predominated in Epicurean and Stoic ethics finds its consequential and scientifically-rigorous carrying-out,—and at the same time Greek and heathen ethics in general, its dissolution and honorable self-destruction,—in *Skepticism*, which declares all judging of good and evil as futile, and all modes of action as indifferent.—*Neo-Platonic* philosophy, which seeks to rescue heathenism as against Christianity, and which perverts Christian ideas to heathen purposes, presents in its but partially developed ethics little more than a dreamy mysticism—a quietistic self-merging into the one universal divine essence; and it is only for non-philosophers that there is need of a, not scientific but, practical code of morals.

Roman philosophy made no original contributions to ethics. Apart from a but slightly independent adoption of the doctrines of Stoicism, it presents nothing more than a feebly eclectic character, and

does not rise beyond superficial calculating observations and opinions.

Skepticism has often been misunderstood not only in its scientific, but also in its world-historical significancy; it arose gradually and, as it were, spontaneously, without any one specially prominent founder, as a protest of the general rational consciousness against the self-sufficiency and presumption of the previously existing philosophies,—and, in the sphere of ethics, as the scientific conscience of heathenism. Subjectivism, when consequentially carried out, leads inevitably to skepticism. Socrates had contended with moral earnestness against the subjectivism of the Sophists, and had attempted to find a solid basis also for ethical philosophy; in this commendable effort, however, he succeeded as little as did, after him, Plato and Aristotle and the Stoics. In these efforts they did not rise beyond mere formal definitions of the moral, and were obliged to derive the material contents of the same from the primarily merely fortuitously-determined essence of the individual subject. The sole thought that leads to a true basing of the moral consciousness, namely, that the moral is the will of God, was only dimly caught sight of, and could not in fact, from the heathen stand-point, be carried out with any degree of certainty. That, now, the vail was torn off from the false method of taking the finite subject as the criterion and the infallible source of universally-valid and objective truth, and of attributing to subjective opinion an absolutely valid objective significancy, and that subjectivism was exposed in all its nakedness and invalidity,—this was the scientific service of Skepticism,—which, having shown traces of itself as early as in the age of Aristotle (*Pyrrho*), attained to greater prevalence in the century before Christ (*Ænesidemus* of Alexandria), and fully developed itself in the second century after Christ (*Sextus Empiricus*), and thus like a devouring rust gradually undermined the last self-confidence of heathen philosophy, save in so far as it did not seek refuge behind the mystical nebulæ of Neo-Platonicism.

Skepticism is in fact simply the product of the antithesis between Epicureanism and Stoicism. The former said: the feeling of pleasure and displeasure alone decide as to the

morally-good ; the latter said : not feeling but thinking decides ; Skepticism lets the two cancel each other, and says : neither feeling nor thinking is capable of any real decision as to what is good. Man cannot *at all* know what is *per se* good ; all our feelings, experiences and thoughts have merely and exclusively a subjective significancy,—furnish no truth in regard to things *per se*. This is not a mere feeble courting of doubt, not a mere, "I know not *whether* this or that is good," but a decisive, "I know positively that I cannot know it, and I know also *that* there is nothing that is *per se* good ;" and this knowledge of the lack of knowledge is the true wisdom and the true virtue. What is good or not good is determined solely by civil law and by adopted custom, and there is no occasion for seeking for another or higher basis therefor. Nothing is *per se*, and in its essence good or evil. This consideration furnishes the basis for true soul-repose and happiness,—seeing that we then need no longer be disturbed by feelings of desire or of disgust, but that we look upon every thing with calm indifference. The true and highest good consists therefore in this, that we be absolutely indifferent toward all things that are usually regarded as goods. As, on one occasion, during a storm, Pyrrho saw some swine very unconsciously devouring their food, he is said to have exclaimed : " The wise man must also be equally imperturbable !"   If there were any thing that is good or evil *per se*, all men would be found to see it ; whereas in fact the judgments of men differ in all things, and the opposing philosophic schools proclaim the most opposite things as good or evil. The truth is, that in every case, the judgment as to good or evil is determined by the spiritual or bodily peculiarity of the person judging, and hence gives no certainty as to the essence of the thing *per se*, but is always simply indicative as to what chances to *seem* good or evil to *him*. Hence a science of the moral, a system of ethics, is absolutely impossible, and all teaching as to the moral is futile. But, as now, notwithstanding this, it is necessary to live and act in some manner, so it is most advisable to act according to the existing laws and customs,—not, however, because they are good, but because this course is most advantageous.—Though Sextus Empiricus,—who has said most on this head,—does not show his best powers on the field of ethics, yet it is not to be denied that his attacks against the re-

sults of all previous ethics contain much truth, and that from the heathen stand-point the Skeptics were, on the whole, justified in their doubts. Their skepticism gives evidence of a significant self-consciousness in heathen science; and even though its results were unsatisfactory, still there was need of just such a radical sifting and exposure in order to bring to sober reflection the falsely-secure and self-deluding spirit of heathenism, and to render it more receptive for a better-founded world-theory.

Neo-Platonic ethics can hardly be regarded as a genuine phase of Greek thought proper. Entering the lists in antagonism to the new world-power of Christianity for the purpose of rescuing heathenism, mingling together into a nebulous conglomerate all the fragmentary notions of Oriental and Occidental religions and philosophies, and supplementing them with Christian thoughts, Neo-Platonic philosophy manifests also in its but crudely-formed ethics little more than the distressful features of a spirit slowly and painfully dying of the mere senility of age,—a spirit which, without considerate choice of its means, is feverishly possessed with the one desire of arousing up by artificial nerve-stimuli its already half-dead life-forces to one last desperate up-flickering into life,—a tragically-grand desperation-effort of a mortally-wounded combatant,—the titanic rebounding of the spirit of antiquity when pierced through the heart by the arrow of a higher form of truth; (*Plotinus*, the greater disciple of Ammonius Saccas, the founder of the school, living mostly in Rome, *ob.* A. D. 270; his disciple *Porphyry*, *ob.* A. D. 304; Proclus, who lived mostly at Athens, *ob.* A. D. 485,—the last philosopher of Occidental heathenism.)

Deviating from all previous Greek philosophy, the Neo-Platonists place the idea of God in the fore-ground, and deduce from it, and bring in relation to it, all principles of morality. But this God-idea itself is further remote from the Biblical idea of God than is even that of Plato and Aristotle. God is no longer the infinite personal Reason, but the absolutely undetermined abstract Unity, which unfolds itself, in Pantheistic emanation, into the world of multiplicity,—which world is consequently not a separate reality different from God, but simply the shadow of God himself,—the reverse-side of the divine, the fading-away of the pure divine light, and hence of essentially

negative essence.—Now as all knowledge must aim at beholding all things in God and God in all things, hence also all moral
activity is directed exclusively to this one end, namely, to unite
one's self with God, to press one's self out of the world of plurality, to renounce one's self as an individual being, to wish to
be and actually to be nothing more than a transient phase of
the alone truly-existing unitary divine essence. The moral
activity aims not at the producing of a real world of the good
different from God,—aims not at realizing any thing which is
not already real and perfect from eternity, but, on the contrary,
aims at reducing back the soul from its immersion in the world
of reality into the solely and the alone-existing good, that is, into
God. God is not merely the highest good, but in fact the absolutely sole good; and whatever is different from God is, in so
far as it is so, not truly good. Hence the sole path of salvation
is the return from plurality to unity, and the first and most essential condition thereto is the beholding of God, an indulging
in a mystical speculation, which is possible only in that one forgets one's self,—spiritually dies away,—so as to permit God
alone to prevail. The more I am a particular self-hood claim-
ing personality, so much the more remote am I from God.
Morality consists, therefore, not in a developing of this personality, but in a suppressing of it, not in a becoming like God,
but in fact in becoming God himself. The self-conscious personality is not the God-like, but the God-foreign; for God himself is not a personality—is not this or that—has no manner of
determinateness, but is that which is sublime above all determinateness, all quality, and hence also above spiritual personality; whatever is in any manner determined is not God, but
has gone out from God, and hence is, in so far, extra-divine;
and the same path which reality has traversed in passing from
undetermined unity to manifoldly-determined plurality, morality traverses again in the opposite direction,—passes back from
plurality and determinateness to the unitary and undetermined.
In all these phases of thought, an Indian influence is unmistakable.

As true cognizing is not dialectical but contemplative, namely, a spiritual beholding of God, so also true morality is not an
outward-going activity, but rather a non-acting, a restraining
of active volition, a dissolving of all particular personal voli-

tionating into the one divine essence. Whoever has the highest good needs and wishes for no other good. But the highest good exists in no sense whatever apart from God, in the world but solely in the reality-transcending and indeterminate God. For such an outward working, such a creating of a real kingdom of the good, there is no occasion whatever; for all that really exists is good already in so far as it is the divine essence, and hence cannot be an object of change or resistance; and in so far as it is the divine essence as self-estranged, it is evil, and hence should not be loved and confirmed; there remains, therefore, for the moral activity no other work than simply to withdraw itself from the world and, not so much into itself as much rather, into God. Hence there is no need of striving, of combatting, and of laboring, but only of reposing; to the eternal keeping-silence, the eternal repose, of God, corresponds the silent repose of the sage and moral man. Active virtue is not the highest form of morality, but is only a praiseworthy moral quality of such as have not yet risen to the stage of true wisdom.—Such are the chief fundamental thoughts of this Neo-Platonic philosophy, the influence of which made itself felt as late as in the Christian mysticism of the Middle Ages. On the whole, we could not properly expect from this last attempt of heathen philosophy at self-preservation, any rigorous consequential carrying-out of fundamental principles; and hence we in fact often find thoughts in it which but imperfectly harmonize with it as a system. Still, the most of these seemingly irreconcilable views are doubtless to be accounted for in the light of the distinction which it made between wisdom proper (which is attainable only for the elect few) and the moral instruction of the populace at large. For the latter there is in fact need of other moral precepts, seeing that men at large are not yet in such a condition as to be able, through beholding and yielding, to merge themselves into the absolutely One.

Roman philosophy, though enjoying high repute in the Middle Ages, and even as late as in the last century, has, however, for the philosophical development of the science of ethics scarcely any significance. The Stoic Romans did little more than indulge in general popular discussions on the philosophy they had adopted from the Greeks; the Epicurean Romans simply applied their views practically. *Cicero* is simply a discreet

Eclectic, though without speculative genius. He discusses moral questions in clear but superficial processes of reasoning, without finding for them a firm philosophical ground, or a really scientific solution. The rhetorical form of his ethico-philosophical writings does not redeem them from that tediousness which inheres in any verbose display of unprofound observations. Zealously opposing Epicureanism, Cicero holds fast in general to the Stoic system, modifying it with Platonic, Aristotelian and other elements, and this too not without many instances of misunderstanding. His most important ethical work is his *De officiis*, which is based mostly on the Stoic Panaetius. In this work he examines, first, the notion of the morally-good (*honestum*), then that of the useful (*utile*), and the mutual relation of these so often conflicting principles. The "useful" he finds to be only seemingly different from the good; the fact is, whatever is good is also useful, and whatever is truly useful is also good, not, however, for the reason that it is useful, but the converse; hence to strive after the good renders necessarily at the same time also happy. Of the other writings of Cicero, belong also here the *Quaestiones academ.*, the *Disputationes Tusculanæ*, and his essays: *De senectute*, *De amicitia*, *De legibus*, *De finibus.*—Cicero blames, in the Stoics, that they conceive of the good only partially, that they regard not the entire man, but only his spiritual phase, and lightly esteem the corporeal, so that in fact while professing to follow nature they do not do her justice,—that they place on an equal footing all the virtues as well as all the vices, and admit no intermediate gradations, and also that because of their one-sidedness they involve themselves in many contradictions. Though finding the source of the moral consciousness in reason,—which is an efflux from the divine reason, and by which therefore we become like God,—he yet derives ethics only in a very slight degree from the essence of reason itself, but rather from the experience of life. From this lack of a firm philosophical foundation, we can understand why Cicero placed an especially high value on his discussion upon the *collision* of *duties*. On the condition of a real deduction of the various forms of duty from one fundamental principle, there would be no possible place for such a discussion; but to the moralist who takes his starting-point from empirical observation, this field appears as of especial difficulty and

importance. The question: Which of several morally good actions which cannot be reconciled with each other is to be chosen as the better? Cicero answers very unsatisfactorily and unphilosophically, on the mere ground of the social comfortableness resulting therefrom (*De off.*, i, 43 *sqq.*) Nor does he succeed in all his sonorous periods on universal benevolence, etc., in rising beyond the narrow views characteristic of heathen ethics.—*Plutarch*, a Greek with Roman education (about A. D. 100,) furnishes in his numerous moral writings many good observations on the moral life, and gives evidence of a noble disposition of soul, though he does not rise beyond popular essays and observations, relating for the most part to particular moral topics,—gives neither a system, nor rigorous, clear principles. In general he follows Plato, and rejects the extremes both of Epicureanism and Stoicism.

B.—OLD-TESTAMENT AND JEWISH ETHICS.

SECTION XXVII.

The ethics of the Old Testament presents, in its entire essence, a direct contrast to all heathen ethics. Without systematic form and without scientific development, it is yet perfectly self-consistent in its ground, its essence and its end. In harmony with the idea of God as a spirit absolutely independent of nature, and himself omnipotently conditioning the whole sphere of nature, the *ground* of all morality is absolutely and exclusively God's holy will as revealed to the free personal creature; the *essence* of the moral is free, loving obedience to the revealed divine will; the ultimate *end* of morality is the realizing of perfect God-likeness, and hence also of perfect God-sonship and bliss, not merely for the individual, not merely for the people Israel, but for all humanity,— and hence the realization of a humanity-embracing *kingdom of God;* the most immediate historical end,

however, is to impart a knowledge of the need of
redemption from depravity as incurred by the sin of
man himself. Hence the law appears in fact predominantly, not as an inner natural one, but as a
purely positive, objective, historically-revealed one,
in order that man may become conscious of his natural estrangement from the truth. In this form it does
not have an ultimately definitive, but a transitory
and essentially disciplinary end; and the realization
of the kingdom of God can only be prepared for, but
not fully accomplished, by the Israelitic people; it is
a morality of hope.

As in the presentation of Christian ethics, further on, we shall
have to glance in considerable detail also at its historical antecedent, namely, Old Testament ethics, hence we need here give
only the general characteristics of the latter.*
The antagonism of the moral idea of the Old Testament to
the views of collective heathenism, is radical and fundamental;
there is here no shadow of a transition from the latter to the
former. Pre-Christian revealed ethics did not, however, have a
scientific, systematic form, and indeed could not have it, inasmuch as the key to its correct understanding was to be given
only in the days of the Messiah, and as the Hebrews were not
to be a perfect, independently-developed nation, but to find
their full truth only in Christianity.—The Hebrews do not undertake to find the ground of the moral consciousness in the
human spirit itself, for the man whom they know as real is no
longer the pure image of God,—has no longer the unobscured
natural consciousness of God and of the moral,—and even unfallen man needed to be awakened to this consciousness by the
revelation of God. The entire ground of the moral consciousness is therefore sought in God's positive revelation to man, as

* In addition to general works on Old Testament theology, which
treat mostly of the ethical phase only incidentally, and to the works
mentioned in § 5, may be cited, *G. L. Bauer: Bibl. Moral des A. T.*,
1803, 2 vols.,—extremely Rationalistic; (*Imm. Berger: Prakt. Einl. ins
A. T.*, continued by *Augusti*, 1799–1808, 4 vols.)

indeed the ground of the moral on the whole is absolutely the holy will of God,—not as an abstract law immanent in, though partially hidden from, human reason, but as an express *command* of the personal God and made known to man by a historical act of revelation. God speaks and man hearkens; and the moral activity is in its entire essence a child-like *obeying* of the divine command made upon man. Here there is no longer any room for a doubt, unless it be a sinful one,—no need of a philosophical analysis. In case there is need in particular conjunctures for a more definite decision, then God gives it himself, either directly, as with the patriarchs and the divinely-called and enlightened prophets, or, mediately, through the same, or indeed also through specific signs, such as the lot [Num. xxvi, 55, 56; xxxiii, 54; xxxiv, 13; Josh. vii, 14 *sqq.;* xiii, 6; xiv, 2; xviii, 6 *sqq.;* xix, 1 *sqq.;* xxi, 4 *sqq ;* 1 Sam. x, 20 *sqq.;* Prov. xvi, 33; xviii, 18], the high-priestly Urim and Thummim [Ex. xxviii, 30; Num. xxvii, 21; 1 Sam. xxiii, 6 *sqq.;* xxviii, 6; xxx, 7, 8; comp. 2 Sam. ii, 1; v, 19, 23 *sqq.*], and others [1 Sam. xiv, 8 *sqq.,* comp. Gen. xxiv, 12 *sqq.*]. The command of God to man presents itself in a strictly positive definite form: "thou shalt," "thou shalt not," "thou mayest." For any other reason than God's will, man has no right to ask; he is simply to *believe* the word of God—this alone leads him to righteousness. To personal free self-determination and maturity, man is to attain simply and solely through child-like faith-obedience to the word of the Father. He who questions and hesitates where God speaks, cannot possibly be moral, since he is lacking in faith. Unhesitating, unreluctant, joyous submission to God's definite command, is the beginning, the end and the essence of all morality. Types of such faith-obedience are Noah [Gen. vi, 22; vii, 5], Abraham [xii, 4], Jacob, Moses, Samuel, David, and others. The simple fact that God wills it, is the absolutely sufficient reason ; the fear of God is the beginning of wisdom. The antecedent condition of the moral, as lying in the bosom of man himself, is, however, the image of God—the pure knowledge and the untrammeled will of moral freedom. Man *should,* but he is not *compelled;* his salvation is placed within his own hand; the thought, "If thou hearkenest to my word, it shall go well with thee," pervades the entire Old Testament from beginning to end.

Between God and man there subsists an absolutely person-
ally-moral relation. Even as God, as the true and perfect
personality, is the holy prototype of all morality, and as the
simple thought of this God is directly presented as the perfectly sufficient ground for all moral life: "Ye shall be holy,
for *I* the Lord your God am holy" [Lev. xi, 45; xix, 2], "I
am the almighty God, walk before me and be thou perfect"
[Gen. xvii, 1],—so also is man's complete personality recognized and respected by God even in the already sin-corrupted
race. God does not himself immediately work all willing
and acting in man, does not force him to obedience, but He
makes a *covenant* with man, with his people,—comes as a holy
personality into moral relation to man as a free moral personality. The fulfillment of the covenant-promise is *conditioned*
on the covenant-fidelity of man.

The purpose, the goal of the moral is not the merely individual perfection of the moral subject, but it is, on the one
hand, the salvation and perfection of the whole human race,
—a thought entirely unknown to heathendom—and, on the
other, the full and blissful life-communion of the person with
God; "I will be your God, and ye shall be my people" [Lev.
xxvi, 12; Jer. vii, 23];—not merely the individual subject
but the moral community, the people of God (entire humanity
is to become this people), is to be received into this communion with God.

Immediately upon the creation of man the thought of the
moral presents itself clearly and definitely [Gen. i, 26–ii, 24].
(1.) The objective presupposition of the moral is presented,
namely, the living personal God as the prototype of man and
of his life, and nature as good and normal and as existing
independently over against man,—and, then, the subjective
presupposition, namely, man as a personal spirit like unto
his Creator.—(2.) The goal of morality as a task, a duty,
namely, the realizing and completing of the divine image, is
expressed under one of its phases, as the dominion of man
over nature; this implies the realization of free personal
spirituality in likeness to God—the *legitimate* "being as
God." In the strong emphasizing of this dominion over
nature, (so utterly in contrast to all actual experience,) there
is plainly indicated the ideal essence of the moral task; its

full realization however is not to be attained to at once, but is the final goal, and lies in the future. In striking contrast to all heathen views, according to which man is either absolutely subject to nature, or at least has nature before him as a cramping, and never-entirely-to-be-overcome power, we have here the true relation of the rational spirit to nature, namely, his complete freedom, his destination to entire mastery over it, that is, we have the full personality of man as the key-stone of the collective morally-religious world-theory. That this dominion of the spirit over nature is not to be a childish magical interfering with nature, is evident from the simple fact that man is called to it only as being an image of the nature-dominating God, and that immediately before and after his call thereto the God-established permanent regularity of nature is alluded to as in some sense a right of nature, and that man is at once directed to the orderly and conserving culture of nature [ii, 15]. The dominion over nature is not the entire goal of the moral striving, it is, however, a very expressive suggestion of the same, and is within the comprehension of the child-like and as yet immature spirit.—(3.) The legitimate freedom of choice and its enjoyment are guaranteed to man as a right, in the sphere of the *discretionary* [i, 28–30; ii, 16].—(4.) The unambiguous declaration is made that morality is not a something belonging merely to the individual person, but that on the contrary man can accomplish his task only as a member of a moral community; it is *not* good that man should be alone; he *ought* not to remain in isolation, but should form a part of a family, should enter into association with moral humanity, and it is only on this condition that the good is truly realizable for the subject.—(5.) In the anticipatory allusion to the observance of the Sabbath as based on the divine example [ii, 2, 3] is presented the ideal phase of human activity,—the re-collecting of the personal spirit from the distractions of the outer life into the calm of meditation; man is not at liberty completely to merge himself into earthly temporal cares,—should constantly have before him, in all his temporal activity, also the eternal as the true and highest good. The heathen either buries himself up in temporal activity and enjoyment, or contemptuously turns himself entirely away from the same; the

saint of the Old Testament lives and acts *in* God's good-created world, but does not merge himself into it,—withdraws himself from it into the Sabbath repose of a heart in communion with its God. In the simple feature of Sabbath observance itself, Old Testament morality presents itself in sharp and definite contrast to all heathen ethics, and places the moral task of man higher than the latter.

Hebrew ethics, however, does not linger, as was almost exclusively the case with heathen ethics, in the purely ideal sphere,—in the consideration of the good *per se,*—does not conceive of *evil* as a mere possibility or as a merely exceptional or isolated reality, or as a nature-necessity back of all human guilt (which are all, in fact, heathen views)—but looks evil earnestly and squarely in the face, and regards it as a sad, all-prevalent reality, the guilt of which lies in the free act of man, and is participated in by all without exception. The morality of the chosen people of God looks, therefore, not merely to a warding off and an avoiding of evil as a something as yet external to our heart, and merely threatening us, but to a zealous, constant combating of the same, not outside of us in an originally defective world, but within in the inmost guilt-laden heart of the subject himself. Sin is of historical origin,—an historical reality and power; and morality, the nature of which presents itself now quite predominantly as a vigorous combating against sin, appears also itself in a uniformly historical character,—is promoted and guided by a divine history-chain of ever richer-unfolding gracious guidances, and gives rise to a moral history, to a redemption-history, to a kingdom of God here upon earth inside of humanity,—at first, in faith and hope, and afterwards (after it has reached the goal promised by God from the very start, and embraced by the people with pious confidence, and kept constantly in view) in full, blissful reality. Heathenism knows indeed evil, knows vice, but it does not know *sin,* for sin is of a morally-historical character; hence it knows also of no historical overcoming of the same, no expecting, no preparing for, nor realization of, a kingdom of God in humanity; the Persians alone have an obscure presentiment thereof, perhaps not without a ray of light received from the people of God, with whom they were in contact, and whom,

from their residence among them, they learned highly to esteem.

On the entrance of sin into the world there arises at once a separation among men between those who permit themselves to be fettered by sin and those who retain God and his salvation in view, between the children of the world and the children of God; God, however. looks in compassionate love also upon the former and plans for them a redemption, the world-historical preparation of which is confided to that people which He separates out from among the men of sin, and paternally guides; God separates to himself the man of faith,—him who trusts in God with rock-like firmness and cheerfully and unconditionally obeys his word even where he is unable to comprehend it and where it diametrically contradicts his own natural consciousness. God places before Abraham, from the very start, not a merely personal, but a *world-historical* goal: "In thee shall all the families of the earth be blessed" [Gen. xii, 3], and he repeats this promise again and again in progressively more definite features; as in Adam all die, so in Abraham are all nations to be blessed and to be brought to the Accomplisher of Salvation. For the first time in the history of humanity we find here, and in contrast to all heathendom, a definite world-historical goal of the moral life; not man, but God has established it in compassionating grace, and has sealed it in successive and progressively richer promises; and an individual man is elected to co-operate in the fulfilling of this promise, which is not given to him as an individual but to *humanity*,—to co-operate in such a sense as that this man, that this people itself, may become capable of really participating in the fruit of the redemption accomplished by the act of grace,—by becoming the maternal womb which is to bear and give birth to the Saviour. But the individual has part in this moral work only when he accepts the promise in faith, and it is only when he accepts the promise in *faith*, and only on the basis of this faith, that he is able to attain to true obedience of life.

This people, so strictly cut off from all the rest of the race, this people hated, oppressed, down-trodden by the rest of mankind, becomes thus, from the very beginning, of *world-*

historical significance, in a much higher sense than any other pre-Christian people. The heathen nations which actively entered into and shaped history sought only *themselves* but not humanity; the Israelitic people, shut up exclusively to the promise and to faith,—a people already spiritually developed and molded into a moral organism before it had as yet where to lay its head, and which was as yet seeking its earthly home,—a spiritual people without any nature-basis, and which received its earthly home only as a gracious gift of God, conferred on moral conditions [Lev. xxv, 23],—this people, in its God-willed and commanded separation from all heathen nations, in its so often, even up to the present day, reproached "particularism," was, after all, absolutely the only people which had in view, from the beginning, the true "universalism," (namely, the salvation of collective humanity), as its highest goal, and which sought to do nothing else than to prepare the way for this salvation of humanity [Gen. xii, 3; xviii, 18; xxii, 18; xxvi, 4; Deut. xxxii, 43; 1 Chron. xvi, 23, 28; Isa. ii, 2 *sqq.;* xi, 10 *sqq.;* xxv, 6 *sqq.;* xlii, 1, 6; xlv, 20, 22, 23; xlix, 6; lii, 15; liv, 3; lv, 5; lx; lxi, 11; lxii, 2; lxv, 1; lxvi, 18 *sqq.;* Jer. iv, 2; xvi, 19; Amos ix, 11, 12; Hag. ii, 7 (8); Zech. ii, 11; vi, 15; viii, 20 *sqq.;* xiv, 16; Micah iv, 1 *sqq.;* Mal. i, 11; Psa. ii, 8; xviii, 49; lxvii, 2; lxxii, 8 *sqq.;* lxxxvi, 9, 10; xcvi, 7, 10; cii, 15; cxvii, 1]. The Israelites had therefore, from the very beginning, the deepest interest for history, and for the goal of history as clearly presented by prophetic promise; the divine prophetic benedictions upon the patriarchs relate much less to their own person than to the history of humanity as proceeding from them; the Hebrew is clearly conscious that all his moral striving contributes to conduct the God-guided current of history to the God-promised realization of salvation; instead of the gloomy, despairing tragic consciousness of the most highly cultured of all the heathen nations, we find here a full confidence in the ultimate fulfillment of the redemption longed-for by man and promised by God.

The Israelites have and could have this high world-historical mission only because they were made to conceive of themselves from the very beginning as, not a nature-people, but as a spiritual people which obtained for itself its natural

prosperity only through moral fidelity. As the people of
God, they name themselves not Hebrews, from their natural
descent, nor yet from Abraham, nor from Isaac, nor indeed
from Jacob's first name, but from his later God-given name,
Israel, which he received after he had wrestled with the angel
[Gen. xxx, 24 *sqq*]. From Abraham and Isaac descend also
other tribes, which do not belong to the people of God; only
Jacob's descendants belong all thereto. Nor is Jacob the
progenitor of the people of God in his earlier self-willed and
self-confiding life, but solely in his spiritually-transformed
life, after that, praying and beseeching, he had wrestled, in
bitter repentance, with Jehovah as offended at his many sins
and deceits, and after that, in self-denying humility having
put off all self-righteousness, he had thrown himself child-like
at the feet of God and confided all his well-being to His
blessing. It becomes the people of Israel, as a spiritual people, to have also a spiritual and not a merely natural man as
their father, and the true bearing of this father to God is expressed in the words: "I will not let thee go unless thou bless
me." Whoever would belong to this spiritual people of God
must divest himself of all his mere naturalness; this is sym-
bolized by the covenant-token of the people with God, cir-
cumcision.

The Israelite, in his moral strivings, has the *highest good*
hopefully and confidently in view, and not for the individual
person alone, but for humanity. The idea of the highest
good, the fundamental thought of all morality, has, in the
Old Testament history, a very distinct development. It appears in God's *promises*, on the one hand, as a grace, and, on
the other, as a reward for trusting fidelity,—neither of which
is by any means to be separated from, or regarded as contradictory to, the other. In the first blessing after the creation,
as we have already seen, the thought of the highest good is
already indicated; by sin, however, the blessing is changed
into a curse, the highest good is thrown into the far distant,
and is only obscurely alluded to in the promise of the ultimate victory of the seed of the woman over the seed of the
serpent [Gen. iii, 15], and henceforth the thought of the
highest good is associated with the *victory* over evil, with
redemption. And though mankind,—originally destined to

possess the whole earth [Gen. i, 28; Matt. v, 5],—receive now
merely in small numbers, as members of the people of God,
only a very·small space of the earth for their possession, yet
is also this typical foretaste of the possession of the highest
good associated at the same time with promises of victory
over the sin-symbolizing heathen inhabitants thereof; the
highest good even in its feeblest foretastes is conditioned on
trustful struggle and victory. In the blessing upon Noah
[Gen. ix] there are indicated as the highest good, in the first
place, the multiplication of the human race through Noah,
and the dominion over nature (now, after the fall into sin,
under a somewhat changed form), and, then, in the express
covenant of God with Noah, the full personal communion of
believing man with God. To Abraham, the prophetic bene-
diction is essentially enlarged, including the multiplication
of his family under God's guidance, the guaranteeing of an
earthly father-land as a gift of *God*, and the blessing of entire humanity through the people of God as springing from
him. God had expressly called Abraham away from his
natural father-land; he is to receive another one in its stead,
one that is *morally* acquired from God's hand through believing submission to God; all earthly good is to bear also a
spiritual character, is to be an outgrowth from spiritual
good; even the most natural earthly good, the home, is to be
obtained as a grace in reward of faith. Homeless upon earth
for several ·centuries, the people Israel are to find, first,
their *eternal* home, so as, then, after having been trained
by God's hand, and ripened for his service through sufferings
and submission, to receive an earthly one as a gift of grace;
and this home is to be for them a symbol of the eternal one,
a shadow of the highest good. Even in the first promise to
Abraham, there beams out through this earthly good a faint
gleam of the heavenly one: "in thee shall all families of the
earth be *blessed ;*" Abraham is to be, not merely by his example of faith, but also really, by his family, the beginning
of a kingdom of God for entire humanity; to be *himself* in
this kingdom of blessing, and this kingdom *in him*, this is,
for him, the highest good. Exactly similar promises of temporal and likewise spiritual goods, God gives to Isaac and to
Jacob [Gen. **xxvi, 3–5; xxviii**, 13–15; comp. **xxxv**, 9–11;

xlviii, 4]; Isaac's blessing upon his son Jacob relates, it is true, primarily only to temporal good [xxvii, 28,29]; xxviii, 3, 4], but nevertheless with allusion to the higher good. It is true, temporal well-being [Gen. xxxix, 2, 3, 5, 23; Lev. xxvi, 3 *sqq.;* Deut. v, 29; vi, 3, 18, 24; vii, 13 *sqq.;* viii, 6 *sqq.;* xi, 9 *sqq.,* 21 *sqq.;* xii, 28; xv, 4–6, 10; xxviii, 1 *sqq.,* comp. Psa. lxxxi, 13, 14], and a continuance in the land, and long life [Exod. xx, 12; xxiii, 26; Deut. iv, 40; v, 33; vi, 2; xxx, 2 *sqq.;* xxxii, 47], are very often presented,—not indeed with reference merely to the individual, but also to the nation, as a divine blessing for pious fidelity,—as a high good and end; but as early as at the time of the actual conclusion of the covenant of God with the *people* on Sinai, the highest good appears as of a *spiritual* character: "If ye will obey my voice indeed and keep my covenant, then ye shall be a peculiar treasure unto me above all people; for all the earth is mine; and ye shall be unto me a kingdom of priests and a holy nation" [Exod. xix, 5, 6]; the highest blessing is the *peace of God* [Num. vi, 26; Psa. xxix, 11], the love of God, the compassion of God, and his covenant with men [Deut. vii, 9, 12, 13; xiii, 17, 18], so that they "may live long" [Deut. v, 33] and that God might be their "righteousness" [vi, 25]; and in the first commandment: "I am the Lord thy God, thou shalt have no other gods before me" [Exod. xx, 2, 3], the objective phase of the highest good is definitely expressed; any thing else, save God, that man might regard as the highest good, is in fact but a worthless idol; and hence the rejection of the covenant of grace works an everlasting rejection of him who rejects it [1 Chron. xxviii, 9].

In view of this high spiritual conception of the highest good, it appears as in the highest degree a surprising fact that the thought of a *life after death* is not directly brought to bear upon the moral life,—is not presented as a motive of action, or as a phase of the highest good,—a peculiarity that is all the more striking when we consider that the children of Israel had lived for four centuries in Egypt, and that Moses had been educated in the wisdom of this country, where precisely this thought of immortality very powerfully shaped the entire moral and religious life, and when we further consider that this thought itself was most unquestionably recognized among the

children of Israel [Gen. v, 24; xv, 15; xxv, 8; xxxvii, 35; xlix, 26, 29, 33; Deut. xxxi, 16; xxxii, 50; 1 Sam. xxviii; Job xxvi, 5; 2 Kings ii; Psa. xvi, 10; xlix, 15; Prov. xv, 24], as it would also be naturally presumable that a people which places so high a value upon the personality, could not be ignorant of this thought, which so largely prevailed throughout heathendom. This manifestly intentional placing in the back-ground of the thought of immortality as bearing upon the moral life, is to be explained from the peculiarity of the purpose which God had with this nation, in view of the salvation of mankind.—(1.) The people of Israel is a world-historical one as no other ante-Christian people was; the entire hopes and striving of the nation are directed toward the ultimate salvation of the human race as the highest goal; the primarily feeble, but constantly more definite-growing Messianic thought throws temporarily into the back-ground the interest in future life of the *individual* person. The entire hope of Israel looks forward to the highest good, the true salvation, but this highest good consists, even for the pious Israelite, only in the future redemption that is to be accomplished by a world-historical divine act; the Redeemer had first to spring from the line of David before the life after death could have real worth for the saint, or be his highest good; *before* this event, the transmundane life was a beclouded one, not only for the consciousness, but also *per se*,—was not as yet a truly blissful life in the presence of God [Psa. vi, 5; xlix, 15 *sqq.;* lxxxviii, 10–13; cxv, 17; Isa. xxxviii, 18]. As Abraham rejoiced that he should see the day of the Lord [John viii, 56], so also longed Abraham's seed for this day, from which time forth, only, the life after death could be a truly blessed one. The saints of the Old Covenant did not pass their lives as having no hope, but their hope was *primarily* an historical one,—was fixed upon the historical fulfillment of the promises, and aspired toward a heavenly home only from, and on the basis of, this fulfillment.— (2.) Though for the redeemed Christian the thought of a future life is a very important element of his moral consciousness, nevertheless for the as yet not truly regenerated man there lies in the same no inconsiderable danger, namely, the danger of selfish reward-seeking, of a narrow-hearted directing of his moral striving exclusively toward his personal well-being

instead of toward the salvation of humanity. Though the saints of the Old Covenant participated in many gracious gifts, so that they cannot be regarded as merely natural men, still, they were not as yet in the highest sense spiritually regenerated; and, in fact, in the necessary redemption-preparing requirement of strict obedience to the objectively-given law, they stood all the more exposed to this danger of regarding their future salvation as a reward for good works, as is actually evinced by the rise of Pharisaism. From this danger God preserved the Hebrews, in that while He indeed promised them a gracious reward for their fidelity, He yet presented as such reward, on the one hand, only such goods as most evidently could *not* be, for the pious, the highest good, and, on the other hand, the fulfillment of the divine promises within the sphere of history, namely, redemption, so that they were necessarily brought to the consciousness that the highest good was *not* the reward of their own works, but the fruit of a future divine act of grace.

Although the law had essentially also the purpose of awakening the consciousness of the antagonism of the sinful nature of man against the holy will of God, thus implying that the full consciousness of the sinful perversion of human nature was a state that had as yet to be attained to, nevertheless this consciousness exists from the very beginning, and that too very vividly, as we shall hereafter see; and it is especially noteworthy that notwithstanding the high reverence which the Israelites had for their patriarchs and for the prophets of God, still they were very far from regarding them as *moral ideals*. It is true, there are mentioned pious and just men, such as Enoch and Noah; and the faithfulness of Abraham shines forth typically even into the New Covenant; but they are never presented as real holy types of morality, (not even in Gen. xxvi, 4, 5; 2 Chron. vii, 17; Mal. ii, 15); on the contrary, the historical records relate, even of the most revered characters, manifold sins, and sins which the Israelites unquestionably regarded as such; thus, for example, of Abraham [Gen. xii, 11 *sqq.*; xx, 2 *sqq.*], and of Jacob [xxvii, 14 *sqq.*; xxxi, 20], and of Reuben, of Simeon and Levi [xxxiv, 14 *sqq.*; xxxv, 22; xlix, 14 *sqq.*]; and of the other sons of Jacob [xxxvii]; and of Judah, the ancestor of the kings, there is recorded scarcely

12

any thing but evil; he even begets Pharez—from whom David, and hence also the Messiah, were to descend—in unconscious incest and conscious whoredom [xxxviii]; Moses slays the Egyptian and buries him secretly, and this was also certainly regarded as a crime [Exod. ii, 11 *sqq.*]; he resists faint-heartedly the divine call, [Exod. iii and iv] and subsequently wavers in his faith, and is, for that reason, shut out from the Land of Promise [Num. xx, 7 *sqq.*; Deut. xxxii, 49 *sqq.*]; and that which is said to him holds good in another sense of *all* the saints of the Old Covenant, namely: "thou shalt see the land before thee, but thou shalt not enter into it;" and however pre-eminent David and Solomon are in courageous faith and in wisdom, still they were not pure examples even for the Israelites; the Israelites knew of only *one* Servant of God who was perfect and pure and holy, namely, the longed-for Anointed of the Lord. And accordingly the saints of the Old Covenant kept themselves far from all self-glorification, and aspired to a higher goal. The undevout self-righteousness and work-holiness of the later Pharisaism is totally repugnant to the spirit of the Old Covenant; for the law requires most certainly not merely the outward work, but above all and essentially also a morally-pious *disposition,*—bears, in contradistinction to the later Jewish outward legality, a very positive character of *inwardliness.* The basis and essence of all morality are the requirement, that man "should love God with all his heart, with all his soul, and with all his might" [Deut. vi, 5; x, 12; xiii, 3]; he is to take the divine law to his heart, and to observe it with his whole heart and his whole soul [Deut. v, 29; vi, 6; xi, 13; 18 *sqq.*; xxvi, 16; xxx, 2; Josh. xxii, 5]; God desires not merely the external works, he requires our heart [1 Chron. xxii, 19; Prov. xxiii, 26]; the saint not only fulfills the law, but "his delight is in the law of the Lord" [Psa. i, 2; cxii, 1; cxix, 24, 35, 70; Job xxii, 22, 26; Deut. xxviii, 47]; and all obedience is simply joyous thankfulness for God's gracious guidance [Exod. xx, 2 *sqq.*; Deut. iv and v; vi, 20 *sqq.*; viii, 3 *sqq.*; x, 19 *sqq.*; xi, 1; xv, 15; xvi, 12; 1 Chron. xxix, 9 and others]; and therefore not merely the sinful act, but equally also the lust to evil, is sinful and damnable [Exod. xx, 17; Prov. vi, 25].

Old Testament morality has essentially a preparatory character,—refers forward to a higher and as yet to be acquired

morality; hence it bears in part a symbolical form,—expressing by external signs, that, the full realization of which, was possible only after the time of the accomplishment of redemption, and thereby constantly keeping before the eyes of the people what the ultimate moral purpose of the divine economy with Israel was,—although this purpose could not as yet be fully realized. In order to keep constantly awake and to intensify the moral consciousness of the antagonism of the divine will to the sinful nature which had now become natural to actual man, the antagonism of the "clean" and the "unclean" is rigorously insisted upon and carried out, and that too not merely in the sphere of the purely spiritual and moral, but also in that of nature, where the moral is only symbolically prefigured. Man is required to learn, in free obedience, to distinguish and choose between the godly and the ungodly, and that too not according to his natural impulses and feelings, nor by the merely reflective observation and examination of things, but solely by the minutely-particularizing positive divine law. To man, as not yet actually redeemed and sanctified, but as yet involved and entangled in the bonds of sinfulness, the law presents itself, and properly so, as of an objectively-revealed character, as foreign to his natural state, and to which there is nothing correspondent in his inner nature unless it be a loving willingness to unconditional obedience. Educative disciplining to obedience is the essential end of many of the positive laws, which must consequently appear to the truly emancipated and redeemed as a yoke, whereas, for him who is only as yet struggling toward freedom, they are a wholesome discipline.

Old Testament morality presents a moral task not only to the individual person, but it also keeps in view, from the very start, the necessity of moral *communion*. It conceives of the moral significance of the family more highly than any of the heathen systems; in giving to reverence for parents a religious ground, it guarantees at the same time the moral rights of children as against sinful parents; and if it is not as yet able to raise marriage to the height of the Christian view, inasmuch as only the truly spiritually-regenerated are in a condition to appreciate and fulfill its full significance [Matt. v, 31; xix, 8], nevertheless it does give to it the truly religious and moral basis. It changes the slavery of Israelites into a very mild service-rela-

tion, and protects, by extremely humane regulations, that o.
non-Israelites from arbitrary and severe oppressiveness. The
differences among mankind are no longer natural, but spirit-
ually-*moral;* even foreign slaves have part in the worship and
in the blessings of the people of God. The moral organization
of society into the state is presented in the Old Testament, from
the very start, in its highest moral significancy, as a unity of
church and state—as a *theocracy*—in which the entire moral
community-life of the people rests on a religious basis,—in
which Jehovah alone is king, and the God-called and enlightened prophets the organs of his will,—organs to whom the people submit themselves in believingly joyous obedience. But here
also, as well as in the case of marriage, God gives simply the
unambiguous idea, and, because of the hardness of the hearts,
concedes another state-organization more correspondent to the
sinful circumstances of the people, namely, the purely human
institution of an earthly monarchy,—reserving the full realization of the higher idea, for the future. But even this earthly
kingdom is to be an image of the divine kingdom, and the
kings, the faithful instruments of the holy will of God—kings
"after God's own heart;" the Old Testament recognizes neither
despotic nor democratic caprice-domination as morally admissible. Of all this we must speak again further on.

As Old Testament redemption-history presents essentially an
educative preparation for the historical accomplishing of the
redemption-act, hence it is clearly manifest that this preparation must be a historically-*progressive* one, and that consequently Old Testament ethics itself must have an *historical development.* This, as yet, very unsatisfactorily-treated portion of
Biblical theology cannot, however, be fully presented in the
brief space to which the plan of our historical Introduction
confines us; we therefore remark here only two points, (1), that
the *essential* character of the moral view (and the question is
here simply as to essential features) is contradictory to the
heathen view, and different from the Christian, and, throughout
all the writings of the Old Testament, self-consistent and the
same: and, (2), that the prophetic redemption-history is closely
connected with the legislative, seeing that Moses himself was
the greatest among the prophets. The prophets, in the narrower sense of the word, do not give an essentially new moral

revelation, but, on the contrary, uniformly proceed on the basis of that of Moses,—referring, on the one hand, exhortingly to its requirements, and rebuking the unfaithfulness of the people to its spirit, but, on the other, directing attention with constantly greater distinctness to the goal of this moral development-process of the people of Israel, that is, to their world historical destination,—and, above all, they seek to ward against the danger of legal holiness and self-sufficiency, the danger of the selfish contentment of the single moral subject with his own individual development,— which lies in every strictly-developed system of laws,—that is, against the danger of a merely external performing of the works of the law, as was at a later period actually presented in Pharisaism; they earnestly urged to the *inner* purity of the heart, and bring to an increasingly clearer consciousness the morality that transcends that of the mere individual, namely, the general moral task of the totality, of the people of God.   While the earlier ethics has more the character of a doctrine of laws and duties, the ethics of the prophets bears rather that of a doctrine of goods.—The *Proverbs* of Solomon, in contrast to the Mosaic Laws which present themselves as direct revelations from God, consist predominantly in rules of practical life-wisdom and life-prudence, drawn from the rich life-experience of a heart pious, though indeed often erring, and strengthened and ripened in the true fear of God; they appeal therefore less to a believing submission to an express divine command than rather to the free spontaneous assent, natural to a pious God-consciousness; they aim not at the disciplining of a, as yet, morally immature spirit by a legal yoke, but at the purifying, ripening and moral strengthening of the spirit as already consciously dwelling in God; they are not the sternly demanding voice of a prophet, but the witness of a preacher; it is not directly Jehovah, but it is the pious servant of God, who speaks to the pious.   In Moses the question is every-where as to *obedience;* with Solomon the constant theme is *wisdom*, a quality which is scarcely mentioned by Moses, and for the simple reason that the discipline of the law needed to precede and prepare the way, before the free subjectivity of wisdom could come to realization.   This coming into the fore-ground of the thought of wisdom evinces the progress of the moral consciousness out of the child-like condition of subjection to an objective

law, to the riper manhood of a freer self-determination on the basis of *personal* moral knowledge. Wisdom is here by no means mere worldly prudence, but its beginning and essence is the "fear of the Lord" [Prov. i, 7], and complete, hearty, God-confiding is its life-spring [iii, 5; xvi], and soul-repose and God's approbation its fruit [iii, 12, 18, 22 *sqq.;* viii, 17, 35; xv, 24; xxviii]; and hence for individual man it is the highest good [iii, 13 *sqq*]. This wisdom is very far removed from the "magnanimous" wisdom of the Greeks; it takes cognizance above all things of the sinfulness of the natural heart, and requires watchfulness over the same [iv, 23] and humility before God and man [iii, 34; xi, 2; xvi, 18; xviii, 12; xxvii, 2; xxix, 23]. While in the Solomonic Proverbs there is a manifest elevating of Mosaic legality toward the personal freedom of the pious sage, still it is not to be overlooked that there lies in the stand-point they assume, as in contrast to the Mosaic, also the danger that the subjective presumption of the individual person may rise to an unwarranted height, and work detriment to the true heart-humility that springs from a consciousness of one's own want of conformity to the law. And it is not unworthy of note that the *Christian* consciousness of the Apostles found much less occasion to appeal to the *wisdom* of man; they discourse far preferably of self-denying, humbly loving *faith.*—The *Ecclesiastes* of Solomon, after referring to the comfortless experience of a heart temporarily immersed in world-enjoyment, totally overthrows all world-pleasure and the vain hope of finding in the finite any real good; the mere negative knowledge that "all is vanity" prepares the way for a seeking after the true, the highest good, which, however, is but remotely suggested [Eccles. xii, 7, 13] but not fully presented; the skepticism, at first sight so seemingly wide-reaching and so entirely despairing of satisfaction, has a back-ground of very profound educative wisdom.

In the fact that the moral is not derived from the natural conscience of man, seeing that the conscience is no longer the pure expression of the original God-consciousness, but that, on the contrary, the historically-revealed will of God is the exclusive source of the moral command, there lies an essential reason why Hebrew ethics did not develop itself into a philosophy; the very thought of such a philosophy conflicts

with the fundamental presuppositions of the Old Testament consciousness. The time had not yet come when the conscience, and human knowledge in general, had so far become free as to derive truth also from within themselves. As yet man was called simply believingly to obey, but not freely and philosophically to create.

SECTION XXVIII.

The Old Testament *Apocryphal Books*,* abandoned by the fire of the prophetic spirit, and in part affected by foreign philosophical influences, treat predominantly of morality. The moral law,—in the Old Testament canon an essential element of the educative divine revelation as a whole,—is here considered rather in itself and as unconnected with the world-historical goal of the Theocracy, and is thereby degraded into a merely individual, empirically-grounded moral system.—In the *Talmud* the law appears as entirely unspiritualized,—as fallen into complete lifeless externality, dissolved into its ultimate atoms.

The moral thoughts of the Apocrypha give clear evidence of some degree of obscuration of the consciousness of redemption-history, both in respect to its presupposition, namely, the fall and its consequences, and in regard to its true nature in the Ancient Covenant, and also in regard to its historical goal—the expected redemption-act by Christ. With the obscuration of this thought go naturally enough hand in hand a manifest coming into the fore-ground of a certain holiness by works, in the manner of the heathen moralists [comp. Sirach iii, 16, 17 (14, 15), 33 (30); xxix, 15–17 (12, 13); xvii, 18 (22) *sqq.*], a one-sided laudation of wisdom and righteousness in obliviousness of the question whether

---

* Comp. Stäudlin: *Gesch. der Sittenl. Jesu*, i, 358; Cramer: *Moral der Apokr.*, 1814; (also in Keil and Tzschirner's *Analekten*, 1814, ii, 1, 2,); Räbiger: *Ethica libe apocr.*, 1838; Keerl: *Die Apokr. d. A. T.*, 1852, somewhat unfair; comp. Hengstenberg: *Für Beibehaltung der Apokr.*

indeed there are any such wise and righteous persons to be found, and also in many respects a proud self-satisfaction with one's own wisdom and virtue, together with a censorious and contemptuous looking-down upon the unwise and unrighteous many,—a certain coldly-rational self-complacent tone, especially in Sirach,—a suspicious complaining and an almost bigoted abstaining from true love-communion with others [comp. Sirach xi, 30 (29) *sqq.;* xii; xiii; xxv, 10 (7); xxx, 6; xxxiii, 25; *sqq.*],—a zealous cautioning against the wickedness and falseness of others instead of a warning against the wickedness and deceptiveness of one's own heart; and there is frequently a manifest lack of the proper humility of the truly self-understanding conscience; and the obtaining of personal happiness is often presented too one-sidedly as a direct motive to virtue, so that the ethical view is sometimes tinged with a shallow utilitarianism [comp. Sirach xiv, 14 *sqq.*].—The book of *Wisdom*, showing traces of Alexandrino-Platonic influences, and accordingly containing the four Greek virtues [viii, 7], does not keep far clear of work-holy boasting [*e. g.* vii and viii]; and though it admits the sinful corruption and weakness of all men [ix; xii, 10 *sqq.;* xiii, 1 *sqq.;* ii, 24], it yet brings them into a false connection with theories from other sources [viii, 19, 20; ix, 15; *e. g.*, pre-existence of the soul, and dualistic relation of the body as an essential trammeling of the soul]. The book of *Sirach* gives expression both to a deep piety and to a rich practical life-experience, and though in the eyes of Rationalism it is the most valuable book of the Old Testament, it is still very far superior to modern Rationalistic shallowness [comp. xxv, 32 (24); xl, 15, 16; xli, 8 (5), *sqq.;* viii, 6 (5)]; it manifests, however, on the other hand, also a want of depth in its view of sinfulness and of the need of redemption [comp. xv, 15–17; xxxii, 27 (Septuagint, xxxv, 23); xxxvii, 17 (13); li, 18 (13) *sqq.*], and often places the outward ungenerous prudence-rules of a distrustful understanding in the stead of higher moral ideas [*e. g.* viii, 1 *sqq.;* xlii, 6, 7], and, as differing from the book of Wisdom, alludes to no supernatural goal of morality in a transmundane life; it may indeed teach the spiritually regenerated much moral life-wisdom and prudent rational foresight, but it cannot bring the natural man to

self-acquaintance and humility. From the stand-point of Christian ethics, this book is very far remote; the essence of .ove is unknown to it. The book of *Judith* presents in narrative form a highly questionable morality [ix, 2 *sqq.;* comp. Gen. xxxiv; xlix, 5–7].

As in Sirach the vigorously-growing tree of Old Testament ethics begins to show signs of failing vitality, so in the *Talmud* (A. D. 200–600) we find the dead and decayed or petrified trunk.* Abandoned by the spirit of faith and hope, the Jews, in their faithlessness to their Redeemer, lost also the spirit of love; and human ingenuity changed the law which was readily enough borne by hoping faith, into an unspiritual yoke utterly subversive of moral freedom. The strictly objective character of the Old Testament law, so necessary for disciplinary purposes, had its vital complement in an expectant faith. This latter element becomes in the Talmud deceptive and wavering, and gives place almost entirely to the doctrine of the law; and the lifeless, idealess law, multiplied thousandfoldly by the ingenuity of human exegesis and inference, takes even the most insignificant and external actions into a dictatorially-regulative tutelage. Man acts no longer as prompted by his inner consciousness, for his inner life-source is dried up, but according to the outward law as multiplying its branches through all the channels of human life.—The *Talmud* contains, besides its more spiritual elements, which are mostly taken from the Old Testament, a system of casuistry unparalleled for its trivial and childish entering into minutiæ, such as was possible in fact only on just such a soil, namely, matured Pharisaism. For the Jew, the authority of the Scribes takes the place of the moral conscience; to him who honestly holds fast to the law, the multiplicity of precepts becomes a yoke subversive of true morality, while to those who are less sincere the manifold contradictions in the same give pretext for a disingenuous relaxation of duty.

Observation. Islamism,—which finds its place in the history of the religious and moral spirit not as a vital organic member, but as violently interrupting the course of this history, and

---

* *Mishna* translated by Rabe, 1760, 6 vols.—*Talmud Babli*, the Babylonian *Talmud*, by Pinner, 1842.—*Schulchan Aruch* by Löwe, 1836, 4 vols.—Fassel: *Die mosaisch-rabbin. Tugend-u. Pflichtenl.*, 2 ed., 1842.

which is to be regarded as an attempt of heathenism to maintain itself erect, under an outward monotheistic form, against Christianity, and to arm the entire unbroken essence of the natural man against the spirit of an inner new-birth,—has indeed given rise to a peculiar ethical system, though one which has so little of depth peculiar to itself, that we need here only allude to it in passing.* The ethics of Islam bears the character of an outwardly and crudely conceived doctrine of righteousness; conscientiousness in the sphere of the social relations, faithfulness to conviction and to one's word, and the bringing of all action into relation to God, are its bright points; but there is a lack of heart-depth, of a basing of the moral in love. The highest good is the very outwardly and very sensuously conceived happiness of the individual. The potency of sin is not recognized; evil is only an individual, not an historical power; hence there is no need of redemption, but only of personal works on the basis of prophetic instruction; Mohammed is only a teacher, not an atoner. God and man remain strictly external to, and separate from, each other; God—no less individually conceived of than man—comes into no real communion with man; and man, as moral, acts not as influenced by such a communion, but only as an isolated individual. The ideal basis of the moral is faith in God and in his Prophet; the moral life, conceived as mainly consisting in external works, is not a fruit of received salvation, but a means for the attainment of the same; pious works, and particularly prayer, fasting and almsgiving, and pilgrimaging to Mecca, work salvation directly of themselves. Man has nothing to receive from God but the Word, and nothing to do for God but good works; of inner sanctification there is no thought; the essential point is simply to let the *per se* good nature of man manifest itself in works; there is no inner struggle in order to attain to the true life, no penitence-struggle against inner sinfulness; and instead of true humility we find only proud work-righteousness. To the natural propensions of man there is consequently but little refused, —nothing but the enjoyment of wine, of swine-flesh, of blood, of strangled animals, and of games of chance, and this, too, for

---

* Imm. Berger: *Ueber die Moral des Koran* in Stäudlin's *Beiträge zur Phil.*, v, 250, (1799), superficial.—Weil: *Mohammed*, 1843.—Sprenger: *Leben u. Lehre des Moh.*, 1862.

insufficient (assigned) reasons. The merely individual character of the morality manifests itself especially in the low conception that is formed of marriage, in which polygamy is expressly conceded, woman degraded to a very low position, and the dissolution of the marriage bond placed in the unlimited discretion of the man; there hence results a very superficial view of the family in general; the moral community-life is conceived of throughout in a very crude manner. Unquestionably this form of ethics is not an advancing on the part of humanity, but a guilty retrograding from that which had already been attained.

C.—CHRISTIAN ETHICS.

SECTION XXIX.

In Christianity alone morality and ethics are enabled to reach their perfection,—the former being perfected in the person of Christ himself, the latter being in process of self-perfection in the progressive intellectual activity of the church.—The subjective and the objective *grounds* of morality are given, in Christianity, in full sufficiency. On the one hand, the moral subject has attained to a full consciousness of sin, of its general sway, of its historical significancy, and of its guilt; on the other, he has, by redemption, become free from his bondage under sin, and risen again to moral freedom,—has again attained to the possibility of accomplishing his moral task. On the one hand, the objective ground of the moral—God— is now for the first, perfectly, personally and historically revealed to man, and God's will not merely manifested in unclouded clearness in his Word and through the historical appearance of the Redeemer himself, but also, by the holy, divine Spirit as imparted to the redeemed, written into their hearts; on the other, this God stands no longer in violent antith-

esis to the sin-estranged creature, but is in Christ reconciled with him, and, as a graciously loving Father, is present to him and in constant sanctifying and strengthening life-communion with him.

The *goal* of morality has become an other,—has risen from the state of hope to a constantly-growing reality. God-sonship is not placed simply at the remote termination of the moral career, but is from the very beginning already present; the Christian strives not merely in moral aspiration toward it, but lives and acts in it and as inspired by it; he cannot possibly live or act morally if he is not already God's child; he has his goal already from the very beginning as a blessed reality, and his further goal is in fact simply *fidelity* in this God-sonship,—a sinking deeper into it, a strengthening and purifying of it by a constantly greater triumphing over the sinful nature which yet clings to the Christian, namely, the "flesh" which lusts against the spirit; and for collective humanity the moral goal is and has been realizing itself from the beginning in ever increasing fullness, namely, in the fact that all nation-separating barriers progressively fall away, and that the Word of life increasingly assumes form in the God-fearing of all nationalities,—constituting the kingdom of God in its gradual rising to full historical reality in a universal Christian church.

The *essence* of morality has risen from the stage of the obedience of a faithful servant to that of the loving, confiding freedom of the children of God. Man has the command no longer as a merely outward, purely objective one, uncongenial to his subjective nature, but as an inward one dwelling within him, and as become his personal possession, and hence as

no longer a yoke, a burden, but as an inner power at one with his personality itself. Man lives and acts no longer as a mere individual subject, but he lives and acts in full life-communion with the Redeemer, and through him with God,—by virtue, on the one hand, of the love of faith, and, on the other, of the gift of the Spirit: I live, and yet not I, but Christ lives in me. The moral idea is not a mere revealed Word, it is the Son of God as become man, the personal Redeemer himself, not merely in his truth-unvailing doctrine, not merely in his truth-revealing Spirit, but pre-eminently in his person itself, both as the historical, pure example of all holiness, as also as the One who is with us always even to the end of the world.— Love to that God who is manifested in redemption as himself the highest love, is the motive of the moral life—its essence and its power; it is a life of holy communion in every respect,—a life in and with God, a life *with* the children of God and in the communion of the redeemed.—The morality of hope has passed over into a morality of the joyous victory-consciousness,—is rather an actual manifestation of the already-attained, grace-awarded highest good, than a mere longing, aspiring after it. The ideal goal of morality is not in the least of a doubtful character, but is absolutely assured. While the fundamental feeling of the heathen virtue-sage is that of a proud self-consciousness of personal merit, the fundamental feeling of the Christian is the feeling of grace-accepting, thankful, loving *humility;* while the fundamental virtue of the Greeks is self-acquired wisdom, that of Christian morality is child-like *faith* in God's loving revelation both in Word and in historical *act.*

There is no need here of detailed developments or proofs; we desire simply to present the ground-character of Christian ethics as in contrast to heathen ethics. This much is clear from what we have already said, that morality must assume here an entirely other form than in heathendom, and even in many respects a different one from that in the Old Testament. No heathen ethical system looks to the formation of a kingdom of God embracing all mankind; the freedom of the will is either denied or restricted to a very few favored ones, and with these it is regarded as unaffected by the historical power of sin; heathenism knows nothing of personal love to God as a moral motive, and of the personal love of God to all men as its antecedent condition. Christianity takes it just as earnestly with the reality, the power and the guilt of sin, as with the real, historical, overcoming of the same through Christ. Man, as not from nature free, but as become free by historical redemption-act and by the personal appropriation of the same, is the true subject, capable of all true morality; and hence the realization of this morality depends no longer on a mere nature-conditionment, but solely on man's free self-determination for or against his redemption. That which is presumptuously presupposed by the Greek philosophers as already possessed by the elect few who are capable of true morality, namely, true will-freedom and a personal moral consciousness springing from the inner essence of the soul, all this has attained to its full truth only in Christianity, namely, in that the false security of a merely natural freedom and power is overcome and remedied. Both freedom and power are procured for all who wish them, and that not by self-deception, but by a real moral redemption-act of the alone holy One.

That the highest good is not a something to be attained to exclusively by moral action, but, on the contrary, in its essence a power graciously conferred on the willing heart, a power which has true morality simply as its fruit and subjective perfection, and which manifests this morality essentially as faithfulness, as a preserving and virtualizing of the received grace,—this is a thought utterly foreign to all heathendom, and which is placed, even in the Old Testament, only in the promised future; and upon this thought,

as upon the consciousness of personal guilt and divine grace, rests the so distinctively Christian virtue of *humility*, as that of a pardoned sinner. There is scarcely anywhere to be found so violent an ethical antithesis as that between the high-esteemed virtue of magnanimity in Aristotle (which corresponds to the pride of the Pharisee in the parable of Christ,) and the Christian humility of that Publican who ventures no other prayer than this: "God be merciful to me a sinner." Such magnanimity appears to the Christian as mere self-blinding pride, while this humility appears to the Greek as servile-mindedness.

Heathen ethics is always simply of a purely individual character, or, if it relates to a moral community-life, then only of a merely civil character, as consisting in obedience to laws purely human, and valid only for a particular people; or where, as in China, the state is regarded as of divine origin and essence, there individual morality becomes essentially a mere mechanical self-conforming to an eternally on-revolving unspiritual world-order; Christian morality is, on the contrary, never of a merely individual character, but absolutely and always an expression of moral communion—on the one hand, with the personal Saviour and God, and, on the other, with the Christian society; its essential nature is therefore *love* in the fullest sense of the word, and it is never of a merely civil character but belongs to a purely moral community-life,—a life that rests in no respect on nature-limits or on unfreedom,—namely, that of the Church as the historical kingdom of God.—In contradistinction to worldward-turned heathenism, Christians make the foundation and essence of all moral life to consist in the constant direction of the heart to God; and especially in *prayer*—(which, as exalted by the communion of devotion, becomes the principal phase of the entire religious life, and conditions and preserves a direct personal life-communion with God)—the entire moral life shapes itself into an expression of the religious consciousness as certain of its reconciliation with God. The Christian stands not alone in his moral life, nor is he merely a member of a moral society, but he stands in constant vital personal life-communion with God, and derives therefrom constantly new moral power. And precisely because Christian morality

is not of a merely individual character, but is rooted in and
grows out of the holiest of communions, is it truly free; the
law stands no longer simply over against man, so that his relation to it becomes one of mere service, but, as in contrast
to the self-sufficiency of the heathen mind (which finds in the
natural man the pure fountain of the moral consciousness), it
has become a perfectly inward personal law, one that constantly generates itself anew out of the sanctified heart of the
spiritually regenerated.

But prayer, wherein man enters into communion with God, is,
as also the example of the ancient church shows, essentially in-
tercession,—implies moral communion. The development of
morality into a collective life of the moral society,—into a collective morality,—is an essentially new phenomenon. Heathendom knew indeed the indefinite and merely impersonal, abstract
power of national custom, as well as the very definite but un-
free-working power of the civil law and of political rulers, but
it knew nothing of a free moral power of the truly moral community. The Christian community itself is the clearly duty-
conscious upholder, promoter and conservator of the morality
of the individuals; it has the duty of the moral overseeing,
furthering and guiding of all its members, and hence also of
moral discipline, and, as involved in this, also the power of in-
flicting moral discipline upon the unfaithful,—consisting essentially in the withdrawing of communion with them, in the
excluding of them from the moral whole as being non-tolerant
of any immoral element. The community-life is of so purely
moral, so intensely unitary, a character, that the unfaithfulness
of a single member thrills through the moral whole, and, because
of the intimate love of the whole for all the individuals, is painfully felt and reproved and rejected by the society. The totality stands surety for the morality of the individual, and the individual for that of totality; the moral life of the spiritual
organism has attained to its truth. The thought of church-
discipline,—which raises morality above the sphere of mere
individuality, without, however, giving to the community-
life the power of outward coercion, such as that of the
state, but on the contrary preserves and gives effect to this
life as a purely spiritual power,—is an essentially Christian
thought, and is only there practical where the moral idea

and its realization in the community-life are taken really in earnest.

In the emancipation of the human spirit by redemption, in the taking up of the moral idea into the inner heart of the consciousness, there lie, now, the possibility of, and the incentive to, a *scientific* development of the moral consciousness. Heathendom developed an ethical science only on the basis of a presumed freedom and autonomy of the spirit of the natural man; the Old Testament religion developed none at all, because in it the divine law was as yet an absolutely objective and merely passively-given one, to which man could stand only in an obeying relation. But Christianity regains for the human spirit its true freedom,—makes the merely objective law into an also perfectly subjective one, into one that lives in the heart of the regenerated as his real property, one that enlightens the reason and becomes thereby truly rational; and hence there is here given the possibility of shaping this pure moral subject-matter as embraced in the divinely enlightened conscience, into free scientific self-development. But Christian ethics, naturally enough, developed itself as a science only after its presuppositions, namely, the dogmatical questions in regard to God, to Christ and to man had attained to some degree of ripeness in the dogmatic consciousness of the church, and hence it appears for a long while predominantly only in closest involution with dogmatics, and in popular ecclesiastical instruction in the form of rules and exhortations, and in part also in ecclesiastically-defined life-regulations enforced by ecclesiastical discipline. The notion that the ancient church could and should have passed over the great dogmatic questions and devoted itself primarily and predominantly, or in fact exclusively, to the development of a system of morals as the essence proper of Christianity, is very erroneous. If we once perceive and admit that the Christian world-theory in general, in respect to God, to the creature, and especially to the nature of man, is of a character diametrically opposed to the heathen view, and if we admit that morality cannot be of an unconscious and merely instinctive character, but must rest on a rational consciousness, then it is perfectly clear that the consciousness must first be scientifically informed in regard to the reality of existence, before that the consciousness of that which, in virtue of the character of

13

this reality, becomes moral duty, can be further developed The religious consciousness of the moral was indeed given in high perfection in the first form of Christianity, but the scientific development of the moral could realize itself only very gradually and *subsequently to* the development of dogmatics.

The three natural chief epochs of church history constitute also those of the history of Christian ethics.

I. THE ANCIENT CHURCH UP TO THE SEVENTH CENTURY.

SECTION XXX.

Morality, as never separated from piety, and as uniformly based on loving faith in the Redeemer, and as upheld, fostered and watched over by the church-communion, appears in its inner phase as essentially *love* to God, and to Christ and to his disciples as brethren, and in its outer phase as a strict rejection of heathen customs, which latter feature, both in consequence of the persecutions suffered and because of the deep corruption of the extra-Christian world, assumes the form not unfrequently of a painfully-anxious self-seclusion from the same; and when, with the victory of Christianity over heathenism, from the time of Constantine on, worldliness pressed into the church itself, then, as a natural counterpoise against this worldliness, world-renunciation was made to apply, among the more pious-minded Christians, even to the sensuously-worldly phase of the Christian life, and was intensified, in the hermit-life, even to morbidness; and in consequence of the distinction which gradually sprang up in the church itself out of this antithesis in the Christian life, namely, between the moral com-

mands, on the one hand, and the evangelical counsels on the other (which latter were thought to condition a superior degree of holiness), the moral consciousness was essentially beclouded.

The moral views of the early Church are at once distinguishable from those of later Judaism by their profound grasping into the pious heart as the living fountain of a true and free morality, and from those of heathenism by the purity and rigor of the fundamental principles involved; and the unavoidable militant resistance against the demoralized heathen world naturally enough heightened this rigor to a degree which, but for this, seems no longer required. The essential difference of the Christian moral law from that of the Old Testament is fully recognized as early as from the time of Barnabas (*Ep. c.* 19). The rigorous element shows itself especially in respect to all sensuous pleasure and all worldly diversion, to marriage, to temporal possessions, and to political power, and to whatever is in any manner implicated with heathenism. In contrast to heathen laxity, the ancient Christians were all the more anxiously watchful against all dominion of sensuous desire, esteeming fasting very highly, though not as a commanded duty, and eschewing the demoralizing and religion-periling influence of the heathen stage and of other amusements; and the severity of their sufferings under the hatred of the world naturally enough made all worldly pleasure appear as in diametrical antagonism to Christian-mindedness. In a well-grounded persuasion of the dangers involved, the Christians declined to accept official positions in the heathen State. Chasteness even in thought was rigorously insisted upon; marriage was held more sacred than had ever been done before, and the sensuous element of the same was guarded within strict limits; and in view of the troubles of the times, and of the expectation of a near second-coming of Christ (which pretty generally prevailed in the first two centuries), very many inclined to a preference of celibacy, without, however, regarding it as a specially-meritorious course of conduct; second marriages, however, were generally viewed as an infidelity to the first consort. Riches were

mostly looked on as of questionable desirableness; the taking of interest was regarded (in harmony with the Old Testament view) as not permissible; beneficence and generosity to the brethren on a wide-reaching scale, was held as one of the most essential virtues; fidelity to truth, especially in confessing the faith, even in the face of threatening death, was a sacred duty, and its faithful fulfillment was the Christian's brightest testimony before his heathen persecutors. The oath was generally regarded as not allowable. Tender love toward each other, and a noble love of enemies, were the Christian's honor. The moral and warmly-fraternal community-life of the believers was a matter of astonishment even to the passionate enemies of Christianity. Slavery was at once essentially done away with by being transformed into a fraternally-affectionate service-relation; and when the State and laws became Christian, it was also greatly mitigated legally.

Notwithstanding the rigor of the moral view of the Christians, it nevertheless differs essentially from that of the Stoics, because of its fundamental character of joyous faith and love; it is in no respect a harsh, stiff or dismal, but, on the contrary, a thoroughly vigorous, youthful and joyous self-sacrificing life, in the full enjoyment of inner peace and of a conscious blessedness. These features were measurably lost only when the Christian Church itself ceased to be the pure moral antithesis of the un-Christian world, and when, having become a State-Church, it admitted into itself even worldly, and in so far, also, heathen elements. And it was now an essentially correct consciousness which inspired the more pious of the believers with a disinclination to the life and pursuits of the great mass of Christians, and drove them into separating themselves from them. The error, however, was this, that instead of separating the unpious from the Church itself, they chose the separation, within the Church, of the pious from communion with the mass of the Church, and thereby rendered the exclusion of the immoral from the Church more impracticable than ever,—in other words, that, instead of morally purifying the natural elements that inhered both in themselves and in the society, they despisingly withdrew the spiritual from all contact with the natural.

The first theoretical as well as practical separation of the ascetes (as imitated from the distinction, prevalent in the heathen world, between philosophers and the unphilosophical multitude, and as extending even to their costume), who thought by extreme world-renunciation to attain to an especially high moral perfection, and, as consequent thereon, also the distinguishing of a general Christian morality from a higher (and in some sense voluntary) ascetic morality, manifests itself in the third century in the currents of Alexandrian thought which had been so largely influenced by heathen philosophy,—as yet but feebly in Clemens Alexandrinus,* but already very damagingly in Origen.† The victory of Christianity over the heathen state in the fourth century, and the in-rushing both of the great and also of the populace into the Church, occasioned, on the one hand, a progressively growing relaxation of ecclesiastical discipline and a darkening of the moral consciousness in the great masses; and, on the other, in natural antithesis thereto, an increasingly radical exalting of the monastic life, in which the Christian conscience of the multitude found, as it were, an atoning complementing of their own imperfect secularized life. The ordinary requirements made upon the life of the ordinary Christian became less deep-reaching; but all the more rigorous were those made upon the ascetic life—wherein Christian morality was now thought to exist in its highest perfection. The distinguishing of mere ordinary moral duty, as the inferior, from moral perfection, became increasingly more familiar to the general Christian consciousness. The two true elements of Christian morality, namely, the turning away from the sinful world, and the aggressive living and working in and for the same, fell apart into two different channels, which respectively served, for the sum total of moral merit, as complements to each other; the superabundant merit of the sanctity of the ascetes fell to the good of the little-meriting world-Christians. In the sphere of morality a division of labor, so to speak, took place, and, in consequence thereof, there was subsequently developed in the sphere of moral merits a system of labor and traffic so artfully

* *Strom.*, p. 775, 825 (Potter).
† *Comm. in Ep. ad Rom.*, 507 (De la Rue).

organized that it required all the boldly initiatory vigor of the Reformation to bring again to the light of day the plain fundamental principles of evangelical morality. To the present period of the history of Christian ethics belong, however, only the feebler beginnings of this corruption.

The development of monasticism introduced a dualism into Christian morality, in that it proposed for the ascetes a morality essentially different from that of the rest of the Christian world, the latter being based upon the divine *command*, and the former upon pretended divine *counsels;* with this error were more or less affected Lactantius, Ambrose, Chrysostom, Jerome, and Augustine. In consequence of this, general Christian morality was degraded to a mere minimum; the truly good was made to be different from the divine command, and this good was considered no longer as the imperative will of God, but only, as it were, a divine *wish*, the fulfilling of which procures for man a special extraordinary merit, but the non-fulfilling of which awakens no divine displeasure. The more general prevalence of this view involved the overthrow of purely evangelical ethics, and the beginning of the perversion of the moral life of the Church in practical respects. By far the greatest portion even of the dogmatic and ecclesiastical errors of the Romish and Greek Churches has sprung from this very notion of a special sanctity in monasticism.

SECTION XXXI.

Ethics itself appears not as yet in scientific form and apart from the presentation of the subject-matter of dogmatics; it appears more in the popular edificatory than in the scientific writings, and approaches more nearly a scientific form in the works written in self-defense against the heathen. The first connected and somewhat comprehensive presentation of ethics— by *Ambrose*—in the manner of Cicero, is scientifically of little value; while the brilliant, penetrative, and ingenious moral thoughts of *Augustine*, (which, along with Aristotle, formed the foundation of Mediæval

ethics), deviate sometimes in daring originality from the earlier ecclesiastical view, and also bring some confusion into purely evangelical ethics by an over-valuing of monkish asceticism. After the time of Augustine, ethics is for the most part limited to the mere collecting of the views of earlier writers, and to popular instruction. The mystical thoughts of the pseudo-*Dionysius the Areopagite* became influential only in the Middle Ages.*

The strict moral life of the early Christians furnished indeed in its inner experiences weighty matter for ethics; ethics proper, however, confined itself at first to the framing of life-rules, which, resting on the fundamental thought of faith and love, were enforced and supported by Scripture texts and by apostolical tradition, by the example of Christ and of the saints of sacred history, and by spiritual experience, and, at a later period, also by the example and authority of the martyrs, and by the definitions [*canones*] of the synods, but they were not as yet digested into a scientific whole. From the moral philosophy of the heathen the Church Fathers kept themselves substantially clear, though they adopted from the Platonic and Stoic, and from the later popular philosophy of the Eclectics, many forms and thoughts. The earlier Fathers, also Irenaeus, involved themselves in perplexities by the fact that, basing themselves primarily on the Old Testament writings, they often presented the moral life of the Patriarchs too fully as a pattern for Christians, although they recognized, throughout, the merely preparatory purpose of the Old Testament law.

In their genuine writings the apostolical Fathers confine themselves to simple evangelically-earnest exhortations.†—

* The ethical views of the Ebionites and Gnostics offer many interesting phases, but they have too little influence in the shaping of the ethics of the church, and are, without a fuller examination, too obscure to justify us in entering upon the subject here at all: comp. Neander: *Gesch. d. christl. Sittenl.*, pp. 111, 137.

† Heyns: *De patrum ap. doctrina morali*, 1833; Van Gilse, the same subject, 1833.

At a very early date there was manifested an antithesis of such on the one hand, as with full fidelity to the Christian faith yet used in the service of Christianity the best results of heathen culture, and, of such on the other, as regarded it as the primary duty of the Church to emphasize and insist on the total contrariety of Christianity to heathenism, and, above all things, also in the morally-practical life, to break off all yet-existing relations with the heathen world, and to present the holy society as, in itself, a totally new world. Both tendencies—the former prevailing more among Greek, the latter more among Latin Christians—were equally legitimate, but both in equal danger of one-sidedness; the former with the aid of Greek philosophy laid rather the foundation for a scientific construction of the moral consciousness, the latter developed rather a rigorous, and even harsh, legality of the moral life; Origen and Tertullian respectively, are prominent representatives of this antithesis.

The philosophically educated *Justin* the Martyr gives special emphasis, in defense of Christianity, to its high moral (and by him very earnestly conceived) views and practical workings, and to its difference from the merely preparatory Old Testament law; he insists very strongly on the freedom of the will as a condition of the moral; but he manifests already a preference for celibacy as a higher perfection, doubtless not without being somewhat influenced thereto by the Platonic notion of the nature of matter.—*Clemens Alexandrinus* enters more direct upon the nature of the moral. In his Exhortation to the Heathen (*Logos protreptikos, cohortatio*), he exposes the defectiveness of heathen ethics, and in single characterizing strokes contrasts with it Christian ethics as the higher; in his *Paedagogos*, designed for beginners in Christianity, he gives a more specific but at the same time more popular presentation of the subject; but in his *Stromata* he raises the Christian faith-consciousness and morality-consciousness to a much higher scientific form, evidencing truly philosophic ability. The divine Logos,—who manifests himself in fact in all true philosophy of the heathen, but in a still higher degree in the Old Testament, and most fully and purely in the New Testament,—is also the pure fountain of the moral consciousness; with the Hebrews the divine law

was essentially objective; but in Christianity it is, by virtue of the activity of the divine Logos, written into the hearts of all believers. The highest law is love to God, and, as based thereon, love to our neighbor; the highest goal is likeness to, and life-communion with, God; the condition of the moral is will-freedom, which, although hampered, yet not destroyed, by the fall, is now restored in Christianity; the Logos, that is, Christ, is the pattern of salvation and the leader thereto. In his very detailed inquiries in the sphere of the moral life, Clemens shows himself both earnest and judicious; he esteems marriage very highly, and manifests no preference for celibacy. A visible fondness for the rational contemplation of the divine, as in contrast to the lower sphere of mere faith (corresponding to the prevalent Greek distinguishing between philosophers and ordinary men), interferes somewhat, however, with his interest in active outward life.—On the use of earthly goods, he treats in detail in his work: *Quis dives salvetur.*

Origen has rich thoughts on the moral, scattered through his many writings, but especially in his Homilies and Commentaries and in his work against Celsus. His Scripture-exegesis is always pregnant with thought, though often venturesomely interpreting and allegorizing, especially in the Old Testament. Freedom of will he insists on fully as strongly as does Clemens, with whom in other respects he essentially harmonizes. His moral views are rigid, but not harsh; the moral disposition alone constitutes, in his view, the worth of the deed; but his over-estimation of the monkish life and of martyrdom, and his doctrine that man can do more of the good and meritorious than is commanded of him, becloud somewhat the otherwise evangelical character of his ethics. His well-known dogmatical tendency to un-churchly opinion shows itself less prominently in the sphere of ethics, and even his notion of the pre-existence of souls does not essentially interfere with his moral ideas.

In striking contrast to the freer idealistic tendency of the Alexandrians, and in harshest Occidental realism, stands the African theologian *Tertullian.* Greatly delighting in spiritual eccentricities, and inclined to daring exaggerations of *per se* true thoughts, this writer presents Christian ethics in his

numerous moral writings on special topics (especially in his *De idololatria, De pudicitia, Ad uxorem, De monogamia, De exhortatione castitatis, De spectaculis, De oratione,* etc.), in a very rigorously legal spirit, especially insisting upon its self-denying, world-renouncing, ascetic phase,—already far leaning toward the monkish view, and exerting a wide-spread influence on the Occident. And this juristic-minded man, with his strong inclination to rigorous formulæ, is true to himself also in the sphere of morality. His passing over to Montanist views does not essentially modify his previous moral views, as they were in fact from the first not inconsistent therewith.—While, on the one hand, he emphasizes more strongly than the Greek Fathers the natural corruption of all men as resulting from the fall, without, however, doing away with moral freedom, on the other hand, he raises (though not without having the precedent of the church in his favor) the requirement of holiness in Christians so high that he regards as admissible, at farthest, only a single repentance after baptism, and, for reiterated severe sins, such as defection from the faith, adultery, whoredom, murder, knows of no forgiveness whatever; * the distinction—here appearing more strongly than ever before—between venial and mortal sins, received subsequently a somewhat different significancy. The greatest sin is defection from the true faith—idolatry; † hence the Christian must avoid in word and deed every thing which is connected with heathenism,—*e. g.*, he may not crown himself, may not visit theatrical spectacles, etc. Tertullian insists also, and with almost painful anxiety, on attention to all outward actions and manners,—*e. g.*, he gives long and detailed disquisitions on the clothing and decoration of women, whom he would like to see attired in a natural and modest simplicity,—not without many theoretical whims (*De habitu, muliebri, De cultu fœminarum, De velandis virginibus*). *Marriage* he regards indeed as a divine institution, although, in view of the expectation of a speedy second coming of Christ, he prefers celibacy as the more perfect and pure state; and second marriages he unconditionally forbids as a heavy sin,—in the face of the utterances of Paul. *Fasting*

* *De poenit.*, c. 2, 6; *De pudicitia*, c. 2, 19; comp. *Adv. Marc.*, 4, 9.
† *De idolol.*, c. 1 *sqq.*

he requires not merely as a penance, but as a protective means of virtue, conducive to a higher perfection, namely, in that it turns the soul away from the earthly and toward the heavenly; and he attempts to reduce it to definite rigorous rules (*De jejunio*). To accept political offices and to wear the insignia thereof, conflicts *per se* with Christian humility, seeing that because of their connection with heathen religion they are inconsistent with Christian sincerity, as also, because of the function of officers to execute and to torture, inconsistent with Christian gentleness;* military service, the Christian must unconditionally refuse.† The notion of a Christian state is utterly foreign to Tertullian; he knows only of the heathen state. The enduring of martyrdom may, as the highest victory of Christian virtue, by no means be evaded by flight or otherwise; all shrinking is here unworthy cowardice (*De fuga in persecutione; Scorpiacum*). Unshaken patience in all manner of suffering in general, he describes and discusses with great ability (*De patientia*).

Cyprian, a great admirer of Tertullian, but more churchly than he, and in his moral judgments more mild, developed, one-sidedly, still further, the ascetic phase of Christian morality; abstinence from enjoyment, steadfastness in suffering, martyrdom, and beneficence to the poor, appear, to him, as the highest virtues; strict churchliness, obedient submission to the visible church and its episcopal guides, as the foundation of all Christian morality; heretical opinions and schismatic separation, as the ground of all moral corruption. While in Tertullian morality appears more as an individual manifestation of the religious personality, in Cyprian it is rather an expression of the community-life of the church. As to marriage and celibacy, he judges as Tertullian. (*De unitate ecclesiæ; Exhort. ad martyrium; De bono patientiæ; De opere et eleemosynis; De zelo et livore; De oratione dominica;* and many letters).

The severe dogmatic conflicts of the fourth century which so deeply rent the Oriental church, turned the current of thought somewhat away from ethics, so that we here find scarcely any thing but merely popular and not scientific presentations of the

---

* *De idol.*, c. 17, 18, 21. † *De corona militis*, c. 11; *De idol.*, c. 19.

ethical, and that too for the most part simply in homilies and practical elucidations of Scripture.—*Basil* the Great—as yet largely devoted to ethical questions—gives (besides his homilies and several other writings of kindred nature) in his *Ethica* a short, popular, little-digested, but plain and Gospel-inspired synopsis of New Testament ethics,—comprised in eighty rules expressed in strictly Biblical forms. In other respects he manifests indeed an over-estimation of monasticism and of outward works in general, as well as an under-estimation of the natural corruption of man. His brother, *Gregory* of *Nyssa*, likewise emphasized moral freedom quite strongly, even in man while as yet unregenerate, and applied many of the ideas of Greek philosophy to Christian ethics, and moreover found also the moral ideal in the monkish life.—This life was still more exalted by *Gregory* of *Nazianzus*, who also presents already quite definitely the doctrine of the evangelical counsels as distinguished from the universally-binding moral laws,* although in other respects he gives expression to many excellent thoughts on Christian ethics.—The liberally-cultured, *John Chrysostom*,—who was no less profound in feeling than rich in thoughts and in acquaintance with man, and who was inspired with high moral earnestness and moral love,—presents in his masterly Homilies an essentially pure, evangelical and deep-reaching moral view, in a striking, warm and clear style,—to such an extent as no other Church Father has done; and even where, in the delineation of the natural conscience and of its freedom, he presents, by the help of philosophical examples, the favorable phases rather too prominently, and where he treats over-fondly of monasticism and the monkish life, and ascribes, in repentance, too high a value to outward works, especially to fasting and alms-giving, still the evangelical ground-thought is by no means pushed into the back-ground. Love to God is, with him, the ground, the beginning, the essence of all morality. His somewhat idealistic turn of mind betrays him sometimes into unpractical views, *e. g.*, into the wish (born of his love to monasticism) for the introduction of a community of goods.†—Imitating Chrysostom also in his weaker points, the likewise philosophically

---

* *Orat. III, invect. in Jul.*, p. 94 *sqq.* (ed. Col.); *Orat.* iv, c. 97 *sqq.* (ed. Bened.)

† *Homil. in Act.*, opp. (ed. Montf.) ix, 93.

educated *abbot*, *Isidore* of *Pelusium*, treated, in numerous epistles, largely of special topics in ethics, and sometimes bordered
on Pelagian views.

In the more practically-inclined and less dogmatically-rent
Occident, we find, already in the fourth century, more comprehensive treatises on the moral subject-matter of Christianity,
but—as differing from the more idealistic and philosophic
Greek doctors—in a rather realistic, legal, juridical manner;
and it is characteristic that precisely the most excellent of the
ethical writers among the Latin Fathers were originally jurists
and rhetoricians.—*Lactantius*, in his *Institutiones divinæ* (III-
VI), treats of the ethical quite largely, critically assailing heathen ethics, and defending spiritedly the ethics of Christianity.
The highest good, as the ground-question of ethics, he finds in
the blissful communion of the immortal spirit with God, a communion which is to be attained to only in the Christian religion,
and of which, in heathendom, not even the conception is to be
found. Christianity alone, but not heathen philosophy, affords
a knowledge of the moral goal, and of the moral way, and furnishes also in Christ the moral example, and moral strength,
and lastly, in pure unselfish love, the true moral motive. The
unchurchly and dualistically-inclining notion entertained by
Lactantius, of a certain primitively-ordained necessity of evil
(ii, 8, 9, 12 ; vi, 15 ; *De ira Dei*, 55) has not much interfered
with his other moral thoughts.—Ethics attains, in a feeble and
ill-adapted outward imitation of Cicero, to a scientific form,
though without really scientific development, through the labors
of *Ambrose*, whose work *De officiis ministrorum*, though for a
long time highly prized, is yet rhetorical in style, and feeble in
scientific contents; and yet, notwithstanding that it introduces,
undigested, many foreign thoughts and forms into the field of
Christian thought in order to conceal a manifest lack of theological culture, it still commends itself by the warmth of a
sincere heart, by its enthusiasm for active piety and by ingenious trains of thought. Though treating in this work primarily
of the duties of clergymen, Ambrose yet considers also pretty
extensively those of Christians in general ; as a whole, however,
it has little order and consecutiveness, and, notwithstanding its
frequent prolixity and repetitions, leaves many points but
slightly touched. He cites many Biblical examples, especially

from the Old Testament; in his exegetical method he is quite faulty; that which is not expressly taught in Scripture either by word or example, he regards as unallowed, *e. g.*, jesting. The four *virtutes principales* (the expression *virtutes cardinales* occurs only in the manifestly unauthentic work, *De sacramentis*), he adopts from Plato; he gives them, however, a much higher significancy; and, by finding for them a greater unity in piety and love, as also by penetrating deeper into the subjectivity of the love-inspired and morally-acting heart, he demonstrates, despite all his defectiveness in scientific construction, the great superiority of Christian ethics over heathen. He places the highest good in the bliss resulting from a knowledge of God, and in moral perfection, the two being inseparably connected with each other. A preference for celibacy he shares with his contemporaries, but in enthusiastic laudations thereof he even outdoes most of them. The duty of beneficence he pushes so far that, like Chrysostom, he passes over into advocacy of a voluntary community of goods (i, 28); and he regards self-defense, even in case of murderous assault, as unallowable. The scientifically-insignificant exegetical writings of Ambrose deal also very largely with ethical questions.—*St. Jerome*, in such of his writings as treat of the moral, is, for the most part, intent on exalting the, by him, fanatically espoused monastic life, but rather rhetorically than scientifically, and with frequent inconsistencies; treating marriage disdainfully, and in fact hostilely, he finds any good in it at all only because it produces children who may devote themselves to the unmarried life (*Ep.* 22, 20, *ad Eustoch.*, *ed Veron.*, t. i); his passionately violent assailing of *Jovinian* (in Rome) who contested the meritoriousness of the monastic life and of ascetic works, found in the spirit of the age great applause.

Much higher in spirit and penetration than the views of the other Latin Fathers, stand *St. Augustine's* ethical disquisitions,—*De doctrina christiana, De civitate dei, De moribus ecclesiæ catholicæ, De libero arbitrio*, and other works—without, however, presenting a connected ethical system. In Augustine the Occidental church not only manifests her radical antithesis to the fundamental and dangerous errors of the Pelagian school, but she further develops at the same time the ethically-significant and healthful antithesis to the more

dogmatically and theosophico-speculatively inclined Greek church, namely, in that this Father emphasized much more strongly than did the Greek church the antagonism of the natural man to God as well as man's moral impotency, and hence his need of redemption, and also in that he conceived the Christianly-moral life as the expression of a complete spiritual transformation, whereas the Greek Fathers tended to regard it rather as a *bettering* of the, in his moral essence, but slightly-disordered natural man. Occidental ethics makes more reference to the Saviour; Oriental, more to the Creator; the former has therefore conceived more deeply, than the latter, the moral consciousness of Christianity, and has developed it more fully. And from this time on, the history of Christian ethics finds but little that is worthy of attention outside of the current of Occidental thought. As it was the special task of the Greek church to ward off from the Christian doctrine of *God* and of *Christ*, all heathen and Judaistic notions, and definitively to refute them, so was it the task of the Latin church to confute and overcome these same elements in the field of *ethics;* and this task was in the main accomplished by St. Augustine. The freedom of the will as it appears in the Greek church, and especially also in Chrysostom, is by no means identical with the freedom of the regenerated Christian as insisted upon by the evangelical church, and the confidence which many of the Greek Fathers place in the moral inclination of the piously-stirred heart, is not yet free from every trace of that over-estimation of the purity of human nature so characteristic of heathenism; also moral action is as yet obscured by the thought of the meritoriousness of the same. These remaining traces of heathen and Jewish views were, in their ground-thought at least, eradicated by Augustine; the thought of unmerited *grace* whereby man attained to the capability of a moral life, and to the highest good, was placed by him in the foreground, and thus the foundation was laid for a true evangelical ethical system. His doctrine (far exceeding Scripture warrant) of the total unfreedom, for good, of the natural will and of an unconditional election of grace, has a less misleading influence on his moral views than might have been expected,—it simply gives to them the character of deep earnestness, but

does not dampen the power of moral admonition.—Man in his enslavement under sin to moral unfreedom is raised to real moral freedom only on the basis of a divine election of grace, by means of a spiritual regeneration through faith in Christ. Natural man is not able to will and to accomplish the truly good; the virtues of heathen and of unbelievers, though indeed often very admirable, have yet no real merit, no truly moral worth. Between virtue and vice there lies no medium ground; whatever is not virtue, and hence whatever springs not from faith, from the right *intentio*, is necessarily sinful; natural man is free only to evil; even the desire for redemption is lacking to him, and is purely a work of gracious influence. Still there are among sin-dominated humanity great differences of personal guilt, and even the heathen have yet a free choice between the more, and the less, evil; to true righteousness, however, they cannot attain. — The destination of man, and hence his moral goal and the highest good, is to return to God from whom he has fallen away, to become reunited with Him by God-likeness. This is possible only through love to God, which is consequently the ground and essence of all good. The world and whatever belongs to it, is not the goal of moral effort,—is not the highest good itself, but only a means to this end. Love to the world in itself is therefore not true moral love, but is only lust; spirit never has true love save to spirit. But man is not to himself the highest end, because he is not *per se* capable of blessedness; the highest end, and hence the highest object of love, is God, upon whom all blessedness rests. All true love rests on love to God, and to love men otherwise than in God, is sinful; also self-love is only then moral when it flows from love to God. Hence love to God is the first and highest command, and the one from which all others spring; this love works obedience to God's command, wherein alone rests all the moral worth of an action; love is the sole true motive to the good,—fear is only a feeble incipiency of wisdom. Hence virtue is in its essence simply love to God,— is nothing other than *ordo amoris*,* and therefore obedience to the divine will, which will is the eternal law of all morality.

* *De civ. dei*, xv, 22.

Love to God as the ground-virtue unfolds itself into the four cardinal virtues : TEMPERANTIA, *amor integrum se præbens ei, quod amatur;* FORTITUDO, *amor facile tolerans omnia propter quod amatur;* JUSTITIA, *amor soli amato serviens et propterea recte dominans;* PRUDENTIA, *amor ea, quibus adjuvatur, ab eis, quibus impeditur, sagaciter seligens.** It is with great ingenuity that the Greek classification of virtue is thus embraced and presented in higher unity, as an unfolding of love under four forms, but the violence of the process is too manifest not to make felt at once the unadaptedness of the Greek classification for the Christian idea; it is new wine in old vessels. To these virtues, borrowed from Greek philosophy, Augustine adds, as superordinate thereto, the three virtues subsequently known as the *theological* virtues: *faith, love* and *hope,* without succeeding in placing them into a clear relation to the other four;† and this unclear and clumsy twofold classification prevails from now henceforth and until the close of the Middle Ages. Faith springs from the merely germinal love to God; but only from faith springs the true all-dominating love to God, and from faith and love springs hope, namely, a longing for the highest good, for the blissful enjoyment of God in union with Him, in the vision of Him,— in perfected love; objectively therefore the highest good is God himself as the perfect truth, the infinite eternal life itself.

Evil or sin is in essence and origin a lack of true love, that is, a love not to God but to the world and its lusts, and primarily a love to self that does not rest on love to God, that is *self-seeking*. From self-seeking springs evil desire (*concupiscentia*) which becomes a power over the spirit. Evil become real in no sense whatever from God, but through the free choice, through the guilt, of free creatures,—is a guilty ruining of the originally good. The distinction (referring primarily to the administration and practice of penance) between venial and mortal sins (*peccata venalia et mortifera s. mortalia*), Augustine defines in the thenceforth prevailing sense, thus,—that the latter include all sins consciously and

---

* *De moribus eccl.*, c. 15 (25) *sqq.*, 25 (46); *De lib. arb.*, 1, 13; 2, 10.

† *Enchiridion, s. de fide, spe et charitate; de doctr. christ.*, 1, 37; 3, 10, *et al.*

voluntarily committed against the Decalogue, and particularly idolatry, adultery, and murder, which, unless atoned for by ecclesiastical penance, involve damnation, whereas the former may be atoned for, or gotten rid of, by the repentant person himself, without special church-penance, through prayer, alms-giving and fasting.*

As to the requirements of morality in detail, Augustine is no less earnest than judicious, forming quite a contrast to the manifold laxities of the age, and to many errors and extreme views of earlier Church Fathers, and, on the whole, he conceived of Christian morality much more profoundly than had yet been done by church writers; but his more especial merit consists in this, that he brought clearly and definitely into prominence the foundation of all morality, namely, faith and the essence of faith, to wit, love to God, and that he referred the validity of outward works more definitely than had been done before to the inner disposition of the actor. A truly evangelical spirit breathes through the greater part of his moral views; and even where, in harmony with the spirit of the times, he laudingly emphasizes outward good works, and particularly fasting, alms-giving and monastic asceticism, he still always lays greater stress on the state of the heart than on the work itself. His greatest departure from a purely evangelical consciousness is the recognition of the, then, already long-prevalent distinction between the divine commands and the divine *counsels;* the latter refer essentially to the giving up of allowed enjoyments, and especially to the abstaining from marriage. The man who leaves the counsels unobserved, sins not; he who fulfills them, acquires for himself higher virtue; wedlock-virtue is merely human virtue, but virginal chastity is angelic virtue. Marriage is indeed *per se* holy and pure, and prevailed also in the state of sinlessness,† but for the state of sinfulness, from which in fact the redeemed are not as yet totally free, celibacy is higher than marriage; and if all men would but live unmarried, there would thereby be straightway brought about the end of the world and the perfection of the king-

---

* *Sermo*, 351; *Enchir.*, 70, 71; comp. *De fide et op.*, c. 19 (34); *De civ. dei*, 21, 27.

† *De Genesi ad litt.*, 9, 3 *sqq.*, 7.

dom of God.* But Augustine wisely avoids the self-contra-
dictory extremes of Jerome, and tolerates even second marriages.—In contrast to heathen ethics, which looks, for all
salvation, to the State and to its unlimited sway, Christians,
even in the days of Augustine, placed (not without very good
reasons) very little confidence in the worldly State. The
Christian state—to the realization of which the Germanic nations were more especially called—had not yet become real;
and the nominally-Christian Roman State lingered as yet essentially in heathen forms. In his ingenious work *De civitate
dei*, Augustine contrasts with the earthly State the purely
spiritual divine State, deriving the former from the self-seeking of God-forsaking man, as prevailing since the brother-
murder of Cain,—since which time the earthly and heavenly
State have been in a condition of divorce (xv, 5). "The two
kinds of love produced two kinds of state: the earthly state
springs from self-love which ripens into contempt of God;
the heavenly, from love to God which ripens into contempt
of self" (xiv, 28). The divine State develops itself independently of the sinful earthly one, until it attains to its true
manifestation in Christ; this state is not an outwardly force-
exercising one, but a spiritual kingdom, and is indeed destined to sanctify and transfigure the earthly State,—to change
it from a merely world-state into an organ of the divine state,
but not to merge itself into it.

The great decline of the scientific life in the Occident from
and after the close of the fifth century, manifested its effects
also in the field of ethics. Little more was done than to
make collections of the opinions (*sententiæ*) of the Fathers,
and to apply them to purposes of Church-discipline and of
popular instruction. But there was no further creative production. In reducing to greater system the discipline of
penance, the interest was turned rather to the discriminating,
defining and classifying of sins than to the scientific examination of the moral in general. The knowledge of Greek
ethics disappeared almost entirely, and the work of *Boëthius,
De consolatione philosophiæ* (about A.D. 542) †,—which is but
feebly touched with Christian influence, and which for the

---

* *De Sancta virginitate ; De bono conjugali ; De nuptiis et concupis.*
† Fr. Nitzsch : *System des Boëth.*, 1860, p. 42 *sqq.*

most part expresses, eclectively, mere Graeco-Roman philosophy,—passed in the earlier Middle Ages for an excellent work of Christian philosophy.—*Gregory the Great*, basing himself on Augustine, wrote moral expositions (*Moralia*) of the Book of Job, of Solomon's Song, etc., and other rather edificatory than scientific works of the same class; most influential was his *Regula pastoralis*, which treated of the clerical calling more especially under its moral phase. *Isidore* of *Hispalis* (Seville) (*ob.* 636) treats, especially in his *Sententiæ*, on many moral points, mostly, however, by way of judicious digesting from preceding Fathers, especially from Augustine and Gregory the Great,—furnishing for the early Middle Ages a principal help in ethical study.—In the Greek Church *Maximus the Confessor* (*ob.* 622) gives in his "Chapters on Love"* a tolerably complete presentation of ethics; *John Damascenus* (*ob.* 754) furnishes, in his chief work, the ground thoughts for an ethical treatise, and in his "Holy Parallels" a rich collection of patristic sentences.

Standing entirely apart, and of influence only in the Middle Ages, is the pseudo-*Dionysius the Areopagite* (fifth century) who introduced Neo-Platonic mysticism into Christianity, and whose Pantheistically-inclined world-theory invades here and there also the moral sphere.† God is all in all,—is the being in all being, the life in all that lives, is the good absolutely. Hence evil cannot exist by itself, but must always be a negating something on the good,—is not an existing something, but essentially only a lack and more an appearance than a reality, and it turns again into the good. The goal of all life, and hence also of the moral, is the returning into God, the changing into God, of whatever is as yet distinct from God; the highest wisdom is therefore the turning-away of the spirit from whatever is not God,—the unclouded beholding of the one, the nameless, the pure divine light, in which God directly imparts himself to man. An outwardly active morality is, according to this view, the opposite of true wisdom.

* Κεφάλαια περὶ ἀγάπης.
† Especially in *De divinis nominibus; De cœlesti hierarchia; De myst. theol.*

II. THE MIDDLE AGES.

SECTION XXXII.

The ecclesiastical consciousness, as having arrived now at greater repose, but as also in a state of spiritual paralysis, limits itself primarily to the preserving and digesting of the views already-attained to, and to the constructing of systems of life-rules on the basis of the decisions of the Fathers and of church councils, —at best elucidated anew by examples from the Scriptures or from the legends of the saints. The practical decisions on the subject of church penance gave rise gradually, in connection with these collections of rules, to a very minutely-specifying system of *casuistry*, which, however, related primarily chiefly to transgressions. The moral views themselves were already largely estranged from evangelical purity, and an ascetic monk-morality, not binding upon all, passed as the ideal of Christian virtue, while the general morality, binding upon all, was to a large degree neglected.

The *libri pœnitentiales*, for the use of confessors, are based for the most part on the decisions of synods and on ancient practice, but are also in some degree complemented by their respective authors; they give for the most part little more than imperfectly classified and illogically connected registers of single sins and of the church-penances and penalties imposed therefor, the latter of course without established and certain norms (Theodore of Canterbury, Bede, Halitgarius and others). These books form the beginning of a casuistical treatment of ethics, which was subsequently extended to other questions than sins, especially to cases of conscience.—Attempts at a more independent and more connected, but yet, on the whole, purely

practical treatment of ethics—mostly simply on single points,—
were made by *Alcuin* (*De virtutibus et vitiis; De ratione animæ*), largely borrowing from Augustine; also by *Rhabanus
Maurus*, by *Jonas*, Bishop of Orleans (about 828), by the earnestly sin-rebuking *Ratherius* of Verona (*ob.* 974), by *Damiani* (*ob.*
1072), the excessive eulogist of self-castigation, and by the
learned *Fulbert* of Chartres (*ob.* 1029).

In proportion as the zeal of love abated, and worldly-
mindedness increased in the church at large, in the same
proportion arose, as in antithesis to this secularism of the
church, a zeal for a special holiness transcending the general
morality required of all. Directions for the monkish life
form a favorite topic for ecclesiastical moralists; the merits
of the ascetic life are more warmly lauded than the practical
Christian life in the civil or domestic spheres, and wedlock
is progressively more deeply disparaged as in contrast to entire renunciation; consorts are loaded with praise, who divorce
themselves in order to practice such renunciation; and according to Damiani's assertion, even St. Peter had to undergo
the martyr-death in order to wash away the stains of his
wedlock-life (*De perfectione monach*, c. 6).

SECTION XXXIII.

The *philosophy* of the Middle Ages, and especially
Scholasticism, was occupied for a long while almost
exclusively with speculations on dogmatical and
metaphysical questions, leaving ethics almost un-
touched; wherever, however, it brought ethics within
the sphere of its intellectual activity, there it treated
the same merely in connection with dogmatics, and
for the most part in the light of the opinions of
Augustine, and, later, of those of Plato and Aristotle,
—often bunglingly combining the latter with the
former.—The brilliant but idealistico-Pantheistically
inclined mystical philosophy of *John Scotus Erigena*,
which threw its lights, as well as its shades, into the

field of morality, seems—as not understood—to have had little influence on subsequent ethics, save in the mystical school.

The spiritualistico-idealistic tendency of the Schoolmen could primarily treat of the moral only collaterally, at least until the dogmatical and metaphysical fields had attained to some degree of philosophical maturity and self-consciousness. The potent influence of Augustine made itself felt also in the ethical field, and his ground-thoughts re-appear in almost all the Schoolmen. The freedom of the will is, however, distinctly recognized, although, in man after the fall, as in a trammeled condition; but also Greek philosophy was powerfully influential on ethics, not merely as to the form, but also as to the subject-matter. The Platonic classification of the virtues was already early combined with the three theological virtues, notwithstanding the inconsistency and impracticability of such a uniting of two entirely different stand-points. In how far John Scotus' attempted translation of Aristotle's Ethics into Latin was of influence, is doubtful; the application of Aristotle to Christian ethics appears in a more direct form, first, in the thirteenth century.

The deep-thinking *John Scotus Erigena* (at the court of Charles the Bald, then at Oxford, *ob.* 886), who was not understood by his own age, and who had but little connection with it even in his errors, touches in his chief work, *De divisione naturæ*, also upon the more general ethical topics, and molds them to his idealistico-Pantheistical system,—a system based on the Neo-Platonic views of Dionysius the Areopagite, and which—very different from recent naturalistic Pantheism—denies not the absolute personal God, but on the contrary the independent reality of the world. The world is only another existence-form of the eternal God himself; God alone is real; the creature, in so far as it is conceived as distinct from God, is nothing; it exists only in so far as it is wholly identical with God. God is whatever truly exists, because He himself does all and is in all; God in not merely the most excellent part of the creature, but He is its beginning, its middle and its end—the essence and true being in all things. The coming into being of the world is

a self-outpouring of God, a theophany. God is manifest not only in Christ, but also in the entire universe,—in the highest degree in the rational creature, and here indeed most purely in the saints. The believing and cognizing of the saints take place solely through God; God cognizes himself in man as cognizing Him. Man is therefore God's image, because God himself comes to manifestation in him. As now every thing ideal, and hence the ideal world, precedes, in the mind of God, its outward realization, so is also the spirit of man earlier than his body,—which latter is but the shadow of the spirit, and is in fact by it created, and that too as a perfect and immortal one (ii, 24).—Man, however, is now no longer in the condition in which he originally was; the body is frail and subject to death; this condition can have been brought about only by sin. But how is sin possible if God is in fact all in all? Answer: every thing is real only in so far as it is good; but in so far as it is not good, it exists not. Hence evil is a mere non-being, a merely negative something, but in no sense a real entity. God can cognize only that which is, not that which is not, hence He cognizes and knows not evil; for if He knew it, then it would be real, and hence would not be evil (ii, 28). This normal *Dei igno-rantia* banishes evil from the sphere of being into that of mere appearance. All evil is merely the shadow of the good, and is accordingly only upon the good,—is essentially only a lack,—a non-being, not a positive entity. Sin consists in this, that man, as on the one hand identical with, and, on the other, distinct from God, fixes his attention solely upon this distinctness from God,—directs himself toward himself and toward nature, and not toward God (i, 68; ii, 12, 25). Only by this confessedly *per se* inexplicable (v. 36) fall into sin, is it that the body of man became material and mortal and a clog to the spiritual life (ii, 25, 26; comp. iv, 12, 14, 15, 20); man thereby ceased to be truly a spirit,—became subject to natural desires; previously the lord of nature, he now became a slave to it.—The ultimate goal of all life, and hence also of the moral, is the return into God (ii, 2, 11), namely, so that this differentness from God, all corporeality and individuality, ceases and passes over into God himself,— is transformed into Him (i, 10; v, 20, 27, 37, 38). Hence all

moral effort is directed toward this uniting of one's self with God, toward the breaking down of the hampering limits of individual naturality, and realizes itself in a gradually progressive development (v, 8, 39). Morality must accordingly bear a predominantly spiritualistic and ascetic, negating character,—must disdainfully turn itself away from finite reality (iv, 5). Into details Erigena enters but little. It is perfectly consequential in him that he regards marriage, which rests on the difference of the sexes, as having originated solely in consequence of sin, whereas sinless man was sexless (ii, 6; iv, 12, 23). And yet marriage is now allowable, only, however, in view of the propagation of the race, irrespective of sensuous pleasure. Though the mystico-speculative bases of these ethical thoughts were of a very unchurchly character, still the thoughts themselves answered very well to the ascetic spirit of the then prevalent morality.

SECTION XXXIV.

It is only in the twelfth century that ethics is seriously treated of by scholastic science;—first by *Hildebert of Tours* (*ob.* 1134), for the most part in the light of the Roman Eclectic and Stoic philosophies;—then by *Abelard*, who, however, treats, mostly in a mere preliminary manner, of the more general questions, giving proof of great acumen, but also sometimes enfeebling the significancy of sin;—very fruitfully by *Peter Lombard*, who presents, in the light of Augustinian thoughts, and with the help of ancient philosophy, a very clear and well-arranged total of Christian doctrine, of which ethics, though but briefly presented, constitutes an essential part;— but with greatest thoroughness and fullness by *Thomas Aquinas*, who made large use of the Aristotelian philosophy in perfecting a system of Christian speculation, and that, too, without thereby working serious detriment to the Christian idea.—In *Duns*

Scotus a sophistico-skeptical treatment of ethics began already to effect, in many respects, an enfeebling of the moral idea, and to prepare the way for the double-dealing morality of the Jesuits.—Through almost all the scholastic presentations of ethics there prevails a pretty great uniformity of spirit and manner of treatment, springing mostly from Augustine and Aristotle, and subsequently from Peter Lombard and Thomas Aquinas; evangelico-theological and ethnico-philosophical elements are often brought together, without that the latter element is always successfully mastered and molded into a Christian character. Ingenious and often truly speculative processes of thought, but frequently also trivial and fruitless hair-splittings, also a pedantic carrying out of particular schemata, and a preference for certain typical numbers in the distribution of the subject-matter,—such are the general characteristics of scholastic ethics.

Contemporaneously with scholasticism prevailed also the science of *casuistry*, which had also to do with practical life; this science was in fact influenced by scholasticism to a higher development, and it attained to its highest perfection in the fourteenth and fifteenth centuries.

Hildebert of Tours (about 1100) treated ethics for the first time in a special work: *Philosophia moralis de honesto et utili* (*Opp.* Par. 1708, p. 961 *sqq*). In philosophical contents it is as yet feeble and dependent, and belongs rather to the sphere of Roman popular philosophy, especially that of Cicero and Seneca, than to speculative science proper; and the Christian element is thrown largely into the shade by that which is borrowed from heathen moralists; the four Greek virtues are servilely carried out; the relation of the *honestum* and *utile* is extensively discussed; and as a whole the work is immature and superficial. —Nearly cotemporaneously appears *Abelard's Ethica, s. Scito te*

ipsum,—not a comprehensive system, but properly only a phil-
osophico-theological introduction to ethics; it treats somewhat
un-uniformly of general questions, and particularly of the essence
of sin and of its imputation. The toning-down of Christian
thoughts,—elsewhere observable in Abelard, in his over-estimat-
ing the natural capability of man,—shows itself also here. He
distinguishes between a natural tendency to evil (called by him
a "will") and the freely-resolved approving of the same; the
former is not *per se* sinful and forbidden of God, for it has its
seat in the sensuous and fragile nature of man, and it is not
even yet a sin when it overcomes the reason; it becomes sin
only by a real approving of sin; and it is for the simple reason
that there is a natural tendency to evil in us, that the virtuous
opposing of it becomes a moral desert. From this it follows,
on the one hand, that man, in virtue of his very nature, cannot
avoid all evil, though indeed this unavoidable evil is not imputed to him as guilt, and, on the other, that the essence of sin
consists wholly and alone in the conscious choosing of it, and
neither in the evil tendency preceding it, nor in the act proceeding therefrom. By the carrying-out of an evil intention
the guilt of that intention becomes not greater, and by the
omitting of its carrying-out, not less. Moral merit and guilt
lie consequently entirely and alone in the disposition; actions
themselves, *per se* considered, are morally indifferent. Hence
he who does a bad act without a bad intention, does not sin.
True, there is necessary also in order to the truly good not
merely a well-meaning, but also a correctly-cognizing intention.
Therefore it is that, while, because of the heathens' lack of a
correct knowledge of the law and the truth, their unbelief and
even their persecuting of the Christian martyrs cannot be imputed to them as real sins, yet, on the other hand, they cannot
without faith become really saved; and the prayer of Christ on
the cross for his persecutors shows that they did wrong in
ignorance, and were in need of forgiveness.—There are thoughts
here in Abelard which, while *per se* true, are yet one-sidedly
pushed into the extreme, and thereby become erroneous. Thus,
he explains the distinction, prevalent in the ethics of the Middle
Ages, between mortal and venial sins, to mean this, that under
the latter we are to understand those the immorality of which
is indeed known to us in general, but is not *clearly* conscious

and present to our mind at the moment of our consenting to
them, and which are consequently committed rather in a state
of forgetfulness. The ethics of Abelard was, not without reason, severely assailed by Bernard of Clairvaux, and is in many
respects a fore-runner of the system of the Jesuits; but in his
own day the conscience of the church was as yet somewhat
quick and tender, and the synod of Sens (1140) expressly condemned the more questionable features of the same.

The subject of ethics was treated with great skill, but rather
ingeniously than profoundly, by *Peter Lombard* (*ob.* 1160), more
especially in the third book of his *Libri sententiarum,*—a work
which was for later schoolmen a very influential model and a
high authority, though the relatively brief manner of treatment
touches only upon the principal points. With a fully-developed
system we are not as yet furnished; it is rather a dialectical
analysis and examination of ideas than a profound speculative
development from a fundamental principle. The ethical notions
are presented first in definitions, then proved and illustrated by
texts from Scripture and from the Fathers, and thereupon follow dialectical inquiries, comparisons of opposed views, and a
definitive judgment.

The notion "good" has both an objective and a subjective
significancy. The good as object is the goal of the subjective
good, the good will; this good object is blessedness, eternal
life in God, and hence God himself in so far as he comes into
communion with man (II, Dist. 38, 40). The presupposition
of all morally good is will-freedom. This freedom is primarily
a threefold one: freedom from necessity, freedom from sin as a
dominating power, and freedom from misery. The first is un-
forfeitable,—exists also in sinful man; the second is enjoyed by
the redeemed, the third by the saved. Before the fall man had
perfect freedom,—could, by his own strength, keep free from
sin, though not attain to perfection save as aided by divine
grace, as, on the other hand, he could in his own strength also
turn to sin. Hence will-freedom is that capacity of the rational
will whereby it, by the assistance of divine grace (*gracia assist-
ente*), chooses the good, or, by not sharing in the same (*eadem de-
sistente*), the evil. In the rational will there is a natural striving,
though but feeble (*licet tenuiter et exiliter*), to choose the good;
but, by the assistance of grace, it becomes powerful and effica-

⁻ious (*efficaciter*), whereas man *per se* can effectually turn to evil. By the possibility of choice in the two directions, human liberty differs from divine liberty, which latter can eternally choose only the good. After the fall into sin, the truth : *poterat peccare et not peccare*, was changed into, *potest peccare et non potest non peccare;* that is, into a freedom very much trammeled indeed, though not yet sunk to necessity; the inwardly enfeebled and corrupted nature of man impels him constantly to sin, and allows him not to will and to accomplish the truly good. The redeemed, however, is free from this predominancy of evil desire,—has indeed as yet moral weakness, but also the assistance of divine grace; hence he can also yet sin,—in fact it is still true of him : *non posse non peccare*, but only as to venial sins, not as to mortal sins. In his ultimate perfection, however, the redeemed attains to a condition transcending the condition of unfallen man, namely : *non posse peccare*,—where all weakness is overcome, and man has risen to a moral impossibility of choosing evil; thus the threefold freedom becomes a fourfold one (II, Dist. 24, 25).

Virtue is the right quality of the human will as turned toward the good. The ground-virtue is, therefore, love to God, as the substance of all good; and all virtues are closely involved in each other, so that he who truly possesses *one*, possesses them all, and he to whom one is lacking, lacks them all; no one can have simply *one* virtue, for love is the mother of all the virtues, and he who has the mother has also the children (III, Dist. 36). In agreement with Augustine, Peter Lombard presents three chief-virtues, which, however, are only different phases of the one love to God, namely : *faith, hope, love* (*fides, spes, charitas*). (1) FIDES *est virtus, qua creduntur, quæ non videntur*, namely, in the sphere of the religious; this faith is threefold :—(*a*) *credere* DEO, to believe the word of God; (*b*) *credere* DEUM, to believe in the existence of God; both these forms of faith are possible to the evil; (*c*) *credere* IN DEUM, to *love* God in faith, and to unite one's self with him; this is true faith, which leads also to truly good works (III, Dist. 23). (2) SPES *est virtus, qua spiritualia et æterna bona sperantur, i. e., cum fiducia exspectantur.* This virtue is only briefly and insufficiently developed, and is not clearly enough distinguished from the first; for the statement that hope refers only to future good, while faith refers also to

evil and to the past and to the present (III, Dist., 26), gives, after all, only the difference of a part from the whole. (3) CHARITAS *est dilectio, qua diligitur deus propter se, et proximus propter deum vel in deo;* God must be loved for his own sake, but our neighbor (and every human being is such) only for God's sake (III, Dist. 27 *sqq.*).—From another point of view,—and which is not properly brought into harmony with the first, but only joined to it—four other virtues (*virtutes principales vel cardinales*) are adopted, after the example of Plato and Augustine, and presented, namely: *justitia, fortitudo* (which manifests itself in suffering), *prudentia*, and *temperantia* (III, 33); after which, without any further development of these four virtues, are given the seven gifts of the Holy Spirit (taken from Isa. xi, 2, 3, in the Vulgate version, namely: wisdom, understanding, counsel, strength, knowledge, piety, God-fearing), as the conditions of the practice of virtue, and as spiritual virtues. Some further discussion of special points is given in connection with a presentation of the ten commandments and of the sacraments.

In the steps of Peter Lombard follows, in all essential points, *Alexander Hales* (*ob.* 1245), though he develops some points more fully, and contributes thereto original matter,—especially is this the case in his discussion of the moral law, which he distinguishes into the natural, the Mosaic, and the evangelical (*Summa univ. theol., pars III*). He separates the moral part of theology more distinctly than had yet been done from the dogmatical, as the "doctrine of manners," and distributes it into the doctrine, first, of the divine law, second, of grace and the virtues, and, third, of the fruit of virtue.—(William of Paris [*ob.* 1249] discussed the more important points of morality in separate treatises grounded on Augustine and Aristotle). More learned, and especially distinguished by extensive use of Aristotle, are the ethical portions of the writings of *Albertus Magnus* (*ob.* 1280), though in other respects they do not contain very much original speculation, and in some respects they show already a strong casuistical tendency.

It is through *Thomas Aquinas* that scholastic ethics was most highly perfected both in form and in substance, and raised to a system of profound speculation. His great work, *Summa theologiæ, prima et secunda secundæ*, combines, in comprehensive thoroughness, a clear intellectual insight with

deep religious knowledge and moral life experience. The style of presentation is indeed somewhat discursive, especially in the citing and refuting of opposite opinions, and runs often into unprofitable distinctions and splittings of ideas, but the substantial contents are in the main so sound and excellent, that the almost autocratical authority enjoyed by Thomas Aquinas, especially in the field of ethics—(an authority which has maintained itself unabated in the Romish Church up to the present day)—is essentially a well-merited one; the later ethics of the Romish Church could indeed fall below this model, but it has not surpassed it; and also for Protestant ethics have the works of this author been of great influence, and they are even yet of weighty import.

The ethics of Thomas Aquinas, which is directly connected with his dogmatics, is distributed into a general and a special part, of which the former treats of the virtues and vices in general, and the latter of the same in detail, so that the whole is made to appear predominantly, though not exclusively, as the doctrine of virtue.—Man is the image of God principally in virtue of his reason; but an essential element of reason is the freedom of the will, namely, the free determining of our own activity. All activity, and hence also that of irrational creatures, has an end; hence human activity must have a rational end, and one which man knows as such, and which is aimed at by free will-determination, whereas irrational creatures seek their end unconsciously and from natural instinct. But rational ends are such only in so far as they do not constitute a mere interminable plurality, but converge and terminate in *one* last and highest good, upon which consequently all rational activity is directed. This one highest end, and hence the *highest good*, which the rational creature seeks to attain to, cannot consist in outward, perishable, and hence unessential things, but only in the one absolutely imperishable, the divine, namely, in communion with God, and hence in the absolutely perfect life of the rational creature,—in *blessedness*. God is the objective, blessedness the subjective, phase of the highest good. The human soul *per se*, and without being united with God, cannot be happy; hence the highest good is not a something belonging to the soul *per se*,—has its ground not in the soul but in God;

the highest good in its objective phase, considered as an object, is not a created, but an uncreated and divine entity, which, however, is appropriated to himself by man. But this uncreated entity cannot be appropriated by sensuous perception, but solely through a spiritual grasping, through cognizing, through spiritual beholding or intuiting. Hence blessedness rests on an intuiting of God, and toward this, therefore, the rational activity of the soul is directed. This blessedness, as resting on the highest activity of the reason, cannot be wholly reached in this earthly, manifoldly-limited and dependent life, and, moreover, as being of an unending nature, it cannot be merited by finite actions,—it can only be appropriated by religious intuition, by contemplation, namely, in that God lovingly imparts himself, and therewith at the same time blessedness, to man. This appropriating is, however, not a merely passive bearing, not a will-less beholding, but a willing, loving, and love-enjoying embracing of the divine. In that the rational striving attains to perfect satisfaction and rest in God as the highest good, blessedness is *enjoyment*, the feeling of delight; this is, however, but one of the phases of blessedness,—the other is the visional cognizing.—The will of man,—ever directed toward a good,— is indeed free,—can be forced neither through an outward nor through an inward power to a given choice, nor is it so forced by God, for God leaves every created being to act according to its inborn nature; and hence the will can direct itself as well to a false and merely seeming good, as to the true good,—but this true good itself stands *not* within the free determination of man, but is absolutely determined by God and by the inner necessity of the case itself; man can, freely-willing, strive for it or fail of it, but he cannot posit any other good than the true one. There is no other highest good than God. The will is good when it hearkens to the reason; but the reason is truthful only when it hearkens to God and accepts illumination from him. Hence every action is evil which deviates from reason, and is evil also when this reason is in error (II, 1, 19); whatever does not spring from the conscience is sin; but the will that follows an erring reason is also not good, but evil, in so far as the error was avoidable. Hence only that action is truly good which follows,

not merely reason in general as fortuitously determined in this or that particular person, but true reason,—which is conscious of the divine will, and determines itself thereafter.

The *readiness* of the soul for well-acting is *virtue*,—which is consequently to be conceived of not as mere action, but as a permanent power and tendency for acting, as a *habitus*, as a power of the rational will. The virtues are primarily of a *natural* character; that is, such as belong to man as such, to his natural rational being, and are developed by exercise and habituation, although they cannot in themselves attain to perfection (ii, 1, qu. 55–59, 63). They are distinguished as knowledge-virtues and moral virtues (comp. §§ 17, 18); the former are wisdom, science, understanding and, connected therewith, prudence, and, in a somewhat peculiar sense, also art-skill. The moral virtues relate to desire; they fall into four cardinal virtues (ii, 1, qu. 60, 61; ii, 2, 47 *sqq*). (1) Virtue considered as a good of the reason, and as expressing the essence of the same, is *prudence;* this virtue is, as distinguished from wisdom, not the lord, but the servant of morality,—gives not the end proper, but only the means to the end of the practical reason. (2) The virtue which expresses the practical will-direction of the reason toward moral actions, is *justness* or righteousness; it relates to the realizing of the right,—is the constant and fixed will to give to each his right, and hence has to do with what we owe to others. It is true, man can in a certain sense be just also toward himself, namely, when reason holds in proper control the passions. Justness is the highest of the moral virtues, and includes in itself also piety, thankfulness, etc. (3) The virtue which expresses the practical will-direction of the reason toward the checking of all reason-resisting desires and passions, is *temperateness.* It holds within rational bounds all desires and pleasure-feelings which relate to sensuous goods, and all displeasure-feelings which spring from the lack of such goods. Modifications of this virtue are shame, reverentiality, abstinence, gentleness, modesty, humility, etc. (4) The virtue which expresses the practical will-direction of the reason toward the carrying-out of rational purposes as *against* opposing natural inclinations and affections, especially against fear in the face of dangers, is *courage.* It wards off whatever would hinder the activity of the reason, and thus preserves man, as against all

15

sensuous and irrational impulses, within the limits of rationality; it is, on the one hand, defensive, a firm calm enduring of hostile influences, and, on the other, offensive, in that it actually assaults the dangers; the first phase, however, is, for Christian morality, the predominant. The highest stage of Christian courage is *martyrdom*, wherein the main element is love. The several chief virtues are subdivided by Thomas Aquinas in a very far-reaching and excessively detailed manner, into very numerous special manifestation-forms.

Above all the moral virtues, stand (not as co-ordinate therewith, but as in fact exalting them into a Christian character) the *theological* virtues, that is, the supernatural ones—those which have for their object the divine, the supernatural, and are not grounded in us by nature, but given (*infusæ*) to us by God (ii, 1, 62 *sqq.;* ii, 2, 1–46); through these alone is perfection possible to man, even in the other or moral virtues.— (1) *Faith;* this virtue relates not to the finite, but to God, and has as its presupposition, divine revelation. It is a thinking with an inner assent of the will, and must manifest itself also outwardly in *confession.* The object of faith is, in part, purely supernatural, transcending our knowledge and reason, and in part it can be discovered even through natural reason; but also that which is discoverable through reason has in fact been revealed by God out of love, and for purposes of culture. Faith is raised to a vital form only by the increment of love (*fides formata*); without love it is crude (*informis*). As faith is the foundation of all morality, so is unbelief the greatest sin; but as faith is a virtue, hence it is not allowable to bring a non-Christian to faith by force. The matter is, however, very different with heretics and apostates, for these have broken their vow, and hence fall under punishment; heresy deserves capital punishment (ii, 2, 10, art. 8, 9); and when a prince falls from faith and in consequence thereof, incurs the ban of the Church, then are his subjects *ipso facto* free and absolved from his dominions and from their oath of fealty (ii, 2, 12, art. 2).—(2) *Hope* has for its object eternal blessedness, that is, the subjective phase of the highest good; it pre-supposes faith inasmuch as it is only by faith that eternal blessedness becomes known to us. With hope must be associated *God-fearing*, inasmuch as God

is the executor of just punishments.—(3) *Love* is the most perfect of the virtues, and its presupposition is faith and hope. It is an intimate union of man with God, a possessing of God, and the shaping-form of all the other virtues, inasmuch as man is to do all good out of love to God; it endures forever, whereas faith ultimately passes over into sight, and hope into the possession of blessedness. This love, which is primarily love to God, and as such is not in us by nature, but is a divine grace-gift, enlarges itself spontaneously into love to men and to all creatures, as also into a love of man for himself and for his own body as created by God. But all love to the created must spring exclusively from our love to God, and it cannot relate approvingly to the evil that is in creatures, but rather seeks to eradicate it. Our enemies and bad men in general we are to love, not as bad, but as men, and for the sake of their rational nature. The degree of our love to creatures is to be in proportion to the union of the same with God. God himself is to be loved above all things, above even ourselves.

This double classification of the virtues is doubtless the weakest side of the ethics of Thomas Aquinas and of the schoolmen in general. The theological and the natural virtues do not possibly admit of being brought into any clear relation to each other; they are based upon two utterly foreign and heterogeneous stand-points, and can be reduced neither to a condition of co-ordination nor of subordination, but on the contrary, they constantly cross and cramp each other, and lead, on the one hand, to many repetitions, and, on the other, to an arbitrary distribution of the special virtue-manifestations. That love, even love to the creature, should appear solely as a theological virtue, is entirely unnatural. The separating of faith from wisdom is no less erroneous, inasmuch as Christian wisdom rests essentially on faith in God. The distinction made between knowledge-virtues and moral virtues suffers not only under all the defects of its prototype in Aristotle, but becomes more perplexed still by the distinguishing of both these classes from the theological virtues, inasmuch as a very essential part of that which Aristotle ascribes to wisdom must here be transferred to faith. And the matter is made still worse by the fact that the moral virtues are not

presented strictly according to Aristotle, but according to
the four chief virtues of Plato, who does not find any place
for special knowledge-virtues, so that while, now, wisdom
does not, yet prudence does, appear as a moral cardinal virtue, whereas in fact prudence belongs unquestionably along
with wisdom to the knowledge-virtues, as is the case in Aristotle (§ 17). The fact is, the entire Greek schema is totally
inadequate for the expression of the Christian virtues, and
the violence of the process is felt at every step of the attempt.
Even the utterly untenable position of Aristotle, that virtue
always lies in the middle between two opposite aberrations
(§ 17), is adopted by Thomas Aquinas, and applied even to
the knowledge-virtues; to the theological virtues he applies
it only in this respect, that, in them, we are to reach a definite measure corresponding to our nature (ii, 1, 64),—to say
the least, a strange application of the middle-way of Aristotle.

On the virtues in general, Thomas Aquinas makes also the
following observations, mostly in the spirit of Aristotle:
every virtue is heightened in its power by exercise; all of
them stand in connection with each other, and when they appear in their perfection, no one of them is without all the
others. The virtues, according as they are viewed under different aspects, are, as to worth, in part equal and in part unequal; the knowledge-virtues are *per se* nobler than the moral
virtues, inasmuch as reason is nobler than desire; but in respect to their activity, the moral virtues stand higher, as they
are more fruitful in results. The perfect practice of virtue
depends on the directly God-conferred seven *gifts of the Spirit*
(ii, 1, 68), which make the person willing to follow the
promptings of the Holy Spirit,—a thought which occurs already in Ambrose and in Gregory I.; but in respect to which,
even the intellectual acumen of a Thomas Aquinas does not
succeed in making clear the relation of these gifts to the corresponding virtues, especially the theological.

The moral activity determines itself according to a *law;*
this law belongs to the sphere of reason. The eternal law is
the universe-ruling divine reason, not the fortuitous reason
of the individual. The laws of nature, and also those of the
practical reason (*ratio practica*) are an efflux from the eternal

law, and the human laws of the state and of society are in
turn an efflux from both. The laws which lie merely in the
natural reason do not suffice for morality; but there is needed,
in order to the supernatural end of blessedness, also a positive
divine law, which is made known and evidenced to all by
revelation, and which at the same time also preserves the
natural consciousness from all doubt (ii, 1, 90 *sqq*).—In the
field of Christian morality the law proper, which is absolutely
binding on all Christians, is to be distinguished from the
counsels, which are left to free choice, though the following
of them works a higher perfection and leads more speedily to
the goal of salvation. The Old Testament law, as a law of
servitude, had no such counsels; but the Gospel as a law of
freedom has them, in order to bring men rightly to a consciousness of their freedom. The clinging to the earthly
hinders our arriving at the heavenly; hence the counsels
hasten this arriving, in that they free man as far as possible
from earthly enjoyments which are otherwise not forbidden
to him; they therefore require poverty, perpetual chastity
(that is, non-marriage), and the yoke of obedience (*obedientia
servitus*), the latter very erroneously based on Matt. xix, 21
("follow me,") and on John x, 27 (ii, 1, 108, art. 4; comp.
ii, 2, 186).—The Christian law as distinguished from the natural law cannot be fulfilled by our own natural power, but
only in virtue of the grace-gifts infused into the hearts of believers; and in so far man acquires for himself, by his virtue,
no *merit* before God. Without grace no one can acquire the
life of blessedness; on the presupposition of grace, however,
man can in fact acquire a merit before God, and thereby an
increase of grace and of the love of God, and hence also a
heightening of his blessedness (*meritum condigni*) (ii, 1, 114).

Opposed to the morally-good stands *evil;* to the virtuous
act, *sin;* and to virtue as a habit, *vice* (ii, 1, 71 *sqq*.); sin and
vice are in contradiction to true reason, and hence in general
to the essence or nature of man. In reference to the kind of
pleasure felt or sought in sin, sins are divided into *spiritual*
and *fleshly* sins. In reference to their guilt and punishable-
ness, they are classed into *venial* and *mortal* (*peccata venalia et
mortalia*); the former consist in the turning to the finite
without a conscious and designed turning-away from God,

and they involve finite punishments, either here upon earth or in purgatory; mortal sins consist in a conscious and designed turning-away from, and hence in a conscious rebelling against, God and his will,—are contrary to the order of love, and hence involve eternal punishment. The gravity of the guilt is measured by the importance of the object, by the motives, by the degree of consciousness and of freedom, and by the spiritual character and position of the subject in society. In reference to the positive or negative contents of the action, sins fall into sins of commission and of omission (*peccata commissionis et omissionis*). In reference to their manner of commission, sins are sins of the heart, of the mouth, and of act (*peccata cordis, oris, operis*). In sin there is to be distinguished a twofold consent of the rational will, namely, to the pleasure in the sin, and to the sinful deed itself, the latter being the more criminal.—The *causes* of sin, as act, are in part direct, namely, erring cognition and volition—the regarding a seeming good as a real one, and the willing it,—and, in part, indirect, namely, first, inner ones, such as imagination, sensuousness, ignorance, passion, and other already committed sins; and, second, outward or tempting ones, such as evil spirits and bad men; temptation, however, presupposes, in order to its effectualness, a sinful welcoming of it. God is not the cause of sin, though indeed, in virtue of his righteousness, He is the mediate cause of the consequences of sin, *e. g.*, of the hardening of the heart. The sinful corruption which transmits itself from the first man to all following generations, that is, original sin, is, formally, the being destitute of original righteousness, and, materially, the tending of the soul-powers to false goods,—*concupiscentia* (75 *sqq*). The particular sins are severally treated of in connection with the virtues of which they are the violation.

In his, not seldom very casuistical carrying out of details, Thomas Aquinas, notwithstanding his moral earnestness, does not, on the whole, incline to theoretical rigor, but leaves pretty free scope for personal determination in particular cases, and even in the face of outward human law. The right of property, for example, is, in his opinion, not unconditional; and in extreme cases of necessity, where the saving of life is involved, the right of self-preservation takes pre-

cedence of the right of property, and a person sins not when, in such a case, he openly or secretly takes from the refused superfluity of another that which he needs (ii, 2, *sq.* 66, 7).— To take interest for money loaned, he regards, in agreement with general ancient-Christian and Mediæval opinion, as unallowable; otherwise the same thing would be paid for twice; he who sells a loaf of bread, may not demand another special payment for the eating of the same; he who lends receives, in fact, the purchase price with the return of the simple sum lent; however, it is not unallowable, in case of need, to pay interest to others for money.—The duty of truthfulness admits, indeed, of saying less than one knows to be the truth, but not more; for the little is a part of the whole.   All lies are sins, though in different degrees; a conscious lie for the injury of another is a mortal sin, but a lie said in sport or a lie of courtesy (*mendacium officiosum*) in indifferent things, and where it injures no one, is a venial one (ii, 2, *sq.* 110, 4).

Duns Scotus (*ob.* 1308), whose really speculative acumen went but too often astray into sophistical and skeptical reasonings, involved the moral idea, and above all its special application, in more than one respect, in uncertainty, namely, by his sophist-delight in the discovering and in the ingenious solving of contradictions and difficulties.   A minutely spun-out *quatenus* makes room for the most opposite assumptions, and opens the way, to subjective discretion, for a lax construing of the law.   Many elements in Scotus remind us strikingly of the later aberrations of the Jesuitical view. The notion of the freedom of the will he conceives, in opposition to Thomas Aquinas, as essentially a mere norm-less discretion, both in man and in God; while Aquinas held that man, as really rational, has, in his rational knowledge of the good, a motive—not a compelling one, it is true, but a motive—to the good, so that he cannot determine himself equally easily for the rational and the irrational, but has in fact a primitive, a constitutional inclination to the good, and that consequently the will does not by any means stand entirely neutral (ii, 1, 9, 13, 17, 58), Duns Scotus maintains, on the contrary, that according to this view the will is not at all free, but is determined by knowledge; according to his

view, the will, as free, is not in the least bound by rational knowledge, but stands perfectly neutral, and can with like facility decide for, or against, the known good.* Likewise, also, is the freedom of the divine will in nowise to be con- ceived of as characterized by any inner necessity, so that, for example, God could not equally well will the opposite of that which he actually does will. A course of order is not willed by God and established as a law because it is good *per se,* but it is good simply and solely because God has willed it precisely so; but He might just as readily have willed the opposite thereof. Hence also God is not bound by his commands, and He can in fact annul them,—not merely the positive laws of Revelation, but also the natural laws of morals; only from the two first laws of the Decalogue, as re- sulting directly from the essence of God, can God not dis- pense.† It is evidently in the interest of this lax notion of liberty that Duns Scotus admits also of morally *indifferent* actions—not merely such *manners* of action, as, being neither commended nor forbidden, constitute the sphere of the al- lowed,—but also real, positive actions which are neither good nor evil, that is, which are not done out of love to God, but also not in opposition to Him.‡ Hence in regard to particular moral cases, Duns Scotus shows himself often very lax. Falsehood and misrepresentation he declares as, under cer- tain circumstances, allowable.§ An oath of promise obligates to its fulfillment only when the person had at the time of swearing it the intention of fulfilling it,—though of course an oath in which one did not have this intention, is a moral sin.‖

Scholastic ethics, as a whole bears a pretty unvarying out- ward form. The method is, as the several points present themselves, first, to state the various opposing views with the reasons in their favor, and then to pass a decision upon the point itself; mere *dicta* of the Fathers, especially of Au- gustine and of Dionysius the Areopagite, and often also of the *Philosophus,* that is, Aristotle, suffice in and of themselves as conclusive proofs; texts from the Scriptures fall rather into

---

* *Quæstt. in libr. Sentent.* ii, dist. 25, ed. Lugd., 1639, t. 6, p. 873 *sqq.*
† Ibid. iii, dist. 37, t. 7, p. 857.   ‡ Ibid. ii, dist. 41.
§ Ibid. iii, dist. 38, p. 917.   ‖ Ibid. iii, dist. 39, p. 980.

the back-ground.—Despite the undeniable acumen shown by the schoolmen in the development of processes of reasoning, there is yet manifest also a lack of the courage to derive their philosophical systems purely and simply from the Christian consciousness. Graeco-Roman ethics was in fact, to the schoolmen, not a merely preliminary and preparatory study, but it was with them of quite too determining an influence, also in respect to the subject-matter of their science. They endeavor, indeed, with great earnestness to exalt extra-Christian philosophy into the sphere of Christian thought; it proves, however, an element too mighty for them, and they do not wholly escape entangling the Christian consciousness in the heathen, and thus robbing it of its peculiarity. They felt indeed the antagonism, but did not overcome it, and the prevalent lifeless juxtaposing of the two elements shows only their embarrassment, but not their ability to dominate the foreign material.—The almost universal resorting to certain favorite numbers in the division and classification of the subject-matter, particularly to three and seven, and also to four and twelve, is indeed based on an obscure consciousness of an inner order of the spiritual life; but this order does not come to a scientific consciousness, and the real reason for its observance is, after all, the typical significance of these numbers as sacred. That there should be presented precisely seven beatitudes, seven (diversely-stated) mortal sins, etc., seems without inner ground; and frequently this using of numbers sinks to jejune play, as, e. g., when a certain writer introduces every-where the number twelve,—in the dividing of his subject, in assigning reasons, in citing objections, etc.

The ethical subject-matter treated of by the schoolmen was subsequently wrought over in large, though but little systemetized summaries in connection with appropriate citations from the Fathers, and placed within reach of the wider circles of the ecclesiastical world. To the period of Thomas Aquinas himself belongs the *Summa* of *William Peraldus,** an essentially casuistical and pretty well digested appreciation of scholastic science; after which we may mention the *Spec-*

* *Summa s. tractatus de virtutibus et vitiis,* from the fifteenth century, (without date or place of printing, then at Col. Agr., 1479 fol.; Basle, 1497, 8vo.) often reprinted.

ulum morale, attributed to *Vincent* of *Beauvais* (*ob.* 1264), but originating in the fourteenth century;* and also the much used and very complete and erudite *Summa* of *Antony* of *Florence* (*ob.* 1459).†

John of *Salisbury* (*ob.* 1180, as Bishop of Chartres), who opposed scholasticism proper with brilliant ability, but was rather empirical in regard to the source of knowledge, though in other respects of rich philosophical culture, undertook to give to the moral views of the Church a scientific expression; in his efforts he based himself most largely on Gregory the Great. *To be* perfect is God's essence, *to become* perfect is the task of man as God's image; man becomes perfect, and hence happy only by moral activity,—which activity rests, on the one hand, on the knowledge of the truth, and, on the other, on love to God. Since the fall into sin man can know the truth only in virtue of divine revelation and illumination, and he can realize the good only by the assistance of divine grace. Because of the evil desire inborn in all men, there is no virtue without a constant struggle of our love to righteousness, as strengthened by redemption, against our innate evil desires. Even as the essence and source of all sins is the natural desire as developed into pride and presumption (so that consequently all virtuous effort directs itself primarily against the pride of the heart), so the essence of all Christian virtue is that *humility* which springs from love to God, and which seeks to lay aside all self-will and to give God the glory in all things. Hence the moral worth of actions lies not in the work, but in the disposition; but from the right disposition there follows with moral necessity also the right work.—Morality is not, however, a merely individual task, it finds its full truth only in the moral *community-life*, which comes to expression in the church and in the closely therewith-connected Christian state. The State has, as a real moral organism, also a *moral* task, namely, to execute righteousness according to the divine will, and not only to protect the morality of the people, but also to foster and guide it. Hence the law which governs the state is to be

---

* Not in his *Opp.*, 1481, but separately printed as a part of the great *Speculum naturale*, etc., 1473, and subsequently.

† *Summa theol.*, 1477, 1478, 1480, 1496; 1740, 4 vols.

an expression, not of human discretion, but only of the divine will, to which even the prince must absolutely subordinate himself; hence it must rest on God's revealed Word, and the vicegerents of God, that is, the representatives of the religious community-life—the Church,—must be also the animating soul of the Christian state; for, in fact, in its *moral* task, the Christian state is identical with the church. God-fearing is the life-power of the Christian state, and this state must therefore above all things recognize and honor both the moral right of the church and also the priests as the higher and, so to speak, divine element in worldly society. The priests indeed should not and may not themselves guide and administer the state; they are rather simply by their moral example, by doctrine, by exhortation, and by reproof, to influence the same, but the princes to whom by divine ordinance the guidance of the state belongs, have received the sword only from the higher moral community, the church, in order to execute justice in the name of the *Christian* idea; and so likewise stands the military order, knighthood, not merely in the service of the prince, but quite as fully, and in fact primarily, in the service of God, and hence of the church. A prince who breaks away from divine law, who rebels against the divine ordinances, and hence also against the church, has, as a tyrant, forfeited his moral right to the crown, and it is not merely legitimate to offer resistance to him, but also in any manner whatever, even by treachery or assassination, to get rid of him [*Policraticus* iv, 2]. The political doctrine of John of Salisbury is a Mediæval Christian counterpart to Plato's doctrine of the state, with which he was not acquainted, and is in fact an attempt to introduce Augustine's *Civitas Dei* into the worldly state.*

The fondness of Schoolmen for proposing difficult controversial questions led them inevitably into the province of *casuistry ;* and this science—which had sustained itself alongside of scholasticism—subsequently borrowed from scholastic science much congenial material, and in part also a scientific form. Hence at the decline of scholasticism in the fourteenth century, casuistry entered in fact upon its brightest days.

* Especially in his *Policraticus.*—(Reuter: *Joh. v. S.*, 1842). Schaar-schmidt: *Joh. Saresb.*, 1862.

The works entitled *Summæ casuum conscientiæ*, were very
much used in connection with confession and penance, and,
as they generally contained also much matter relative to
church law, also in ecclesiastical administration. In them
we find a very imperfectly digested, and often merely alphabetical, summary of specific single moral questions, which
relate in the main to what is allowed or disallowed, and the
decision of which is given less from general principles than
on the basis of the utterances of the more highly esteemed
Fathers. The questions are often not taken from life at all,
but are simply invented in order to exercise ingenuity, as in
riddle-solving; and in some of these works there is manifested a peculiarly fond lingering over extremely impure subjects. In the presence of the too exclusively considered
individual case, the general principles involved in it are
often wholly lost sight of, and ethics is in danger of degenerating into a sophistry of special-pleading,—into a treating
of the moral merely empirically and skeptically; thus we
find questions often extensively discussed, as doubtful, which
cannot be in the least practically doubtful for the unsophisticated moral consciousness. The best known of these works
are the *Summæ* of *Raymund* of *Pennaforti* in the thirteenth
century,* and of *Astesanus* in the fourteenth† (the *Astesana*,
is cautious and judicious, contains also many general considerations, and is pretty systematic and comprehensive); *Angelus*
of *Clavasio* in the fifteenth century‡ (the *Angelica*, perhaps
the most extensively used; alphabetical, with much worthless matter, and often treating of indelicate questions); *Syl-
vester Prierias*, General of the Dominicans, the well-known
opponent of Luther, gave in his *Summa moralis*,§ generally
called *Summa summarum*, an alphabetical compilation from
others. (The Pisanella [1470 and often], revised by Nicolas
of Ausmo, 1471, '73, '74, '75, '78; Galensis, 1475; Rosella,
1516; Pacifica, 1574. The *Biblia aurea*, 1475, '81,—also in

---

* *Summa de casibus pœnitentiæ*, Verona, 1744; upon this is based the
work of John of Freiburg, Augsb., 1472, and frequently.

† *S. d. cas. consc.* (at first without date or place) about 1468–72 fol.;
then at Col., 1479; Norimb., 1482, and often later.

‡ *S. cas. consc.*, 1486 without place. fol.; Venet., 1487 4to.; Norimb.,
1488, and often.

§ Printed in 1515 4to.; Argent., 1518 fol.

German, alphabetical.)—Also the *Decretum* of *Gratian* contains, in its first part, much that appertains to casuistical ethics.

SECTION XXXV.

The writings of the *Mystics* contain in the field of ethics many profound thoughts, though without rigidly scientific form.   This is the case with *Richard* of *St. Victor* and *Bonaventura*.   Less mystical than simply practical, and strongly emphasizing the subjective phase of morality, was the influence of *Bernard* of *Clairvaux*, and later, of *Thomas à Kempis*; while *Eckart*, and in part even *Tauler*, conceive the moral in the main negatively and quietistically (in the spirit of a Pantheistically-infected mysticism) as spiritual poverty, as the turning-away of the spirit from all that is created.   Occupying a mediating position between mysticism and scholasticism, also *John Gerson* seeks to give form to ethics, but he already begins to show signs of that paralysis of the moral spirit which had spread into the widest circles previously to the Reformation; *Raymund de Sabunde* deals in more popularly-practical modes of thought. In the spirit of the Reformation, and as its precursors, worked, in the field of ethics, also *Wickliffe*, *Huss*, *John* of *Goch*, and *Savonarola*.

In contrast to the growingly-Aristotelian, dialectical treatment of ethics, the mystical anti-scholastic current of theology clings, more or less closely, to the writings of the supposed Areopagite (§ 31), but keeps for the most part clear from the daring speculations of John Scotus Erigena, and gives, in general, thoughtful meditations and profound glances of insight rather than rigorous and clear processes of reasoning.   The freedom of the will is, by most of the Mediæval mystics, pretty strongly emphasized; but the active working

in the outer world is made largely to give place to the purely contemplative life.

Richard of *St. Victor* (about 1150) treats, in several special works, of the inner life of the pious heart in its union with God,—a life which through *contemplatio* as distinguished from *cogitatio* and *meditatio*, passes over into self-forgetting love. The divine is not attained to by laborious thinking and doing, but by an immediate and spiritual, freely self-devoting vision or beholding, to which receptive state of the soul God lovingly manifests himself as in-streaming light. And the soul becomes receptive by the progressive cleansing of it from the dross of the earthly life, from the striving after the creature,—by self-immersion into itself, not in order to hold fast to itself in antithesis to God, but in order to aspire toward him in ardent love-desire; the goal is perfect, blissful rest in God; the condition is the operation of grace and the willing, joyous laying-hold upon the same on the part of the subject.—*Bonaventura* (*ob.* 1274) attempts to fuse dialectics with mysticism, but, notwithstanding his frequently almost overflowing subjectivity of feeling, his mysticism is less sustained and less deep than that of Richard St. Victor, and lingers more in the sphere of practical piety.—*Bernard* of *Clairvaux* (*ob.* 1153),—opposing scholasticism in many respects not without good grounds, and confining himself mainly to the practical sphere,—has also carefully examined the subject of ethics in some of its parts; (*De diligendo deo ; De gradibus humilitatis et superb.; De gratia et libero arbitrio ; De consideratione.*) To true virtue belong two things: divine grace and a free, active embracing of the same; without freedom there is no responsibility. But freedom is threefold: first, freedom of nature as opposed to necessity; second, freedom of grace,—attained to through Christ,—that is, emancipation from the bondage of sin; and, third, freedom of glory which is realized in eternal blessedness, but enjoyed here only in moments of spiritual vision. Freedom of choice is from nature, but by grace it is regulated and attracted toward the good, though not forced. By simple free-will we belong to ourselves; by the willing of the good we belong to God; by the willing of evil, to Satan. The decision lies in our own hand; no one is forced to salvation. Love, as constitut-

ing the essence of the moral, has four degrees: first, man loves himself for his own sake; second, he loves God, not, however, for God's but for his own sake, because without God he can do nothing; third, he loves God for God's sake, out of thankfulness for experienced love; fourth, he loves also himself solely for God's sake; this highest stage, that of true morality, is, however, but seldom enjoyed in this life. The essence of wisdom, on the whole, is, to behold and to love the invisible essence of God in all things, to give up all that we have to God, and to live only in God and for God. All true virtue is an expression of humility, whereby, in true self-knowledge man becomes nothing in his own eyes; humility leads in twelve stages to the truth, which truth in turn develops itself in three stages, the highest of which is the direct spiritual beholding of God. Humility, love, and the beholding of the truth, are the three aliments of the soul, corresponding to the Son, the Spirit, and the Father. The mystical element in Bernard shows itself mainly in the development of the doctrine of contemplation. Many of his principles he borrows from the ethics prevalent in his day, as, *e. g.*, the four cardinal virtues, and also the notion of the middle-way as the essence of virtue.

Master Eckart (a Dominican at Cologne, *ob.* 1329),[*] distinguished for profound insight, but not unfrequently overpassing, in his fervid soarings, the limits of the Christian world-theory, was of very great influence on subsequent mystics; taking his departure from Dionysius the Areopagite, he pushes the thought of the union of the soul with God, as the highest good to such a height as almost to lose sight of the individual existence of the creature, and of its distinctness from God,—not, however, in the sense of modern Pantheism, but in that of John Scotus Erigena. The world is, strictly speaking, nothing at all,—is rather mere appearance than reality; God alone is real in whatever exists; God alone is the object of true love, and in this love all morality is comprehended. Hence the entire striving of man must be directed to this end, namely, to becoming at one with God, to laying aside his

---

[*] *Schriften*, edited by Pfeiffer, 1847,—(mostly sermons; larger scientific works of his appear to be lost. C. Schmidt in *Stud. u. Krit.*, 1839; Martensen, 1842; J. Back, 1864.

separate existence, to turning away from all that is created, to wishing nothing, loving nothing, knowing nothing but God alone—to merging himself into God, to transforming himself into God. If God is to come into the soul, then the creature must be driven out; if man is to become rich in God, then he must become poor in the creature. When man turns himself away from all that is finite, when he forgets himself and the world, and directs his soul exclusively toward God, then God pours himself into his soul,—God is born in the soul, and the soul has eternal rest in God. Virtuous working in the world is not the highest working, for in it man disperses himself into the multiplicity of the finite; he who has found God, who has God dwelling in himself, divests himself also of works,—seeks only the *inner* work, reposes in God alone; nay, he aims not at his *own* blessedness, for in fact this is also a clinging to self, to the created,—he aims only at giving himself wholly up to God, at sacrificing himself to God, at reducing himself to nothing, at cutting off and throwing away from himself whatever is finite or creature-like, or different from God; he breaks himself loose not only from sin, but also from the world and from his own self. Not man is to work, but he is to let God exclusively and alone work in him; such purity of heart, such freedom from all self, also from all personal volition, is the highest good, is the spiritual birth of God in the soul; we possess all good when we are united with God's nature, and a single glance at God "in his nakedness" is of more avail, and unites the soul more with God, than all the works of Christendom could accomplish.

In a similar spirit, although less bold in emphasizing the mystical element, wrote and lived *Tauler*, Eckart's disciple (a Dominican at Cologne and Strasburg, *ob.* 1361). He presented, in his "Imitation of the humble Life of Christ," * a system of pure mysticism, and which, for that very reason, was one-sided and dangerous to the Christian consciousness. The essence of morality is spiritual *poverty ;* the way to life, to "equality with God," is to become spiritually poor, to be separated from all that belongs to the creature, to cling to

* Edited by Schlosser, 1833 (in modern German); his sermons are mostly practico-edificatory. The work, *Medulla animæ*, is not by Tauler C. Schmidt: *J. Tauler*, 1841.

nothing among finite things; as, however, all that is finite must cling to something, hence man is to cling only to that which is above himself, to God. The poorer man is in the creature, so much the richer is he in God; God is intuited only immediately, without any intervention of the creature; in so far as man looks to the creature he is distant from God. Man must put off from himself all that is multiple, manifold, in order to become rich in the One,—must be poor in knowledge in so far as knowledge relates to the finite and is involved in finite forms,—poor in virtue in so far as it is an acting in the finite (only the disposition is divine),—poor even in grace in so far as the soul in its union with God stands no longer in a mere relation of grace to God, but is actively led by God in harmony with himself in a divine manner. The sole true knowledge is the direct spiritual beholding of God. The sole virtue is simple love to God. God is free from every thing that is creatural; in spiritual poverty man becomes also free from and divested of all things,—presses, as a free soul, into the uncreated good, into God, and is no longer affected by earthly pleasure or by pain. Hence true divine freedom springs from poverty and humility; false freedom, from pride. God is a pure activity—a mere working; therefore also poverty is a pure working with God; now there are three kinds of work: (1) *natural* work, in part bodily and sensuous; this work must take place with moderation and in the Holy Ghost, and the senses must be indulged in their necessary wants; and in part, spiritual, as knowledge and love; also this work must take place only in so far as necessary, must be turned aside from all not absolutely essential things; otherwise it leads to pride. (2) *Grace*-work; in man, this work is primarily learning, namely, acquiring a knowledge of the Scriptures and of all the efficacy of the Holy Spirit, and hence also a knowledge of good and evil. When man permits himself to be guided by the divine Spirit that dwells within him, then he becomes a friend of God; as such, he must divest himself of all temporal things, and renounce them, for they are all null and void; he must simply follow Christ, and in so doing he attains (3) to the *divine* work in man; man is now *one* spirit with God, and seeks nothing but God; his work is God's work, and God's work

16

is his own work; and God's spirit speaks to him no more in symbol and form, but in full life, light, and truth. All the powers of the soul keep holiday, and are at rest, and let God alone work, and this is the highest work of which they are capable. The human spirit loses finally its own self, loses itself in God and knows no longer any thing but God; God puts himself in the place of reason in man, and works man's works; the soul merges itself into God and remains eternally hovering in God,—drowns itself in the unfathomable sea of divinity. Hence by the renouncing of all that is temporal, by true poverty, man becomes divested also of outward works. He who has no longer any thing wherewith to help his fellow-man, is in fact no longer required to do so; also external works belong to the sphere of the temporal, and hence man must pass through them and beyond them up to true poverty and vision; in this *one* work he works all works, and in this one virtue he has all virtues.—In Tauler the one phase of the moral, namely, union with God, is pushed one-sidedly into untruth, so that the right of the creatural individuality is relatively lost sight of, and hence we find in many respects Pantheistical forms of thought.—*John Ruis-broch* of Brussels (*ob.* 1381) wrote in a similar spirit, but strayed into a still more transcendental heart-mysticism, though his works abound rather in allegorizing portrayals and confident assertions than in scientific demonstration.

The comprehensiveness of a *Gerson* (*ob.* 1429) could not bring to a check the decline of the inner spirit of the church, which was now seriously affecting also the general moral consciousness. Scholasticism and casuistry had, by their interminable subtleties, largely obscured the more simple moral modes of thought; and while puzzling themselves in fruitless speculation over the imaginary difficulties of cunningly-invented cases of conscience, they lost all sense for moral straightforwardness, and found abundant pretexts for making exceptions from the moral rule. The Franciscan, Jean Petit of Paris, was able, on occasion of the murder of the regent, the Duke of Orleans, in 1407, to find reasons for openly justifying the murder of tyrants, and the Council of Constance did not venture to pronounce a decided disapproval of this doctrine; and not only that, but it gave, for the first

time, serious countenance to the notion of moral *probabilism*, that is, the doctrine that a morally doubtful action is permissible on condition that several esteemed Fathers can be cited in its favor.* Gerson, who opposed the doctrine of Petit with but half-heart, was also himself involved in the general laxity of the moral consciousness; he also countenanced probabilism. He held that the vow of celibacy was violated only by actual marriage but not by fornication, and for this sin he shows an excessive leniency.† The notorious morality of the Jesuits is not peculiar to them, but is only the further development of a spirit that was already powerful in the Romish church before the time of the Reformation. In other respects Gerson seeks, in his numerous writings on specific moral topics, to mitigate the erroneousness of the prevailing moral views; the monastic life and the doctrine of the divine counsels, he does not esteem so highly as did the spirit of his age; he finds the difference between venial and mortal sins rather in the subjective intention than in the objective nature of the sin. The mystical element appears in Gerson under a very moderated form.

Thomas à Kempis (*ob.* 1471), the author of the most widely known of all books of devotion: *De imitatione Christi* (translated into all European languages, and published nearly two thousand times), shows himself in this book as a thoroughly practical, moderated mystic, of deep moral life-experience, and of genuine, heart-felt, morally-vigorous piety; and hence his work is not less prized in the Protestant than in the Romish church. The thoughts are presented in a clear, genuinely-popular style, and the rich heart-depth is thereby thrown all the more brightly into relief.—The book known as *German Theology*, published first by Luther in 1516, but springing from an unknown author of the fifteenth century, is based on Tauler, and is characterized by a somewhat more strongly speculative mysticism than that of Kempis,—emphasizing in an almost one-sided manner the turning-away from self and from the world, and the becoming united with

---

* Marheineke: *Gesch. d. christl. Moral*, etc., 1806, p. 161 *sqq.*; Stäudlin: *Gesch. d. ch. Mor. seit. d. Wiederaufl.*, etc., p. 63 *sqq.*; Wessenberg: *Kirchenversamml.*, 2, 247.

† *Opp.*, Antv., 1706, t. iii, 917 *sqq.*

God as the one eternal good, so that the moral right of the
personality is thrown quite too far into the back-ground, and
too little distinction is made between the personality itself
and the "selfhood" that is to be done away with.

Less peculiar in contents than in form, and differing equally from scholasticism and from mysticism, are the moral
views of *Raymund de Sabunde* (of Toulouse, about 1430).*
Appropriating to himself the results of preceding theological
and philosophical thought, he undertook, rather from the
stand-point of experience, of the observation of nature, and
of the common sense of mankind, to place these results within reach of the understanding of the masses. The freedom
of the will as directed toward the good is the highest possession of reason; called to the highest place in the scale of
created beings, man should, by free conduct, show himself
worthy of this calling,—should establish and preserve the
harmony of the created. As man has received nothing from
himself, but every thing from God alone, hence his first duty
is thankful love to God who first loved him (tit. 96 *sqq.*, 109
sqq.); love to self becomes moral only through love to God.
Other creatures give us good only in so far as God works
through them, and hence our love to them must be subordinated to our love to God; but out of this love to God follows
also a love to that which He has created, and hence, first of
all, to man as God's image; hence the requirement to love
one's neighbor as one's self (120 *sqq*). Through love to God,
man constantly grows in God-likeness, for *amor convertit
amantem in rem amatam* (129 *sqq.*), though this is not to be
taken in the sweeping sense of the Mystics. Evil consists in
this, that we honor and love the creature not in God but for
itself, and is consequently idolatry; the root of all evil is
this impious love to self, that is, it is self-seeking and self-
will; the devil seeks nothing but himself.—As in consequence
of sin a general corruption of man's nature has been brought
about, and as the power of sin over man is paralyzed only by
redemption, hence Christian morality rests entirely on loving
thankfulness to Christ, and involves a constant struggle
against the remains of sin that still infect us.

The *evangelical* tendency which during the time of the

* *Theologia naturalis*, Solisb., 1852.—Matzke: *R. v. S.*, 1846.

universal domination of the Romish church had never entirely disappeared, and which, especially since the appearance of the Waldenses, had been growing more positive in its opposition to the corrupted church, directed its efforts from the very first against the anti-scriptural and arbitrary ordinances of said church, especially against the work-holiness of monastic morality, in order to vindicate the moral freedom of the Christian personality, and also against the sophistical laxity of the more recent period; this tendency insists above all upon faith-born love as the source and essence of all true morality, and rejects the notion of supererogatory merit as arising from the observance of the so-called evangelical counsels.—So taught *Wickliffe* in his *Trialogus*, but rather as assailing than as positively building up; all sin, he refers to a lack in true faith; a correct knowledge of faith precludes sin; true virtue is not possible without true faith; a correct knowledge of faith precludes sin; true virtue is not possible without true faith; hence by a man's virtue one can judge of his faith. Wickliffe's over-rigid and almost deterministic predestinarianism simply stands, unmediated, along-side of his moral views, and merely impedes their freer scope.—Also *Huss* combats, in the ethical field, chiefly only against the errors of Romish dogmas and morals, without himself establishing any thing essentially new.—Violent and keen, and generally, though not always, purely evangelical are also the assaults of *Nicolas de Clamengis* [Clemangis] in France—*ob.* about 1440—against the corruption of the moral consciousness of the church).*—*John of Goch*, of Malines (*ob.* 1475) assailed, from an Augustinian stand-point, the commingling of the evangelical with the Mosaic law, also the system of vows, and outward work-holiness in general; faith as working by love is the essence of Christian freedom and morality.† The influence of *Savonarola* in Florence lay more in his fiery zeal for pure evangelical morality than in fruits of scientific thought; in his mode of thinking, the phase of the God-possessed affections stands forth with most prominence; a mystical subjectiveness is combined with a fervent work-activity.‡

---

* *De corrupto eccl. statu*, and in briefer essays and letters, *Opp.*, 1613.
† Ullmann: *Reformatoren vor d. Ref.*, 1841, i.
‡ Rudelbach: *Sav.*, 1835; F. C. Meier, 1836.

If we leave out of view these teachers of the church who were forerunners of the Reformation, we find in general in the ecclesiastical ethics prevailing before the opening of this Reformation a threefold character: a casuistical, a scholastic, and a mystical one, corresponding to the three phases of the soul-life, namely, to the empirical understanding, to the speculative reason and to the loving heart. The mystical form of ethics is the pure antithesis to the casuistical; the former rests on heart-union with God, the latter on the analyzing understanding; the former, upon an inward ineffable vision, the latter, upon outward calculating observation; the former strays at times into the borders of Pantheism, and hence has some points of contact with the cosmic theory of India; the latter is rather in danger of repeating, in the Christian sphere, the Jewish externality and chicanery of Pharisaism and Talmudism;—the former reduces all plurality, all heterogeneousness, to a homogeneous unity,—endangers the practically moral working-life in the world; the latter dissolves the moral idea into an atomistic plurality of single cases devoid of uniting bond;—mysticism turns itself away disdainfully from all objective reality even of the moral life; casuistry threatens to bind up and to smother the moral in narrow legal forms; mysticism turns away from the circumference toward the center, but does not return again from the center to the circumference; casuistry proceeds and stumbles by a reverse course;—the former tends to a lightly-esteeming of the active life, the latter to a hypocritical and external work-holiness. Speculative ethics, especially in Thomas Aquinas, stands higher than in either of the other two forms, but lacks too much in evangelical directness and simplicity; and because of its double dependence on Greek ethics, on the one hand, and on the evangelical church-creed, on the other, it has not only compromised its legitimate and essential freedom, but, at the same time, also its truth. Notwithstanding this, however, it stands (especially in its highest perfection in Thomas Aquinas) far more closely to the evangelical consciousness than the later form of Roman Catholic ethics as presented by the zealous champion of the Romish church, the Jesuits.

III. THE EPOCH OF REFORM.

SECTION XXXVI.

The antagonism of the evangelical ground-thought to that of Romanism manifested itself also in ethics. In the evangelical or Protestant church the sinful corruption of the natural man was conceived much more deeply, and consequently the moral task of the Christian much more earnestly; and, as a consequence of the impossibility of meriting salvation by our works, Christian virtue was conceived, in much greater freedom from self-seeking, as the simple fruit of faith; and the notion of supererogatory works became impossible in view of the decided recognition, that the life even of the most holy always falls short of moral perfection. The Scriptural view excludes a very essential portion of Romish ethics from that of the evangelical church.*

The semi-Pelagian enfeebling of the effects of sin that prevailed in the Romish church, deprived ethics of its proper deep-reaching foundation. The more deeply the moral corruption of man is conceived of, so much the greater becomes also the significancy of redemption, and likewise also of the moral struggle of the regenerated Christian against sin. Hence the, at first thought, surprising phenomenon that the rigid predestinarianism of Calvin did not lead to a decline in moral effort, but on the contrary to a very vigorous moral life. In the deep earnestness of their conception of the moral task, both evangelical churches, the Lutheran and the Reformed, stand alike.

The Holy Scriptures are the sole fountain of Christian ethics, just as, living faith in Christ as the sole cause of salvation, is

---

* Comp. H. Merz: *System der christl. Sittenlehre in seiner Gestaltung nach den Grundsetzen des Protestantismus im Gegensatze zum Katholicismus*, Tüb., 1841,—ingenious, but prepossessed by speculative theories, and doing injustice to both sides.

also the subjective ground and the living fountain of morality.
All blessedness is imparted to us without our meriting it, and
solely of grace; but good works, as the necessary effects of true
faith, are the certain verification of the same. The moral law
is not, as in the Romish church, predominantly objective, but
is of a strictly inward character. No one can do more than
what God requires of him, for man is called to perfection; all
that is truly good is a requirement of the divine law and not
of any mere counsels, which, without the forfeiture of a God-
pleasing life, might in so far be left undone,—all the good that
we can do, we are also under obligation to do. The so-called
counsels of the Romish church are rather a hindering than a
furthering of the good, for they stand in the way of active love,
and nourish the delusion of personal merit. Monastic vows are
not consistent with vital faith. As man is saved only in virtue
of redemption through Christ, hence his salvation rests solely
on the worthiness of Christ, and not on personal merit; all true
virtue must be simply a fruit of faith, and hence of an already-
acquired divine sonship, and consequently, though it may verify
this sonship, it cannot first acquire or heighten it.

Evangelical ethics is therefore apparently much less comprehensive in its subject-matter than that of the Romish church,—
treats a not inconsiderable portion of the latter merely con-
demnatorily, as, e. g., the entire subject of asceticism, and of
opera supererogatoria as fulfilling the counsels; on the other
hand, however, it has a deeper ground and a higher earnestness. Romish asceticism simply hides from view the inner
lack of a truly evangelically moral depth. He who has understood the entire and profound earnestness of the moral life-task,
and is conscious, how far the reality still falls below the moral
prototype, can never come upon the thought of attempting,
in addition to the moral task proposed to us by God, to perform still other additional works, in order to attain to a still
higher degree of sanctity. All these self-imposed works are
really an implication that God placed the moral goal of man
too low, and that He is thankfully pleased to accept the
voluntary and non-owed over-payment of those who feel themselves superior to the ordinary assessment.

SECTION XXXVII.

The Reformers themselves treat the moral con
tents of the Christian consciousness for the most part
only practically; *Melanchthon* develops in his *Loci*
merely the ground-thoughts, though he also attempts,
on the basis of Aristotle, a philosophical establishing
of the foundations of ethics; *Calvin* gives only
brief outlines, independently of the earlier scholastic
method. The antithesis of the two evangelical
churches manifested itself also in wide-reaching differences of ethical views. As an independent theological science, ethics was somewhat earlier treated
in the Reformed than in the Lutheran church. In
the latter, it was at first either combined, in its mere
ground-principles, with dogmatics, or treated merely
practically and popularly; *G. Calixtus*, however,
treated it as a science distinctly separate from dogmatics, though only in its scanty beginnings. From
this time forward it was frequently treated independently, though for the most part, even as late as into
the eighteenth century, only as casuistry; and *Pietism*,
which embraced so earnestly the ethical contents of
Christianity, although with some formal narrowness,
prepared the way for a profounder scientific treatment of ethics.

Luther himself, who embraced the evangelical ground-truths
so clearly and distinctly, was not called by the general scope of
his activity to the preparing of a system of scientific ethics
proper. His warfare against Romish work-holiness, and against
the formal, subtle and freedom-hampering casuistry of the Ro-
manists, must have awakened in him a certain disinclination to
a rigidly-scientific development of ethics, and an anxiety lest
such a work might sink the free moral activity of the Christian

from the sphere of faith-communion with Christ into unfree and juridical forms. He expressed it repeatedly, that the true believer needs no law at all, because faith itself is both law and power, and spontaneously works the God-pleasing out of free love without being hampered by an objective law. As the apple-tree bears its fruit not in virtue of a law given to it, but out of its own proper nature, so are all Christians so tempered by faith that they spontaneously do well and righteously better than all laws could teach them to do. Even as the tree must exist antecedently to its fruit, and as the fruit does not make a tree good or bad, but the tree makes the fruit, so must man be good or bad before he does good or bad works. The Christian's love is to be an outward-gushing love, flowing from within out of the heart, out of his own little fountain; the spring and the stream are themselves to be good,—are not to derive their waters from without. Christ was a Redeemer, not a Lawgiver, and the Gospel is not to be turned into a book of laws. With such views, so directly antagonistic to the common Romish teaching, if we except the Mystics, it was natural that a rigidly-drawn-up system of ethics might seem a hampering to faith-born freedom,—might seem like an adulterating of the teachings of the Gospel with the doctrine of the law. This period of agitated contest was therefore little adapted to the scientific development of a system of ethics; this science was in fact the fruit of the evangelical life as having come to inner peace and stability, and as grown ripe through long experience in faith.

Of the chief Reformers, only *Melanchthon,*—who was of solid classic culture, and who gave proof, at the time of his scientific maturity, both of decided fondness for, and of a thorough understanding of, Aristotle,—indicated, in his theological writings not only the ground-thoughts of evangelical ethics, but gave even the outlines of a system of philosophical ethics. Besides his valuable comments on the Ethics and Politics of Aristotle,* he wrote, on the basis of Aristotelian principles, *Philosophiæ*

---

* *In Ethica Arist. comment.*, 1529, treating only the 1st and 2d books; n 1532 were added the 3d and 5th; re-written in 1545 as *Enarratio aliquot librorum Eth. Ar.*, etc.,—in the *Corpus Reformatorum* of Bretschneider and Bindseil, t. xvi, p. 277–416.—*Comment. in aliquot politicos libros Aristot.*, 1530, in *Corp. Ref.*, ib., p. 417 *sqq.*

moralis epitome, 1538.* In this work Melanchthon keeps philosophical ethics and the Christian knowledge of the moral strictly separate. The former is capable of comprehending and presenting only a part of the divine law; it gives only the natural law; but this is also a true divine law, which is implanted in human reason; and the philosophical knowledge of the same is a legitimate requirement and is an education toward the higher truth, as also the true foundation of all civil legislation, and is consequently by no means to be despised; moral reason is the mirror from which the wisdom of God is reflected forth [*Corp. Ref.*, pp. 21–27; comp. 277]. The method of the work follows the plan of the ethics of Aristotle, but presents far more solid principles. Man is the image of God, and his goal is the true development and manifestation of this image. Hence the end of man is to know and to recognize God, his prototype, and to manifest, in and through himself, the glory of God, by willing and complete obedience [28 *sqq*]. Of the virtues that fall within the scope of philosophical ethics, righteousness or justness takes first rank, and this virtue is pretty fully discussed [63 *sqq*.], especially in its civic significancy; more briefly are treated the virtues of truthfulness, beneficence, thankfulness, and friendship.—His philosophical ethics appeared, in 1550, entirely re-written and more independent of Aristotle, as *Ethicæ doctrinæ elementa et enarratio libri quinti Ethicorum*, and afterward in 1554, '57, '60, and frequently after Melanchthon's death.† This excellent work, though not comprehensive,—shorter even than the previous work, and presenting only the general bases of the moral, and examining more fully only certain special and, in part, civic questions,—is written in a clear, concise, and beautiful style, and is a worthy commencement toward a system of evangelical and, in fact, essentially philosophical ethics,—since the seventeenth century undeservedly laid aside, and also in more recent times almost forgotten.—A knowledge of the virtues is necessary, because it shows *that* God is; for the eternal and immutable distinction of the moral and the immoral in our reason cannot be fortuitous, but must proceed from the eternal, prescribing reason itself; it shows also *how* God is, namely,

---

* *Corp. Ref.*, xvi, pp. 21–164. The following editions, 1539, '40, are largely changed; three later ones, 1542–'46, are like that of 1540.

† *Corp. Ref.*, xvi, pp. 165–276; not printed in the earlier *Opp.*

wise, free, truthful, just, beneficent, merciful, etc. ; it is a witness
of God's justly retributing judgments, and is a life-norm for
men in outward (not spiritual) actions and in discipline.   Natural reason, however, can discover neither the ground of the
enfeeblement which has resulted from sin, nor the means of salvation therefrom ; hence philosophy, without the Gospel, does
not suffice [*Corp. Ref.*, 165–167].   Moral philosophy is the scientific presentation of the moral law of nature in the sphere of
external morals and discipline, and is, in this field, in harmony
with the Decalogue, and in so far also with the Gospel; for the
moral law is the eternal and immutable wisdom and measure
of the justice of God, obligating all rational creatures, and con-
demning those who come into conflict with it; but the Gospel
preaches repentance, and promises forgiveness of sins on the
ground of redemption by grace.   Now, though moral philosophy knows nothing of this promise, yet, as being a part of the
law, it also, on its part, leads toward the Gospel, and is therefore not to be despised [*C. R.*, 167–170].—Ethics inquires first
of all after the *goal* of the moral course.   This goal or end is
God himself, who lovingly communicates himself to us, and
hence the true knowledge and reverencing of God.   God created
man unto his image, hence He wills that He should himself be
manifested in and through man, namely, in that man becomes
morally like unto Him; only in a derived sense can it be said
that virtue is the end of man, as the highest good.   The good
is that which harmonizes with the God-set goal; hence evil is
a disturbing of the divine plan; and evil is primarily a *malum
culpœ*, in pure antagonism to the divine will, and then, second-
arily, a *malum pœnœ*, which by the divine, righteous will is
made to follow upon the guilty *malum culpœ;* God is in no
sense whatever the author or accomplice of sin,—to affirm this
would be blasphemy,—though He is indeed the author of the
punishment [*C. R.*, 170–183].—Virtue, as an acquired tendency
to obey right reason, is conditioned on the fact that, on the one
hand, reason guides the will by a right judgment, and that on
the other the will freely, persistently and firmly lays hold upon
this judgment, and has pleasure in so doing.   A knowledge of
the law and a free-will are the characteristics of the divine
image as created in man by divine love; virtue is the moral
realization of this image,—is thankful, answering love for re-

ceived love. In reason, as darkened by sin, this knowledge and freedom are indeed enfeebled, but not annihilated, and there remained in man a moral consciousness of right and wrong, and some degree of freedom to act conformably to this consciousness. Hence, the will is then truly good when it corresponds to the moral consciousness in so far as this consciousness harmonizes with the divine will. Hence virtue—more definitely stated—is the tendency of the will constantly to hearken to the moral consciousness for God's sake and out of thankfulness toward him [183 *sqq*]. The thought of the moral freedom of the will is, now, thoroughly, carefully, and very emphatically developed by Melanchthon, and an attempt made to establish it by Scripture (in harmony with *Loci*, iv, edition of 1559). Man as man, and hence even unredeemed man, has in the moral sphere a free discretion to prefer morality to crime, to perform outward moral works and to preserve discipline, and it is God's will that such discipline and order be freely preserved—not merely from fear, but also for conscience' sake. Indeed, genuine God-fearing, right trust and right love to God, steadfastness in confession, and hence, in fact, all the truly God-pleasing spiritual virtues, are impossible without the assistance of the Holy Spirit; in this assistance, however, man is not purely inactive like a statue, but reason must attentively lay hold on the Word of God, and the will must not resist, but must yield to the gracious workings of the Holy Spirit, and aspire after divine support. Absolute predestination and Stoic fatality are equally to be rejected. The passions—by which Melanchthon understands both the impulses of feeling and the desires—are not to be suppressed as irrational, as the Stoics teach, but are to be taken into the service of the moral reason, and those that have become evil by sin are to be resisted [201–207].—The distribution of the virtues is best made according to the Decalogue. But the commands of the first table cannot be adequately known in a purely philosophical manner; nevertheless, some points may be made. Every effect is dependent on its cause, and must remain in harmony therewith; man is an effect of God, consequently he ought to remain in harmony with God, and not break off the bond that unites him with God. Moreover, as the image of God, man has the duty of remaining in likeness and harmony with God [214, 215]. In the commandments of the second

table appears, first, the virtue of justness, and in fact primarily in a general character, in the relation of those who guide and those who are guided, in which relation obedience to parents and to the magistracy, and piety in general, appear as a moral law of nature. Justness in its special form—that which gives to every one his dues—appears in the three following commandments, which require the preserving of every one in his rights, in respect to life, to wedlock-fidelity and to property. The second chief virtue, as expressed in the eighth commandment, is truthfulness, which is a necessary requirement of the rational nature of man; for in fact reason consists essentially in a knowledge of the truth, and consequently it also requires the truth. The two last commandments enjoin temperateness, but they are not developed in detail. To these three chief virtues the others are joined as branches, namely, steadfastness to truthfulness, and thankfulness, beneficence, diligence, etc., to justness, especially justness toward God [215–222].—In his second book, Melanchthon gives a development of the virtue of justness in detail, with the omission of the other virtues. Justness, or righteousness in the evangelical sense—the virtue which acquires for man eternal salvation—cannot be attained to by mere human effort because of the prevalence of sin, but is imparted to man by grace in virtue of redemption; in moral philosophy the question is therefore only as to the justness which consists in the outward fulfilling of positive laws. This justness is, in part, of a general character, consisting in obedience to law both human and divine [as in Rom. ii, 13; Psa. cxix, 121], and in part of a special character; the latter is, in its turn, of a distributive and of an exchanging character; as distributive it relates to social order, as well to social superordination and subordination as to the calling of the proper persons to particular offices, and to rewarding and punishing, and hence, in general, to the upholding of proper discipline,—as exchanging it relates to the moral intercourse and commerce of men among each other as equals. The practice of justness, and hence also obedience toward those holding office and authority, takes place not merely in virtue of human laws, but also in the fulfilling of the divine will; the proper human ordinances of society are God's ordinances. A violation of the law of nature, and hence also disobedience toward the legit-

imate ordinances of civil authority, is consequently not merely
a civil misdemeanor, but also a sin against God, a mortal sin.
The ordinances of the natural law are in part unconditional,
and hence divine and perpetually-valid commands, such as
obedience toward God, parental duties, the virtue of truthfulness; and, in part, only conditionally-valid, such as the
keeping of peace and the communistic use of property; the
latter feature, in fact, would be obligatory only on condition
that mankind were not corrupted by sin; in consequence of
sin, however, the forcible protection and distinct separation
of property become necessary [222–234]. The guilt of transgressions of the law is different according as the person does
or does not act with a clear consciousness of the law and of
the deed; guiltily-incurred error excuses not the deed, but
rather heightens the guilt, inasmuch as it is our duty to seek
after the truth. Also violent passions do not make the un-
lawful action an involuntary one, for man may and ought to
control his passions [237–240].—Hereupon, and *apropos* to
the assumption of power on the part of the Pope over secular governments, Melanchthon treats of the nature of, and
the difference between, the spiritual and the temporal powers, in essential agreement with what he had said in his
Loci [20, 21]; this is followed by disquisitions on questions
of civil right, on taxes and contracts.

In his *Loci* Melanchthon gives the general bases of the moral
consciousness in strictly Biblical form [*Loci* 3–6; 8–11]. The
Old Testament law is not identical with the eternal moral law,
but contains besides this law (which is indeed not fully included
in the Decalogue, but only indicated in its chief features) also
the ceremonial and the civil law, both of which had validity
only until the advent of Christianity. The moral law is the
immediate and pure expression of the divine wisdom and justness themselves, and hence was not first given by Moses, but
was always valid from the very beginning. Melanchthon's somewhat extensive examination of the several divine laws in the
order of the Decalogue, may serve in many respects to complement his philosophical ethics. He writes, here, free from the
cramping fetters of the long-observed schemata, and reckons
among the "works" of the first commandment: a proper knowledge of God, God-fearing, faith, love, hope, patience, and hu-

mility. The Romish doctrine of the counsels he refutes and rejects. The distinction between mortal and venial sins he indeed retains, but he conceives it much more deeply,—understanding under the latter such sins as are committed by Christians without evil intention and with inner resistance to the evil, and are followed by honest repentance, and under the latter those which are committed premeditatedly and against conscience [*Loc.*, 11]. In addition to this, Melanchthon examines in special treaties and letters many particular, and especially practico-moral, questions,* in a very judicious manner.

In his scientific conception of the ethical task, Melanchthon furnishes an essential complement to that of Luther, who fixed his attention simply on the fact of the moral life of the regenerated as such, without shaping the development of this fact out of the inner heart of the Christian life, into an ethical science. Melanchthon himself, however, did not complete this task, but simply began it; and although we find in him frequently a slight over-estimation of Aristotle, still we perceive in the vigorous manner in which, in his last ethical writings, he breaks loose from all cramping and foreign forms and thoughts, and lays an entirely new, purely Christian foundation, how clearly he comprehended his task,—the carrying-out of which was delayed by the soon-following inner struggles of the evangelical church; only a few writers—*Chytræus,* Victorin *Strigel* and Nicholas *Hemming*—followed, in, as yet, feeble attempts, upon the path marked out by Melanchthon.†

The rigid predestinarianism of *Calvin* seems at first thought still more unfavorable for the development of ethics than the stand-point of Luther; in reality, however, the Reformed church developed an independent system of ethics earlier than the Lutheran. The juridically-dialectic ground-character of the Calvinistic world-conception necessarily led sooner than the more mystically-inclined subjective Lutheran view, to a rigorous development of the practical phase of religion. In his *Institutio* [iii, 6–10] Calvin gives a short, plainly-biblical presentation of the bases of Christian morality,—which, of course, can be actually practiced only by the predestinated, but which

---

* *De conjugio; quæstiones aliquot ethicæ, de juramentis,* etc., 1552; in *Corp. Ref.,* xvi, 453 *sqq. Consilia s. judicia theol.,* ed. Pezellii. 1660.

† J. C. E. Schwarz in *Stud. u. Krit.,* 1853; Pelt., ib., 1848.

is however for them, as being called to purity, an unconditional duty. That virtue cannot actually obtain for us salvation—communion with God—but is simply the necessary fruit of the salvation already obtained by grace, and the constant bond of this communion as established by grace, Calvin affirms very definitely. Therein, precisely, consists, in his view, the essential superiority of Christian to philosophical ethics, namely, that the former gives much deeper-reaching motives for the good than the latter, to wit, thankful love in return for God's love as revealed in redemption, and confiding love to the Redeemer, in whom we have at the same time the perfect personal pattern of the moral life. Out of this love to God in Christ flows a love of justness or righteousness (in the Biblical sense of the word) as the basis of the entire religious life. But the essence of Christian righteousness consists in perfect *self-denial*, that is, in the renunciation of all self-will and self-reason as opposed to God,—in an unreserved surrender to God and his will; it draws us away from love to the world, but must not sink into self-mortification and false asceticism. Man must not, by arbitrary non-Scriptural ordinances, impose upon himself a yoke. The moral life manifests itself [according to Titus ii, 12] in three chief virtues: soberness, righteousness and piety; to the first (*sobrietas*), which relates to the subject himself, belong also chastity, temperateness and the enduring of privation; the second relates to other men, and gives to each his dues; the third separates us from the impurity of the world and unites us with God.—Calvin gives expression, on the whole, also in his other numerous moral essays, especially in his exegetical writings, to a moral view which is no less earnest than sound, and generally keeps clear of all un-Biblical austerity. To the Romish seeking of holiness by abnegation, he opposes the thought, that the goods of this world are designed not merely for our absolute wants, but also for our moral delight; their enjoyment is not forbidden, but it should be made to contribute to the glory of God. The strict church discipline established and exercised by Calvin was indeed an offense to a gainsaying world, but was morally perfectly justifiable. His unevangelical view of the right of capital punishment against heretics, belongs less to the sphere of ethics proper than to that of civil right.

In all essential points the ethical systems of the Reformed

and of the Lutheran churches are in harmony; there is manifest
throughout, however, a general characterizing difference in the
coloring given to the otherwise essentially harmonizing forms;
this difference we cannot here follow into its finer shades; * a
few of the more general traits will suffice. The ethics of the
Lutheran church bears predominantly an anthropologico-sub-
jective character, that of the Reformed a theologico-objective
character; the former proceeds from the inner life-source of the
regenerated heart, and constructs, therefore, only hesitatingly
an ethical system proper,—as, in some degree, superfluous; the
latter sets out from the unconditional will of God to man, and
hence felt much earlier the need of a scientific expression of the
moral law, objective to the consciousness; the former wears
rather a Paulino-free stamp, the latter rather an Old Testament
stamp; in the Reformed church sermons on morals have a much
more prominent place than in the Lutheran. Lutheran ethics
expresses, also in its christology, the transfiguration of the human through indwelling grace, Reformed ethics, rather the
glorifying of God in and through the elect. With both, the
goal of morality is the glory of God,—in the Lutheran church,
however, more through the witness of the salvation-experience
of the redeemed, in the Reformed, more through the offering
of willing obedience under the law; in the former predominates
rather the manifestation of the filial relation, in the latter,
rather that of submissive service; in the former there is greater
freedom in the self-determination of the believing subject, even
to the danger of Antinomianism, in the latter greater rigor of
outward discipline, incurring danger of Puritanic rigorism and
pedantic externality. The moral life of the Lutheran church
bears, so to speak, a lyric character, that of the Reformed a
practico-juridical one; hence the former expressed itself, naturally enough, in the sublimest soaring of church hymnology,
the latter crystallized itself into a sharply-defined and regular
church discipline; in the former predominates the mystical
heart-element of union with God, in the latter predominates a
rational contrasting of God and man. In the former all that is
natural is ethically exalted and taken into the service of the

---

* Comp. Schneckenburger: *Vergleichende Darstellung des luth. u. ref.
Lehrbegriffs*, 1855; Tholuck: *Das kirchl. Leben des .7 Jahrh.*, i, 199 *sqq.*,
218 *sqq.*, 301 *sqq.*; ii, 140 *sqq.*, 239 *sqq.*

holy; whereas, in the latter, the spiritual is exalted by being divested of the natural. The morality of the Lutheran church develops itself rather from the fullness of inner life toward knowledge, that of the Reformed rather from knowledge toward life-fullness; the former is more immediate, natural and unconscious, the latter is more mediate, calculating, doctrinary; the former is directed more inwardly, the latter more outwardly; the former is more an outgush out of the deep and overflowing feeling of love and bliss, the latter, more an intentional act of the earnest but calm will,—as also, in the Lutheran view of salvation, the attention is fixed more upon the all-embracing love of God, and in the Reformed more upon the decrees of the will of God; Mary and Martha are types of the respective ethical tendencies. The Lutheran Christian does good works *because* he is certain of his salvation through faith; the Reformed does them *in order that* he may become certain of his saving faith, and hence of his election,—good works are to him necessary unto salvation, though not its cause. The Lutheran needs the law and its discipline, strictly speaking, only in so far as he has as yet in himself sinful elements which need to be taken into discipline; but to the Reformed, the law is a real and necessary guide for the regenerated heart itself. Hence, to the Reformed, the Gospel wears essentially also the character of law in the Old Testament sense, and the Old Testament law is taken literally as yet binding,—hence the rigid observance of the Sabbath and the prohibition of statues and pictures. In the Lutheran catechism the ten commandments precede the confession of faith; in most of the Reformed churches they stand after the same, and constitute, in the French and English service, an essential part of the liturgy. This seemingly insignificant circumstance is in fact very significant; in the Lutheran view the law has essentially the purpose of educating toward the true freedom of the children of God, which freedom itself, when once attained to, has no longer any need of an outward law; in the Reformed view the law is an essential part of the Christian faith-life itself, but an objective, purely-divine element still external to the regenerated subject. The Lutheran is fearful rather of work-holiness, the Reformed rather of non-conformity to the law; the former

has the law rather as his inward personal property, the latter rather as a categorical imperative external to his own subjective will. To the Lutheran, Moses and Christ stand in sharp contrast to each other; to the Reformed they are most intimately united; "one must live as if there were no Gospel, and die as if there were no law," says, very significantly, the Reformed divine Baile (*Praxis pietatis*, 1635). To the Lutheran, Christ is, in ethical respects, rather the beloved Saviour, out of love to whom and in communion with whom he lives in holiness; to the Reformed he is more the moral pattern by which man is constantly learning, and which he endeavors to imitate. Hence Lutheran ethics appears predominantly as the doctrine of virtue and of goods, Reformed ethics as the doctrine of the law. The Lutheran Christian conceives the good essentially as the morally-*beautiful*, and hence he has also appreciation and love for the beautiful in general,—gives expression to art, and makes it even a moral agency; the Reformed conceives the good essentially as the *right*, and hence he has little taste or love for art as a moral power, but all the higher an appreciation for the legally-disciplined development of the church and of moral society; to the former the highest virtue is believing love; to the latter, righteousness. The moral consciousness of the Lutheran conceives the highest good rather as a power directly given by grace and reflecting from itself the moral life; the Reformed consciousness makes the moral life an essential factor in the obtaining of the highest good. Hence, in the ethical sphere, the antithesis of the Lutheran doctrine to the Romish is more violent than that of the Reformed; hence also the Reformed church, but not the Lutheran, developed a theocratical form of the church, and placed in general much greater emphasis on the legal and governmental development of the purely moral community of the church as in contrast to the state, and as a determining power for and over the same, whereas the subjective inwardliness of Lutheran Christians manifested little interest for such development. Such are the differences which, while they indeed manifest a general ethical antithesis of the two forms of doctrine, yet in fact constitute only two corresponding and manifoldly-complementing, but not mutually-ex-

cluding phases of the same unitary evangelical consciousness.

The theological ethics of the evangelical church was treated as a separate science,* first by the learned Reformed divine *Danæus* (Daneau, *ob.* 1596) in his *Ethica christiana* (1577, '79, '88 and 1601),—in a rigidly Calvinistic sense, with a large using of Augustine, Aristotle, and the Schoolmen, in strong opposition, however, sometimes to the two latter sources, resulting in a learned and thoughtful work, though as yet somewhat immature. He endeavors especially to solve the apparent contradiction between the doctrine of predestination and the requirements of the moral consciousness, though not with very happy results; the special treatment of duties he bases on the Decalogue; in respect to Church-discipline he requires the greatest rigor,—for heretics, capital punishment. (In connection with this ethics stands his *Politica christiana*, 1596–1606). The antithesis which Danæus makes between Christian ethics and Aristotelian philosophical ethics, was rejected by *Keckermann* (*ob.* 1609 in Heidelberg), who considered ethics as essentially a philosophical science, and Aristotle as its true founder;† while the severely Puritanical *Amesius* (in Holland, *ob.* 1634) emphasized again very strongly the distinction of Christian from philosophical ethics, placing Christian ethics along-side of dogmatics.‡ (The distinguishing of ethics and dogmatics as the two parts of the body of Christian doctrine, appears also in the Reformed divine, *Polanus* of Basle.)§ *Walæus* (in Holland, *ob.* 1639) attempted in his compendium of the ethics of Aristotle (1620) to imbue this work with a Christian spirit. More important, despite its rather popular style, is the peculiar work of the moderate Calvinist *Amyraud* (Amyraldus, at Saumur, *ob.* 1664).‖ He distributes ethics historically, into the ethics of the pure unfallen state, into that of heathenism, and of

---

* On the history of the earlier Reformed ethics, see Schweizer in *Stud. u. Krit.*, 1850.

† *Systema ethicæ* in his *Opp.*, 1614.

‡ *Medulla theologiæ*, 1630, and frequently, a brief compendium; *De conscientiæ et ej. jure vel casibus*, 1630, and subsequently,—casuistical.

§ *Syntagma theol.*, 1610.

‖ *La morale chrestienne*, 1652 *sqq.*, 6 t.,—rare in Germany; see Stäudlin iv, 404 *sqq.;* Schweizer in *Stud. u. Krit.*, 1683.

Judaism and of Christianity; the first part contains the general philosophical considerations. The historical treatment of the subject gives a just appreciation also of heathen ethics, without intermingling Christian ethics therewith.— The ethics of the Reformed church was casuistically treated by the Puritan *Perkins* (of Cambridge, 1611), also by the above-mentioned Amesius, and by the German *Alsted* (1621, 1630), who distributed the subject-matter according to the chief heads of the Catechism. Also *Forbesius à Corse* treated the subject in the order of the Decalogue, in his learned though quite practically-written work on moral theology, considered as the special doctrine of duties.* Ethics was treated in a popular, edifying manner by La Placette, Pictet, Basnage, and by the Englishman Richard *Baxter*. The scientific and purely theological form of Reformed ethics was still further developed, in the eighteenth century, by Hoornbeek (1663), by Peter of Mastricht (1699), who follows Amesius, by Heidegger (1711), by Lampe (1727), and by others. In the middle of the eighteenth century the rigid form of Calvinistic ethics begins to give way, and the influence of the philosophy of Wolf commences to break down the confessional antithesis in the field of morals.

In the Lutheran church there was at first but little done beyond the already-mentioned further developments of the philosophical ethics of Melanchthon, with the exception of a single, though not purely theological, attempt of the Melanchthonian Hamburger, *Von Eitzen :*† theology is so involved in dogmatical controversies as to have in general but little inclination toward a scientific development of ethics; it treated the weightier and more general questions only briefly, in dogmatics, in connection with the doctrines of free-will, of sin, of the law, and of sanctification, leaving the more detailed treatment of the subject rather for such practical writers as worked toward the Christian edification of the masses,—writers who were in some respects related to the Mystics, and among whom two deserve especial attention. The first of these, John Valentine *Andreæ*, of Wurtemberg (*ob.* 1654), is a very morally-earnest spirit, thoroughly devoted to practical Christianity, of slightly mystical tenden-

---

* *Opp.*, Amst., 1703.   † Comp. Pelt in *Stud.* u. *Krit.*, 1848.

cies, of thorough scientific culture, and of deep acquaintance with human nature. Strongly impressed with the Calvinistic church discipline in Geneva, Andreæ devoted his unwearying efforts to the bringing about of moral discipline also in the German church, though he found a rather unreceptive age, and was much deceived in his, at times, somewhat idealistic hopes. His numerous moral writings,—often clothed in poetical and especially allegorical forms, and sometimes satirical, though always hiding, even in hilarity, a very deep and often melancholy earnestness,—are always directed to definite special objects, and hence present no connected whole. Holding fast to the faith of the church, he yet rebuked indignantly the unfruitful hair-splitting spirit of dogmatic controversy, and insisted on the one thing needful; at the same time, it is true, he occasionally too lightly esteemed man's scientific right to a clear knowledge of the contents of faith, as well as the significancy of the doctrinal differences between the churches; and, in his desire for a moral reformation of the church, he too little considered the importance of pure doctrine, and was too indulgent toward many opposers of the same.—The second, John *Arndt*, (*ob.* 1621), was spiritually kindred to Andreæ and held him in high esteem; Arndt was an evangelical Thomas à Kempis, and combined evangelical fidelity of faith with mystical subjectivity and practical zeal for morality, and exerted a deep-reaching, beneficent influence on the evangelical churches. His work entitled *Four Books of True Christianity* (at first in 1605–10)—with the exception of the *Imitation of Christ,* the most widespread of German books of devotion—bears indeed sometimes a rather strong mystical coloring (in this respect following somewhat in the path of Tauler and of the "German Theology"), and under-estimates, in many respects, the significancy of the objective means of grace, and lays chief emphasis on the mystical, direct union of the soul with God; nevertheless it constituted so essential and so salutary a complementing of the somewhat one-sidedly theorizing theological spirit of the age, and so powerfully stirred up the partially-dormant moral consciousness, that Arndt will always occupy an eminent place in the history of morality and of practical ethics.

A *per se* unimportant and yet fruitful attempt at a purely

theological system of ethics, unconnected with dogmatics, was made by George *Calixt* of Helmstädt; his *Epitome theologiæ moralis* (p. I, 1634; 1662,) is only a short, incomplete outline, giving in fact only an introduction. The purpose of ethics is, to describe the way to blessedness, the life of the already spiritually-regenerated Christian; regeneration itself is presupposed; the foundation, even of Christian morality, is the ten commandments, which are a revealed re-establishment of the original law of nature; but the difference of Christian ethics from Old Testament ethics is not made prominent enough. In the footsteps of Calixt followed J. C. *Dürr* of Altdorf, who, for the first, gave a tolerably complete and learned treatise on ethics;* he distinguishes between virtues toward God, toward others, and toward ourselves; in regard to theatrical spectacles, to jesting, etc., he shows a less rigid severity than the ethical writers of the Reformed church; and this difference of view is manifest also among the other Lutheran moralists, if we except the Pietists. Of the same tendency was also G. T. Meier, of Helmstädt, whose erudite and profound introduction to ethics† examines, for the first time, with critical discrimination the presuppositions of this science. (*H. Rixner*, in a briefer work in 1690.) Aristotle is used also in these theological treatises on ethics, without, however, damagingly influencing their theological character.

The ethics of the Lutheran church was treated more frequently casuistically than in a systematic form; it bore this character even as late as into the eighteenth century, and forms, properly speaking, only an amassment of material for a subsequent scientific development. As occasioned by the casuistry of the Romish church, the casuistry of the evangelical church, in express antithesis thereto, manifests, on the basis of Scripture and of spiritual experience, a greater certainty and simplicity, and preserves a middle-ground between the sophistical laxity of the Jesuitical view and the rigid severity of the Calvinistic. Many of these works contain also many dogmatic questions together with their decisions. The distribution of the subject-matter follows, for the

---

* *Enchiridion theol. mor.*, 1662; later as: Compend., 1675–98 4to.

† *Introd. in univ. theol. mor. studium*, 1671, And as the beginning of a development of ethics itself: *Disputt. theol.*, 1679,

most part, the order of the catechism; the answer is given on the basis of the Scriptures, and then confirmed by the decisions of the Fathers and of later writers, especially of Luther and of the other Reformers. The first work of this kind, after the already-mentioned *Consilia* of Melanchthon, is by *Baldwin* of Wittenberg,* and obtained great popularity; it treats chiefly of the *casus conscientiæ*, that is, of such moral questions as the common conscience cannot immediately and satisfactorily decide, but in regard to which it may fall into doubt, and which consequently can be decided only by a careful weighing of the word of God. He classifies these cases according to the moral objects: God, angels, the subject himself, and other men. (L. Dunte of Reval, gave a thousand and six decisions on conscience-questions of a moral and dogmatical character, in 1643.) *Olearius* of Leipzig, who had already previously presented ethics in tabular form, examined thoroughly, and with the most minute and discriminating exactness, the purpose and the nature of casuistry;† casuistry was more fully carried out by Dannhauer,‡ by G. König,§ but especially circumstantially by John Adam *Osiander*,‖ who introduces into the subject almost the entire body of dogmatics; he classifies the cases in the order of the Decalogue; under the sixth commandment, *e. g.*, he proposes the question whether in a case of extreme necessity it is allowable to eat human flesh, and, in opposition to the Jesuits, negatives it (ii, p. 1367). The work of *Mengering* (superintendent in Halle) *Scrutinium conscientiæ catecheticum*, that is, a "Reproving of Sin and Searching of the Conscience," etc. (3 ed. 1686, 4to.), more especially intended for moral self-examination, is classified minutely and circumstantially according to the Decalogue, and is morally earnest and judicious, though it presents also a few peculiarities (*e. g.*, p. 752, as to the inadmissibility of tobacco-smoking, then called tobacco-drinking). Only in part, belongs in this place the voluminous work: *Consilia theologica Witebergensia*, that is,

* *Tractatus luculentus*, etc., 1628, '35, and later.

† *Introd. brevis in theol. casuisticam*, 1694.

‡ *Liber conscientiæ*, 2 ed. 1679, 2 t., and *Theologia casualis*, 1706.

§ *Casus consc.*, Altdorf, 1676, 4to.

‖ *Theol. casualis*, 1680, 6 t., 4to.

"Wittenberg's Spiritual Counsels," etc.—(Frankfort on the Main, 1664)—which contains, in an immense folio, judgments of Luther and of his co-laborers, and decisions of the Wittenberg faculty on doctrinal points, moral and ecclesiastico-legal questions (also matrimonial questions). Of a similar character is the *Opus novum quæstionum Practico-Theologicum* (Frankfort, 1667, fol.), which treats, in the order of the common *Loci*, sixteen hundred and sixty-seven questions, —also that of *Dedekenn : Thesaurus consiliorum theol. et jurid.* (1623), revised by John C. Gerhard (Jena, 1671, 4 vols. fol.).

Also the theological "Bedenken" of the eighteenth century belong to the sphere of this casuistical ethics. Among these works those of Spener occupy a peculiar and significant place, and constitute, together with his other more or less ethical writings, a turning-point in the development of the evangelical moral consciousness. Their significancy rests less in their single judgments than in their peculiar ground-thoughts. *Spener*, —who was imbued with the spirit of Thomas à Kempis, of Andreæ and of Arndt, and in part, even of Tauler, and who restlessly labored in the path trod by these men for a moral bettering of the Christian church,—called forth by the *Pietism* which proceeded from him, a deep-reaching, beneficent movement in the moral life and in the moral views of the evangelical church, although indeed in consequence of his one-sided emphasizing of the practical, he treated science itself somewhat too lightly, and set too high an estimate on certain outward forms of devout morality, and thus needlessly limited the legitimate liberty of a regenerated Christian. Spener's *Pia desideria* * are directed essentially to an improving of the ecclesiastical life, to a stronger emphasizing of holiness in the spiritual activity of the church, to a stirring-up of the church-membership to churchly spontaneity, to the bringing about of a more edifying manner of doctrinal preaching, and, on the other hand, against the misuse of the doctrine of justification by faith. His ethical works proper, though only bearing on particular cases, especially of the inner life, are found in his *Theo-*

* Appearing first in 1675 as a preface to Arndt's *Postille*, afterward separately,—often printed.

*logical Considerations,** which exercised a wide-reaching and wholesome influence on the church.—Spener insisted with much more earnestness on the significancy of spiritual regeneration for the moral life than did the orthodoxy of the day, in its one-sided emphasizing of theoretical faith. The man of the Holy Spirit has nothing in common with the sinful world and its lusts; his total life-stream flows from a new and absolutely holy fountain; worldly pleasure is foreign and uncongenial to him, and therefore to be avoided. The morality of the Pietists was distinguished primarily by an especial rigor in regard to the sphere of the allowed, inasmuch as it viewed as absolutely unallowable many worldly enjoyments which in the Evangelical Lutheran church had, thus far, been regarded (too unsuspiciously, it is true) as *adiaphora*, and consequently as not strictly unallowable, especially such as dancing, card-playing, theater-visiting, banqueting, gayness of dress, and the like; it denied altogether that there are any morally indifferent things; whatever is not done to the glory of God, and springs not of faith, is sin; and these amusements cannot consist with a pious frame of the heart,—cannot take place in faith, and to the glory of God. This is, however, only an outer manifestation of a very deep-reaching antithesis of Pietism to the hitherto prevalent views of the Lutheran church. The high evangelical thought of Gospel-freedom and of justification by faith alone, had in fact, in the time of the declining church-life, led, in many respects, to erroneous courses, and had often allowed the moral earnestness of holiness to give place to mere formal orthodoxy, and also sometimes occasioned, in contrast to the severe earnestness of the discipline of the Reformed church, too careless a regard for the outward forms of the moral life, and had enlarged beyond measure the sphere of morally-indifferent things. The notion had obtained for itself vogue, that whatever is not forbidden in Scripture is allowable. It was the reaction of a truly Christian conscience, which caused Pietism to discard this somewhat presuming maxim, and, in any case, the thought which it opposed thereto was strictly legitimate, namely, that there is nothing indifferent in the entire life-sphere of a regen-

* *Theologische Bedenken*, 1700, 1712, 4 vols.; *Letzte theol. Bedenken*, 1711, 3 vols.; *Consilia et judicia theol.*, 1709, 3 vols., and many other smaller works.

erated person, but that every thing without exception must stand in living relation to the new spiritual life-principle, and that whatever does not admit of a true association with the same is not simply indifferent, but is un-Christian. Pietism may have made many mistakes in the application of this thought, but the thought itself had, as in contrast to the one-sided orthodoxy then prevalent, its own good right. Furthermore, Spener brought again into the fore-ground the thought which, while indeed dogmatically admitted, had yet never been sufficiently emphasized morally, namely, that faith without works is dead; the sanctification of the heart and life does not simply follow upon, and stand in connection with, true faith, but is in such faith already itself directly contained; there are not two spiritual life-streams, but only *one;* the moral personality itself as justified by faith admits of no falling apart of faith and morality; all religious life is immediately and necessarily at the same time moral,—is not simply followed by the moral as a second collateral element. In the eyes of declining orthodoxy, religion had become too much a mere objective something by which the religious subject is simply embraced and influenced, but not thoroughly permeated; Pietism brought religion and its divine spirit-principle again entirely within the Christian subject, and caused the subject, as now transformed, to create a new Spirit-witnessing, objective morality. The Christian conscience is quickened and made more vigorously active by Pietism; the views thus far prevalent in the Lutheran church are, in the eyes of Pietism, not strictly conscientious, seeing that they tolerate many manners of action which do not flow from the Christian conscience, and are not consistent with it.— The morality of Pietism is by no means of a predominantly outwardly-active working character,—is in fact very different from the more recent activity of the "inner mission," but is predominantly subjective,—is one-sidedly directed toward the morally-pious heart-condition of the subject, and sustains to the outer world rather a rejecting, negating and uninterested relation; the ascetic tendency which constantly grew more prominent, especially among Spener's followers, rose even to a manifest preference of celibacy to marriage, and to an avoidance of political offices (in the spirit of Tertullian), and to a refusing of military service. When its orthodox opponents re-

proached Pietism with an unevangelical seeking of sanctification by works, with a tendency to the monkish spirit and the
like, they did not do it full justice; and it was in vain that
they undertook to check the historically-justified movement,
and, notwithstanding all their hostile exaggerations, they saw
very clearly the questionable narrownesses of the movement
they opposed—more clearly than they saw their own; and it is
not exclusively through Pietism, but also in virtue of the oppo
sition which it awoke, that the religiously-moral consciousness
of the church was stimulated to a higher life.—The Pietistic
tendency proper, because of its disinclination to abstract science, produced no ethical works of importance; most important are: *Breithaupt: Theol. moralis* (1732, 4to.; *Institt
theol.*, 3 parts, 1716), and the moral parts of Joachin Lange's
Œconomia salutis (1728.) But the popular Pietistic works,
written for the masses of the church, were more influential.

SECTION XXXVIII.

The ethics of the *Roman Catholic* church, after
the Reformation, was treated for the most part as a
constantly increasing and more minute-growing body
of *casuistry*. The highest development of the same,
and at the same time the greatest perversion of Christian ethics, also in regard to its moral contents, appeared in the semi-Pelagianizing ethics of the *Jesuits*.
The place of the unconditional validity of the moral
idea is here largely usurped by outward adaptability
to the weal of the visible church, as the highest end;
the place of the unshaken authority of the Scriptures
and of early Christian tradition, by the authority of
certain special Doctors; the place of moral conviction, by *probabilism;* the place of moral honesty,
by a sophistical construing of the moral law to the
present fortuitous advantage of the church and of the
individual, and by the falsehood of *reservationes
mentales;* and the place of the moral conscience, by

rational and cunning calculation; thus the essence of the moral law becomes entirely unsettled; and the practical application of moral principles, an unserious exercise of sophistry.

At first thought we are surprised at the exceeding fruitfulness of the Romish theology of the sixteenth and seventeenth centuries in ethical writings, in comparison with which the evangelical church, and especially the Lutheran, is very barren. Opposition to the faith-principle of the Evangelical church, led the Romish church to an especial development of the practical phase of religion, as in fact, in the order of the Jesuits, a vigor of activity hitherto unknown in the Romish church makes at this time its appearance; and precisely this order was the chief representative of Romish ethics.—The more purely scientific form of ethics lingered in general strictly within the limits of the scholastico-Aristotelian rut. Francis *Piccolomini*, a much-lauded Aristotelian, in Italy (*ob.* 1604) produced a comprehensive and discursive moral philosophy * based on Aristotle and Plato; but his writings do not give proof of any independence, and fail to satisfy the Christian consciousness.

The *Order of the Jesuits*, as calculated in its very nature for action, for the championship of the endangered Romish church, was called by its fundamental principle to the development of a special system of morality,—a system the highest end of which is the glory of God through the exaltation of the visible church. The majority of the Jesuitical presentations of ethics treat, for the most part, only of the more or less classified circle of single cases, while the more rare systematic works follow very closely the traditions of scholasticism.†—Very soon after the Reformation the Jesuits appeared in the field of ethics; we will mention only the more important. Among the Spaniards were: Francis *Tolet* (a cardinal, *ob.* 1596, *Summa casuum conscientiæ*, often printed); *Azorio* (*Institutiones morales*, 1600, 3t.; 1625, 2t.); *Vasquez* (*Opusc. mor.*, 1617); *Henriquez* (*Summa*, 1613 fol.);

---

* *Universa philosophia moribus*, Venet. 1583; Frkf., 1595, 1627.

† Perrault: *Morale des Jes.*, 1667, 3t.; Ellendorf: *Die Moral und Politik der Jesuiten*, 1840—not sufficiently scientific; *Pragm. Gesch. d. Mönschsorden*, 1770, vols. 9 and 10.

Thomas *Sanchez*, whose learned work, *De matrimonio,** was highly esteemed, (but which, in the invention and discussion of indelicate questions, transgresses the bounds of all propriety), and who by his sweeping doctrine of probabilism deeply unsettles the foundations of all morality; (of him are further: *Opus morale s. Summa casuum*, Col. 1614, 2t.; *Consilia s. opuscula mor.*, Lugd. 1635, 2 fol.); Francis *Suarez*, in numerous very ingenious works; Alphonso *Rodriguez* (*Exercitium perfectionis*, etc., 1641); Antonio de *Escobar*, one of the most important of the casuists (*Liber theol. moral.*, etc., Ludg., 1646; *Universæ theol. moral. problemata*, Ludg., 1663, 7 fol.); and *Gonzales* (*Fundamentum theol. moralis.*, 1694, 4to.) Among the Italians were: *Tamburini*, and *Filliucci* (*Moral. quæst.*, 1622, 2 fol.) Among the French: *Bauny*, and *Raynauld*. Among the Germans: *Layman* (*Theol. mor.*, 1625, 3 4to.); *Busenbaum*, of Munster, whose *Medulla casuum consc.* has had, since 1645, more than fifty editions,†—an able, clear, compact manual in tolerably systematic order, and authoritative almost throughout the whole Order, although in many respects assailed, even by popes, and in some countries proscribed. Among the Netherlanders: Leonard *Less* (in several works), and *Besser* (*De conscientia*, 1638, 4to.) The contents and manner of treatment of most of these works are very similar.

The peculiar character of Jesuitical ethics rests on the fundamental purpose of the order as a whole, namely, the rescuing of the Church, the bride of Christ, as endangered by the Reformation in its very foundations, and hence the rescuing of the honor of God from a most pressing danger. In a struggle of life and death one is not very careful in the choice of means, and in all warfare the sentiment holds good, though involving manifold violations of ordinary right, that the end sanctifies the means. The rescuing of the Romish church at any price is the task, even should it involve an entering into alliance with the dark powers of this sinful world, and with the passions and sinful proclivities of the unsanctified multitude. The one

---

* Genuæ, 1592? 1602; Antv. 1607, 1612, 1614, 1617, 3 fol.; Norimb. 1706; the first edition has become rare; in the later editions, after 1612, the smuttiest passages are omitted or modified.

† Rewritten and enlarged by Lacroix, 1710, 9t., Col. 1729, 2 fol., and frequently.

exclusively aimed-at end makes use of the systematized totality of moral ends as mere means, and the morally-contracted view taken of this one end leads naturally and of itself to morally unallowable means. The real, visible church is not measured by the idea of the true or ideal church, but all moral ideas are measured by the visible church. The Jesuits were well aware that they were an essentially new phenomenon of the churchly life,—that they stood upon purely human invention and power; we need not be surprised therefore to find that in their moral system human invention and human authority stand in the foreground. The expressed opinion of a church doctor forms a sufficient basis for a legitimate moral decision. The eternal and objective foundations of the moral are exchanged for the subjective view of individual persons of eminence. The contradictions thereby resulting render the single subject all the less trammeled,—enable him to follow the decision which he most prefers. Another of their peculiarities is their discipline; the required unconditional obedience to the commands of superiors takes the place of the personal conscience, and paralyzes its power; it becomes a duty of the members of the order to have no personal conscience whatever, and to subordinate the individual conscience unconditionally and blindly to the general conscience of the order; a collective conscience, however, is a poor one, and poorest of all when it is represented by one single person. Thus the Jesuit accustoms himself from the very start, blindly to follow the authority of a single eminent man, and Probabilism is, in his moral theory, an inevitable matter of course.

This, then, is the distinguishing characteristic of Jesuitical ethics,—that in the place of the eternal objective ground and criterion of the moral, it substitutes subjective opinion, and in the place of an unconditional eternal end, a merely conditionally valid one, namely, the defending of the actual, visible church against all forms of opposition,—that in the place of the moral conscience, it substitutes the human calculating of circumstantial and fortuitous adaptation to the promotion of this its highest end,—that it attempts to realize that which is *per se* and absolutely valid by a wide-reaching isolating of the means, but in so doing subordinates morality to the discretion of the single subject.—While the ethics of the Jesuits appears

as lax and quite too indulgent toward worldly, sinful proclivities and fashions, yet this is only one phase of the matter. A merely worldly-lax moral system, in the usual sense, seems but little applicable to the members of a brotherhood the first rule of which is a perfect renunciation of personal will and personal opinion and self-determination, in a word, unconditional obedience to every command of superiors, and which has actually accomplished in the missionary field the grandest of deeds, and numbers, among its members, multitudes of heroic martyrs. This lack of strictness in one direction rests by no means on mere worldliness, on pleasure in the delights of this life, but follows, on the one hand, of necessity (as well as does also the rigor of obedience) from the subjectively-arbitrary presupposition of the entire order, from the lack of an objective, unshaken foundation, and rests, on the other hand, strictly on calculation,—is itself a cunningly-devised means to the end,—is intended to awaken, especially in the great and mighty of the earth (and the masses of the people are such under some circumstances), a love to the church, to the mild, friendly, indulgent mother; and these concessions to the world formed a contrast to the severer moral views of the evangelical church, and especially to the over-rigid discipline of the Reformed church; and the contrast was tempting.—The purpose—zealously pursued by the Jesuits in the interest of Romish domination—of becoming soul-guarding fathers and conscience-counselors, especially for men and women of eminence, required, on the one hand, that the Jesuits themselves should acquire for themselves the highest possible repute in ethics,—and hence it was requisite that they should become the literary representatives thereof,—and, on the other, that this ethics should be molded *in adaptation* to this end,—should make itself not disagreeable and burdensome, but should become as elastic as possible in view of different wants, —should be a "golden net for catching souls," as the Jesuits themselves were wont to call their own pliableness. The more ramified and complex the net-work of casuistic ethics became, so much the more indispensable were the practiced conscience-counselors, or more properly, conscience-advocates; the more stairways and back doors they were able to turn attention to in conscience affairs, so much the more prized and influential they became. This explains the great compass and the peculiar

character of Jesuitical ethics. The becoming accustomed to slippery and precipitous ways, and the pleasure in the ready-finding of sophistical authority for morally novel positions, led of itself unconsciously into still deeper error. "Accommodation" was the magic word which opened the way for a surprisingly-rich storehouse of moral rules. Confession, where made to Jesuits, lost much of its seriousness, and nowhere else was absolution so easily obtainable for those who were to be won over, nowhere penance and satisfaction so readily done with,— and this not merely in fact, but also from principle. Penance is to be chosen as light as possible; the confessor may impose as penance, on the confessing one, the good or evil which he can do or suffer on the same day or in the same week; the penance may, when there exists a sufficient reason, be even performed for one person by another, etc.* Also in most cases it is not a very serious matter even if the absolved one neglects entirely the imposed penance.

The development of Jesuitical ethics is by no means a phenomenon essentially new; the bases therefor were already long extant; it is only a further building upon the same foundations. The Pelagianizing view of the moral ability of the human will and of the meritoriousness of outward works lay already at the basis of the entire system of monkish holiness, and the Jesuits went only one step further when they, in contradiction to Thomas Aquinas, taught often almost entirely as Pelagius. The earlier casuistry in its lack of fixed principles had already shaken the moral foundation; and the too great indulgence in sophistry on particular, and, in part, entirely imaginary, cases, had beclouded the unsophisticated moral consciousness; the doctrine of probabilism had been already sanctioned at Constance, and in many respects practically applied. The entanglement of the church with the then so manifoldly-complicated state of European politics, with worldly passions and rancors, and its very worldly struggles against the worldly state, had already long since undermined the purity of the ecclesiastical conscience, and the maxim, that the end sanctifies the means, had already been long practiced and approved by the church before it was, by the Jesuits (if not sanctioned in express words,

---

* Filliucci: *Moral. quæst., I, tract.* 6 *c.* 7; Escobar: *Liber th., VII,* 4 c. 7 (especially *n.* 181,182), comp. Ellendorf, 263 *sqq.*, 312 *sqq.*

yet in fact on the largest scale) put into practice; the *per se* not incorrect distinguishing of venial from mortal sins offered easy opportunity of indefinitely enlarging the sphere of the former by a limitation or a ready transforming of the sphere of the latter, while at the same time the ever-growing readiness in granting indulgences was making the sphere even of mortal sins of a less terrifying character, especially for those at whose command stood the keys to the treasure-chambers of indulgence; and in fact it was these especially, namely, the rich and noble, who enjoyed the advantages of the generosity of Jesuitic ethics. Jesuitic ethics did not indeed harmonize with the moral consciousness of the ancient church; its representatives were also well aware of this, and they hesitated not to admit that they did not recognize ancient church tradition as a criterion for morality, but wished rather to lay the foundations for a new tradition.

The chief means used for the purpose of lightening moral duty was the so-called *moral probabilism*, namely, the principle that in morally-doubtful cases the authority of a few eminent church-teachers, or also even of a single one (if he is a *doctor gravis et probus*), suffices to furnish a *sententia probabilis* as to a moral course of action, and hence to justify the performing of it, even if the opinion followed were *per se* false; nay, according to some, even if this teacher himself had declared it as only morally possible, without really approving of it. Hence, as soon as I can hunt up for an action which seems to me of doubtful propriety, or even positively wrong, a consenting opinion of an ecclesiastical authority (and of course it is best if I find it among the Jesuit doctors themselves), then am I perfectly screened by the same;* in which connection it is to be taken into account that there is scarcely any one moral question which is not answered by different doctors in an entirely contrary sense. That thus the most opposite manners of action may be equally readily justified, the Jesuits knew very well; and Escobar even found, in the actual variety of views as to the moral, an amazing trace of Divine Providence, inasmuch as thereby the yoke of Christ is in so agreeable a manner rendered

---

* Laymann: *Theol. mor.* 1625, i, p. 9; Escobar: *Liber th.*, *prooem.*, *exam.* 3; Bresser: *De consc.* iii, c. 1 *sq.*, and in almost all the others.

easy.* Although probabilism was not so immoderately extended by all the Jesuits, nevertheless it was the decidedly dominant teaching; and when the general of the order, Gonzales, in 1694, disapproved of it, many were minded to regard him as thereby deposed because of heresy, and only the protection of the Pope saved him.†

Probabilism is not a merely fortuitously discovered expedient, but it is in fact an almost inevitable consequence of the historical essence of Jesuitism. As the order itself arose neither on the basis of Scripture nor of ancient church-tradition, but sprang absolutely from the daring inventive power of a single man breaking through the limits of ecclesiastical actuality, hence it is not at all unnatural that it should make the authority of a single spiritually preëminent man its highest determining power, and subordinate to this the historical, objective form of the moral consciousness. When the learned moralists came to be regarded as the determining authority in morals, then the Jesuits were the masters of the world, for they were themselves the most excellent doctors. Though they absolved the inquirer from so many burdensome chains of commanding duty, though they led him in the selection between opposed authorities to a subjective discretion of decision, yet at least this point was reached, that he recognized the Jesuit priests as his liberating masters. The doctrine of probabilism can by no means be explained as a simple sequence of the Romish tradition-principle; for here the deciding element is not the authority of the church, but simply individual teachers and in fact not, the majority of authorities, but it is expressly permitted to follow ‡ the lesser authority in face of the greater, and to select among several authorities the one which best pleases, even if it be the less probable one.§ Hence also the father-confessor is not at liberty, as against the probable opinions of those who confess to him, to appeal to other and higher authorities, but he must admit the former

* *Quia ex opinionum varietate jugum Christi suavita sustinetur* (*Univ. theol. mor.*, t. i, *lib.* 2, 1, c. 2 in Crome, **x**, 182.)

† Wolf: *Gesch. d. Jesuit.*, 1, 173.

‡ Escobar: *Th. mor.*, *proœm.*, iii, n. 9, and many others.

§ Sanchez: *Op. mor.*, i, 9, n. 12 *sqq.*, n. 24.

even should he hold them for entirely false,* and a doctor, when asked for moral advice needs not to impart the same exclusively according to his own judgment, but may also suggest the judgment of another though contradictory to his own, in case it is more favorable to, or more desired by, the inquirer (*si forte hæc illi favorabilior seu exoptatior sit*)*;* hence he may give to different persons a directly contrary answer to the same question, "only he must in this matter use discretion and prudence." † Many go so far as to maintain that I not only need not follow the opinion most probable to me, but that I may even follow that one of which I hold only that it is probable that it may be probable (Tamburini).—But how is the doctrine of probability to be reconciled with the Catholic doctrine that the assent of the church is necessary in order that any course of action may be ecclesiastically valid? *Bauny* gives the answer: All that doctors teach in printed books has, in fact, the assent and approval of the church, provided that the church has not expressly declared it as invalid.

Though probabilism *per se*, as a mere formal principle, endangers morality in a high degree, substituting in the place of the moral conscience individual and arbitrary authority, and rocking the soul into false security, still it were possible that the danger of this principle should not actually realize itself, in that it might be presupposed that the theological authorities would, in all essential moral thoughts, harmonize with each other and with the Scriptures, and would show some difference only in regard to more external, unimportant questions. In this case the erroneousness of the formal principle would in some measure be remedied by the correctness of the material contents. The question rises therefore: What do the doctors who are presented as moral oracles, positively teach as to the moral?

One would be largely deceived were one to expect to find in the moral writings in question merely the loose world-morality of moral indifference, selfishness, and pleasure-seeking; on the contrary, they often present anxiously, minute

---

* Escobar: *Th. mor. prooem.*, iii, n. 27; Laymann, i, p. 12; so also Diana: *Resol. mor.*, ii, *tract.*, 13,11 *sqq.*, Antv., 1637; *Summa*, 1652, p. 216.

† Laymann, i, p. 11.

and strict prescriptions, especially in churchly relations, so that the evangelical liberty of a Christian man would feel itself thereby in many respects largely cramped. One must here distinguish, however, between the ordinary popular morality—as it were, for home use, and indeed also for show—and the higher morality which relates to the fundamental purposes of the Jesuit order, that is, to the furtherance of the Romish church, and which is chiefly practiced by the great, in church and state, and hence also by the Jesuits themselves.—To the semi-Pelagianizing explaining-away of the sinful corruption of human nature, corresponds, on the other hand, a lowering of the moral requirements made of man; for the natural man, downy cushions are spread. We are not obligated to *love* God throughout our whole life, in the full sense of the word, nor even every five years, but more especially only toward the close of life.* In fact, the French Jesuit *Sirmond* denies the obligation of love to God on the whole; it is sufficient if we fulfill the other commandments and do not hate God;† and he found in his Order warm concurrence. So also is the love of neighbor, and especially of enemies, lowered to a degree corresponding to anti-Christian, heathen ways of thinking. And even the duties of children are placed lower than is the case among the Chinese. The fourth commandment is fulfilled by the fact that one shows due honor to his parents, though without loving them; for love is not required in the commandment. To be ashamed of one's parents, to banish them from one's presence, to treat them as strangers and the like, is not a severe sin; but, on the contrary, it is allowable for the son to accuse his father of heresy before the Inquisition (Busenbaum), and according to a majority of the Jesuits, as also in the opinion of Diana, he is obligated thereto; and the same holds true of brothers and sisters, and of consorts.‡ Some of them declare it even as allowable that a son should wish his father's death, or should rejoice at the occurrence of his death, because he has now the happiness of coming into his inheritance (Tamburini, Vasquez), or that a mother should wish the death of her daughter, in case the latter is ugly (Azorius). Malignant

* Escobar: i, 2, n. 7 *sqq. ;* v, 4, n. 1 *sqq.*   † *Defensio virtutis,* i, 1.
‡ Diana: *Resol. mor.* i, *tract.,* 4, 4, 5.

revenge is indeed forbidden, but not the taking revenge in vindication of one's honor.

In respect to moral imputation and condemnation, most of the teachers make—in view of rendering moral desert easy—the remarkable distinction, that the action answering to the divine law is good and meritorious as such, without it being requisite thereto that the intention should be good; and that, on the contrary, sin exists only where there is really an intention of sinning. Hence if the intention is a good one, that is, pro-motive of the weal of the church, then the act which serves to its carrying-out cannot be sinful; and there can be a mortal sin only where the person in the moment of the act had the definite intention of doing evil, and a perfect knowledge of the same. But passion and evil habit becloud one's knowl-edge and hence render the sin venial, as does also weighty evil example;* and a probable opinion entirely excuses even a mortal sin. In an unimportant matter even the transgres-sion of a divine law is not a mortal sin. Ignorance of the law excuses the mortal sin; and inveterate ignorance, the father-confessor may overlook in silence. Repentance over a com-mitted sin is indeed necessary to the forgiveness of the same, but a very slight degree of repentance suffices, or even a de-sire to have repentance, or the fear of eternal punishment; and, in case of repeated sins, it is enough to feel repentance for only one of them, provided that all are confessed; nay, it even suffices that I should feel pained, not because of the sin, but because of its bad consequences, e. g., disease, dishonor;† it is therefore not to be wondered at when some of the doctors assert, in contradiction to others, that it is suf-ficient in order to the obtaining of absolution that we feel a regret at our lack of repentance (Sa, Navarra). An actual bettering of one's life needs not to follow immediately upon repentance, as in fact the habit of sinning renders the sin itself venial. Venial sins (and in the eyes of the Jesuits this field is uncommonly large) need not to be confessed, and it is not even necessary, in connection with the sacrament of penance, to repent of them, and to form a resolution to avoid them.

---

* *E. g.*, Laymann: i, 2, c. 3; i, 9, 3; Escob.: i, 3, n. 28; *Conseuetudo absque advertentia letale peccatum non facit.*

† Escobar: *Tr.* 7, 4, c. 7.

Not undeserved is the notoriety of the chapters in Jesuitical ethics on *falsehood*, on the *sexual sin*, and on *murder*. One may intentionally use ambiguous words in one sense though knowing that the hearer understands him otherwise; and one may for a legitimate end, *e. g.*, for self-defense, or to protect one's family, or to practice a virtue, utter words, which, as uttered, are entirely false, and which express the true sense (which may be the opposite to the sense really expressed) only through mental additions *restrictio s. reservatio mentalis*); of such cases the moralists abound in remarkable illustrations;* *e. g.*, when some one wishes to borrow something of me which I do not like to let him have, I am at liberty to say, "I have it not," namely, by adding mentally, "in order to give it to thee;" if some one asks of me something which I do not wish to tell, I am at liberty to answer, "I know it not," namely, as obligated to communicate it; if I am asked as to a crime of which I am the sole witness, I am at liberty to say, "I know it not," mentally adding, "as a thing publicly known;" if I have hidden away a quantity of provision of which I have need, then I may swear before the court, "I have nothing," mentally adding, "which I am bound to disclose." A priest threatened with death may, without real *intentio*, that is, merely in appearance, pronounce absolution, administer sacraments, etc. An adulterous wife, when questioned by her husband, may swear that she did not commit adultery, adding mentally: "on this or that day," or "in order to reveal it to thee." He who comes from a scene of pestilence, but is convinced that he is not infected, may swear that he does not come from such a place. When a poor debtor is pressed by a hard creditor, he may swear before the court that he owes nothing to the other, in that he adds mentally, "in order to pay it right away." I may deny, before the court, every trespass or crime which has any manner of excuse, namely, by adding mentally, "as a crime." *Is, qui ex necessitate vel aliqua utilitate offert se ad jurandum nemine petente, potest uti amphibologiis, nam habet justam causam iis utendi* (Sanchez,

---

* Sanchez: *Opus mor.*, iii, 6, 12 *sqq.; Summa:* i, 3, 6 ; Diana: ii, *tr.* 15, 25 *sqq.;* iii, *tr.* 6, 30, where many cases are cited and approved ; Ellendorf: pp. 42 *sqq.*, 52 *sqq.*, 124 *sqq.*, 157 *sqq.;* Crome: x, 142 *sqq.*

Diana). In general, all such untruths are allowed EX JUSTA CAUSA, namely, *quando id necessario est, vel utile ad salutem corporis, honoris aut rerum familiarum,* or when an improper question is addressed to us; on the contrary, to swear falsely *without* a good reason is a mortal sin (Diana); this is—though not in express words yet certainly in sense—the maxim which is disavowed by the more recent Jesuits, namely, that the end sanctifies the means. A promise obligates to its fulfillment only when one actually had, at the time of promising, the intention of fulfilling it.* Hence an *oath* is binding only when one meant it earnestly; otherwise it is to be regarded as a mere blame-worthy indeed, though not obligating, piece of trifling (Sanchez, Busenbaum, Escobar, Less, Diana), and it obligates only in the sense in which, by mental reservations, it was intended, and not in that in which, by its form of expression, it would have to be understood by the other; and knowingly to mislead any one into a false oath, who, however, acts in good faith, is no sin, since in fact he who *unknowingly* swears falsely does no evil thereby;† to swear falsely from bad habit, is only a venial sin. If any one swears that he will never drink wine, then he seriously sins only when he drinks much, but not when he drinks but little (Escobar). He who swears before a court that he will tell all that he knows, is not bound to tell that which he alone knows (Less).‡

The *sexual* relations are discussed by the Jesuits in a so immorally-detailed circumstantiality that the laxity of moral judgment (elsewhere without parallel) is rendered thereby all the more pernicious and condemnable.§ A maiden who has committed unchastity for the first time is not required, even when she is, as yet, under the oversight of her parents, to give, in making her confession, this circumstance, namely, that it is the first and hence more serious case, for the freely consenting virgin does a wrong neither to herself nor to her parents, inasmuch as she has discretionary power over her virginal purity.

* Escobar: iii, 3, n. 48.　　　　　　† *Ibid.*, i, 3, n. 31.
‡ Compare Diana: iii, t. 5, 100 *sqq.*
§ Escobar: i, 8; v, 2; Busenbaum: iii, 4; especially Sanchez; *De matrim.;* so also Diana; comp. Ellendorf: 30 *sqq.*, 95 *sqq.*, 288 *sqq.*, 331 *sqq.*

(*Quum sit domina suæ integritatis virginalis*).* For all possible kinds of unchastity, apologies and excuses are invented;† and Tamburini even fixes with great exactness the taxes for public women. The discussions of the moralists on these subjects are, in many respects, of so indelicate a character, that the judgment of the Episcopal censor, printed in the work of Sanchez, (t. 2.), namely, *summa voluptate perlegi*, sounds almost too naïve.—Under the head of *murder*, the Jesuits had the task of accommodating themselves to the then prevalent moral notions of the South-European nations, and the result of their labors was an ingeniously constructed code of murder.‡ The murdering of a person, even of an innocent one, may under circumstances be allowable, not indeed simply in case of self-defense, but also in other cases,—for example, in case of severe insult, inasmuch as the insulted one would otherwise pass as dishonored; and even when the insulted one is a monk or priest, he may, according to some authorities, kill his opposer (Escobar i, c. 3, Less, and others); and several Jesuits directly maintained that any one, even a priest or monk, is entitled to anticipate an intended slander or false accusation by secret murder; for this would not amount to murder, but simply to self-defense; § and this was expressly applied to the case where a monk should have reason to fear the disclosures of his mistress. When a knight, in fleeing from the enemy, cannot otherwise rescue himself than by riding over an infant child or a beggar, then is the killing of these innocent persons allowable, save only in case that the child is not as yet baptized (Escobar, c. 3, 52),—which would apparently be rather difficult for the knight to know. Killing in self-defense is allowable even where the self-defender is caught in a crime, and that, too, where the killing is beforehand intended, *e. g.*, when he who is caught in adultery kills the injured husband (Escobar i, 7, c. 2, 5, 13; 3, 35; i, 8, n. 61). A woman may stiletto her husband when she knows definitely that this same fate threatens her from him, and when she knows no other escape (Less). He who has secretly

---

* Escobar: *Liber*, etc., *princ.* ii, n. 41; so also Bauny.

† *E. g.*, Diana: ii, t. 16, 54; 17, 62 *sqq.*; iii, 5, 87 *sqq.*; iv, 4, 36, 37,—in the spirit of many of the Jesuits.

‡ Especially Escobar: i, 7; comp. Ellendorf: 72 *sqq.*

§ Sanchez: *Summa*, t. i, 2, 39, 7; Amicus: *De jure et justitia*, v, sec. 7, 118; comp. Diana: iii, *tr.* 5, 97, ed. Antv. 1637.

committed adultery may kill the single witness thereof who is
on the point of accusing him, for this witness is not under obligation to make this accusation; however, adds the Jesuit,
civil law has unfortunately not assented to this probable opinion (Escobar i, 7, n. 39). He who without his own fault is required to accept, or to challenge to, a duel, does wisely to put
his opponent out of the way by secret murder, for thereby he
protects himself from the assault, and his opponent from a
serious sin.* Escobar is unwilling to see him who murders
his enemy secretly shut out, just like a common murderer,
from the right of asylum (6, 4, n. 26). According to some
teachers—the majority, however, think otherwise—a pregnant
maiden may procure an abortion in order to escape the shame.†
According to Azor, a physician may administer a less certainly
effectual medicine although he has with him a more certain
one, and even when it is more probable that the less effectual
one may do harm; for he has after all some probability on his
side.‡ Tamburini justifies the castration of singers for the
service of the church. The doctrine—notorious in church-his-
tory—of the justifiableness of tyrant-murder, we need only
mention in passing, as well as also the almost demagogic doctrine of the merely-relatively valid and purely human right of
princes, and of the right to disobey law on the part of the
people, as being themselves sovereign.§ In this political
respect is especially notorious the work of the Spanish Jesuit,
Mariana, (De rege, 1598, 1605), according to which, a king
who oppresses religion or violates the laws of the state may
be killed by any of his subjects, openly or by poison; the
murderer, even if his attempt fails, renders himself meritorious in the eyes of God and man, and wins immortal renown
(comp. the view of John of Salisbury, § 34). It is chiefly
these revolutionary doctrines that brought the order to its
fall; with its other moral views the secular world could have
put up with much better grace.

The maxims of the Jesuits disseminated themselves like

---

* Sanchez: *Opus mor.* ii, 39, 7.

† Crome, x, 229; Escobar, i, 7, n. 59, 64.

‡ In Escobar: *Princ.* iii, n. 25,—who, however, himself disapproves
thereof.

§ Perrault, ii, 304 *sqq.;* Stäudlin, 503; Ellendorf, 360 *sqq.*

an infectious disease far beyond the circle of their own Order, as is shown by the comprehensive works of the already mentioned Sicilian, Antony *Diana* (*clericus regularis*),[*] who taught, under the express *approbatio* of his ecclesiastical superiors, and also of the Jesuits, the doctrine of probabilism in its worst forms. One may act according to a probable opinion and disregard the more probable one; man is not under obligation to follow the more perfect and the more certain, but it suffices to follow simply the certain and perfect; it would be an unendurable burden were one required to hunt out the more probable opinions;[†] the most of the Jesuits taught the same thing. In relation to murder, he teaches like Escobar; I am at liberty to kill even him who assails my honor, if my honor cannot otherwise be rescued.[‡] When some one has resolved upon a great sin, then one is at liberty to recommend to him a lesser one, because such advice does not relate absolutely to an evil, but to a good, namely, the avoiding of the worse; for example, if I cannot otherwise dissuade a person from an intended adultery than recommending to him fornication instead thereof, then it is allowable to recommend this to him, not, however, in so far as it is a sin, but in so far as it prevents the sin of adultery; Diana appeals in this connection to many like-judging Jesuit doctors.[§] If a priest commissions Peter to kill Caius, who is weaker than Peter, but nevertheless Peter comes out second best and gets killed himself, still the priest incurs no guilt, and may continue in the administration of his office.[||] He who resolves upon committing all possible venial sins, does not thereby involve himself in any mortal sin.[¶] He who *ex aliqua justa causa* rents a house to another for purposes of prostitution, commits no sin.[**] To eat human flesh, in case of necessity, he holds with the majority of the Jesuits, as allowable.[††] He who in virtue of a promise of marriage induces a maiden to yield to him, is not bound by his promise, in case he is of higher rank or richer than she, or in case he can persuade himself that she will not take his promise in serious ear-

[*] *Resolutiones morales*, Antv., 1629–37, 4 fol., Lugd. 1667, Venet., 1728.
[†] *Res. mor.*, Antv., 1637, ii, *tract.* 13 ; iv, *tr.* 3 ; Summa, 1652, p. 214.
[‡] *Ibid.*, iii, 5, 90 ; *Summa*, pp. 210, 212.   [§] *Res. mor.*, Antv., 1637, iii, *tract.* 5, 37.   [||] *Ibid.*, ii, *tract.* 15, 17.   [¶] *Ibid.*, iii, *tr.* 6, 24.
[**] *Ibid.*, iii, *tr.* 6, 45.   [††] *Ibid.*, 6, 48.

nest.* Marriage between brother and sister can be made legitimate by Papal dispensation.†—In such moral perversity of view Diana seems only to have been surpassed by the Spanish Netherlander Cistercian, *Lobkowitz*,‡ who, in his skepticism, entirely breaks down the moral consciousness, and declares that nothing is evil *per se*, but only because it is positively forbidden; hence God can dispense even from all the commandments (comp. the views of Duns Scotus, § 34),—can, *e. g.*, allow whoredom and other like sins, for none of these are evil *per se*. Monks and priests are at liberty to kill the female misused by them, when they fear, on her account, for their honor. This writer declares himself expressly and decidedly in favor of the views of the Jesuits.—Also the Franciscan order became infected with the maxims of the Jesuits, as is proved by the very voluminous work of *Barthol. Mastrius de Mandula*,§ which was published under the express sanction of the officers of the order, and who justifies *restrictiones mentales* even in oaths,‖ and also the murder of tyrants,¶ the murders of the slanderers of an important person, castration and similar things,** as well as also probabilism.

The moral system of the Jesuits is not, strictly speaking, that of the Romish church; many of their more extreme maxims the church has condemned, and the more recent Jesuits themselves find it advisable no longer fully to avow their former principles. Nevertheless Jesuitism, together with its system of morals, is the ultimate consequential goal of the church in its turning-aside from the Gospel, just as (though in other respects widely different therefrom) Talmudism was the necessary goal of Judaism in its rejection of the Saviour. The error consists in the placing of human discretion and authority in the stead of the unconditionally valid, revealed will of God. Even as earlier Catholicism had intensified the divine command by self-invented, ascetic work-holiness into a seemingly greater severity,—had aimed

---

* *Resol. mor.*, Antv., iii, 6, 81; in the spirit of Sanchez and Less.

† *Ibid.*, iv, *tr.*, 4, 94; sanctioned by several Jesuits.

‡ *Theol. mor.*, 1645, 1652; the work itself I have not been able to find; comp. Perrault: i, 331 *sqq.*   § *Ibid.*, 1626.

‖ *Disp.*, xi, 52, 171, 172, 183, (ed. Ven. 1723.)   ¶ *Ibid.*, viii, 27.

** *Ibid.*, viii, 25, 28; xi, 110 *sqq.*

at a higher moral perfection than that required by God,—so Jesuitism with like presumption lowered the moral law, out of consideration to temporal relations, to a merest minimum requirement,—contented itself with a much lower moral perfection than the divine law calls for, and sought out cunning means for lightening even this minimum. Jesuitical ethics is the opposite pole of monastic ethics; what the latter requires too much, the former requires too little. Monastic morality sought to win God for the sinful world; Jesuitical morality seeks to win the sinful world, not indeed for God, but at least for the church. Monasticism said to God, though not in an evangelical sense: "if I have only thee, then I ask for nothing else in heaven or earth;" Jesuitism says about the same thing, but says it to the world, and particularly to the distinguished and powerful. The former turns away in indignant contempt from the worldly life, because the world is immersed in sin; the latter generously receives the same into itself, and turns attention away from guilt, by denying it. It is true, the Jesuits represent also a monastic Order, but this order is only a means to an end, and resembles the other nobler orders about as much as wily Renard resembles the pious Pilgrim; and the well-known hostility of the older orders to this brilliantly rising new one, was not mere jealousy, but a very natural, and, for the most part, moral protest against the spirit of the same.

Other casuists are: *Jacobus à Graffiis*, a Benedictine (*Consiliorum s. respons. cas. consc.* 1610, 2, 4to.); *Pontas* of Paris (*Examen general de conscience*, 1728; Latin, 1731, 3 fol., alphabetical); the French bishop *Genettus* (*ob.* 1702, *Theologie morale;* also in Latin, 1706, 2, 4to., earnest and rigid); the Dominican *Perazzo*, in his *Thomisticus ecclesiastes* (1700, 3 fol.), digested the ethics of Thomas Aquinas into an alphabetical register; *Malder* of Antwerp treated it more systematically (*De virtutibus theologicis*, 1616).

In a more systematic form, a purer Christian spirit, and, in many respects, opposed to Jesuitical views, and corresponding rather to Mediæval ethics, is the moral treatise of the French bishop *Godeau* (1709); *Natalis Alexander* (1693) treated the same subject in a similar spirit, in connection with dogmatics.

SECTION XXXIX.

In striking antithesis to the morals of the Jesuits, stand the teachings of the Augustine-inspired *Jansenists*, who, in opposition to the subjectively-individual character of the Jesuitical system, hold fast to the immutable objectivity of the moral law, and teach the latter in a very rigid manner, much resembling that of Calvinists; but yet because of their leaning upon the earlier mysticism of the church they come short of carrying fully out the Reformatory principle. —The *mystical theology*—present in Jansenism only as a co-ordinate element—perpetuated itself in the Romish church, in natural antagonism to the cold casuistic morality of the Jesuits, but rather in a popularly devotional than in a scientific form, and rose, in the *Quietism* of *Molinos*, to a one-sided turning-aside from all vigorous moral activity, while *Fénelon* shaped a modified and moderated mysticism into a noble, moral system of devout contemplation.

Jansen of Louvain (afterward bishop of Ypres), presses, in his *Augustinus* (1640), the doctrine of Augustine against the semi-Pelagian system of the Jesuits, and occasioned thereby a powerful theological movement which led almost to schism, and which demonstrated again by historical results that even the most rigid teaching of predestination brings about higher moral views than the doctrine of Pelagianism and semi-Pelagianism,—and for this simple reason, that, in the former system God is brought absolutely into the fore-ground, while, in the latter, the individual subject is put forward into a false position. Love to God and to his will is the essence of all morality; where God is not loved in an action, there the action is not moral; mere love to created things is sinful; but our love to God is poured out into our hearts by God himself, and hence stands in need of grace, which inclines the will directly and irresistibly to the working of the good.

The four chief virtues and the three theological virtues, as adopted from Augustine, are only different manners of loving God; God is their ultimate goal, as also their source; his gracious working and our love, both inseparably united, constitute their impelling power; fear does indeed bring about order, but not virtue.—Although the book of Jansen was burned at Rome, and forbidden by Papal bulls, still his opinions continued to disseminate themselves in the Netherlands and in France, and bade defiance to Jesuitism. The writings of *Arnauld, Pascal, Nicole, Quesnel*, developed the moral principles of Jansen still further, and though they in fact remained far remote from evangelical purity of faith, and even defended as a high virtue the afflicting of the body by fasting and other severe acts of penance, even to self-mortification, still they were thoroughly in earnest for moral purity,—required complete moral self-denial out of love of God, and placed the moral worth of all actions, and even of their ascetic practices, essentially in the disposition of the heart; and their ground-principles were definite and clear, and proof against all sophistry.* *Arnauld* assailed effectually the ethics of the Jesuits. *Pascal's* (*ob.* 1662) "Pensées" (1669 and later), consisting of thoughts on religion without any very close connection, attained to a very wide circulation. That the presentation of these quite plain thoughts could produce so great an impression, is evidence of how deeply had sunk the Christian life, and of how great was the necessity of reformation. Peter *Nicole* (*ob.* 1695) worked effectually, through his numerous popular and essentially Scripture-inspired writings on special moral topics, toward a purer form of ethics;† and this was done in still wider circles by *Quesnel's* "Moral Reflections" (at first in 1671, on the Four Gospels, afterward on the entire New Testament) which were affected with a slight tinge of mysticism;—(Sainte-Beuve: "Resolutions," etc., 1689, 3, 4to.). The open or underhanded opposition of the Jesuits to these writings simply awakened the attention of the people all the more to the great difference between the parties, and that, too, not to the

---

* Comp. Reuchlin: *Geschichte von Portroyal*, 1839, and the same author's *Pascals Leben*, 1840,—neither work entirely unprejudiced.

† *Kirchenhistor. Archiv. v. Stäudlin*, etc., 1824, 1, 127.

advantage of the Jesuits.—The chief strength of Jansenism lay in its opposition to the Jesuits; its own positive contents, as an emphasizing of the practical phase of Augustinianism, was not consequentially carried out; it was not able to disenthrall itself from the unevangelical ground-thoughts of the corrupted church, but halted at half-ways; and hence though it had a wide-reaching, it did not have a permanent and profound, influence. Discarding the system of external work-holiness and insisting on the inner element of the moral life, it yet did not clearly and purely embrace the evangelical thought of faith, which first lays hold on grace and then freely carries out the life of grace; but it regarded morality not merely as an evidence of salvation, but also, though without merit in itself, as a means of salvation; hence its insisting on painfully-anxious ascetic practices.

The *mystical* current of ethics, with which the Jansenists always manifested a sympathy, was represented by *Francis de Sales* (bishop of Geneva, *ob.* 1622, and subsequently canonized) in several works;* by *Vergier* (abbot of St. Cyr, *ob.* 1643) a Jansenist, who was already powerfully working in the direction of Quietism, and who encouraged the severest, and even cruel, self-mortifications; † and by Cardinal *Bona* (*ob.* 1674.) ‡ Most remarkable, however, though quite consequential, was the manner in which mysticism was transformed into *Quietism* § by the Spaniard, Michael *Molinos* (afterward in Rome,) whose work entitled "Spiritual Guide," originally (1675) in Spanish, soon disseminated itself throughout Romish Europe.§ As the goal of morality is union with God through an entire turning away from the creature, hence true morality must manifest itself, not in acting in the outer world, but in turning away from it. Such is the doctrine which Molinos derives from his favorites among the earlier mystics, from Dionysius the Areopagite down. In contemplation, in the path of faith, in immediate spiritual vision of God, without the intervention of an inferential process of thought, the soul already possesses eternal truth. True vision, inward

---

* *Œuvres*, Paris, 1821, 16 t., 1834.　　　† *Opp. theol.*, 1642, 1653.
‡ *Manuductio ad cœlum*, 1664, and frequently; *Opp. Antv.*, 1673, 1739.
§ Walch: *Einl. in d. Rel. streit. ausser. d. ev. K.*, 1724, ii, p. 982; Stäudlin u. Tschirner: *Archiv.*, i, 2, 175.

rest and inward composure,—the remaining silent in the
presence of God, the beholding of God without figure or
form, and without distinguishing between his attributes, as
the absolutely One,—all this is not a self-acquired active
state, but a passive one imparted by God himself to the soul,
so that consequently God alone works in man, and the soul
itself remains motionless and inactive,—yields itself entirely
to the solely-working divine activity,—is entirely united
with God; this is the true, pure manner of prayer, which
cannot be uttered in words, but is a holy keeping-silence of
the soul. Satiated in this union with God the soul is entirely filled with the divine, and hates all worldly things,—feels
a repugnance to every thing earthly, forgets every thing
created, is divested, in its inner solitude, of all affections
and thoughts, of all inclinations and all creature-will,—withdraws itself into its most innermost depths, and enjoys, in
its total self-forgetfulness (entirely merged into God), perfect
inner rest, and holy peace; self-mortification and self-denial
are but disciplinary helps for beginners in the acquiring of
salvation, but do not themselves lead to perfection; this is
attained only through sinking into one's own nothingness,
through " self-annihilation," through the putting on of, and
becoming united with, God.—Molinos, though at first favored
by the Pope, was afterward delivered over, by the influence
of the Jesuits, to the Inquisition, and was required to disa-
vow his doctrines (1687), and died in prison. Many of the
propositions condemned were only inferences drawn from
his writings, though not expressly taught by himself.—In
spite of this and other persecutions, mysticism still continued
to exist, also in its quietistic form, in the Latin nations.
(Madam *Bouvier de la Mothe Guion*—*ob.* 1717—represented it
in numerous writings, mostly published by Poiret, in which
she sometimes goes in fervent mystical depth of love, even
beyond Molinos,—the out-gush of a glowingly enthusiastic
womanly heart.)—*Fénelon*, archbishop of Cambray, favored
the doctrine of Madame Guion, and endeavored by moderating
her quietistic views to conjure the opposition; and his writings, which portray in simple, noble eloquence the pious life
of the Christian, and keep free from the extremes of one-
sided mysticism, and uniformly place love to God in the fore-

ground as the essence of the moral, offer and propose, in opposition to the pettifogging dialectics of Jesuitical morality, the Christian spirituality of the heart. His mystical masterpiece (*Explication des Maxims des Saintes*, 1697, and often subsequently) was condemned by the Pope and proscribed; Fénelon yielded.

SECTION XL.

Independently of the Reformation,—because averse to Christianity itself, and standing rather in connection with the already previously existing breaking-loose from the evangelically-moral consciousness which showed itself, as godlessness on the one hand, and as humanism on the other,—there was developed, in antithesis to the Christian religion and to Mediæval philosophy (as also in antithesis to the riper Greek philosophy, and consequently to the historical spirit in general) an essentially new *philosophical* movement, which, while moving forward under manifold modifications of form, gradually won a progressively greater influence on theology, and in fact chiefly also on theological ethics, leading the same astray, on the one hand, into deep-reaching errors, but also, on the other (and in fact because of these errors) bringing it to a riper self-examination and to a clearer self-consciousness. Showing a preference,—in contrast to the precedent of the better form of scholasticism,— to those ancient moralists who already represented the decadence of Greek thought, namely, to the Epicureans, the Stoics, and the Skeptics, or indeed also, merely in a general way, to the so-called humanistic spirit of antiquity,—this movement (which found favor especially in Italy and France, because of the there-increasing demoralization of the higher classes), shows itself at first, for the most part, simply in the

form of general maxims and sentiments, and attained only rarely to a more scientific shape. Scarcely anywhere save in Germany did this current of thought rise to scientific earnestness and philosophical development, and thereby to a more substantial moral character. *Spinoza* broke off all connection with ancient and Mediæval philosophy, and developed a consequential Pantheistic system, in which ethics assumes the form of an objective describing of the absolutely unfree, purely mechanically-conceived moral life, as determined with unconditional nature-necessity by the life of the universe, although, because of the unhistorical originality of his manner of thinking, he exerted but little influence upon his (for this element, yet unreceptive) age. All the greater, however, became the influence of the philosophy of *Leibnitz*, representing as it did a world-theory the opposite of that of Spinoza, and placing itself rigidly on monotheistic ground, and standing in a much closer connection with history;—especially was this influence extended through the labors of his somewhat independent disciple, Christian *Wolf*, who created a very detailed and morally earnest system of ethics, essentially under the form of the doctrine of duties, which, as a purely philosophical opposition-movement to the above-mentioned non-Christian and anti-Christian current, attained to a not undeserved influence on Christian ethics in Germany, and gave rise in *Crusius* to an evangelically deeper, though not philosophically carried-out, development of moral science.

It is utterly incorrect and anti-historical to deduce the collective, and (as some have done) even the anti-Christian philosophy of modern times from the Reformation, or even to regard it as standing in any close connection therewith.

The essence of the Reformation is not the freeing of the individual subject from all objective authority. Historically, we are forced to hold fast to the fact that both before, and during, and after, the time of the Reformation, there were prevailing still other entirely different spiritual influences than the religiously-evangelical one,—influences which were in part entirely independent of the Reformation and of its spirit, nay, even utterly opposed thereto, and in part, though occasioned in their development by the movement of thought going out from the Reformation, were yet not caused thereby. The renewed cultivation of ancient classical literature, especially of the belletristic as distinguished from the philosophy of Plato and Aristotle, played, in the Reformation-movement, only a very subordinate and essentially negative rôle, namely, in that it undermined the credit of scholasticism. The deep earnestness of the religious life in the evangelical church, the required inward purity, and the repentance of regeneration, consisted but illy with a love for the exaltation of the natural man, as exhibited in Greek literature; and it was much easier for humanism to find an undisturbed patronage within the Romish church,—which, though indeed not theoretically approving of the movement, had yet practically already long since accorded it favor. Humanism was the name self-assumed by this movement, which in antithesis to the Christian world-theory placed *man*, in his natural development, into the fore-ground even of its moral world-theory, and threw as far as possible into the back-ground his need of redemption, and which had consequently in Christianity only a scientific,and æsthetic interest. The unbelieving impiety which prevailed widely in the Romish church of that age, and which found its way even into the Papal chair, had a much more lively sympathy for heathen literature than the evangelical church. The Pelagian character of humanism stood in fact nearer to the view of the Romish church than to that of the evangelical. Luther turned the unevangelical Erasmus indignantly away; Rome offered him a cardinal's hat.

It was quite natural, although it had nothing at all to do with the evangelical Reformation, that there should now rise in opposition to the one-sided idealism and spiritualism of

scholasticism, an equally one-sided realism and naturalism, which would naturally enough find encouragement in the spirit of the age as weaned off from the Mediæval ideals of chivalry and poetry, and as immersed in material interests and in the prose of politics. This thoroughly non-Christian naturalistic tendency, which attained to a more spiritual content only in the sphere of German thought, manifested from the very start a decided aversion to all history, an aversion which constantly grew more marked and positive. This anti-historical spirit began already to show itself in the attempt to call again into life, in disregard to the entire history of Christian thought, an ante-Christian world-theory, namely, to effect a rehabilitation of the spirit of the heathen thought of Greece and Rome. At a later period the movement went still further,—broke even with the history of philosophy, pushing it entirely aside even in its ancient form,—and the "philosophical" century thought to display its strength in speaking disdainfully of the spiritual products of a Plato and an Aristotle, and in regarding as philosophers only third and fourth rate minds, such as Cicero, and in basing itself, in boundless self-sufficiency, purely and simply upon itself. It required all the pretension of the so-called philosophical century to accept men, such as Rousseau and Voltaire (who had in fact scarcely the faintest conception of solid philosophical thought-work), as the greatest philosophers of the world's history. From the history of thought, these men were unwilling to learn any thing, but solely from nature; every one wanted to philosophize on his own responsibility; every thing had to be entirely new; the new era wished to owe nothing to the past, but contemptuously to tread it under foot; and the reaction from this anti-historical, and hence unspiritual tendency, begins only quite late—with Schelling. Now as the Christianly-moral world-theory has a thoroughly *historical* character, hence the history of this essentially *naturalistic* form of ethics admits of no possible organic incorporation into the history of Christian ethics; it simply moves side by side with the Christian current,—breaks, especially at a later period, disturbing, confusing, and perverting, into it,—but is with only slight exception not a furthering element of its development.

Erasmus, who enters the ethical field in several treatises,[*] does not as yet himself directly assail the Christianly-moral consciousness, but only presents with prudent reserve the ethics of Plato and Cicero as very closely related to Christian ethics, and mingles faint Christian views with Grecian, and thereby reduces them to the level of Pelagianism. His assaults on the moral abuses of the church are devoid of Christian depth.—*Pomponatius* (of Padua and Bologna, *ob.* about 1525),[†] who, under the patronage of the Papal court, assailed the doctrine of personal immortality, professed, in point of ethics, to belong to the Stoic school,—taught absolute determinism, and presented the Christian view only ambiguously along-side of the heathen.—*Lipsius*, in the Netherlands (*ob.* 1606) went still further in the exaltation of Stoicism,[‡] though his opinions received no very favorable commendation from his unbridled life and from his threefold change of faith—Romish, Lutheran, Reformed, and then Romish again.—In all essential features belongs here also the Socinian ethics of *Crell*, which is in many respects kindred to the later Rationalistic system, and presents (in a spirit of pure Pelagianism) Christian ethics simply as improved Aristotelian ethics, and prefers the latter to the ethics of the Old Testament.[§]— *Agrippa of Nettesheim* (of Cologne, *ob.* 1535), undermined, by a far-reaching skepticism, the certainty of all moral consciousness, and explained this consciousness simply by mere fortuitous habit and by fortuitously-adopted public manners;[||] his magico-alchemistic superstitiousness forms the back-ground thereto. (Giordano *Bruno*, the forerunner of Spinoza, produced no system of ethics.)

Less influential upon his own age than upon recent times, was the philosophy of *Spinoza*. His chief work, *Ethica* (1677), which appeared only after his death, constitutes almost an entire philosophical system, of which the ethical

---

[*] *Enchiridion militis christ. ; Matrimonii christ. institt. ; Institt. principis christ. ;* and others.

[†] *Opp.*, Bas. 1567, 3 t.

[‡] *Manuductio ad Stoicam philosophiam*, 2d ed., 1610.

[§] *Ethica Aristotelica*, etc., Selenoburgi, s. a., 4to.,—later: Cosmopoli, 1681, 4to.

[||] *De incertitudine et vanitate scientiarum*, 1527 (?) then in Col., 1531.

part proper forms indeed the largest but not the most philosophical and important. This perspicuous and mathemati-
cally-exact treatise presents not so strictly a speculative development of the subject-matter as, rather, rational elucidations
and proofs of assumed propositions, among which, however,
some very important ones, which needed to be demonstrated,
are presented merely as axioms not needing proof, or are dis-
guised in definitions. That the Jewish, but also Judaism-
rejecting, philosopher should feel himself obliged also to
ignore the history of the human spirit in general, was naturally to be expected; his system (if we except the philosophy
of Descartes, which had likewise but little connection with
earlier philosophy, and whose monotheistical character Spinoza assails) has no historical antecedents proper, but in
fact begins anew the philosophical thought-work from the
very beginning, and develops the Pantheistic world-theory
so consequentially and undisguisedly as is nowhere else to be
found.—God, as the solely existing substance whose two attributes are thought and extension, has not a world different
from and outside of himself, but is this world himself, as
considered simply under a particular aspect. All particular
being is only a mode of the existence of God; and all these
modes are conditioned by the absolute necessity of the divine
life, and cannot be otherwise than as they really are; all that
is, is what, and as, it is, from necessity; of every thing which
is or takes place the principle holds absolutely good: *omnia
sunt ex necessitate naturæ divinæ determinata*. Hence this holds
good equally also of man, who is likewise a particular mode
of the being of God. When we say: "the human soul thinks
something," this is the same as to say: "God thinks," not
however in so far as God is infinite, but in so far as he constitutes the essence of the human spirit. Hence human
thought is just as necessarily determined as is all being in
general, —and hence knows *per se*, and necessarily, the truth.
—Now, thinking has two phases: knowing and willing. Of
willing the same holds good as of knowing, namely, it is absolutely determined in all its activity. Every will-act has a
definite cause, by which it is absolutely determined. Willing can never contradict knowing, but is the immediate and
necessary product of the same, and is, strictly speaking,

dentical therewith; willing is affirming, and non-willing is denying. He who believes that he speaks, or keeps silent, or does any thing else, by free choice, dreams with open eyes. Men delude themselves into thinking that they are free in their volitions, only because they are not conscious of the cause which absolutely determines them; all that takes place through the activity of the will is necessary, and therefore good. This doctrine renders the heart calm and makes us happy; with it we have no longer any occasion for fear, for we know that every thing takes place according to the everlasting decree of God, with the same necessity as it follows from the idea of a triangle, that its three angles are equal to two right angles,—teaches us to hate, to despise, to mock no one,—teaches us unlimited contentment (ii, *prop.* 48, 49).

All this is clear and consequential; but how can the existence of a moral consciousness be reconciled therewith? How can any thing be morally required or done, if every thing takes place with unconditional necessity, and if will-freedom is only a false appearance? That there can be no question of a moral command proper, of an "ought," Spinoza himself virtually admits, inasmuch as he declares it his purpose to speak of human actions just as if the matter in question were lines, surfaces, and solids (iii, *prœm.*) We are active in so far as any thing takes place within or without us, of which we are the perfect cause; and the more we are active, and the less we are passive, so much the more perfect are we. Even as all other things, so also the spirit strives to retain and to enlarge its reality; its striving is its willing; the end is not different from the cause—from the unfree-acting impulse of nature; the passing-over to a higher reality awakens the feeling of pleasure; the opposite, that of displeasure. Pleasure in connection with the consciousness of its cause, is *love;* the opposite is *hate.* For a real difference between good and evil there is, in this world-theory, no place whatever. Neither good nor evil is a reality in things themselves, but both are simply subjective conceptions and notions, which we form by a comparison of things, and are hence only *relative* relations having their basis not in things but in ourselves,—are only modes of our thinking; for example, a particular piece of music is good for a melancholic

person, not good for a different one, and is of no significancy
at all for a deaf one; hence it is *per se* neither good nor bad,
(iv, *præf.*)   Hence we cannot say in general that any thing
at all is good *per se ;* it is only by comparing one thing with
another higher entity, or with a notion formed by ourselves,
that we find any thing to be good; good and evil are only
expressions of our subjective judgment as to that for or
against which we have a desire or an aversion.   *Per se,* however, every thing is good, because necessary; nothing is or
transpires without God or against his will; every thing is
just as, according to eternal, divine destination and necessity, it *ought* to be; hence the notion of evil is only a limited
and ungrounded manner of thinking on the part of our own
understanding,—is nothing on the part of God.   Evil is in
fact, even in our own conception, only a negative something,
a privation; but God knows no mere negative something,
hence God knows absolutely nothing of evil (comp. the view
of Erigena, § 33), and hence there is in reality no such thing as
evil; for what God does not know does not exist, and outside
of God's thinking there is no other thinking. "Moreover,
were evil or sin a real something, God would necessarily not
only know it, but also be the *cause* of it, for God is the substance and the cause of all that is; and what is of God cannot be evil.   Hence it is only a false manner of looking at
things, an imagination, when we find any thing evil in the
real world,—false, in that we bring things into relation to
ourselves, to our fortuitous feelings of pleasure and displeasure, instead of contemplating them in their own nature; in
and of itself, and hence in truth, every thing real is good and
perfect.   In all seemingly free action nothing else can take
place than what results with necessity from the existing circumstances of the acting subject.   Even the stings of conscience are a self-deception, and are nothing other than a
sadness or chagrin which we feel over some kind of a failure.
Let it not be objected to this, that if men do every thing
from necessity, and hence, also, sin from necessity, they cannot consequently be blamed therefor, but that all men would
then be necessarily happy.   On the contrary, man can be
without guilt, and, notwithstanding that, be also devoid of
happiness.   The horse is not guilty for its not being man,

and nevertheless it still remains a horse; and he who is bitten by a mad-dog is also not guilty therefor, and yet he goes mad; he who is blind was in fact destined in the concatenation of beings to be blind and not seeing (*Ep.*, 32, 34.) This is surely the most wonderful justification of the moral order of the universe which one could possibly fall upon; for, in fact, whence can mad-dogs originate in an absolutely necessary and good world ? If every thing is necessary, and the entirely innocent can be made mad by mad-dogs, this is evidently a very bad sort of world-order. And we must ask : if all human thinking is the thinking of God himself, and is absolutely necessary, how is there in fact possible any manner of *false* thinking and imagining ? If men really regard evil as real, then this is, in fact, an error on the part of God himself, which our philosopher should endeavor to account for; but if there *is* no evil, then there is also no error, and the system thus entangles itself in its own meshes. And when Spinoza makes error to be just as necessary as truth (ii, *prop.*, 35, 36), he still cannot evade this contradiction by declaring error to be merely relative, for a merely seeming error would yet in reality be the truth, and hence would not admit of the turn here taken by Spinoza.

Hence—so infers Spinoza—all is good which is useful; and all is evil which hinders from a good (iv, *def.*, 1, 2.) Hence virtue is the power or capacity of acting in conformity to our own nature; *virtus nihil aliud est, quam ex legibus propriæ naturæ agere;* hence every one must follow the necessity of his nature, and by it judge of good and evil. Hence sin is avoided for the simple reason that it is contrary to our nature; but why sin is yet in fact committed, Spinoza needs not to answer, because sin in the proper sense of the word cannot be committed at all; of sin there can be any question only in the State, and, there, it is disobedience to civil law (iv, 37, *schol.* 2). As reason can require nothing which would be against nature, hence it requires that each should strive for that which is useful to himself; and useful is that which brings each to a higher reality. Hence morality requires that each should love himself, should seek to preserve as much as possible his existence, and to bring it to higher perfection and reality; and man is all the more

virtuous the more he seeks after that which is useful to him, (iv, *prop*. 18).—As the essence of reason is knowledge, hence knowledge is the most useful of things, and the rational man holds nothing for truly useful save that which contributes to knowledge. Hence the highest good is the knowledge of God, and the highest virtue is the striving thereafter; and every man has the strength necessary thereto; and as the body is directly connected with the spirit, and as the spirit is all the more vigorous the more vigorous the body is, hence it is useful and virtuous to make the body skillful.

The good always awakens delight; hence delight is *per se* necessarily good, and sadness necessarily evil, as well as whatever leads to sadness. Hence *compassion* is, for the rational man, evil and irrational; true, it often inclines us to beneficence, but this we should do at any rate even without compassion, (this is the virtue of *generositas*); and the truly wise man knows indeed that nothing is or takes place in the world over which we could grieve; moreover compassion easily leads astray to false acting (*Eth*. iv, 50).—Also *humility* as including a feeling of sadness is not a virtue, and springs not from reason, but from error, inasmuch as in it man recognizes himself as, in some respect, powerless, whereas, in virtue of the prevalence of universal necessity, he has all the power necessary to his destination (iv, 53). *Repentance* over committed sin is not only not virtuous, but it is irrational, because it rests on the delusion of having done a free and, that too, evil action, whereas the action was in reality necessary, and hence good; he who feels repentance is consequently doubly miserable. However, our moralist appears to shrink back from the practical consequences of this doctrine; he declares it as very dangerous when the great masses are not kept in bounds by humility, repentance and fear (iii, 59, *def*. 27; iv, *prop*. 54),—an apprehension which is, of course, entirely inexplicable from the ground-principle of his system, and must be banished, as a mere "imagination," into the sphere of unreason; for how can there be, in Spinoza's world, a dangerous populace to be curbed only by false notions, seeing that indeed every thing that takes place is absolutely a necessary divine act ?—The notion that any thing is bad or evil is, according to Spinoza, *per se* already an evil;

if man is truly rational and has only correct ideas, then he can have no notion of evil at all, for it in fact does not exist; whatever affects us as pain or suffering, is such only in virtue of an erroneous, confused conception, an "imagination;" if we have correct knowledge, then are we free from all pain; the more we recognize all things as necessary, so much the less are we subject to suffering; every painful state of the emotions disappears so soon as we form to ourselves a clear notion thereof. Hence, according to Spinoza, the sole evil is false conceptions, but how these could arise we are not informed.—He who truly knows himself and his circumstances, has necessarily joy; and as in all true knowing he also knows God, and as this knowing is attended with joy, hence he also *loves* God; hence in the knowledge and love of God consists the highest joy. God himself, however, (conceived as the universe) is without states of emotion, without love or aversion. God can neither love nor hate, save in the love or hate of man himself; and when any one who loves God desires to be loved in turn by God, he desires in fact that God should cease to be God. True, we may indeed speak of God's love, but not in such a manner as that God as a personal spirit should love man, but only that God loves in our love; God loves not me but God loves himself, namely, in that I love Him.

Spinoza's ethics appears at once as very widely different from all preceding ethics; its essential characteristic is, unhistoricalness. Greek philosophy, and also scholasticism, are the fruit of a long and vigorous development of an historical current of human thought,—presuppose an already historical moral consciousness, for which they aim to create a scientific form. Spinoza's ethics sprang, in no sense whatever, from the spirit of an historical people,—has no historical antecedents, no historical consecration, and hence wears in its lofty, reality-spurning bearing, also the character of historical impossibility. Plato's idealistic state is historically possible on a Greek basis; Spinoza's ethics can absolutely never and nowhere be the expression of the moral consciousness of a people,—can be appropriated only as their isolated moral consciousness by single persons, who in proud selfishness imagine themselves far above the morally-religious conscious-

ness of the masses, whereas in fact they owe the very possibility of their moral existence in society simply to this consciousness of the masses. Spinoza has learned nothing, whether from the philosophers of Greece, from the Middle Ages, from the religion of the Old Testament, or from Christianity; his ethical speculations are devoid of preparatory antecedents,—are an absolutely revolutionary breaking-off from all historical spirit-development,—base themselves purely upon individual thinking. His unimportant dependence on Descartes is not in conflict therewith. If he had had even the slightest appreciation for the significance and the rights of history, he would have been required, on the very ground of his own system, to recognize the Christian world-theory as a highly important revelation of the alone-ruling God, and to regard history in general as a normal and necessary life-manifestation of God. Whereas in fact he turns himself contemptuously away from all history of thought, as if God had come to true self-consciousness alone and solely in himself. He does not free himself in any sense from the contradiction of declaring, on the one hand, all reality as necessary and good, and all evil as mere appearance, and of regarding on the other hand, all previously-existing *spiritual* reality as absolutely wrong, senseless, and irrational.

Plato and Aristotle, for the reason that they stand more within the current of history, stand also far nearer the Christian consciousness than Spinoza. In his wide-reaching antithesis to the real essence of spirit which is in fact necessarily history, he is the father of the *Naturalism* of more recent times. Only the unfree, the nature-entity, is real; the free, the spiritual, and hence also the moral, in general has no existence whatever. Though indeed he contrasts thought and extension in space, as being of different nature, yet this thinking is in fact not free and spiritual, but bears absolutely a nature-character,—has not ends before it, but simply presents manifestations of a necessary ground; so in the case of God, so in the case of man. Ethics is therefore degraded to a mere describing of necessary nature-phenomena; and where it falls into the tone of moral exhortation in view of rational ends, then this is to be understood either in a merely improper sense, and is indulged in simply in view of the

unwise multitude, or it comes into irreconcilab.e contradiction with the ground-thought of the system. The Jew continues a Jew, in this Christian age, only through hatred against
history, which has in fact pronounced his condemnation; he
is either the petrified guest in the midst of living society,
or the insolently mocking despiser of all historical reality,
utterly devoid of reverence and respect for the historical
spirit,—a champion of the wildest radicalism. Spinoza,
breaking loose from the petrified form of Talmudic Judaism, stands entirely isolated in the world of the historical
spirit; he can find for himself no proper place in this world,
—makes only an attempt to build up an entirely new world
out of himself. The same self-delusion which prevails
throughout post-Christian Judaism, namely, in that it dreams
of still having an historical character, whereas it has in fact
sunk utterly into mere lifeless matter, is also potent in Spinoza. He dreams of creating a system of ethics, whereas it
proves to be really nothing else than the theoretical describing of a moral instinct devoid of a rational end. Where
the "must" dominates, there all "should" and "would"
cease. In sharp contrast to the pure idealistic Pantheism of
Erigena, who really recognizes only God and not the world,
and who, like the Indians, finds evil only in the distinguishing
of the worldly and finite from God, Spinoza holds in fact fast
to the reality and divinity of the finite,—merges God into the
world, and regards the real, simply as it is, in its isolated
separateness, as good and perfect. The Pantheism of Erigena leads to an ascetic turning-away from the world; that of
Spinoza, to a contented and absolutely satisfied merging of
self into the world; and the "akosmism" which Hegel
thinks he discovers in Spinoza is not to be found in him,
but rather in the nobler and far more spiritual John Scotus
Erigena.

Spinoza exerted in his own age but little influence. Notwithstanding the deep spiritually-moral declension of that
dark period, the religious God-consciousness was as yet too
vital to fall in with this naturalistic Pantheism; and the requirement to recognize all reality as necessary and good,
could find little response at a time of profound disorganiza-
tion and far-reaching material, misfortune in Germany. It

was reserved for a later age, when a wide-spread irreligious sentiment was attempting to create for itself a scientific justification, to emphasize the doctrine of Spinoza not merely in its undeniable (though yet not to be overestimated) philosophical significancy, but also to attempt to exalt it to a religious character, nay, even to a pretended transfiguration of Christianity, and "to offer a lock to the *manes* of the holy Spinoza"—(Schleierm., *Reden; 2 ed.*, p. 68).

That from this doctrine there could arise for the moral life itself only a perverting influence, needs for the unprejudiced mind no proof. The letting of one's self alone in his immediate naturalness and reality, is here even lauded as wisdom; repentance and sanctification within, and sanctifying activity without, become folly, because no one has either the right or the ability initiatively to interfere with the eternally necessary course of things. That Spinoza himself was an upright man, proves nothing in favor of his system; the weight of custom and the natural moral sentiments are often stronger than a perverse theory; nor is, in fact, mere uprightness in our social relations the full manifestation of the moral.

Leibnitz,—though also stimulated by Descartes, but opposed to Spinoza in his fundamental thoughts, and more imbued with an historical spirit, and standing in closer connection with the results of precedent spiritual development, —did not produce a system of ethics proper, though he broke the way for the development of such. Though highly respecting the Christian consciousness, he yet had no very deep appreciation for the same, and hence his thoughts in relation to religion and morality are of a somewhat external character. He is unable to comprehend evil in the purely spiritual sphere, but seeks for its roots, beyond this sphere, in the essence of the creature as such. God as the absolutely perfect rational spirit has indeed realized, among all possible conceptions of a world, the best one; but as the world does not contain the fullness of all perfection, which in fact exists in God alone, nor yet all possible perfections, as in fact all that is possible has not become real, hence there lies in the conception even of the best world still at the same time the necessity of a certain imperfection, without which a world is

in fact not conceivable, and which consequently belongs to
the essence of the world as such, and is a *malum metaphysi-
cum;* this is, however, not *per se* a reality, but only a non-
being, a limit. The reality of the morally evil is fortuitous,
is the fault of man; only the possibility of it is necessary.
In his popularly-written work " *Théodicée* " (1710), he further
develops this thought, although elucidatorily rather than
scientifically.—Though Leibnitz recognizes the freedom of
the will and the guilt of man in relation to sin, still he does
not sufficiently deeply conceive of this guilt, and above all
of the significancy and workings of sin as an *historical* world-
power, otherwise he would have constructed his theory quite
differently. He constantly seeks the roots of evil elsewhere
than in committed sin. The naturalistic determinism of
Spinoza, however, he utterly rejects; to the free personal
God, corresponds the freedom of the rational creature. The
rational man never acts from mere fortuitous fancies, but
only from rational grounds. But this moral necessity does
not interfere with liberty, because the possibility of irrational
determinations still remains.—Leibnitz conceives of ethics
essentially as the doctrine of right, inasmuch as moral duty
is a right of God upon us. Right, in the wide sense of the
word, has three stages: mere *right*, which requires that we
injure no one; *equitableness*, which leaves and imparts to
every one his own; and piety, which fulfills the will of God
and thereby preserves the harmony of the world. Hence
faith in the personal, almighty and all-wise God is the foundation of all right; and the essence of piety is love to God,
from which all other forms of love, constituting the essence
of justness, receive their power. To love signifies to be rejoiced by the happiness of another, or to make that happiness one's own. The proper object of love is the beautiful,
that is, that, the contemplation of which delights; but God
is the highest beautiful. Piety as the highest stage of right,
creates also the highest moral communion—the *church*—which
is destined to embrace entire humanity. The three forms of
society, corresponding to the three stages of right, have also
a threefold uniting-bond: mere power, and reverence, and
conscience; but also the first two receive their real character
of right, only through the latter. Love to God leads us into

20

the way of the highest happiness,—is in itself already the beginning of the same in the "this-side," and works a constant progress in perfection also in the "yon-side." *

In an original spirit, and, in the moral sphere, almost independently of Leibnitz, wrote Christian *Wolf*. He created a complete ethical system.† His great reputation, and the authoritative character which he enjoyed with his contemporaries, were, however, almost entirely overthrown in the Kantian period; that over-estimation, as also the subsequent under-estimation, were equally unjust. A many-sided boldly-exploring spirit, and, though in many respects deceiving himself as to the scientific value of propositions which he uttered with the greatest confidence, and attempted to demonstrate in a not unfrequently stiff mathematical form, he yet attained to an extraordinary influence, because of the clearness and precision of his ideas, and of their manner of presentation, and gave rise, also in the sphere of ethics, to a very vigorous scientific movement; and though his commendable effort to remain in harmony with Christian revelation was not by any means always realized, yet it helped to preserve for a long while in Germany, as in contrast to the frivolous hatred of Revelation prevalent in France and in England, a more earnest Christian and scientific spirit. Precisely in the field of morals Wolf was greatly influential toward the independent shaping of German science; and he broke off the excessive dependence, also of theological ethics, on Aristotle. While Wolf, in his decided, scientifically-grounded recognition of the personal God—whom he conceives of indeed rather merely, in his relation to the world, as Creator and Governor, and less, in relation to himself, in his inner essence—holds fast to the objectively-religious basis of ethics, he yet at first view seems to en-

---

* In various essays, especially in the preface to *Cod. juris diplom.*, 1693; Gubrauer: *Leibnitz*, 1842, i, p. 226 *sqq.*

† *Vernünft. Gedanken v. d. Menschen Thun u. Lassen* (1720); more elaborate is: *Philosophia moralis s. Ethica, methodo scientifico pertractata* (1750), both works forming the first part of a whole which he presented in his *Philos. prac. univ.* (1738), the second part of which embraces the doctrine of society or politics; also in his *Jus naturæ* (1740) there is much ethical matter.

danger the subjective foundation thereof, namely, the moral freedom of the will, by his *determinism*.

Whatever takes place, also the seemingly fortuitous, has a sufficient ground, either in itself or in its connection with other things, and is in so far determined; there takes place no change whatever which is not conditioned in the peculiarity of the concatenation of the universe, and determined by the antecedent circumstances thereof, just as a clock, set in motion for a whole year, is determined in each moment of its movement by this its first starting; the world is just such an absolutely, determined clock-work,—is a machine. Also in the freedom of the human will, every real determination has its sufficient ground, and is not arbitrary. This freedom consists in the possibility of choosing and doing the opposite of what we really do, but that the opposite possible should become *real* pre-supposes motives, and in so far as the motive is sufficient, this determination to realization is also conditioned by the motive. It is impossible that a person who knows something as better, should prefer to it the worse, and hence in such a case it is *necessary* that he should choose the better; but the will is free in this nevertheless, as in fact man has the ground of his determination of will in himself. —This sounds at once very questionable, and, as is well known, Wolf was, because of this doctrine, driven from the Prussian states, as politically dangerous. However, it is not to be overlooked that when man is considered as a rational creature *per se* irrespective of the already-existing depravity, his freedom is in fact not a groundless and irrational caprice, but is determined by rational knowledge, and that, for the really moral man in possession of correct knowledge, there does in fact exist a moral necessity of following the rational. Hence Wolf's thought is not *per se* incorrect, but only too unguarded, and therefore liable to misunderstanding. As, however, Wolf expressly declares himself against determinism as held by Spinoza, and as he distinctly and repeatedly asserts the real, free will-determination of man, though indeed not as irrational caprice,* we are consequently not at liberty to attribute to him the full determinism of Spinoza.— The question as to whether, and in how far, our knowledge is

* Introduction to the 2d ed. of his *Moral.*

conditioned by and dependent on our moral nature, and hence as to whether this knowledge is freely, or absolutely unfreely, determined, Wolf does not answer, but simply holds, that our willing is conditioned and determined by our knowledge; and with him, as with Socrates, the essential point is simply to correct and disseminate knowledge, and then the corresponding moral action follows of itself with inner necessity. Hence we can explain the almost unbounded pretensions which the Wolfian ethics makes, and hence also the *per se* correct, but (in view of the actual condition of humanity) erroneous thought that ethics is not simply a scientific consciousness of the moral life, but also an essential motive *to* the moral life itself,—that, properly understood, ethics is the source of virtue. This thought stands forth more or less clearly throughout Wolf's writings; practice follows theory of necessity. The moral life is like a mathematical question proposed for solution; it is only necessary to have clear notions of virtue and vice and of duty, and then evil disappears of itself, and man becomes virtuous. "I have," says Wolf, (in the preface to his second edition), "not a little lightened the entire practice of the good and the avoidance of the evil, by the fact that I have shown that when one wishes to turn the will, it is just the same as when one disputes, namely, in that one has at all times in the one case, as in the other, simply to answer to one of the premises of an inference;" and later (in the preface to the third edition) he says: "When my writings on world-wisdom and, among them, the present one on what men are to do and what not to do, appeared, those who are able to understand and judge of the matter for themselves, and who were not prepossessed by unfavorable prejudices, judged that thenceforth reason and virtue would become *universal*, and that *every body* would strive, by this means, to attain to happiness of life." Wolf, however, expressly deprecates the misconception, that in his ethics he "ascribes too much to nature and leaves no room for grace; the doctrines taught by me," says he, "serve much rather to make clearly understood the difference between nature and grace, and especially the great help which the latter is to the former, so that consequently they are guides to grace;" the Christian religion offers more

than world-wisdom can do; rather does man learn by this
rational morality, that his natural powers do *not* suffice, and
hence he perceives all the better the necessity and excellency
of the grace which is offered to us in the Christian religion,
and which supplies that which nature lacks. How it can be
that the natural powers do not suffice, and how, on the presumption of such a lack of strength, the philosophical ethics
of Wolf can yet be, independently, effectual in itself, we are
not informed.

Ethics has to do with the *free* actions of men as distinguished from the necessary ones; and freedom consists in the
possibility of choice between several possible things. The
condition of a man is perfect when his earlier and later
conditions agree with each other, and all of them with the
essence and nature of man. The free actions of man promote or diminish this perfection, that is, they are either *good*
or *bad*. When, therefore, actions are to be judged according
to their moral worth, then we must inquire what change they
bring about in the condition of our body or soul. Hence
free actions become good or evil in virtue of their *effect;* and
as the effect follows from them necessarily and cannot fail,
hence actions are good or evil in and of themselves, and are
not made so simply by God's will; hence if it were possible
that there were no God, and that the present inter-depend-
ence of things could exist without him, still the free actions
of men would nevertheless remain good or evil.—Here the
per se correct ground-thought of the moral receives an external and therefore misleading application, inasmuch as the
result of our actions is dependent on other powers than these
actions themselves; only in an ideal and as yet not sin-per-
verted condition of humanity, would such a judging of the
moral worth of actions from their result, hold good, though
even then it would be certainly more appropriate to determine this worth from the essence of the action itself and not
simply from its result. In this respect Wolf clings so fast
to the merely-outward that he says: "Thus, he who is
tempted to steal learns that stealing is wrong, because it is
followed by the gallows." Equally one-sided is the contrasting of the goodness *per se* of an action and of the will
of God. The general maxim of ethics is therefore this: "Do

that which renders thee and thy condition, or that of others,
more perfect; avoid that which makes it more imperfect;"
this is a universal rule of nature. [This "or that of others"
is only thrust in, and is not at all derived from the ground-
thought; the dualism involved therein, and the possible contradiction, are in no manner reconciled.]—The sufficient
motive of the will is the knowledge of the good; and it is
impossible that one should *not* will a *per se* good action, when
one only clearly comprehends it; hence when we do not will
it, it is for no other reason than that we do not comprehend
it." Likewise is the knowledge of evil the motive of non-
willing or aversion, and hence it is likewise impossible that
one should will a *per se* evil action when one clearly understands it. Hence all moral willing and doing of the good or
of the evil rests absolutely on our knowing or non-knowing.
True, man can indeed act contrary to his conscience, but this
takes place only when, because of special circumstances, he
regards the good as evil, or the evil as good, and hence,
after all, from error. The ultimate end of all moral actions,
and hence of our entire life, is the perfection of ourselves and
of our condition, or happiness, which is consequently the
highest good for man.

Ethics proper, Wolf treats as the doctrine of duties. Duty
is an action which conforms to law. Law is a rule to which
we are bound to conform our free actions; it is either a natural, a divine, or a human law. Reason is the teacher of the
law of nature; this law fully embraces the whole moral life,
and is, for this life, sufficient and absolutely valid and unchangeable, for it rests on the harmonizing of our actions
with our nature. But as this our nature is established by the
divine creative will, hence the law of nature is at the same
time also a divine law, an expression of the divine will,
though this will is not to be conceived of as an arbitrary
one, so that, for example, God's will might declare the *per se*
good for evil, and the *per se* evil for good. The duties are:
(1) duties of man toward himself, and more specifically,
toward his understanding, toward his will, toward his
body, and the duty in regard to our outward condition
(that is, our social position); (2) duties toward God, and
more specifically, love to God, fear and reverence, trust,

prayer and thankfulness, and outward worship; (3) duties toward other men, and more specifically, toward friends and enemies, duties in regard to property, and duties in speech and in contracts. This general classification of duties became subsequently very usual.—Upon ethics is based *natural right*, which treats of the allowable, as ethics proper treats of the obligatory; all rights rest on duties. The ground-thought of right is: thou mayest do whatever sustains and promotes the perfection of thy own condition and that of the condition of others, and thou mayest do nothing which is contrary thereto. In the further application of right to society, and hence as politics, the welfare of society is the norm of action.

Wolfian ethics has manifestly, both in form and in contents, great defects. In respect to form, it may be reproached with a manifold commingling of empirical maxims with speculation; notions derived from experience are often simply analyzed and then used as bases for further inferences, and that, too, with the pretension of philosophical validity; also there is abundant philosophical dogmatism, inasmuch as the thoughts are very frequently not really developed in regular process from the ground-thought, but are only associated and joined with it. In respect to matter, there prevails throughout this ethics, despite all its monotheistic presuppositions, a naturalistic tendency; Wolf knows only the immediate natural existence of the moral spirit, but not the history thereof, that is, the life proper of the same. His ethics has a history of the spirit neither as its presupposition nor as its goal; there is created by the moral activity not a moral history of humanity, but only a state of the individual. Hence the question as to whether indeed the actual nature of man is not already in some respects a product of such a moral history of humanity,—whether or not it is a pure unchanged original nature,—falls outside of this circle of thought, and in fact remained unheeded by philosophical ethics, and hence also to a large degree by theological ethics, throughout the eighteenth and a part of the nineteenth century; and in this respect Wolf was, in fact, the forerunner of the modern Rationalistic school. And what he says of sinfulness, of divine grace and of Christianity, by way of guarding against this naturalistic ground-tendency, is rather mere personal

good-will than a consequential result of his system. All real interest is directed here to the sufficient reason, and not to the end; there is lacking to morality and to history the vital heart-blood of free spiritual productive creation. Christianity can be, to this world-theory, at best only a higher revelation of the truth, a furthering of knowledge, but not an historical history-creating fact. Hence in the further theological development of this stand-point, Christianity constantly sunk more and more to a mere revealed system of morals, which, however, contained and could contain nothing other than the Wolfian doctrine itself. Positive contents proper, Wolf does not really give to the moral law; he does not rise beyond mere formal definitions. What the good is, in and of itself, we are not informed; we learn only that it stands in harmony with reason and makes us happy; hence it is embraced only in its relations to something else, but not in its inner contents.

In the spirit of Wolf, though with some independence, *Canz* labored further, in Tübingen; his *Disciplinæ morales omnes*, 1739, is an able survey of the entire ethical field as then known; more theological is his *Instruction in the Duties of Christians*, (1745, 4to., presenting ethics as "duty-imposing God-acquaintance" and prefacing the doctrine of duties simply by an essay on the four chief springs of all human action and omission, namely, the flesh, nature, reason, and the gracious workings of the Holy Spirit). Alexander *Baumgarten* (a brother of the noted theologian) perfected, in his *Philosophia ethica* (1740, 1751), the Wolfian ethics, especially in formal respects; he places our duties toward God (as those which condition all the others) at the head.—G. F. *Meier* of Halle wrote, on the basis of Baumgarten's book, a fuller and more popular work: *Philosophical Ethics* (1753).—(The voluminous and superficial *Eberhard* appears in his *Ethics of Reason* (1781) merely as a feeble, barren imitator of Wolf.)

Nearly contemporaneously with Wolf, had *Thomasius* (of Leipzig and Halle) presented ethics from the stand-point of mere common sense in a very popular form,* offering indeed

---

* *Von der Kunst vernünftig. u. tugenhaft zu* LIEBEN, etc., 1710; *Von der Artzenei wider die unvernünftige Liebe*, 1704; comp. Fülleborn: *Beitr. z. Gesch. d. Phil*, 1791, iv.

many good observations, but containing neither precision of thought nor a really scientific development. He places Christian ethics higher than philosophical, but conceives of the former very superficially; Aristotle and the schoolmen he despises and combats without understanding them. The essence of virtue is love, or the desire naturally inherent in man to unite himself to, and to remain in union with, that which the understanding recognizes as good; in this love lies blessedness, that is, repose of soul and absence of pain, as the highest good; love is irrational when it aims at vain, transitory, and hurtful things, or when it is too violent, or wills the impossible; from such love spring all the vices. General love to man, as the essence of morality, embraces five chief virtues: sociableness, truthfulness, modesty, forbearance, patience; self-love should rest only on love to man. The necessity of revelation, Thomasius recognizes; philosophy does not supply its place, but leads to it, in that it leads to self-acquaintance.

Clear-headedly and with deep Christian knowledge, Christian August *Crusius* (of Leipzig, *ob.* 1776) opposed the Wolfian philosophy, but was abler in criticizing than in creating, and hence of more limited influence than Wolf, ("Directions for Living Rationally,"* etc., 1744; third edition, 1767). He declares himself very definitely against the determinism of Wolf; the human will is not absolutely determined by its knowledge, but remains, in relation thereto, free, and can act contrarily thereto; he appeals in proof thereof to the perfectly unambiguous evidence of consciousness, and to the full responsibility of man for his sins. The determinations of the will are indeed, as rational, not arbitrary and fortuitous, but have, on the contrary, a sufficient reason; but this reason is by no means a necessarily-determining one, but the will has always the possibility of acting contrarily even to a sufficient reason; and Crusius goes, in this respect, so far as to find perfect freedom only in holding that the will can determine itself *as easily* for the one course as for the other. All duties he considers as contained in our duty toward God, and hence he does not co-ordinate, but subordinates, them to this duty. Moral effort has indeed happiness and perfection for

* *Anweisung vernünftig zu leben.*

its goal, but it has its law in the divine will, which likewise aims thereat. Man's relation of dependence to his Creator directs him to make his entire life dependent on the holy will of God; our striving toward the rational God-willed goal, becomes truly moral only when it is the expression of loving *obedience* to the revealed divine will. Hence it is incorrect that the good is good *per se* even without reference to God's will; rather is it good simply because God wills it, though this divine willing is not irrational caprice, but a morally necessary act of his holy essence. Hence morality rests in its very essence on religion; and the moral law may not, as in Wolf's system, stand apart from the religious consciousness, but requires a free God-obeying course of acting answering to the divine will, and therefore also to the end of the perfection of the creature. A natural, though not absolutely sufficing manifestation of the divine will, is given in the *conscience*, which, however, does not, as with Wolf, simply form a theoretical judgment, but contains also at the same time a feeling of joy or anguish, and hence an impulse. Crusius separates *prudence* from the doctrine of morality proper, as the ability of finding, for rational ends, also the special appropriate means.—A more popular presentation of this view is contained in the so-long-esteemed, widely-read, and influential "Moral Lectures"* of *Gellert* (1770), which, however, are estimable more for their noble sentiments and warmth of feeling than for depth of thought; and which, in their rhetorically verbose and often dull and tedious manner could have made so great an impression only in an age which had lost all taste for strong food; discursive discussions on "the utility of health," etc., were then regarded as interesting reading. Gellert addresses himself more to the feelings than to the cognizing understanding, but the former are not embraced in Christian depth, but rather as mere feeble sentimentality.

Since the middle of this century the taste for really philosophical thinking had been declining in Germany, in the precise measure in which the pretension to the name of "philosophical century" was put forward; instead of a spiritually-vigorous, constantly-progressing development of thought, we

* *Moralische Vorlesungen.*

find, for the most part, only a self-complacent superficial criticising tendency and arbitrarily-brought-together, ungrounded assertions and observations, derived more from outward experience than from reason, and often delighting in rhetorical bombast.—The voluminous *Feder* of Göttingen (*Prakt. Philos.*, 1776; *Unters. üb. d. menschlichen Willen*, 1779–85), reminds indeed often of Wolf by his pedantic minuteness, but not by depth of thought; and he bases himself in the main on the empiricism of Locke.—*Garve*, who was highly esteemed by his contemporaries, derived the most of his matter from the English moralists, and limited his own moral thoughts to annotations on other writers (Cicero), and to disconnected but clear and elegantly written, though neither profound nor ingenious, dissertations.

SECTION XLI.

In England and France an anti-Christian tendency gave rise to a progressively-degenerating *moralism*, which,—resting on an idealess empiricism, and, though vigorously resisted, yet maintaining a rising influence for a long time,—based itself in part on a superficial deism, but also in part, and more consequentially, advanced to pure atheism and materialism, and exalted into a moral law the lowest form of Epicurean self-seeking. But it was especially reserved to the *French* mind to draw the ultimate consequences of these premises, and to seek in the wildest demoralization the highest civilization and "philosophy," and, through a destruction-loving dissolution of all moral consciousness in the higher classes (a dissolution which swept over devastatingly into the un-German circles of the German literary world) to prepare the way for that general convulsion in Europe which at length attained, only through horrors and anarchy, to some presence of mind and to some degree of calm. *English* moralism lingered

in general in a state of capricious wavering between
the principle of happiness and the principle of spiritual perfection, between the principle of subjective
eudemonism and the principle of objective spiritualism. The reaction of this freethinking on *Germany*
shows itself mostly in the superficial utilitarian
morality of the period of self-styled "*illuminism.*"

Quite otherwise than in Germany was philosophical ethics
shaped in England and France. While in Germany, notwithstanding the deep spiritual and moral disorder consequent
upon the Thirty Years' war, there prevailed, for a long
while still, a predominantly Christian spirit, (which remained
proof against the Spinozistic Pantheism, and sought to develop philosophy in harmony with Christianity, and only
gradually and at a late hour was enervated by French freethinking through the un-German culture of the higher
classes), in England the religious contests had resulted in a
deep spiritual laxity and in a growing aversion to Christianity
and to the spiritual in general. The unspiritual empiricism
of *Bacon* and *Locke* seconded this superficial empirical turning-away to the immediately visible and prosaic reality of the
world. At first it was regarded as a progress to disregard
the doctrinal contents of Christianity and to insist only on
its *morals;* then it followed very naturally that this morality,
as divorced from its doctrinal basis, should be divorced also
from its historical presuppositions in general, and be derived
only from the consciousness of the natural man, and that religion in general, as in contrast to the Christian religion,
should be conceived simply as a system of *moralism,* over
which then, not as a foundation but as a protecting super-
structure, a superficial *deism* was constructed;—or, indeed,
this tendency was followed out further, and men rejected
also this deism, and contented themselves with the superficial
morality of individual self-love; and it must be regarded as
a real progress (as in contrast to this spiritual superficiality),
when clearer thinkers skeptically undermined also this pretended natural religion and natural morality, and insisted on
the vanity of all human knowledge.

Bacon of Verulam, though not himself constructing an ethical system, opened, by his empiricism (which opposed all previous philosophy, and according to which there is absolutely no knowledge *à priori*, but only such as springs from immediate and primarily sensuous experience), a current of thought which was dangerous to the Christian world-theory, although he himself did not in the least oppose the Christian consciousness, but rather placed Christian faith above all philosophical knowledge. However, he was not clearly conscious of the tendency of his fundamental thoughts. On this basis, *Locke* (*ob.* 1704) subsequently developed a system of philosophy which attained, especially in England, to a wide-reaching influence, but which is in fact, properly speaking, the very opposite of all speculation. True knowledge arises only from the experience of our sensuous existence; general notions are not the first but the last; the human mind *per se* has and produces neither notions nor ideas, but is rather a *tabula rasa* upon which the experience of the objective world first writes its characters; and it is only through impressions from objective existence that the spirit attains, through abstraction, comparison, and analysis, to ideas. Out of this empiricism, however harmless and pretentionless it might seem at first examination, was destined logically to result a system of religion and morality essentially different from the Christian world-theory; and historical facts realized this logical sequence. It sweeps away, in fact, at a single blow all ideal contents of the scientific and religious consciousness, in so far as these lie outside of sensuous experience. But experience furnishes not ideas, but only impressions; and at furthest one attains only to abstracted notions, which, however, have no general and unconditional validity; for the ideas of the divine and eternal, there is no place. But man must have *something* ideal; if he has it not in and above himself, so that he has simply to accept it in his rational self-consciousness and in religious faith, then he must have it *before* himself,—must practically and productively create it, in action; the ideal is indeed not yet real, but it is to become so. It is consequently, at least, a presentiment of reason which turned this idealess empiricism toward ethics. But precisely this one-sided moralism shows most evidently,

the incorrectness of the ground-principles; an idealess morality sinks at once to a morality of the most ignoble self-
seeking and materialism. A moral consciousness is, according to this system, derived only from direct experience;
what is good I know only from the fact that it makes upon
me a pleasant impression, affects me, as a particular individual,
with the feeling of pleasure; individual happiness becomes
the measure of the moral, and thus Epicureanism has again
attained to validity.

Already before the more complete development of the
Baconian empiricism by *Locke*, Thomas *Hobbes* had drawn
the natural and clear consequences of the same.* Only what
we experience is true; but we can experience only through
the senses, and hence only the sensuous; only this is true and
real, even in man himself. Human action has not a *purpose*,
for a purpose is a mere idea without reality, but only a *ground*,
namely, in his sensuously-material reality, and, in virtue of
this ground, it is also fully determined; hence the moral law
is in no respect different from the law of nature. Good or
evil is the agreeable or disagreeable state of the individual
person, and hence is determined by our immediate feelings,
and has in no sense a general significancy beyond the individual being; what is good for me is not so for another;
hence, in regard to the good there can be no general decision;
every one determines this according to his feelings and experience; every one strives, and rightly too, to have the most
possible feelings of pleasure, and in this he is rational and
moral. Self-love in this sense, namely, of referring every
thing to one's own enjoyment of the agreeable, is the highest
moral law; each has a right to all. From this it follows, indeed, that through mere morality no harmonious life of men
in common is possible, but that, on the contrary, all strive
against each other,—a war of all against all; but this leads
not to a proof of the unreality of the moral law, but only to
the necessity of the *State;* but also the state, because of the
lack of a universally-valid objective norm of morality, can
rest only on the individual will of the strong. The unlimited
despotism of a single person is alone capable of bringing

* Especially in his *Leviathan*, 1651, and in his *De cive*. 1647; comp.
Lechler: *Gesch. des engl. Deismus*, 1841, p. 67 *sqq.*

order and harmony into the chaos of individual strivings;
and all individuals must submit themselves unconditionally
to the will of this ruler,—a will which knows no other law
than its own pleasure, and which consequently is always
right, let the ruler decree what he will, and which is for all
the citizens of that state the unassailable law and conscience,
and which has consequently to determine what shall constitute right and morality.   Also all religion in the state depends exclusively on the will of the ruler; and he alone has
to determine what shall be believed and not believed; no one
has a right, in the state, to hold any thing else for good and
true in the moral and religious sphere, than what the king
declares as good and true; sin is only a contradiction to the
king's will.   Whatever is not by him prescribed or forbidden,
is morally indifferent.—We cannot deny to this system full
consequentiality, and the unabashed nakedness of the same
is at least more honest than those more recent views, which
seek to bemantle the very same ground-thoughts with more
moral forms and disguises.

In express antagonism to this materialism, *Cumberland*
made general benevolence the principle of morality; * but he
rendered it difficult for himself to refute the consequential
Hobbes, by the fact that he placed himself essentially upon
the stand-point of sensuous experience, and undertook therefrom to rise to higher religious and moral ideas.   He attains
thus to the principle which he makes the foundation of all
morality, namely, that the striving for the common good of
the entire system of rational creatures leads to the good of
all the single parts of the same, whereof our own happiness
constitutes a portion.   Hence the chief end of moral effort
is not one's own but the general good, although the former
is contained in the latter.   This moral law, to the observance of which man is obligated by nature itself, is especially
seconded by religion, and sanctified by the will of God, as
Lawgiver, who associates with the law rewards and punishments.   But the idea of God is not already pre-supposed in
the moral consciousness, but this idea pre-supposes this consciousness.—Hobbes was opposed from a stand-point diametrically opposed to this, and related to that of Plato, and

* *De legibus naturæ*, 1672, 83, 94.

hence also more effectually and consequentially, by *Cudworth,*[*]
who entirely rejected the empirical basis of the moral, and
appealed to original moral ideas given in reason itself.　He
assails materialism and atheism in a learned and ingenious
manner, and declares the moral ideas which transcend all
experience, and which can never be adequately explained by
experience, as a self-revelation of God himself, impressed
upon finite reason; and in his opposition to empiricism, he
goes so far as to hold that the moral idea stands even above
the will of God, so that this will does not determine the
good, but is determined by the *per se* valid idea of the good
as existing in God.　A complete moral system Cudworth did
not carry out; and his influence was less extensive, because of
the prevalent tendency of the English mind toward empirical
reality, than it deserved to be.—Basing himself upon Cudworth's theory, Henry *More* presented a brief but comprehensive treatise on philosophical ethics.[†]　(The end of morality is the perfection, and therefore the happiness, of man,
which rests essentially on virtue; sensuousness has no right
in itself, but stands under the dominion of moral reason; the
antecedent condition of morality is the freedom of the will,
as itself not determined by any thing, not even by knowledge.)　In a similar spirit, Samuel *Clarke* (1708) insisted on
the view, that creatures are for each other.　Morality consists in conducting one's self, by virtue of free rationality, in
harmony with the universe, and in the proper relation to
one's self and to the rest of the world, even as irrational
creatures do from inner impulse.　This relation cannot be
arbitrarily fixed by man, but is fixed by the nature itself of
things, and man is morally to conform himself to this relation; thereby he realizes his happiness.

Locke endeavored to avoid the inferences which Hobbes
had drawn from the ground-thought of empiricism, at least
in the moral sphere.[‡]　Inborn moral ideas, or ideas that lie
in the essence of reason itself and in the conscience, do not
exist; all moral laws are derived simply from the observation
of real life,—are inferred from the benefit which certain

[*] *Systema intellectuale*, etc., in English in 1678.
[†] *Enchiridion ethicum*, in his *Opp. omn.*, 1679, 2 fol.
[‡] *Essay on the Human Understanding*, 1690.

modes of action have for the well-being of the actor or of others, and hence may, under different circumstances, be very different; and the actual differences, nay, even contradictions, of moral views that do exist, prove that these views do not lie in reason itself. It is only through education and dominant custom that moral opinions rise into pretended fixed moral principles,—into laws of conscience; there is no innate primitive conscience; the approval or disapproval of a particular organized society is the sole sufficient measure of virtue and vice. Here, however, it is natural that such modes of action as are useful not merely to the subject himself, but also to others and to the community, should also be regarded in general as praiseworthy, and hence virtuous, so that for a certain circle of actions, there may indeed be found an essential agreement of moral judgment, and hence a certain natural law lying in the nature of the thing, which is to be regarded as also God's law. However, Locke derives this law not from the nature of the moral thought itself, but in fact, simply from public opinion, and hence from experience, and he rises only through inferences *from* facts of experience to more general notions, which, however, have by no means a validity absolutely and *per se*. Hence the moral idea does not transcend reality,—does not so much say what *should* be, as rather what already *is;* a moral judgment upon the actual moral consciousness of a society is, according to Locke's theory, impossible; for not the idea is the measure for reality, but reality is the measure for the idea. The question whether indeed the condition and the moral consciousness of society themselves might not be perverted and untrue, is entirely out of place,—is indeed absurd,—as it would assume to measure moral reality by an idea independent thereof; the moral consciousness of society is always right.—The limiting of these far-reaching assertions by the interposing of a superficially-conceived divine revelation is without any sufficient foundation in Locke's system.—The Lockian view has indeed, as compared with that of Hobbes, a somewhat more respectable tone, but it has on the other hand less inner consequentiality. The thought of self-love, or, more properly, self-seeking, is at least intelligible and clear; but the taking, as a basis, the judgment of society must be regarded as en-

tirely ungrounded, and is in reality utterly meaningless, inasmuch as, in every society, moral views the very opposite of each other are represented, so that consequently the individual is, after all, referred to his own private judgment, which, as it rests upon no *per se* valid idea, can in fact be based only on the feeling of pleasure or displeasure.

The consequences of this unspiritual ethics showed themselves very soon. The position of *Wollaston* * is as yet moderate, but for that reason all the more indefinite and unclear. He reduces all religion to morality; religion is only the obligation to do the good and avoid the evil. The good is identical with the true; every action is good which gives expression to a true proposition, that is, which actually recognizes that a thing is as it really is, and which hence corresponds to the nature or end of a thing; things should be treated as being what they are. The destination of man himself is happiness; but happiness is pleasure,—the consciousness of something agreeable, of that which is in harmony with the nature of man; hence true pleasure springs only from that which corresponds to the destination of man, and consequently to reason. Morality or religion is, therefore, the seeking of happiness through the realizing of truth and of reason.—The next advancement of this tendency consisted in this, that the thought of happiness was fixed more definitely in view. Man *wills* by his very nature to be happy, that is, he has inclinations the fulfillment of which renders him happy. These inclinations man does not give to himself, but he has them from nature,—finds them in a definite form existing within himself; they are the norms of man's actions, that is, he is good when he follows his natural inclinations. This advance to Epicurean ethics is made by the plausible and fashionable writer, Lord *Shaftesbury*.† Every action springs from an inner determinateness of the actor, from a proclivity or propensity; hence the moral worth of an action lies essentially in this propensity; the propensity aims at that which gives pleasure, and avoids that which gives displeasure; that which by its presence gives pleasure, and by its absence displeasure, is *good;* the opposite thereof is *evil;* as objects of effort, the former is the good, the latter the evil; between these

---

    * *The Religion of Nature Delineated*, 1724.
    † *Characteristicks*, (1711), 1714; comp. Lechler, p. 240 *sqq.*

there lies the sphere of the indifferent. The decision as to good and evil is not arbitrary; but that is good which corresponds to the peculiarity of a being, and, for that very reason, gives pleasure to the being experiencing it. Happiness is the greatest possible sum of satisfactions or experiences of pleasure; spiritual pleasure-impressions stand higher, however, than the merely sensuous; and the generally-useful or benevolent propensities are, in turn, the better among the spiritual ones, for they duplicate the enjoyment by the participation of others; and they do not stand in contradiction to our own personal good, because they relate to the whole of which we ourselves form a part. Hence true morality consists in the striving after the proper relation and harmony of the individual and of the whole; the one is not to be merged into the other, for man is just as much an individual as he is a member of the whole, and self-love is *per se* just as legitimate as the propensity of general benevolence. Hence virtue consists in a rationally-calculated weighing out of the measure of the reciprocally limiting propensities, that is, in preserving a proper equilibrium. The decision in this case is given primarily by our *innate feeling* for good and evil, by the moral *sense* or instinct,—not taken in the sense of a conscious thought, but of a feeling, a feeling of pleasure in the presence of the good, and of displeasure in the presence of the evil. This moral sense is developed by exercise and reflection into a *moral judgment*. Virtue is indeed independent of religion, and even atheism does not directly endanger it; but yet it receives its proper force and life only in the belief in a good, all-wise and justly-governing God.— Shaftesbury endeavors to rise above the fortuitousness of the determination of the moral in Hobbes and Locke, and to attain to a *per se* valid determination of the same; but after all, he also finds the deciding voice only in the fortuitous feeling of pleasure or displeasure; his empiricism is essentially subjective. That, as differing from Locke, he regards the moral feeling as innate, does not yet guarantee its objective truth, and, at all events, the objection of Locke holds good against it, namely, the actually-existing diversity of moral views. But this moral feeling is not a moral idea; it has no contents, but utters itself only in each separate case, when it is stimulated by an action or an object, even as a piano gives a note only when it is struck; other-

wise this feeling is silent and dead, whereas an idea is living and conscious even in the absence of any reality affecting it; this subjective feeling itself is moreover incapable of being tested by á *per se* and absolutely valid idea.

While *Collins*, the eulogist of Epicurus, a disciple and friend of Locke, and the first who called himself Freethinker, denied the freedom of the will and regarded human action as absolutely determined by the influences surrounding us, *Hutcheson* (of Glasgow) endeavored to rectify the moral system of Shaftesbury by assuming good-will toward *others*, in contradistinction to self-love, as the contents proper of the innate moral sense. To the purely empirical foundation of ethics, however, he held fast in his "System of Moral Philosophy" (1755). We find that certain actions in men, even when these men are not affected by the consequences of the same, meet with approbation or disapprobation; from this it follows that the ground of this judgment is not personal advantage or disadvantage, but a natural moral sense, which perceives the moral irrespective of personal interest, and has therein pleasure, and which therefore also, equally disinterestedly, impels to moral action. This inborn moral sense is not a conscious idea, but an immediate feeling which differs from the interested self-feeling,—just as we have an immediate pleasure in a beautiful, regular form, without being conscious of the mathematical laws thereof, or having any benefit therefrom. The moral approbation and striving are consequently also all the purer the less our personal interest is involved in the case. The selfish and the benevolent propensities mutually exclude each other, for benevolence begins only where personal interest ceases. Therefore we have to make our choice between the two propensities, and as the benevolent one is the purer, hence the moral proper consists exclusively in it. Virtue is not practiced for the sake of a benefit or an enjoyment, but purely out of inner pleasure in it; our nature has an inner innate tendency to promote the welfare of others without having any regard therein to personal benefit. This benevolence toward others is the essence of all the virtues; for even our care for our own welfare is exercised in order to preserve ourselves for the good of others; the degree of virtue rises in proportion to the happiness procured for others, and to the number of persons benefited by us. The preliminarily-

ignored moral relation of man to God, Hutcheson afterward brings—not without violence—into his system, by holding that the moral sense leads also to the union of the moral creature with the Author of all perfection.—The fundamental thoughts of this ethical system are indeed well meant, but they are scientifically weak and arbitrary; from the Christian view they are far remote, for the self-complacent mirroring of self in the pretendedly pure virtuousness of one's own benevolent heart, and the easy contenting of self in a certain circle of benevolent outward actions, are, in one direction, quite as dangerous for correct self-knowledge, as is the system of pure self-seeking in the other.—A related system, but one manifoldly complicated in unclear originality, was developed by Adam *Smith* (1759, and later). He emphasized, more strongly still, the element of feeling for others in the innate moral sense, and conceived of it as the feeling of sympathy, in virtue of which we share in natural participation in the joy and in the pains of others, and strive for the participation and harmony of others with our own feelings and actions; in this harmony we find the good, and in the opposite the evil. The morality of our action we recognize by the fact that it is adapted to awaken the sympathies of others; a perfectly isolated man could not possibly have a moral judgment as to himself, because he would lack the criterion, the mirror. Hence man must always so act that others not standing in the same fortuitous relations, that is, impartial persons, can sympathize with him. The obscure conviction that the moral consciousness must rest on a *per se* valid idea, brings the empiric to this strange and certainly very difficult and inadequate procedure, which, however, though expressly intended to throw off the accidentality of individual being, yet cannot, after all, get rid of it.

Also David *Hume* treats of the subject of ethics, though with less acumen than that wherewith, in the sphere of religion and of theoretical philosophy, he skeptically undermines the certainty of all knowledge.* While, in the field of philosophy, he ingeniously exposed the feeble superficiality of the prevalent empiricism, he yet hesitated to introduce his skepticism, with like consequentiality into the practical sphere of morals. A real science of the moral there cannot be, in the opinion of

* *Treatise of Human Nature*, 1730; *Essays*, etc., 1742.

Hume, seeing that the moral is not an object of the cognizing understanding, but only of mere feeling or sensation. The ultimate end of all action is happiness; but that which renders happy can be determined only by sensation; hence a sense, or tact, or feeling innate in all men, decides as to good and evil, in that the good excites a pleasant, and the evil an unpleasant feeling. Hence we must learn by way of pure observation what actions violate, or answer to, the moral feeling; and we find, now, that the *useful* excites moral approbation, and more particularly, that which is useful to the community. General and necessary moral ideas there are none; and even the moral feeling is very different in different nations; hence moral conceptions have always only a varying worth and rest essentially upon custom. The obligation to virtue rests on the fact that in virtue there is furnished the greatest guarantee for actual happiness; and also the working for the good of others reacts in the end upon our own good. Thus Hume coincides essentially with Locke. That he regards suicide as allowable is easily explainable from his ground-thoughts.—By means of a feeble and unfounded eclecticism, Adam *Ferguson* (of Edinburgh)* endeavors to avoid the one-sidedness of other moralists, but only involves himself in worse confusion. To the moral he gives three fundamental laws: the law of self-preservation, the law of community or society, and the "law of estimation," (the latter relating to the *per se* excellent),—without reducing this threefoldness to any kind of clear unity. He attains to an unpredjudiced consideration of the moral in detail only at the expense of the consequentiality of his system.

The ultimate consequences of empiricism were not drawn by the systematic moralists, but by other so-called Freethinkers who wrote more for the general public. Such was the case especially with the most influential among them, Lord *Bolingbroke*, the chief representative of deism (*ob.* 1751),† who declared Plato to be half crazy, and all philosophy proper to be mere narrow-mindedness. The moral law is, as the law of nature, clearly revealed to all men through the observation of existence. All morality rests on self-love; this law incites to marriage, to the family, and to society, and to the duties that result therefrom. The end of all effort is the greatest possible

* *Institutes of Moral Philosophy*, 1769.   † *Works*, 1754.

happiness, that is, the greatest possible number of pleasure-sensations. But this natural law teaches Bolingbroke some very strange things; shamefulness, *e. g.*, is only an aspiration of man to be something better than the brute, or it is a mere social prejudice; polygamy is not immoral; on the contrary, it harmonizes with the law of nature, because it effects a greater increase of the race; wedlock-communion is disallowable only between parents and children; all other degrees of relationship admit of it, for the highest law and end of marriage is propagation. The pretentious superficiality of this writer obtained for him in the " cultured " world the highest repute.

English moralism checked itself, for the most part, at half-ways; it found as yet too much moral consciousness alive among the masses, not to feel bound in general to hold fast still to a respectable code of morality, even though at the cost of the consequentiality of the system. In *France*, on the contrary, the demoralization had made sufficient progress among the cultivated classes to be enabled to throw off all reserve, also in the sphere of theory. The scanty remnants of religious and moral contents still retained in the freethinking ethics of Englishmen, had to be thrown out, in the further fermenting process, as discoloring dregs, in order that the unmingled wisdom-beverage of the natural man might attain to its life-giving purity; deistic moralism had to pass over into atheistic materialism. The French ethics of frivolity became, also for German ears, a sweet-sounding music; and French parasites at the little German ducal courts charged themselves with the task of distilling the decoction of trans-Rhenane moral notions also into the lower strata of the German population.

Shaftesbury and Hutcheson had endeavored to secure the innate moral feeling against the threatening overthrow of all morality, by placing over against the feeling for self, a feeling for the social whole, either as of like worth, or as of a still higher validity. This course was arbitrary, and not grounded in their fundamental principle; for every man is, as an individual, the nearest to himself. And a feeling inborn in *me* relates, after all, first and last, always to *myself ;* as a merely natural being inspired by no higher idea, I feel for others only in so far as I am myself interested in them. Feeling clings absolutely to the subject, and egotism is the inner essence of any natural

moral feeling which is not willing to be dominated by an idea.
In order to this further development of ethics, there was need
of a still further carrying out of empiricism as a theory. This
we meet with in *Condillac*, a French nobleman, an abbot and
prince-educator,—one of the most superficial and, therefore,
most preferred authors of the middle of the eighteenth century.—All knowledge rests on sensuous impressions; man is
acted upon and filled with spiritual contents, simply as a machine, through outward impressions ; of all the senses the sense
of touch is the highest; it alone gives us certainty as to the
objective reality of things, and raises man above the brute,
with whom in other respects he is essentially identical. The
pleasure and displeasure of impressions work desire and repugnance, and hence awaken and determine the will. It is incredible what stupid absurdities Condillac offers in the name of
metaphysics ; and it is a significant index of the spirit of the
age, that he was one of the most influential and fêted writers
of France. The ethics of this world-theory was easily inferred,
and was pronounced with open boldness. Long previously
Gassendi (of Paris, *ob.* 1655) had presented the satisfaction of
desire as the end of human life; this satisfying is rational when
it is orderly, natural, and not excessive; and it effects peace of
heart and painlessness of body. He recommended, consequentially enough, the doctrine of Epicurus as the highest wisdom.
—The full and clear consequence of empiricism, however, was
drawn by *Helvetius*, who expressly based his doctrine on the,
by him, highly esteemed theory of Locke. As an affluent gen-
tleman of leisure, and living only for his pleasures, he became
greatly renowned by his work, *De l'esprit* (1758), throughout
the luxurious fashionable circles of Europe. His book was
proscribed in France, but all the more circulated throughout
Europe; and the author, in his travels to different courts, especially the German ones, was fêted as a great philosopher. His
second more important work, (a further development of the
first one,) *De l'homme*, appeared only after his death (1772). The
highly-colored and daring tone of his writings, with their rich
setting of wit, and of indelicate anecdotes, furnishes a clear
image of the then prevalent spirit of the higher classes of cultivated Europe.—All thoughts, according to Helvetius, spring
from sensuous perceptions, and our knowledge extends only so

far as the senses extend; of any thing super-sensuous, and hence also of God, we know nothing. The motives to activity are essentially the *passions*, which spring from our inclination to pleasure and our aversion to displeasure. The fundamental stimulus of all moral activity is *self-love*, the expression of which is, in fact, the passions; nothing great is accomplished without great passion; he who is not passionate is stupid. As, now, all thoughts rest on sensuous impressions, so rest also all self-love and all passion, and hence all morality, on the impulses of *sensuous* pleasure; and even the decision as to truth is entirely dependent on the interest of the self-loving subject. Should the case arise, says Helvetius, that it would be more advantageous for me to regard the part as greater than the whole, then I would in fact assume this to be the case. The good, or the moral, is neither an absolutely valid idea, nor is it any thing arbitrarily assumed, but the determination as to it rests in the experience of the individual; but experience teaches that each regards as good that which is useful to him; and consequently each judges of the morality of actions simply according to his own interest; hence the best actions would be such as corresponded to the interest of all men; but there are no such actions. Hence we must limit our view; and, on closer examination, we find to be truly good that which promotes the interest not merely of the individual but of our nation; the political virtue is the highest, and the political transgression, the highest sin; that which does not contribute to the public good of the nation, as, for example, the so-called religious virtues, is not a virtue, and what does not conflict therewith is not a sin; virtues which profit nothing must be regarded as virtues of delusion, and be discarded. Hence, true ethics has its norm essentially in the civil law-book and in public utility; that which lies outside of these is, for the most part, morally indifferent; when it is useful to the public weal, even inhumanity is just. The motive to moral activity remains, even in this so narrowly limited sphere, self-love; the thought of doing the good for the good's sake, is antiquated and exploded. To sacrifice my own private advantage to that of the public, I am under no obligation; rather must I seek in the best manner possible to combine the two. When any one helps an unfortunate, out of compassion, this is only self-love, for he simply aims to

rid himself of the sight of misery, which is unpleasant to him. Ethics is utterly fruitless and vain so long as it does not definitely regard personal interest, and hence sensuous pleasure and the avoidance of sensuous pain, as the highest principle of morality; nothing is forbidden but what causes us pain; with religion, ethics has nothing whatever to do. Morality is therefore also, at different times and under different relations, essentially different; there is no crime which under some circumstances—(when it should be useful)—would not also be right. True, the vicious man seeks also his own advantage, and the only trouble in the matter is that he deceives himself as to the means thereto; hence, he is to be pitied because of his error, but not to be despised. The fact that among all nations, some actions are regarded as virtuous which offer no profit whatever for this life, is simply a hurtful delusion. As self-interest is the ground of all virtue, hence it is also entirely legitimate that the state should stimulate its citizens to obedience by rewards and punishments; in fact, it thereby hits upon the solely correct moral motives to the good; rewards and punishments are the gods which create virtue. All statesmanship consists in awakening the self-love and self-interest of men, and in thereby stimulating them to virtue.

The intellectual revolution—represented by great names—made sweeping advances in France and also in the fashionable world servilely dependent on France, at the courts of the rest of Europe, and especially of Germany, and had already long since reached its ultimate results, before the political revolution enabled also the lower classes to speak their word in the same sense. It was fashionable at this period to designate by the word "*esprit*" (as the privilege of the giddy, freethinking world) that which was subsequently called "revolution" among the great masses, and which was, in fact, simply the consequence of the former. Every thing which hitherto had passed as philosophy, (with the exception of the Epicurean), was regarded as nonsense; the most stupid superficiality, provided only that it ridiculed sacred things, passed as philosophy; wit and frivolous fancies took the place of earnest science. The "philosophical" century sank, in the appreciation of really philosophical thought, deeper than even the earlier and as yet barbarous

Middle Ages had sunk. The higher the encomiums they
heaped upon what they called "spirit," so much the more
utter became the spiritual vacuity; men extolled reason more
pretentiously than ever, and yet they placed in her temple,
as goddess, a public woman. Rousseau and Voltaire passed
as the profoundest thinkers of all ages; their spiritual tri-
umphs and attainments were unparalleled, and Voltaire's renown transcended in glory all renown ever heaped upon an
author. The history of the human mind has no second
century to refer to in which un-reason dominated with such
complete omnipotence.

Jean Jacques *Rousseau* produced indeed no system of
ethics, but he exerted in the sphere of moral opinion an
influence such as no author before or after him ever exerted,
and felt even up to the present day,—not indeed because he
uttered deep thoughts, but because he gave expression to
what lay in the spirit of the age,—himself an utterly un-
genuine character—under the form of a severe moralist
undermining all morality, under the form of earnest thought
bidding defiance to all philosophy and science, under the
form of a censorious sage, in hermit-like seclusion from the
world, preparing soft cushions for the vices of the "cultured"
great. And precisely in this his peculiar character he chimed
in with the tastes and desires of the age; he simply made, in
the dike of the as yet somewhat cramped current of the age,
the little breach through which its pent-up waters dispersed
themselves over the low-lands so as subsequently, as morasses,
to exhale the pestilential miasma of revolution. Of scientific
ground-thoughts there can in Rousseau be no question; bold
assertions and rhetorical phrases take almost every-where the
place of scientific demonstration. The writings of Locke
exerted upon him the greatest influence; sensuous experience
is also for him the source of all ideas. His moral views receive their proper commentary in his utterly immoral life.
His *Contrat social* (1761) became the theoretical basis of the
French Revolution; his narrow-minded sophistical work,
Emile (1762) had an immeasurable and bewildering influence
on education, and is yet to-day the catechism of all un-Christian schemes of education. Rousseau's religion of nature, as
he called it, is a shallow idealess deism grouped around the.

three thoughts: God, virtue, and immortality, in high sounding rhetorical phrase. He bases morality upon the natural *conscience*, which, as a direct feeling for the moral, renders unnecessary all instruction and all science as to the moral, and guides man with unerring certainty. All immorality springs simply from "civilization," and from perverted education; true education consists in non-educating. Let the child be simply let alone in its naturalness; let it be guarded against perverting influences, and then it will spontaneously develop itself as normally as a tree in a good soil. In the nature of man there lies nothing evil whatever; all natural impulses are good; every child is by nature still just as good as the first man was in coming from the hands of the Creator. The sole inborn passion is self-love, and this is good. The child should learn every thing through personal experience, and nothing through obedience; the words "obey" and "command" must be erased from its dictionary, as also the words "duty" and obligation;" the child must by all means be kept in the belief that it is its own lord, and that its educator is subordinate to it. Make the child strong, and it will be good; for all defects, the educator alone is to blame. The sole moral instruction for the child is: "Do wrong to no one;" of love and religion there should, in education, be no question whatever. Instruction should by no means be imparted before the twelfth year, and even after this period only at the desire of the pupil; at twelve years it should yet be incapable of distinguishing its right hand from its left. It should never believe or do any thing on the mere word of another, but must always do simply what it has found to be good from personal experience. The end of this "inactive" method of education, as Rousseau himself designates it, is the end of human life, namely, freedom; but true freedom consists in this, that we wish nothing other than what we can do or obtain; and in this case we will also do nothing other than what pleases us; and this is always the right. Hence the essence of all morality is the giving free scope to our natural propensities. The highest moral law is; "seek thine own highest welfare with the least possible detriment to others." Christianity is the natural enemy of true morality and of human society, for

it desires the absolute purity of human nature,—directs man away from the earthly, and preaches only servitude and tyranny.   These were sweet words for the ears of the great multitude, and they did not die away unheeded, but found enthusiastic welcome.—Although the almost apotheosized prince of the "philosophical" century, *Voltaire*, whose pretended philosophy rests almost exclusively on Locke, wrote both moral phrases and un-moral poems, yet in neither case has he produced any thing peculiar or original, much less philosophical, notwithstanding his frequent allusion to his "metaphysics."   Morality, he repeats time and again in the strongest affirmations, is entirely independent of religious faith,—rests upon a natural innate impulse, and is consequently in all men and in all ages, so soon as they use their reason, uniform and the same.*   Virtue or vice, the morally good or evil, is always and every-where that which is either useful or hurtful to society; incest between father and daughter may, under circumstances, be allowable, and even a duty, as, for example, when a single family constitutes an isolated colony; falsehoods uttered out of a good purpose are legitimate, and the same holds good of almost every thing that is in ordinary cases unallowable.   Divinely-revealed moral laws there are none; but a certain benevolence toward others is inborn in man, at the same time with self-love.   To the objection, that with so uncertain a basis, one might seek his own welfare by stealing, robbing, etc., Voltaire has the ready answer: then he would get hanged.†
And all this he calls metaphysics.

What little of a superficial religious consciousness had yet remained with Rousseau and Voltaire, entirely vanished with the *Encyclopedists*, and especially with *Diderot* (*ob.* 1784). Diderot endeavored, above all things, entirely to divorce morality from religion; the latter is for the former rather a hindrance than a help.   In morality itself he wavers, undecided, between naturalistic determinism and a very superficial society-morality.   The Epicurean view he regards as the most true.   All the vices spring from covetousness, and hence they can all be got rid of by the abolition of property,

* *Œuvres*, Paris, 1830, t. 31, p. 262; t. 12, p. 160; t. 42, p. 583.
† *Ibid.*, t. 37, p. 336; t. 38, p. 40.

by a community of goods; for the discovery of this universal panacea of human ills, he takes to himself great credit.— Naturalistic morality appears in its most gross form and in shameless nakedness in *La Mettrie* (*ob.* 1751),* whom even Voltaire despised, but whom Frederick the Great, from some incomprehensible caprice, made his reader and daily companion (from 1748 on), and even nominated him, ignoramus that he was, to membership in the Academy of Sciences. Religion and morality stand in irreconcilable antagonism to philosophy; they rest only in politics, and serve for the bridling of the masses who are yet unable to rise to philosophy, just as, for a similar reason, there is as yet need also of hangman and death-penalties. But humanity as a whole cannot be happy until all the world embraces atheism. Religion has poisoned nature and cheated her out of her rights. Where the truth, that is, atheism, prevails, there man follows no other law than that of his particular natural propensity. And thus alone can he be happy. Man is not essentially different from the brute, not even by any peculiar moral consciousness; he stands in many respects below the brute, and has only this advantage, that he has a greater number of wants, whereby a greater culture becomes possible. Man—as sprung from the mingling of different races of animals, and as formed from matter of the same kind as that constituting the brute, save only that it has simply gone through a higher fermentation-process, and as being of a merely material organism (for the soul is only the brain, which is itself only a slightly organized piece of dirt),—is simply a mere machine, and is set into motion by outward impressions, and hence he is necessarily determined in all his volitions, and is not responsible for any of his actions. Repentance is folly; for individual man is not at fault for his being a poorly constructed machine. Hence also we should not despise the seemingly vicious, nor judge them severely. As, at death, all is over, hence we should enjoy the present as much as we possibly can. To defer an enjoyment when it offers itself, is the same as waiting at a banquet without eating, until all are done; enjoyment, and indeed primarily and principally, sensuous enjoyment, is our highest and sole destination.—It was

---

* *L'homme machine; L'art de jouir.*, 1751.

precisely during his stay in Potsdam that La Mettrie wrote his most audacious glorification of the wildest and even unnatural wantonness. His writings were very much sought after in the higher circles of society.

The total result of materialistic ethics is summed up in a work written very probably by Baron Holbach with the co-operation of Diderot and other Encyclopedists: *System de la nature, par Mirabaud* (1770), constituting the gospel proper of atheism, and presenting nakedly and undisguisedly, in a dull and spiritless form, the results of the philosophy of Locke, Hobbes, and Condillac, who are in fact expressly cited as sources. As man is only a material machine, hence there is between the physical and the moral life no difference; all thinking and willing consist simply in modifications of the brain. All propensities and passions are purely corporeal states—are either hatred or love, that is " repulsion or attraction;" the absurd doctrine of the freedom of the will has been invented simply to justify the equally absurd one of divine providence. Man is only a part of the great world-machine, determined in all his movements,—a blind instrument in the hands of necessity; the concession of freedom even to a single creature would bring the whole universe into confusion; hence whatever takes place takes place. necessarily. Religion and its ethics are the greatest enemies of man, and occasion him only torment. The system of nature alone makes man truly happy,—teaches him to enjoy the present as fully as possible, and gives him, in relation to every thing which is not an object of enjoyment, the indifference that is essential to his happiness. Hence there is no need of a special moral system. Its fundamental principle would necessarily be: " enjoy life as much as thou canst;" but every man does this already of himself without instruction. Self-love, one of the manifestations of the law of gravitation, is the highest moral law. The chief condition of happiness is bodily health; the true key of the human heart is medicine; the most effectual moralists are the physicians; he who makes the body sound, makes the man moral. Every man follows by nature and necessarily his own special interest, a course of conduct which in fact follows immediately and necessarily from his bodily organization; vice and crime

are but consequences of morbid corporeality,—are not guilt
but necessity. Hence only the unwise can repent; in any
case repentance is only a pain arising from the fact that an
act has had bad consequences for us. Now as the instincts
and passions are the sole motive of human action, hence we
can influence other men only by working upon their passions.
Each is obligated only to that which procures him an advantage. Hence a good man is he who satisfies his passions in
such a manner that other persons must contribute to this
satisfaction so as that they also thereby satisfy their own passions and interests. Hence the atheist is necessarily a good
man, whereas religion makes men bad in that it embitters to
them the passions. That suicide is held as legitimate for
those who are weary of life, is a matter of course.—This
godless world-theory disseminated itself in rapid development deeper and deeper among the masses; and the ten
years of the French Revolution are the practical realization
of this ethics as a social power.

It is characteristic of the difference of national spirit that
the naturalistic tendency could not, in its stark crudity, take
hold upon the *German* people, but came to expression only in
association with other higher principles, with Christianly-moral
elements, namely, in the Rationalistic "*illuminism*" of the
eighteenth century. Open unbelief proper and materialistic
morals spoke, in Germany, almost exclusively French; and the
sycophant court-atheists were too much despised to find hearty
favor with the masses. The demoralizing revolution which proceeded from the upper classes, met with a powerful opposition
in the German national spirit. Even while a popular school of
poetry divorced itself from the Christian consciousness, still
this school held fast to the antithesis of the spiritual and the
naturalistic world-theories, recognizing the former as the higher; "let him who cannot believe, enjoy; let him who can believe, deny himself."—The superficial deistic ethics attains to
greater influence in Germany than the materialistic, though
without giving rise to any important scientific works. On the
basis of the uncorrupted purity of human nature there was
developed a superficial utilitarian morality without deeper contents; and this morality was looked upon as the essence proper
of Christianity. *Basedow's* demagogic attempt at world-reno-

vation by a new system of education based on Rousseau, became very soon too ridiculous to exert any enduring influence, *Steinbart* * (professor of theology at Frankfort on the Oder) in his utterly superficial but greatly lauded *System of Pure Philosophy or Christian Doctrine of Happiness* (1778, '80, '86, '94), regarded the chief contents of the Christian religion and of Christian ethics as simply the answering of the question: " What have I to learn, and to do, in order to have the greatest possible sum of pleasure ? " " Happiness is the end of the entire human life, and consists in the heart-state of a continuous contentment and of frequently recurring enjoyment." Every man is by nature perfectly good and pure, though indeed not as a spirit but as an animal, and he rises only gradually from the animal to the man. Self-love is the ground of all morality, and morality is the infallible way to a state of enjoyment; of a checking of self-love there can be no occasion ; hence Christian virtue is " nothing else than a preparedness to enjoy one's existence to the highest degree, under all circumstances " ; the highest state of enjoyment is of course only in the life after death, where alone we can really survey the consequences of our beneficent, meritorious actions ; " but our glimpses into that life encourage us to a better using of the present one, and the fullest enjoyment of *this* life enlarges our receptivity for higher degrees of happiness in the future world." This is the pure doctrine of Jesus, which unfortunately has, for eighteen centuries, been lost sight of.—Steinbart was favored in the highest degree by the Prussian government, and aided in his plan of founding a " general normal school in which teachers might be educated for the true enlightenment of the nations."

It was only the revival of the Pantheism of Spinoza in the nineteenth century that gave rise, in Germany, to a scientific form of ethics; but also this system, though of a far higher character than the freethinking of France, yet, in its later unscientific offshoots, ultimated in like results ; and the fact that in our own day a resuscitated materialism, resting, however, more on natural science than on philosophy, presents us again with the ethics of the " System of Nature," is certainly no indication of progress in spiritual development, though indeed an

---

* *System der reinen Phil. oder Glückseligkeitslehre des Christenthums.*

evidence of a progress of the intellectual blight consequent on the too great stagnation of the religious and philosophical spirit in the present age.

SECTION XLII.

The theological ethics of the evangelical church of the eighteenth century made but a quite temperate use of German philosophy before the time of Kant, and insisted but little (not without some influence from Pietism) on the antithesis of the two evangelical churches in the sphere of ethics. *Buddæus* furnished the first scientific system of ethics, though in its philosophical elements it is rather eclectic. *Stapfer, Baumgarten* and others, applied the Wolfian philosophy in pedantic minuteness to Christian ethics; while Mosheim constructed it more upon a purely Biblical basis, and upon that of practical life-experience. Toward the close of the century the superficiality of Rationalism began already to make itself felt.

Francis *Buddæus* of Jena, one of the most learned and sound theologians of the eighteenth century, a man of comprehensive philosophical culture and who wrote also a thoughtful, evangelically-inspired system of practical philosophy (*Elementa philosophiæ practicæ*, 1697, and often), prepared the way, with his *Institut. theologiæ moralis* (1712, '23, 4to.; in German as "Introduction to Moral Theology," 1719), for a more thorough, systematic treatment of ethics. The rich, carefully and some times rather lengthily treated subject-matter rests upon sound Scripture exegesis and careful observation of human life. Influenced somewhat by Spener, this writer combines practical sense with a scientific spirit. He begins at once with the thought of the corruption of human nature and with that of divine grace, and hence gives not a general philosophical, but only a specifically-Christian system of ethics, in view of man as regenerated. The ground-thought of morality is: man must do every thing which is essential to a constant union with God

and to the restoration of God's image, and must avoid the contrary thereof. The whole subject-matter is distributed, (1), into moral theology (in the narrower sense of the word), which treats of the nature of regeneration and sanctification in their collective development,—(2) into *jurisprudentia divina*, which treats of the divine laws and of the duties resting thereupon,— and (3) into the doctrine of Christian prudence, which presents the practical carrying out of the moral in detail, and especially by clergymen. For the future development of evangelical ethics, the thorough treatment of the first part is especially valuable; Buddæus finds in Christian ethics not merely the manifestation, but also the progressive development of the spiritual life of the regenerated. He presents as chief virtues : piety, temperateness and justness. (Buddæus has been much used by other writers, also by J. J. Rambach, 1739, and by J. G. Walch, 1747).

The Reformed divine, John F. *Stapfer* of Bern made, in his rather comprehensive than scientifically-important system of ethics (1757), a very moderate use of the Wolfian philosophy. The earlier Calvinistically-rigorous spirit is here already very much modified. Sigismund Jacob *Baumgarten* (of Halle, a brother of the philosopher) follows, in his discursive "Theolog-ical Ethics" (1767, 4to.), the painfully-minute manner of Wolf, which is applied also in his numerous other writings, and which leaves absolutely nothing unsaid, not even that which every reader could supply for himself; and this pedantic discursive-ness detracts considerably from the otherwise real thoroughness of the treatment.—(The Wolfian philosophy was applied to theological ethics by *Canz* (§ 40), by Bertling [1753], and by Reusch [1760]; J. C. *Schubert* [1759, '60, '62] is more indepen-dent.)—The not sufficiently prized P. *Hanssen* (of Schleswig-Holstein) gave in his "Christian Ethics" (1739, '49) a very clear and sound presentation of the evangelical doctrine,—a work which gives evidence of a truly philosophical spirit, and protests against the one-sidedness of Wolf; in the first general part, he develops the threefold form of the moral life—in the state of innocence or perfection, in the state of sin, and in that of regeneration. T. Crüger (of Chemnitz) develops, in his *Apparatus theol. moral. Christi et renatorum* (1747, 4to.), the thought of the moral pattern as found in Christ, and hence of

an ethical Christology and of its application to the life of Christians, with great profoundness and uncommon erudition, though in a somewhat stiff, over-carefully-classified, scholastic form.

Mosheim's comprehensive "Ethics of the Holy Scriptures," * though in its sometimes almost hortatory discursiveness, often unnecessarily detailed, yet differs from works of the Wolfian and the earlier schools by a beautiful, animated and popular form, free of all stiff scholastic-elements, and gives evidence of a close observation of life, of impartial and profound study of the Scriptures, of a simple, mild, evangelical spirit, and of a thorough and careful attention to details; but the scientific demonstration and development are frequently feeble, and, despite all his insisting on the rationality of Christian morality, the philosophical element is almost entirely overlooked; the antitheses of view, as developed in the two churches, are not made prominent. The whole subject is distributed into the consideration of the inner holiness of the soul, and into that of the outer holiness of the walk. Miller's continuation of the work, though furnished with more learned apparatus, is less mature and also less inviting in form.—*Crusius*, whom we have already mentioned as a philosophical moralist, wrote also a " Moral Theology " (1772) which is inspired with a philosophical spirit, and gives evidence of deeply Christian knowledge.— *Töllner*, 1762, wrote rather on the treatment of ethics than on ethics itself,—already quite Rationalistic; *Reuss*, 1767, uncompleted; the work of G. *Less*, (1777, and subsequently), is not important; H. C. *Tittmann*, 1783, '94, endeavors to be strictly Biblical but is without depth; *Morus'* work, 1794, is imperfectly edited from his lectures,—partially based on Crusius, frequently rationalistic. The Englishman, Thomas *Stackhouse*, wrote on Christian ethics in a plain and Biblical spirit, treating mainly only of general questions. The Reformed divine, *Endemann* of Marburg, closes the series of Reformed moralists (1780), but he bears the distinctively Reformed character only in very feeble traits.

* 1735-70; continued by Miller, 1762; Miller wrote also a special *Einleit. in die theol. Moral*, 1772, and a short *Lehrbuch*, 1773.

SECTION XLIII.

In the system of *Kant* philosophical ethics put off the naturalistic or subjectivistic character; the moral idea attained, on the basis of the freedom of the will, to an objective significancy, and became an end *per se*, and not simply a means to the end of individual happiness. Independently of the theoretical reason and of the God-consciousness, the moral idea became the presupposition and basis of all speculation on the supersensuous, and hence also of rational religion. The universal validity of the moral law became the formal, and, pretendedly also, the material principal of morality. But the one-sided rational character of this morality left essential phases of the moral unaccounted for; and the merely formal character of the moral law admitted of no consequential carrying-out in detail.—The application of Kantian ground-thoughts to theological ethics was of two-fold effect,—raising it indeed above the utilitarian ethics of the "illuministic" current, but robbing it, in its divorce from religion, of a part of its Christian character.

Previous philosophical ethics had gone astray in two respects. The two equally true and necessary thoughts, that, on the one hand, the moral idea has a universally valid significancy, that it cannot be dependent in its obligating character on the chance caprice of the individual subject, and that yet, on the other, it has in fact for its end the perfection of the person, and hence also his happiness, had been one-sidedly held fast to, each for itself. Naturalistic Pantheism gave validity simply to the objective significancy of the moral,—absolutely annihilated the freedom of the will, and conceived by the moral law as a mere fatalism unalterably determining every individual; and when, with the champions of materialistic atheism, this notion of the unfree

determination of the individual, ultimated practically in an entire letting-loose of the passions, it was not without the countenance of strict consistency with the ground principle. The opposite tendency proceeded from the subject, emphasizing his free will, and hence looking less to the ground than to the end of the moral activity; man was to be determined by nothing which does not leave him absolutely free, which does not contribute to his own individual advantage, in other words, by the thought of individual happiness. While the first tendency undermined morality by the fact that it annihilated the moral subject, sinking him into a mere unfree member of the great world-machine, the other tendency imperiled morality in its innermost essence, in a no less degree, by the fact that it required no self-subordination of the subject under a *per se* valid idea, but emphasized the absolute claims of the individual personality, so that in fact in their ultimate consequences the two opposite tendencies resulted, equally, in the letting-loose of the individual in his unbridled naturalness.—Christian ethics could not, save by letting itself be led astray by philosophy, fall into either of these errors. That the moral idea is valid *per se*, that it has an unconditional, universally-obligating significancy, is here a point settled from the very start, inasmuch as it conceives this idea as the holy will of God. He who inquires first as to himself, and only afterward as to the will of God, has absolutely reversed the moral relation. On the other hand, it is, in Christian ethics, not in the least doubtful, that this will of God has in view the perfection of man, and hence also his perfect happiness,—that man, in fulfilling God's will becomes also truly happy, and does not lose his freedom but brings it to perfection.—It was high time, toward the end of the eighteenth century, to set bounds to the decline of philosophical ethics; the two opposed currents had attained to their last corrupt consequences, subversive of all morality. The "eudemonistic" tendency could oppose nothing else to the frivolous enjoyment-seeking and conscienceless self-seeking of the materialistic tendency, than an insipid utilitarian morality essentially identical at bottom with the other, and which differed from it only by an air of external decency, but not by profundity of thought or moral worthiness. It was a great forward-step of philosophical thought-development when

Kant, with mighty hand, dashed to atoms both these moral structures, and built up a new firmer-based system; although his own age, in its enthusiasm for him, no less than he himself, sadly deceived themselves as to the perfection and durability of the same.

His first and by no means unimportant service consists in the fact that basing himself primarily on the skepticism of Hume, he annihilated, at a single stroke, all confidence in previous methods of philosophizing, whether speculative or empirical, and deprived both empiricism and the pure theoretical reason, in so far as it had thus far been developed, of all right to pretend to establish, in respect to the supersensuous, or the ideal, any thing whatever as philosophical knowledge. Though in his "Critique of the Pure Reason" (1781) Kant had ascribed to the speculative reason, in the sphere of theoretical knowledge, really only the function of formal thought or logic, he yet attained in fact to a positive knowledge of reality in the sphere of the *practical* reason, that is, in that of morality.* Reason is not merely a cognizing, but *also* a volitionating power; hence there is not merely a rational knowledge of that which *is*, namely, theoretical or pure reason, but also of that which, through rational volition, *ought* to be, namely, practical reason; the former seeks in every given reality for the rational beginning, the ground; the practical reason seeks for the rational goal, the *end.* This end can, as a rational one, not be fortuitous, arbitrary, or doubtful, but must have an unconditional absolutely-valid character. The office of reason is here entirely other than in the sphere of pure theoretical cognition; the practical reason directs itself toward something which is not yet real, but which should through reason become real, and which, consequently depends upon reason; hence reason is here, as in contrast to the other sphere, in its own sphere proper, where it itself actively creates its own object,—is free and responsible. Man, as a spirit, *can* choose whatever object of action he pleases, but as a rational spirit he *should* set before him-

---

* *Grundlegung zur Metaphysik der Sitten,* 1785; *Kritik der praktischen Vernunft,* 1788, the chief work of the Kantian form of ethics; *Metaph. Anfangsgründe der Rechtslehre,* 1797; *Metaph. Anf. der Tugendlehre,* 1797.

self only a rational, and hence absolutely valid object. As he acts here in a sphere determined by himself, hence he is dependent only upon himself; in willing and acting, man is *free*. A rational end is such a one as must be recognized by every rational man, as his own end; for reason is not a merely individual quality, but is in all men the same; hence the rationality of the end consists in its universal validity. Hence the highest principle of all rational moral action is the law: "act in such a manner that the maxim of thy conduct is adapted to become a universal law for *all* men." (Maxim is here taken as the subjective principle of moral action in contradistinction to the objectively-valid law.) The obligatoriness of such action lies exclusively in my rationality, and is hence entirely unconditional: should I act otherwise I would not be rational; hence this law of the reason is the "*categorical imperative.*" I am here to inquire not after my own happiness, but only after that which is rational; I ought to be rational; to this end I need no other motive than my own rational nature itself. To make my own happiness the end of my moral activity—eudemonism—is irrational and immoral; for, because of the fortuity of the outward conditions of happiness, and of the heterogeneousness of claims upon happiness, the moral would be rendered dependent upon accident and caprice. The moral reason is absolutely free only when it has absolutely within itself the law and the motive of action, and where it makes itself dependent on no other conditions not given within itself. "Autonomy" constitutes the essence of reason and the dignity of human nature. Reason, in a practical law, determines the will directly, and not by means of an intervening feeling of pleasure or displeasure. To be happy is indeed the legitimate and naturally-necessary striving of every rational being, but such a ground for action can be known and recognized only empirically, whereas the moral law must necessarily have objective unconditional validity. What is good or evil cannot be known through any thing outside of reason, but only through reason itself; but feelings of pleasure and displeasure belong not to reason, but to the lower sphere of the spirit-life.

Though morality as resting exclusively upon the categorical imperative of the reason has not happiness for its motive,

yet it earns a *right* to happiness; virtue is the subjective fitness for and worthiness of happiness, that is, for that condition of a rational being to whom, in its entire existence, every thing goes according to wish and will, and where consequently also the outward relations, including those of nature, harmonize with the spiritual and moral reality of the person. Neither virtue *per se*, nor happiness *per se*, but happiness as attendant upon virtue, constitutes the true, perfect life-condition of man—his *highest good*. The moral law *per se* is the sole true motive of the will, while the idea of the highest good is an *object* of reason. Happiness depends not merely upon our rational will, but also upon outer conditions which lie not within our power. Hence happiness and virtue are not identical (as the Greek moralists taught), but have primarily nothing whatever to do with each other; the virtuous man may possibly be very unhappy, namely, in so far as his condition is not dependent upon himself,—which is in fact another proof that the striving after virtue and the striving after happiness are not one and the same thing, and that the striving after happiness *per se* is neither moral nor leads to morality. In this distinction lies the dialectics of the practical reason; happiness is not already included in virtue itself,—stands therewith not in analytical but in synthetic connection; and hence we are brought to the important question: how is the highest good practically *possible?* that is, how can the two essentially different elements of this good be brought into perfect harmony?—The highest good is a demand of the practical reason; the demand of happiness *for* the virtuous is just as rational as that of virtue itself; but its realization rests not (as that of virtue) within our free power, but is rather a morally necessary demand upon the moral government of the world,—a "*postulate* of the practical reason." The demand, the postulate, of a perfect morality which is not fully to be attained to in this temporal, sensuously-limited life, and of a correspondent happiness, that is, the demand of the highest good, finds its fulfillment only in the assumption of an *immortality* of the rational personality, and of a universal government of an all-wise, just and almighty *God*. These postulates have, in virtue of the moral nature of man, entire moral certainty, because it is only on the assumption

of their truth that the morally-rational life can attain to its goal. Thus the moral law leads, through the idea of the highest good as the object and end of the practical reason, to *religion*, that is, to the conceiving of all duties as *divine* commands,—not indeed as arbitrary prescriptions of an external will, but as essential and morally-necessary laws of every free rational will *per se*, which, however, must be looked upon as divine commands, because it is only on the supposition of a moral Infinite Will that we can attain to the highest good. Thus the moral striving is preserved from becoming selfish, and the thought of happiness is not made the motive of morality, but this motive is and remains absolutely nothing else but the moral law; but, through the religious consciousness, our reason attains to certainty and confidence in its moral aspirations. Ethics will never become a doctrine of happiness, an art of becoming happy; it becomes simply the doctrine as to how we may make ourselves *worthy* of happiness. Hence the moral idea rests not upon religion, but, conversely, religion rests upon the *per se* certain and necessary moral idea,—follows by moral necessity from this idea. Man is not moral because he is pious, but he is pious because he is moral. Morality in so far as it rests upon the idea of a free and rational creature, *has no need*, *per se*, of religion, because it has no end nor motive outside of itself, but it *leads* necessarily to religion, and thus gives rise to the idea of an almighty moral Lawgiver and world-Governor.—A special carrying-out of philosophical ethics, Kant has not really given; we find only a scanty approach thereto in his "Doctrine of Virtue," a work of no great importance, and which already betrays marks of intellectual senility. He contents himself mostly with the mere general foundation-laying, whereas in fact, the chief question is: in how far the general thoughts admit also of being carried out in detail? Duties toward God belong, according to Kant, not to ethics proper, but to the doctrine of religion.*

Unquestionably there lies in the ethics of Kant a decided advance beyond antecedent philosophical ethics, and especially beyond the empirical and naturalistic. He raised it from the low region of a self-seeking or external utilitarian

* *Met. d. Sitten*, ed. 1838, p. 355 *sqq.*

morality into the dignity of the science of a purely rational idea transcending all mere reality,—rejected all inferior self-seeking motives to morality, and insisted on the unconditional validity and obligatoriness of the moral law. While there lies in this a decided approximation to the Christian conception of the moral, still the great difference of this from the Christian view, and the inner weakness of the Kantian system as a whole, are unmistakable. The independence of morality on religion which follows from Kant's theory of rational knowledge, makes it impossible for the moral principle to obtain positive contents; his much admired moral law, and for which he puts forth such high claims, says in fact absolutely nothing, and does not lead, save by arbitrarily calling in aid from without, a single step further; and it is manifestly not without good reason, that Kant developed no system of ethics proper. The above-mentioned formula expresses not, properly speaking, the moral law itself, but only the universal validity of the law which is yet to be discovered,—says, in fact, nothing else than: "act according to rational, and hence universally-valid law;" but if we now ask, what then is this law, we are left entirely without answer. The application of this formal principle becomes in each particular case an experiment, an examination of the question: can I will that all men should act according to the same maxim by which I act? But we have absolutely no clue or criterion as to whence and on what basis the answer is to be given, inasmuch as the moral law is utterly destitute of positive contents; we could at best only start the inquiry as to what the result would be in case all men acted as we; but this, as a judging of morality by the result, would be in contradiction to the other moral views of Kant, and would be the worst of all empiricism,—as in fact not the real, but only the possible or probable result could be taken into consideration. But in case, now, some one should, in view of some *per se* immoral action, come to the manifestly possible, though erroneous conviction, that such action is adapted to be practiced universally, then such a person would be entirely unassailable and unreformable from the stand-point of Kant, and thus an error in the calculating understanding would jeopardize the entire moral conduct of the person. And in fact Helvetius and La Mettrie affirmed

without hesitation, that their own maxim was adapted to be
a universally valid law; what could Kant then object to them,
seeing that they recognized his formal principle? The Kantian
moral law, which he himself declared to be purely formal, is
moreover incorrect even in formal respects. Inasmuch as,
according to Kant, a maxim is the subjective rule which lies
at the basis of my conduct, hence it is for that very reason
per se utterly unadapted to be made into a *universal* law for
all men; a maxim is the law as subjectively conditioned and
shaped, and has in fact, in its subjective form, validity *only*
for this particular subject. The moral maxim of an educator
and guide is *not* adapted to be also the maxim of him who is
to be guided and led,—that of a warrior cannot be that of a
clergyman. Although it is true that the *law* which forms the
basis of my maxim must be universally valid, yet I cannot
derive the law from the maxim, but only the maxim from the
law. Kant gives not the contents of the law, but only the
way in which the contents may be found; this way, however,
is in contradiction to his entire system, and is not merely a
purely empirical or rather experimental one, but also an entirely false one. In the very attempt at rejecting every
merely individual element as determinative, Kant exalts it in
fact to the solely determining one.

Kant undertakes, now, actually to advance further by the
aid of this formal principle, and infers from it, as a second
formula, the principle: "act in such a manner as to consider
and use rational nature, that is, humanity in general, both in
thy own person and also in the person of every other one,
always, at the same time, as an end, and never merely as a
means,"—namely, because rational nature is personality, and
personality is an end in itself. Kant himself admits that
this formula is merely formal; but precisely in this fact lies
its defectiveness, for it is just as impossible to attain to positive contents from merely formal principles as to obtain a
real value from a purely algebraic equation. When the principle is only a mere empty space which is first to be filled
from without, and not the fountain which unfolds itself into
a stream, there is no possibility of advancing a step further.
And hence, the above formula may be applied equally well
morally and immorally; the whole question depends on, *what*

the end is, for which I consider the person; it might in fact
be an end of Satanic malice. This second principle is, in its
arbitrarily-determined form (and which in fact embraces only
a limited part of morality) still less adapted to its purpose
than the first, with which in fact it stands in no logical connection.

Another wide-reaching defect of Kantian ethics is this, that
morality appears as a mere one-sided affair of the understanding, while the heart entirely disappears, and is left utterly
unexplained. This one-sidedness results of course from the
divorce of morality from religion. It sounds plausibly, and
is likewise very easily said, that the good must be done for
its own sake, that the law of the reason must be *per se* the
direct motive to moral action; but as Kant positively admits
elsewhere the possibility that man can act also against his
better knowledge, and consequently against his conscience,
hence this undeniable fact proves that rational knowledge is
not *per se* a sufficient motive to moral action. The thought
of *love* is wanting; man can indeed act against his knowledge,
but not against his love. It is only in a *love* of the good that
a sufficient motive for moral action is found; but in this God-
ignoring morality of the understanding, love has no ground
and no place. The love of the living God can enkindle love,
but an abstract thought cannot. Kant demands simply unconditional obedience, but not love; he expressly declares
that the law must often be fulfilled even *against* our inclinations, yea, in the face of decided repugnance; but this would
amount only to an outward fulfilling of duty. Kant's morality is possible only for beings who have in themselves no
manner of sin and no germ of sin; but so soon as even the
mere possibility of an already-existing sinfulness is admitted,
this ethical system loses all foundation; for both the certainty
and also the potency of the rational law as a motive, are thereby undermined. And now Kant in fact admits,—in his remarkable work: "Religion within the Limits of Pure Reason" (1792, '94)— (which, with the exception of the one point
here in question, became the catechism of Rationalism)—the
indwelling of an *evil* principle in man along-side of the good
one, a "radical evil in human nature," existing there already
anterior to any exercise of freedom,—a tendency to evil in-

hering in all men without exception, as a subjective motive-power antecedent to all action,—a *peccatum originarium*, which he describes with such dark colors that even the strongest presentations of the orthodox doctrine of hereditary sin would fail to depict the natural man so unfavorably; but by this admission, Kant undermines his entire moral system, for he thereby renders it entirely incomprehensible, how the mere knowledge of the moral law (if indeed, under such circumstances, such a knowledge could in fact be certain and unclouded) could be the motive to a willing fulfillment of the same, seeing that, in fact, the love of man is turned in the direction of evil. And though it is true that often precisely in the contradictions of a system, the deeper presentiment of the truth is in fact contained, still the system itself is thereby overturned and proven untrue. And in general the antithesis of reason and sensuousness, which extends through Kant's entire world-theory, is in no respect rendered comprehensible, nor conciliated; it appears simply as a fact, broadly prominent and defying all comprehension.—Another peculiarity of Kantian ethics is its utter lack of appreciation for history, although this was in fact characteristic of the entire epoch; his ethics has history neither as its presupposition, nor as its end, nor as its contents. Each man stands unconnected with the historical development of the spirit,—is considered only as a rational unity, and acts only as such; and there is also a lack of all appreciation for an historical goal of the moral, for a morality of humanity, for the rational moral significancy of universal history.

The Kantian ground-principles of ethics were further carried out and applied, with partial modifications, by *Kiesewetter* (1789), by K. C. E. *Schmid* (1790), by the Roman Catholic *Mutschelle* (1788, '94), by *Snell* (1805) in smooth, popular style, by L. H. *Jacob* (1794), by *Heydenreich* (1794), by *Tieftrunk* (1789 and later), and by others.

Kant's moral system was, in its general character, very poorly adapted to be applied to Christian ethics. Its absolutely unhistorical character, its merely formal principle the application of which rests simply on reflective calculation, its lack of any other moral motive than the authority of an abstract law, and above all the reversing of the Christian relation between mor-

ality and religion,—all this could not, on its application to theological ethics, fail to endanger the Christian character thereof, notwithstanding the fact that it opposed with moral earnestness the insipid utilitarian morality of deistical "illuminism." Precisely this divorcing of morality from religion— a direct contradiction to the Christian view—was very much in harmony with the dominant spirit of the age; and this in fact accounts in part for the warm welcome which Kant's moral system met with also within the sphere of the already deeply sunken theological world; and upon this adoption of Kantian views rests the general development of the system of Rationalism. The dogmatic element of the Christian religion,—reduced now to the ideas of God, of immortality and of Christ as the ideal of virtue,—sank into secondary importance—into dependence on the morality given with full certainty in reason itself; the historical phase of Christianity was without worth; Christ himself was admired only in so far as he had realized in himself the moral law given already in reason,—only as a teacher of "illuministic" morality, and as a living exemplification of the same. It was not evangelical faith that could lean with confidence upon Kant, but rather only the anti-Christian tendency, which had thus far been represented in "illuminism," and which now, in fact, received from Kant a more earnestly-ethical and scientific character. We have no wish to deny this scientific impulse given to theology; but when (as is done by Daniel Schenkel in his Dogmatics) Kant is exalted into an essential and necessary reformer of the whole field of evangelical theology, through whom there has been wrought " a deep-reaching reaction on the part of the ethical factor against the fanatical-grown doctrinism of the dogmatics of the seventeenth century " which had annihilated all interest in ethics,—such a manner of viewing the matter simply indicates a forgetfulness of the fact that this orthodoxy in question had been already. for almost a century devoid of vitality, and that in the meantime the philosophy of Wolf and the movement of Pietism had given theology an entirely other direction, and that Pietism especially had in fact almost onesidedly emphasized the moral phase of Christianity,—so that there could hardly have been need of the Kantian moralism as the sole salvation against said doctrinal " fanaticism."

The most important theological presentations of ethics from the Kantian stand-point are: J. W. *Schmid* ("Spirit of the Ethics of Jesus," 1790; "Theological Ethics," 1793; "Christian Ethics," 1797), who presents the founding of ethics on Kantian principles as the sole mission of Jesus; J. E. C. *Schmidt* (1799), in a similar spirit; S. G. *Lange;* S. *Vogel.* *Stäudlin* treated theological ethics (from and after 1798) with constant changing of title and stand-point, until in his "New Treatise on Ethics" (1813, third edition, 1825) he despaired of any superior principle at all, and brought together, in a wavering eclecticism of heterogeneous thoughts, a feeble whole. The self-metamorphosing C. F. von *Ammon* repeated at first (1795–'98) simply the ethics of Kant, but soon after (1800) broke entirely away from him, without yet getting rid of his own superficiality.

SECTION XLIV.

The philosophy of *Fichte,* resting upon Kant, but, with rigid consequentiality, proceeding beyond him, manifested itself predominantly upon the ethical field. Fichte endeavored indeed to complement the formal principle by a material one, but both of them are so absolutely devoid of ethical contents, and the material principle stands even so positively in antagonism to the contents of a really moral consciousness, that an actual ethical development of these principles became impossible; and the occasionally sound and morally-earnest contents of the development in detail could only be loosely associated with these principles, but not scientifically developed from them. The immaturity of the entire stand-point rendered it also impossible that any important ethical tendency in philosophy or theology should arise therefrom. Fichte labored indeed fruitfully in a time which had lost all solid philosophical foot hold, but he formed no school.

Fichte's "System of Ethics according to the Principles of the Doctrine of Science" (1798) is the most important attempt to apply the ground-thoughts of the "Doctrine of Science" to one particular science. We would do injustice to the Fichtean philosophy were we to consider its unfruitful eccentricities apart from their connection with the immediately-preceding philosophy; his philosophy is a scientifically-justified and necessary advance beyond Kant. As Kant had denied to the pure reason all objective knowledge, and also placed all contents of the practical reason exclusively in the subject, and derived the objective validity of the law of reason simply from the subject; so Fichte simply made the validity of the individual subject, the *ego*, all-predominant,—conceived all objective existence merely negatively as the non-ego, and based cognition and volitionating absolutely on the individual ego. The ego and the non-ego reciprocally determine each other, and hence stand in reciprocal relation. The ego posits itself as determined by the non-ego, that is, it *cognizes ;* and it posits itself, on the other hand, as determining in relation to the non-ego, that is, it *volitionates.* The two are only two phases of the same thing, inasmuch as the non-ego in its entire being exists only in so far as it is posited by the ego, so that, strictly speaking, the ego is its own object. The ego should in all its determinations be posited only by itself,—should be absolutely independent of all non-ego. Only as volitionating, as absolutely determining the non-ego, is the ego free and independent. The ego as rational, *should* not permit itself to be determined by any non-ego independent of it,—should be absolutely independent, should make all non-ego absolutely dependent on itself,—should exercise absolute causality upon the same. In freedom, in volitionating, I am rational; and in that I determine my freedom as an absolutely self-poised power, that is, affirm my freedom, I am moral; hence morality is self-determination to freedom. I should act freely in order that I may become free, that is, I should act with the consciousness that I determine myself in absolute independence. Hence the formal principle of morality is: "act according to thy conscience," or "act always according to the best conviction of thy duty;" and as material principle of ethics, there results this: "make thyself into an independent or free being." "I should be a

23

self-dependent being; this is my destination; and the destination of things is, that I use them in furthering my independence."

So absolutely void a principle of morality was probably never before proposed. The formal principle expresses nothing other than: act according to a yet unknown material principle. As to what the "conscience" is and contains, we are as yet utterly uninformed; and the material principle gives only the formal presupposition of morality, but not its contents proper; I must in fact already be free, in order to be able to act morally; freedom is not the contents, but the form, of moral action. If this material principle is to be taken in its entire significancy (and according to the philosophical presupposition this is strictly consequential), then the very opposite of all morality would be thereby expressed, namely, the acting absolutely without law, the virtualizing of freedom in its simple form without contents, and hence as mere individual caprice—amounting to a radical absolutism of the individual subject, whereas all morality consists in fact most essentially in a determining of individual freedom by an unconditionally and objectively valid law,—is a subordinating of the subject to a universally-obligating idea standing above the subject. From Fichte's principle there results, not a system of ethics, but, consequentially, only a theory of license. While it is true that in his examinations of particular moral questions only loosely connected with his system, Fichte shows himself, for the most part, high-minded and earnest, though indeed often strangely unpractical, still there lies, at least in his ground-principle and in his general system, no justification thereof. The cold, heartless, non-loving, intellectual character of his discussions, is moreover not very well adapted to awaken a moral interest.

What Fichte says on moral questions in his later, more rhetorical than scientific, writings, bears in general the same unfruitful stamp,—often widely misunderstanding the reality of life; we need only call to mind the new system of education proposed in his much admired "Addresses to the German Nation," which was presented with the assumption of world-regenerating significancy, but at which, in fact, no experienced educator can avoid smiling, and also his "Doctrine of the State" which is even more than fantastical. The public often allowed itself to be deceived by the ring of his periods,

and by the loftily enigmatic character of the expression. And it is doubtful whether the fanaticism of the philosopher himself, or that entertained for him by others, was the greater; certain it is, however, that very soon there was a vast sobering-down of both. We will here only refer to the fact that Fichte was personally very far from drawing the very natural consequences of his dangerous moral principle, but that on the contrary in his rhetorical "Direction for a Holy Life" (1807), in which he already largely departs from his earlier views, and takes a rather mystico-Pantheistic turn, he expressly presents, as the goal of morality, complete "self-annihilation"—not, however, in the Christian sense of moral self-denial, but rather in the sense of the religion of India. The belief in our self-existence must be absolutely destroyed; by this course the ego that was, sinks away into the pure divine essence; we should not say: let the love and the will of God become mine, because in fact there are no longer two, but only One, and no longer two wills but simply one. So long as man yet desires to be any thing himself, God comes not to him; but so soon as he annihilates himself fully, utterly and radically, then God alone remains and is all in all. In annihilating himself man continues in God, and in this self-annihilation consists blessedness. The scientific justification of this (in some respects) not unambiguous requirement, is not given.—Notwithstanding the enthusiasm which Fichte's pretentious philosophy excited, especially among the youth, it was unable to create any long-enduring movements of thought. Feeble attempts to develop it further, or, in fact, to apply it to Christian ethics (Mehmel: "Elements," 1811), fell very soon into deserved oblivion.

SECTION XLV.

Schelling, after passing from Idealism to Pantheism, and from Pantheism to a dualistic Theosophy, endeavored, in this his third development-period, to reconcile the freedom of the individual with the sway of necessity, and indeed of necessary evil, by regarding individual man as determining himself for evil in an ante-mundane self-determination as influenced

by a principle of darkness lying in God himself,—
but as necessary for the self-revelation of divine love.
The presentations of philosophical ethics which based
themselves on Schelling, have been unable to attain to
any permanent significancy.—The imperfectly developed anti-Schellingian philosophy of *Jacobi* answered,
in its ethical phases, more to the Christian view, but
it also has given rise to no real ethical system.

Schelling, appearing at first as a disciple of Fichte (at a
period which was very receptive and thankful for philosophy,
even for a youthfully unripe one), and then, in a more highly
speculative spirit passing beyond him, and also in constant
metamorphoses progressively rising above even himself,—never
settled, never bringing any thing to perfection,—did not develop in his earlier period any ethical system, and, at furthest,
only gave, on purely Pantheistic foundations, more or less clear
suggestions toward an ethical system; however, in his last productive period (when, under the stimulation of Jacob Böhme
and Francis Baader, he plunged into a current of phantasy-
speculation not un-akin to Gnostic dualism), he furnished, in
his "Philosophical Inquiries as to the Essence of Human Liberty" (1809), a less dialectically developed, indeed, than theo-
sophically-portrayed, though certainly deeply suggestive, presentation of the presuppositions and bases of a system of philosophical ethics.—In God there exists, before all reality, his
eternal ground, his *per se* unintelligent nature, out of which in
all eternity the divine understanding generates itself as the
eternal antithesis to this ground-nature, which understanding
stands dominatingly over against this nature,—rules creatingly
in it, and by its acting upon it creates the finite world.   Every
creature has consequently a twofold nature in itself: an essentially dark principle corresponding to the nature-element in
God, and also the principle of light or understanding.   In the
highest creature, man, there exists the entire power of the dark
principle, namely, the unintelligent self-will, and also the entire
power of light—the deepest abyss and the highest heaven.
From the fact of his springing from the ground or nature-
element in God, man has in himself a principle relatively inde-

pendent of God, which, answering to this ground, is darkness, but which becomes transfigured by the light, the spirit. But while in God the two principles are indissolubly united, in man they are separable, that is, man has the possibility of good and evil. The dark principle can, as selfishness, separate itself from the light; self-will can endeavor to be, as a separate will, that which it truly is only in unity with the universal will,—can endeavor to be, also in the periphery or as a creature, that which it is only in so far as it remains in the divine center; this self-severing of self-hood from the light is *evil*. Evil, as the dissevering of the two principles, is necessary in order to a revelation of God; for if these principles remained in man as unseparated as they are in God, then there would be no difference between God and man, and God could not manifest his omnipotence and love; but God must of necessity so reveal himself. For this reason, the self-will of man is influenced by that dark unintelligent principle in God,—man is tempted to evil, in order that the will of divine love may find an opposing element, an antithesis, wherein it can realize itself. Hence evil exists in man as a natural tendency, for the reason that the disorder of his powers, as occasioned by the awakening of self-will in the creature, communicates itself to him in his very birth; and this ground-element in God works also constantly in man, and excites his self-hood and individual will, in order that in antithesis to it, the will of divine love may find scope for action. Hence results a general necessity of sin, which, however, by no means does away with the personal guilt of man, for the dark ground in God realizes not evil as such, but only prompts thereto. The actions of actual man result, indeed, with necessity from his essence, but this essence man himself has determined by an act of self-determination beyond all time and co-incidently with creation itself. Man is indeed born in time, but he has, himself, determined his life and character before his temporal life, yon side of time, in eternity. Hence our actual actions are, on the one hand, necessary, and, on the other, within our own responsibility. That Judas betrayed Christ, was absolutely necessary; neither himself nor another could have changed the matter; and nevertheless it was his own guilt, for he had so determined himself from eternity. As every man now acts,

so acted he, as the identical person, already at the beginning
of creation; he is not simply now forming his character, but
his character is already formed. All men have determined
themselves from eternity to egotism and self-seeking, and are
born with this dark principle essential in their being. Evil,
however, ought not to remain, but to be overcome by the
good principle.

Schelling promised a fuller development of these ground-
thoughts, but did not carry it out. The enthusiasm with
which this philosophy of his (which promised the solution of
all the enigmas of existence), was received,—an enthusiasm
which was not dampened, but rather heightened by its orac
ular tone and by the boldness of assertion which often assumed in it the place of scientific proof,—gave occasion also
in the ethical field, to various, though mostly feeble, fruitless and soon abandoned, attempts at a further carrying out
of his ground-principles,—some of them in greater approximation to the Christian consciousness; (Buchner, 1807; Than-
ner, 1811; Klein, 1811; Möller, 1819; *Krause*, 1810, though
deviating considerably from the master, and rather independent).—The facility with which other kindred currents of
thought admitted of being joined into Schelling's theosophi-
cal outbursts, was indeed very tempting to the book-prolific
spirit of the age, but it also soon awakened in the sobering-
down spirit of the time a degree of distrust; and the fame
obtained by the master in his meteoric flight, showed itself
less partial for his zealously-imitating scholars; and when
Daub, after welcoming, in their regular order of succession,
all the philosophies from Kant to Hegel, advanced in his
" Judas Iscariot " (1816), on the principles of Schelling, to a
sort of personality of evil, to a philosophical Satanology,
which indeed is yet far different from the Christian view,—
then, at last, the predominantly Rationalistic spirit of the age
began to lose confidence in the worth of the more recent
philosophy as a whole.

F. H. *Jacobi* of Munich, who, in antithesis to all Pantheism,
took his departure from the stand-point of the free personal
spirit, has given in his miscellaneous and unsystematic
writings* only hints and suggestions toward an ethical sys-

* *Werke*, 1812, 4 vols.

tem. He opposed to the Pantheistic philosophy, however, rather, merely the consciousness of its untruth than a scientifically-constructed theory. He emphasized very strongly the personal, moral will-freedom of man as opposed to all necessary determination, without, however, creating for it a really scientific basis, appealing here, as also in the case of the idea of the personality of God, to inner spiritual experience—to feeling. Morality, he based on a primitive feeling for the good, which is independent of the striving after happiness; the good must be accomplished for its own sake, and not as a means to happiness. In general, Jacobi did not rise beyond the views of Rationalism.—The few moralists who followed in his wake, defend indeed the Christian stand-point as against the Pantheistic tendency, but they have no very great scientific significancy. Among them belongs essentially also the Roman Catholic theologian, *Salat* (1810 and later).

SECTION XLVI.

The philosophy of *Hegel* knows nothing of ethics under this name; upon its Pantheistic ground no really personal freedom can find foothold, although it makes all possible endeavors to find scope therefor. The reality of freedom appears essentially only under the form of necessity, as that *right* which, on the part of the subject, is *duty;* ethics appears only as the *Doctrine of Right;* its scientific significancy lies in its decided advance beyond the previous subjective stand-point (which appears even yet in Kant) to the objective validity and reality of morality in the family, in society and in the state, as real moral forms of humanity. In the fact, however, that only the *State* is conceived as the highest realization of objective morality, lies also the one-sidedness of the view, inasmuch as the full reality of moral freedom remains unrecognized.—The Hegelian school has not developed philosophical ethics beyond the positions

of the master; its application to theological ethics by *Daub* and *Marheineke* presents the unrefreshing picture of a vain attempt at harmoniously reconciling irreconcilable contradictions.—The school of Pantheistic *radicalism*, which is nominally connected with Hegel but is in reality based rather on Spinoza, has produced no real system of ethics, but only narrow-minded and absurd essays on particular ethical topics.

The ethics of Hegel, as presented in his "Philosophy of Right," (1821; better by Gans, 1833),—the field occupied by which constitutes a part of the Philosophy of the Spirit,—rests on the Pantheistic current set in motion by Spinoza, and appears in higher scientific maturity than in Schelling.—The rational spirit, as the unity of the objective consciousness and of the self-consciousness, is the true free-become spirit; it cognizes every thing in itself and itself in every thing,—is, as reason, the identity of the objective All and the ego. In that the rational spirit recognizes rationality in nature, and hence nature as objective reason, it is *theoretical* spirit. But reason knows its own contents also as its object, objectivizes the same, posits them outwardly, that is, the spirit is *practical* spirit—*volitionates*. But in so far as it is determined to this volitionating by no other object foreign to itself, but determines itself simply by virtue of its rational being, it is *free* spirit. Hence the spirit posits itself outwardly from within, objectivizes itself in freedom, realizes itself in an objective manner. This its realization is not nature, but is essentially of a spiritual character, is a spiritual world, a kingdom of the spirit which exists not merely in the ego, but has an objective reality the creator of which is the free rational spirit; the objective-become spirit is the *historical* world in the widest sense of the word. The freedom of the rational spirit is, however, with Hegel, by no means a real freedom of choice; such a freedom finds in the Pantheistic world-theory no legitimate place; it is only the spirit's active relating to itself, its being independent upon any other external entity, but it is nevertheless essentially at the same time

necessity. Thus the free spirit creates a world as the objective reality of freedom, a reality, however, which has a general significancy transcending the individual being,—becomes a power over the individual spirit, assumes the form of necessity, whereby the individual subject is determined in his freedom and which consequently must be recognized by the individual as the higher factor,—is a general will over against the individual will,—is *right*, which becomes for the individual, *duty*.

The Philosophy of Right falls into three parts. (1) The free will is primarily immediate, as individual will. The subject of right is the *person*, which stands to other persons primarily in an excluding relation. The person confers upon itself the reality of its freedom posits a special sphere of its subjective freedom in *property*. I declare an objective entity as my own, and hence as that upon which another has no right. This is primarily as yet an outward and not necessary action; it lies not in the essence of the thing itself that I declare it as my property; hence right in this sphere is the merely *formal, abstract* right. The freedom of the subject is assured and recognized by the fact that other subjects must concede the validity of *my* freedom, my property, my right; freedom receives thus a general significancy, becomes right. The freedom of individual subjects is regulated by law, is reduced to general harmony. But that the reality of this right rests primarily on the subjective will, and that the general will is the product of the individual will, is as yet an irrational state of things, and abstract right advances now, (2), to *morality*, wherein the individual will becomes the product and expression of the general will, but on the basis of freedom, through free recognition. In the first sphere the subjective freedom of the individual is bound by the right of the other, and hence trammeled. But in the free recognition of this right, the bondage, the trammeling element, is thrown off; right and law are no longer a merely outward limiting element, but become the personal law of the subject, the contents of his free self-determination. In the mere fulfillment of right the disposition does not come into question; I may concede to another his right unwillingly, and hence immorally; so soon, however, as right becomes morality, the disposition, the intention,

becomes the chief thing, and the outward act a merely secondary matter. A man may be forced to right, but not to morality; only free, cheerful action is moral. That which in the
sphere of right is wrong, becomes in the moral sphere moral
guilt. The intention of the moral action directs itself primarily upon the rational subject himself, wills his *welfare;*
but, as rationality has a general significancy, this intention
looks also to the general welfare, to the realizing of the
rational will and hence of rationality in general, that is, to
the *good.* To realize the good, is for the individual subject,
duty,—is no longer a merely outward law, but an inner,
freely appropriated one. The good as the unity of the notion of the rational will and of the particular will of the
individual subject, is the end, the goal of the universe.

But in the accomplishing of this duty of realizing the
good, the subject finds himself involved in a multitude of
contradictions and conflicts; the outer objective world is,
as related to the subject, a something different from and independent of him; hence it is doubtful and fortuitous
whether or not it is in harmony with the subjectively moral
ends,—whether or not the subject finds his well-being in it.
The abstract right was a merely outward and formal one;
morality is a merely inward subjective something,—has
harmony only as a postulate, as an "ought;" the good
is, as yet, only the abstract idea of the good; hence there
is need of a third, higher stage wherein the subjective and
the objective phases are united, where the postulate of the
harmonizing of the two spheres is realized, where the ought
is also reality, where the good is no longer an abstract general something over against which the subject stands as yet
as an isolated individual, but where the good has attained to
reality, where freedom has become nature, and law has become *custom.* This brings us, (3), to the sphere of *customariness*—the completion of the objective spirit. In customariness
the spirit enters into its true reality; the person finds the
good outside of himself, as a reality to which he subordinates
himself, as a *moral world.* Thus Hegel, deviating from the
ordinary usage of language, distinguishes morality [moralität]
from customariness [sittlichkeit], conceiving the former as
the merely subjective and individual morality, and the latter

as civic or *social* morality. In the sphere of morality man is considered as an individual who determines himself according to abstract moral laws; in that of customariness he is considered as an essential member of a moral community, of a moral whole, so that he now fulfills not abstract laws, but the requirements of the concrete-become spirit of a moral, social reality. Hence the end of customariness is primarily and immediately, not the individual, but the moral whole. The moral organisms constituted by reason as become object-ive, present themselves in the three development-stages of the *family*, of *civil society* (in which the individual subjects are bound together only by legal relations), and of the *state*, in which appears the full reality of morality.—The state is the moral substance as conscious of itself,—the objectively-realized moral and rational spirit, the union of the principle of the family and of civil society, the outer full realization of freedom,—inasmuch as here the moral reality rests no longer (as in the case of the family) upon a nature-ground, and no longer (as in the case of civil society) upon merely outward legal relations, but upon the common conscious-ness wherein the individuals are conscious of themselves as organic members of the whole. Hence the state is the *per se* rational existence, the highest manifestation of moral reason in general.—Hegel conceives the state in higher significancy than antecedent philosophers, namely, not as a mere means for the end of the individual citizens, but as end *per se*, to which the individual must sacrifice his particular and finite ends. This is a decided advance, especially in contrast to the utterly perverse and entirely anti-Christian state-doc-trine of the eighteenth century, when it was regarded as perfectly self-evident that the state has no other task than to serve the interests of individuals, whether the interests of the individual citizens of a state, or the interests of a class in society, or those of a prince, but not to fulfill a moral idea. But the state is also here the ultimate and high-est form of all morality, as, indeed, Hegel recognizes no higher existence yon-side the finite reality of the natural All, but not an absolutely self-existent, infinite, personal spirit. The purely moral reality of the *church*,—which in its purely spir-itual interests is far *above* the necessary outward limitations

of the state, far above classes of society and national boundaries, and has a super-mundane eternal goal, and which, as
resting absolutely upon freedom, does not exert coercive
power,—finds no room for itself in Hegel's system. *All*
morality, without exception, appertains to the state, and all
reality of the church must be merged into it,—a doctrine
which of course was especially favorable to the absolutism
of politics then in vogue. All that was usually ascribed to
the church in its significancy for the moral, falls here to the
state, while religion is regarded only as the basis, but not as
the essential reality, of the moral spirit. "The state should
be reverenced as an earthly-divine element; the state is
divine will as present and developing itself into the real
form and organism of a world." Hence with Hegel, as also
with the Greeks, morality is merged in the state, and has no
significancy beyond it. "What man has to do, what the duties are which he has to fulfill, is, in a moral community, easy
to determine: nothing else is to be done by him than that
which is prescribed, expressed, and made known, in his relations." That this moral community may also be morally a very
perverted one, and that consequently man may be morally
obligated to resist it, and that even the most perfect actual
state, does not embrace the whole field of the moral community-life,—of all this the Hegelian system takes no account.

In the carrying-out of the classification of the moral subject-
matter, the "Philosophy of Right" varies largely in many
places from the presentation given in the "Encyclopedia"
and in the "Phenomenology of the Spirit." The transition
from morality to customariness seems artificial and very ar
bitrary. The freedom of choice here largely brought into
requisition is entirely without justification in the system, and
even contradictory thereto. The classification itself is also
not rigorously kept apart, nor indeed can it be; the sphere
of right falls largely into that of civil society, in so far as
there is any real attempt at carrying it out; and the protection of right, which according to Hegel falls into the sphere
of civil society, is utterly impossible without the state.
Furthermore, it is worthy of note that Hegel, in perfect consistency with the principle naturally following from his system, namely, that "all that is real is also rational," regards

war, not as an evil, but as a phenomenon necessarily connected with the highest moral community-life or the state, and, hence, as entirely rational, and which simply expresses in act the frailty and finiteness inherent in all finite being, and which has in the moral sphere the same inner necessity and normalcy, as death in the nature-sphere; war is death exalted into the moral sphere.*

The Hegelian school, dividing itself soon after the master's death into a right wing, which progressively drew nearer to the Christian consciousness, and into a left wing, which sank lower and lower in the direction of radicalism and destructiveness, has not produced any very important results in the ethical field. (*Michelet* gave a "System of Philosophical Ethics," 1828; *Von Henning* presented the "Principles of Ethics," historically, 1824); *Vatke* ("Human Freedom in its Relation to Sin and to Grace," 1841) develops, in opposition to Julius Müller's "Presentation of the Christian Doctrine of Sin," the Hegelian view in a very ingenious manner, without, however, succeeding in reconciling the unfreedom essentially inherent in the Pantheistic System with the general consciousness of moral freedom of choice; evil, though regarded as ultimately to be overcome, is yet held to be an absolutely necessary incident of the good. *Daub* and *Marheineke* undertook, in their ethical works,† the vain and thankless task of giving to the Pantheistic ground-thoughts of Hegel such a turn, and of clothing them in such forms of expression, as to make them appear as a higher scientific expression of the Christian doctrines. But the rapidly disenchanted age soon saw clearly enough the impossibility of this undertaking. Daub's *Ethics*, as edited from his lectures in an easy and often conversational style, though proposing to present Biblical ethics, is yet unwilling to derive the moral law from the Scriptures, but seeks for it only in reason, regarding it as inherent therein, and forces the Biblical teachings, frequently with violence, into conformity to the already adopted system; the lofty self-complacency of the philosophizing theologian looks often contemptuously down upon

---

* *Phanomenol.*, p. 358; *Phil. des Rechts*, pp. 417, 427, *sqq.*

† Daub: *Prolegomena zur Moral*, 1839; *System d. theol. Moral.*, 1840; Marheineke: *System d. theol. Moral.*, 1847.

the churchly consciousness, and oftener still, artfully explains away its significancy. Marheineke divides ethics into the doctrine of the law as the objective phase, into the doctrine of virtue as the subjective phase (virtue being taken as the harmonizing of the will with the law) and into the doctrine of duty. Despite a very pretentious style, the positive contents, consisting in many places merely in a loose series of single, and not always ingenious, and sometimes even insipid, observations, are really quite barren, and often involved in violent self-contradiction.

The left wing of the Hegelian school,—which strayed still further from the master in the direction of a vulgar Pantheism based on Spinoza, and which does not rise in the ethical field even to the honest consequentiality and earnestness of Spinoza, but, for the most part, sinks back into the most vulgar freethinking of French materialism,—has shown itself utterly unfruitful in ethical works; it has made itself felt, on the field of ethics, less by scientific productions than by impudent assertion. David *Strauss* is unwilling to admit the fatalistic necessity of all the individual phenomena of life, so consequentially affirmed by Spinoza; but he gives scope, without hesitation, to chance and to arbitrary discretion, and affirms (of course without any justification in his system) even the freedom of the human will. What the world had not as yet known, Strauss presumes to assert, and takes the liberty of blankly contradicting the principle of Spinoza, that the human will is a *causa non libera, sed coacta*. In his view, Pantheism alone guarantees the free self-dependence of man. If God is immanent in the world, and hence also in man; if, as in the Christian world-theory, the finite stands over against the absolute Agent as a distinctly different object, then is this finite (the world) only in a condition of absolute passivity; but in Pantheism the absolute actuosity lies in the collectivity of finite agencies, as their own activity. While in monotheism it holds good, that as truly as God is almighty so truly are men unfree, in Pantheism it holds good that as certainly as God is self-active so truly are men also so, in whom He is so.* What the drift of this special-pleading inference is, appears at once from the following observations:

* *Glaubenslehre*, ii, 364.

"This holds good, of course, only of our conception of the divine essence; whether it holds good also in the reciprocal relation of finite things, where Spinoza denies it, is another question, and one which does not concern us in this place." He makes, however, in this connection, in order to maintain against Spinoza the freedom of the will, also the following very curious observation: "Spinoza declares individual man as unfree, for the reason that only that determinedness of his essence and activity remains to him which all other things leave to him; but in this connection he overlooked the fact that also, conversely, only that much remains to all other things which the individual leaves to them; this is of course not freedom of choice, but it is also not coercion." The honest Spinoza would doubtless have shaken his head in astonishment at this naïve objection.—Strauss, naturally enough, recognizes also, as the highest moral reality, the state as separated from the church and as entirely swallowing it up within itself; in the place of the worshiping of God must be substituted art, and especially the theater; for genuine morality, that is, for the life in the state, religion is not only superfluous but hurtful; for whoever thinks he has, outside of his duties as a citizen of the state, still other duties as a citizen of heaven, will, as a servant of two masters, necessarily neglect the first class of duties.* In this expression of opinion he gives to governments a very significant hint, as to how dangerous for the state is an ecclesiastically pious disposition in the people, and how great is the duty of an enlightened government to guard against it.—Lewis *Feuerbach*, who finds in religion only a morbid delusion, namely, in that man regards his own being as a divine object, declares religion, and especially the Christian religion, as the destruction of morality, inasmuch as it makes the validity of the moral law dependent on religious faith. Nature is every thing, and exclusively so; to follow the voice of nature is the highest principle of morality. This voice, however, teaches us love to our fellow-men, whereas religion teaches only hatred against those who believe differently from us, and directs the love and activity of man, not toward other men, but toward a non-existing being—God, only the religionless man

* *Glaubenslehre*, ii, 615 *sqq.*

can have universal love to man, which is *per se* always practical atheism, namely, a denial of God in heart, in sentiment, and in act. For a scientific justification of these wonderful assertions we seek in vain; morbid bombast supplies its place. That this theory of morality must lead to the vulgarest enjoyment-seeking, is perfectly natural; and Feuerbach himself explains himself as to the nature of this morality of human love, very clearly, thus: "When I am hungry then nothing is more important to me than the enjoyment of food, —after the meal, nothing more than rest, and after rest, nothing more than exercise; after exercise, nothing more than conversation with friends; after the completion of the work of the day, I court the Brother of Death as the most beneficent of beings; thus every moment of the life of man has something,—but *nota bene!*—something *human in it.*" *

Thus the philosophy of "modern science" has returned, in rapid circuit, back to the morality of French materialism, to the practical morality of Philip of Orleans under Louis XV. The more advanced and almost insane productions of the still more "radical" circle, especially of the circle of "emancipated" ones,—which formed itself around Bruno and Edgar Bauer, and by whom even Feuerbach was soon stigmatized (Max Stirner) as belonging among "theologians," "believing hypocrites" and "slavish natures,"—belong not in the sphere of a history of science, but, at best, only in that of the history of the morals of the nineteenth century.

We will mention additionally, in passing, only the *materialistic* world-theory, which, though not directly springing from the Pantheistic philosophy, yet coincides with it in its ultimate results, and which has its origin more in the empirical study of nature than in philosophy, and which in its moral views has sunk back to the French materialism of the *Systéme de la Nature* (Moleschott, Vogt, Büchner, etc.). If spirit is simply a phenomenon of brain-force, and if man is nothing more than a highly organized animal, then the moral catechism is very easy and short. Vogt declares it as presumption in man to pretend to be any thing essentially different from the brute; man belonged originally to the ape race, and has only gradu-

* *Werke*, i, 355.

ally developed himself somewhat more highly. Man is guided and impelled, just as the brute, by his own nature, that is, by the laws of his material existence, and with inner irresistible necessity; every so-called act of the will is strictly a necessary product of the material conditions of the brain and of the outer sensuous impressions, as determined by nutrition and by the peculiarity of the brain-substance. Hence also there can be no manner of moral responsibility; all so-called sins and crimes are only "consequences of a defective nutrition and of an imperfect organization of the brain." The distinguishing between morally good and evil actions is merely a self-deception; "to comprehend every thing involves also the justifying of every thing," says Moleschott. Hence, the moral amelioration of man takes place solely through suitable and strengthening nutrition. "The more fully we are conscious that by the proper proportioning of carbonic acid, ammonia, and the salts, etc., we are contributing to the highest development of mankind, so much the more are also our efforts and work ennobled." Upon eating and drinking, these writers naturally enough lay very great emphasis; it appears to them as a sacred rite, and Moleschott is not ashamed even to compare it with the holy eucharist. It was also reserved for this writer to stigmatize the Christian world-theory and Christian custom as detrimental to the public good, and for this, among other reasons, that thereby the national wealth suffers a considerable loss from the practice of burying corpses in special graveyards, whereas the bodies of the dead should rather be used for manuring the fields. Those who look always for the truth simply in a "progress" beyond that which has hitherto been known and practiced, can perhaps inform us what the next further progress beyond this world-theory will lead to.

SECTION XLVII.

The philosophical ethics of the two last decades, based in general on Hegel or on Herbart, shows a manifestly growing approximation to the Christian world-theory; but because of the rather unphilosophi-

24

cally-inclined spirit of the age, it has exerted less influence upon society at large than the immediately preceding philosophy.

The most recent times have suddenly shown, after an excessive and almost morbid intensity of enthusiasm for philosophy, an all the greater lack of earnest interest therein. The excessive expectations were soon followed by discouraging disappointments; and while at the beginning of the century the most crude products of philosophy, if they were only presented with assurance, were sure of an enthusiastic welcome, the, in general, far more mature and more scientific and profound works of recent times have met with but cold indifference; and though the philosophers of the present day have some reasons to complain of the thanklessness of the educated world, and that only ambitious rhetoric is now able to win applause, nevertheless this state of things is clearly explainable as a reaction from the wild intoxication of the past.

Nearly contemporaneously with Hegel wrote *Herbart* of Königsberg. Taking up his position outside of the historical development-course of philosophy, and, in keen skepticism, discarding the unity of the principle of reality, he had in his elegantly written "Practical Philosophy" (1808) thrown open a new path. In his view the previous treatment of ethics, as the doctrine of goods, of virtues and of duties, makes the will of a twofold character—a norming or commanding one, and a derived or obeying one,—and hence makes of the will its own regulator; but this is impossible and absurd. On the contrary, a will-less *judgment* as to willing precedes all actual willing; this judgment cannot command, but only approve or disapprove; but it never acts upon the will as strictly isolated, but always as a member of a relation. Hence all willing presupposes moral taste, which has pleasure in the morally-beautiful; thus the moral is conceived essentially *esthetically*. The esthetical judgment as to the will leads it to action, but not necessarily; the will *should* be obedient, but it *can* be disobedient; taste is immutable, the will is flexible; thus manifests itself the idea of inner freedom. Together with this idea Herbart assumes still others,—ideas

which are connected, but reduced to no real unity, with this
idea, and which precede all exertion of will, namely, the
ideas of perfection, of benevolence, of right, and of fitness;
by virtue of these five ideas the moral taste passes upon an
act of the will, directly and involuntarily, a judgment of approval or disapproval. The full realization of the moral is
society, as expressing itself in different stages.—This work
of Herbart, though little regarded in its day, contains in its
details many profound and ingenious thoughts; the violently
original character of the whole is very stimulating, but not
satisfying; the unity of the theory as a whole is defective.—
Hartenstein wrote in the spirit of Herbart, his "Fundamental
Notions of the Ethical Sciences," 1844, a work full of
thought, and presenting a much more candid view of the
realities of life than the writers of the Hegelian school, and
not unfrequently assailing Schleiermacher and Hegel with
keenness and success. As primitive ethical ideas, he assumes
those of inner freedom, of benevolence, of right and of fitness.
Similarly also *Allihn:* "Fundamental Doctrines of General
Ethics," 1861.—(*Beneke:* "Elements of Ethics," 1837, entirely empirical, and only partially based on Herbart.—
Elvenich: "Moral Philosophy," 1830, based on evangelically-
modified Kantian views.)

The "Speculative Ethics" (1841) of *Wirth* sprang from
the Hegelian school, but deviates therefrom in many respects;
the Pantheistic fundamental view is not entirely overcome;
(ethics is "the science of the absolute spirit as will realizing its absolute self-consciousness into its likewise infinite
reality;" in details it offers many good thoughts, though also
many mere empty phrases, especially where it treats of religious morality; to close the development of ethics with an
amateur-theater as one of the most important moral agencies,
is surely a very odd fancy).—*Chalybäus* of Kiel: "System of
Speculative Ethics," 1850,—doubtless the most important
treatise on philosophical ethics in modern times. Chalybäus,
in his work, breaks entirely away from the Pantheistic view
of Hegel, and treats ethics on the basis of the idea of personal freedom, and does not, as Hegel, regard the ideal and
the real as in perfect harmony, but on the contrary recognizes evil as merely possible in virtue of freedom, and hence

its reality as only fortuitous and guiltily-incurred, but not as necessary. A candid, sound view of reality is combined with an ingenious development of thought in clear vigorous language; and notwithstanding a few cases of the lowering of Christian doctrines, this philosophical ethics expresses the Christian consciousness, in many cases, more faithfully than does Rothe's "Theological Ethics."—Also J. H. *Fichte* (son of the philosopher) places himself in his "System of Ethics," 1850, upon a decidedly theistical stand-point, and strongly emphasizes the idea of personality, which in Hegel falls into so dubious a back-ground. (The essence of the moral appears as love, which, as an "unselfing of the personal ego," is carried out somewhat one-sidedly so far as to throw the validity of self and of right quite too much into the back-ground.) —K. P. *Fischer* (of Erlangen): "Elements of a System of Speculative Ethics," 1851,—briefer than the preceding works, freighted with thought,—likewise an essential advance of recent philosophy toward a deeper comprehension of the Christian consciousness. (*Martensen:* "Outlines of a System of Moral Philosophy," 1845. *Schliephake:* "The Bases of the Moral Life," 1855,—inspired by Krause, empirical toward the close, but keen and judicious).—In this place belongs also, in part, the ingenious and deeply Christian work of *Stahl:* "The Philosophy of Right—"* based in the beginning rather on Schelling, but afterward more independent; the idea of the human personality as a copy of the personality of God is, in contrast to all naturalistic philosophy, raised to the full significancy and to the foundation of all morality and of all right.

(The preposterously original *Schopenhauer* goes back to Indian conceptions, and finds morality only in an annihilating of the individuality. The will to live is the root of all evil; the denying of this will is virtue. The will must turn away from existence, must turn to will-lessness; for existence is absolutely null, and the will a delusion, from which we must become free. Vulgar suicide is indeed not right, for it is a phenomenon of a strongly-affirming will; on the contrary, a voluntary starving of one's self to death is a real moral sacri-

* 1830, 3 ed., 1851.

ficing of the will to live. "The two Fundamental Problems of Ethics," 1841; "The World as Will and Conception," 1819, '44, '60.)

SECTION XLVIII.

The *Theological* ethics of the nineteenth century, in so far as it came not into a relation of complete dependence upon some particular philosopher of the day, remained either upon a purely Biblical ground, making no use or only a very moderate use of philosophical thoughts, or assumed a rather eclectico-philosophical character. Rationalism proved surprisingly unfruitful.

Ethics was treated in a predominantly original manner by *Schleiermacher*, in a widely differing and irreconcilable double-form of philosophical and of theological ethics,—in the former case entirely irrespective of the God-consciousness, and in the latter, from the inner nature of the pious Christian consciousness,—with great richness and ingenuity of thought, but also without a rigidly scientific form, and, in a violently-revolutionary originality, in many cases beclouding the Biblical view with foreign thoughts.—*Rothe* shaped his "Theological Ethics" into a system of theosophic speculation, resting upon the philosophy of Hegel and Schleiermacher, but carried out in an unclear originality, covering almost the entire field of Christian doctrine,—constituting a work in which a pious mind, and exotic thoughts deeply endangering the Christian consciousness, go hand in hand.

Although the scientific treatment of the subject-matter of ethics in the earlier and (in the main) Biblical moralists of the nineteenth century, may be regarded as relatively feeble,

yet they have this not to be despised significancy, that in an age almost entirely estranged from Biblical Christianity they kept alive the consciousness of this estrangement, and faithfully held fast to the indestructible bases of Christian Ethics. *Reinhard's* "System of Christian Ethics" (1780–1815) has indeed neither any special depth of thought nor a rigidly scientific form, and contains many insipid and useless discussions, and furnishes no just comprehension of the inner essence of the moral idea; but yet it gives indication of a thorough examination of the Scriptures, and of an unprejudiced observation of real life, furnishing often in detail good and morally earnest discussions, and avoiding all eccentricity. His classification of the whole is poorly adapted to give a clear steadily-progressive development of the subject-matter. In his third edition Reinhard declares himself very decidedly against Kant.—*Flatt* of Tübingen in his "Lectures on Christian Ethics" (published by Steudel in 1823) gives only carefully-compiled, purely Biblical material, without impressing upon it a scientific form.—F. H. C. *Schwarz* of Heidelberg in his "Evangelically-Christian Ethics," 1821, presents ethics in two different forms, in the first volume in a scientific, in the second in an edificatory form, but which is designed to serve at the same time in elucidation of the first,—presenting for the most part a simple evangelical view, brief, clear, but without deeper foundation.

De Wette has furnished a threefold treatment of ethics, which more than the above-mentioned works is imbued with philosophical thoughts (from the stand-point of the Kantian Fries). His "Christian Ethics" (1819) one half of which is occupied by the history of ethics (which is introduced between the general and the special part), is more ingenious than profound, and does not appreciate the full significancy of the evangelical consciousness. His "Lectures on Christian Ethics," 1824, are intended for a wider circle of readers. (His Compendium of Christian Ethics, 1833, is only a brief outline.) With the exception of this rather Rationalistic than evangelical treatment of ethics, Rationalism has, contrary to what might have been expected, produced but very little in the ethical field. The next most noticeable work is *Ammon's* (comp. § 43) later "Hand-book of Christian

Ethics." (1823, '38), scientifically very unimportant, and containing, besides many examples and anecdotes, mostly only commonplace thoughts and mere objective observations, without in any degree going into the depth of the subject.— *Baumgarten-Crusius* in his "Compendium," * breaks already, in many respects, with Rationalism; his work is ill-digested, but in many respects instructive. *Kähler*, in his "Christian Ethics" (1833; a "Scientific Abridgment," 1835) hesitatingly endeavors to rise beyond the Rationalistic stand-point, and gives much that is peculiar, and also much that is superfluous.

Philosophical and theological ethics were treated very profoundly and very peculiarly, but in a manner violently revolutionary and different from all precedent treatment of the subject, by *Schleiermacher;* indeed in no other science does the inner and unmediated scientific dualism of this writer appear so prominently as here. His critical acumen, his restlessly changing and almost fitfully metamorphosing productiveness, showed itself here under the most brilliant forms; but there is for that reason all the greater need of a cautious guarding against being deceived by the arts of his dialectic genius. Introduced into the field of philosophy by the study of the Greeks, and especially of Plato, enthusiastic for Spinoza, and building mostly upon him, but also powerfully incited by Fichte and Schelling, and uniting in himself the collective, anti-historical and anti-Christian culture of his day, Schleiermacher was not able to harmonize his Pantheistic and unhistorical metaphysics with his heart-Christianity, which latter, though sometimes drooping and wounded, yet grew constantly more and more vital with the advance of his years; he left these two forces standing side-by-side in his soul, and honestly entertained and expressed religious convictions with which his philosophical opinions stood in irreconcilable antagonism; and it would be a great mistake to undertake to interpret the ones by the others. Schleiermacher did not rise above this inner dualism,— a state which not every mind would be able to endure. In his first period, he manifested in the field of ethics a keen critical power, but also as yet great unclearness as to the

* *Lehrbuch*, 1826.

positive essence of Christian morality; and he did not keep
free from some of the serious errors of the uncurbed spirit
of the age. The moral laxity of the "geniuses" then reign-
ing supreme in the world of letters, threw its dusky shadows
also over this mighty spirit. His justificatory "Letters" on
Schlegel's immoral "Lucinde," 1800, were of a nature to be
used, and unfortunately not without ground, by Gutzkow in
countenancing the "rehabilitation of the flesh" which was
then taught by this writer, and in casting reproach upon the
sacredness of wedlock.*—In his "Discourses on Religion,"
1799, which breathe a Spinozistic spirit under the drapery of
poetic rhetoric, Schleiermacher declares also evil as belonging
to, and co-ordinate in, the beauty of the universe. Morality
rests upon religion. In his "Monologues," 1800, which emphasize the ethical phase, there is manifested a bold, high-
aiming self-feeling,—the full, overflowing self-consciousness
of the youthful genius. Self-examination appears here as
the basis and fountain of all wisdom,—not indeed in the
sense, that man is to compare himself in his reality with an
idea or a divinely-revealed law, in order to arrive at humility
and at a consciousness of his need of redemption, but on the
contrary it is an immersing of self in one's own immediate
genial reality as the fountain of all truth and strength,—
a full, self-satisfying enjoyment of self, a pride-inspired self-
mirroring of a nobly-aspiring spirit.† Though this unhumble
spirit of self-enjoying was not peculiar to him, but was
rather the spirit then dominant among the excessively self-
conscious "geniuses" of the day, still there lay therein the
germ of an ethico-scientific peculiarity of Schleiermacher,
as against the Kantian school. In the latter, individual man
is a mere moral exemplar shaped after a general pattern,
merely a single fulfiller of an impersonal moral law, the
essence of which consists precisely in *not* recognizing the
peculiarity of the person, but in throwing it off, and in giving validity only to the general. Schleiermacher maintains,
on the contrary, that every man is to represent humanity in a

* Comp. Vorländer's: *Schleierm.'s Sittenlehre*, p. 69 ; C. H. Weisse
in Tholuck's *Litter. Anz.*, 1835, 408 *sqq. ;* Twesten, in his preface to
Schleiermacher's *Grundriss*, p. 76 *sqq.*

† Compare the dissenting judgment of Twesten, idem, p. 83 *sqq.*

peculiar manner, and that, accordingly, it is the very opposite
of correct to propose to one's self simply the question,
"whether this my maxim is adapted to be exalted into a
law for all men." Even as the artist does not produce an
object of beauty by representing simply abstract, mathematic-
ally-correct forms, but by expressing that which is individu-
ally-peculiar, so is also the moral man to be an artist, an
artist whose task it is to develop himself into a personally
peculiar art-work, and not merely into a monotonous expression of the species. He is not to strip off, but, on the contrary, artistically to develop, his personal peculiarity,—he is
not to cast himself down before duty as a thought different
from his individual personality, but rather on the contrary
"constantly to become more fully *what he is;* this is his sole
desire." Thus Schleiermacher, in opposing the Kantian one-
sidedness, involves himself in the opposite one; both positions are equally true and equally untrue, and the Christian
view stands in the middle-ground between them. If the
Kantian view answers rather to the Old Testament law-system,
then that of Schleiermacher would answer rather to the Christian idea of the freedom of the children of God (at least,
—in case it were applied to spiritually-regenerated children
of God, which, however, is not the case), so that consequently the presentiment of the higher truth turns into untruth,—
into a perilous holding-fast to self, and this all the more so
for the reason that it is absolutely and independently based
upon mere self, for "from within came the high revelation,
produced by no teachings of virtue and by no system of the
sages."

The "Elements of a Criticism of Preceding Ethics," 1803,—
able but in a heavy and often unclear style, and hence more
celebrated than known,—relate only to philosophical ethics,
and discard, in keen but sometimes unjust criticism, all previous methods of treating this science, and present (as opposed
to the more usual method of treating of ethics as the doctrine
of virtues or duties) the doctrine of goods as the basis of the
science, and, hence, ethics as an analysis of the highest good;
the good is the objective realization of the moral. The criticism of the work is applied not so much to the contents as to
the scientific form, and seeks to show that the contents can be

true only when the form is perfect; there is no other criterion of truth in ethics than the scientific form. Plato and Spinoza are esteemed most highly. In explaining away the almost unbounded self-feeling of the author, large account must be made for the spirit of the times; less care is given to the demonstration of his own view than to the many-sided assailing of the views of others.

The "Sketch of a System of Ethics" (published in 1835 by Schweizer, from Schleiermacher's posthumous papers, in an imperfect digest of different sketches ; in a briefer and more general form in 1841 as "Outlines of Philosophical Ethics" with an introductory preface by Twesten) * rests upon the philosophy of Spinoza and the earlier views of Schelling, but contains speculations in many respects peculiar, and not always sufficiently developed. In this philosophical ethics Schleiermacher leaves entirely out of consideration the Christian consciousness, and indeed the religious consciousness in general,—knows nothing of a personal God as moral Lawgiver, nor of an immortal personal Spirit independent of nature ; this religious basis is left so entirely in the background that Schleiermacher (as late as in 1825) answered the question: whence, then, arose in the moral law the idea of a "should," which seems to refer to a commanding will ? by saying, that in the *Jewish* legislation the divine will had been conceived as of a magisterial character demanding obedience; and that this *form* had also been adopted in Christian instruction, and "thus arose the custom of associating with moral knowledge also the 'should,' and this custom was retained even after men had begun to reduce moral knowledge to a general form, wherein there was no longer any reference to an outwardly-revealed divine will, but human reason itself was regarded as the legislating factor." † The two manifestation-forms of God in Spinoza, namely, thought and extension, and the primitive antithesis of Schelling, reappear here as the antithesis of the universe in reason and nature, in the ideal and the real. The highest antithesis in the world is the antithesis of material (known) and of spiritual (knowing) existence. The existence in which the former element predominates

---

* Comp. Vorländer: *Schleierm.'s Sittenlehre*, 1851,—keen and clear but not evangelical.   † *Werke*, iii, 2, 403.

is *nature;* the existence in which the knowing element predominates is *reason,* the two appearing in man as body and soul. Hence reason is essentially knowing, and, in so far as it is self-active, willing. Speculative reason is *ethics,* which has, then, *physics* over against itself, the two embracing the whole field of science, so that ethics appears essentially as the collective philosophy of the spirit,—an entirely unjustifiable deviation from all previous nomenclature.* Ethics presents the collective operation of active human reason upon nature. Hence the aim of moral effort is, the perfect interpenetration of reason and nature, a permeation of nature by reason, and indeed of all nature in so far as standing in connection with human nature. This interpenetration is the highest good,† the sum total of all single goods; it is embodied in the thought of the Golden Age, where man dominated absolutely over nature, and in the thought of everlasting peace, of the perfection of knowledge, and in the thought of a kingdom of heaven, and in a free communion of the highest self-consciousness by means of spiritual self-representation. In the individual the attainment of the moral goal appears as personal perfection, as a perfect unity of nature with intelligence, and hence as a perfect blessedness.—But the unity of reason and nature is to be conceived in a threefold manner: (1) In reference to the *end-point* of the moral striving, namely, the real unity of reason and nature, as the *highest good;* herein is embraced the multiplicity of particular manifestations of said unity, and hence of *good;* this is ethics as the *doctrine of goods* or as the doctrine of the highest good; (2) in reference to the *beginning-point* of the moral striving, namely, the efficiency of reason in human nature, and hence said unity conceived as *power,* that is, as virtue,—the *doctrine of virtue;* ‡ (3) in reference to the relation *between* the beginning-point and the end-point, and hence in the movement of the power toward the goal, and consequently a *modus operandi* of reason in realizing the highest good; this is the *doctrine of duties.§* Hence a threefold

* See his discussion of the difference between natural and moral law: *Werke,* iii, 2, 397.

† *Ueber das höchste Gut,* 1827, '30; *Werke,* iii, 2, 446.

‡ Comp. *Abh. üb. d. Behandlung des Tugendbegriffs,* 1819; idem 350.

§ Comp. *Abh. üb. d. Behandlung des Pflichtbegriffes,* 1824; idem 379.

manner of presenting ethics is possible and necessary ; each
embraces really the whole field of the moral, but as considered
from a different point of view; each, however, refers to the
others. In giving all the goods, one must give at the same
time all the virtues and duties, and the converse. However,
the doctrine of goods is the most self-based and independent,
because it embraces the ultimate goal. "Every definite existence is good in so far as it is a world for itself, a copy of
absolute being, and hence in the disappearing of the antitheses ";* a good is "every harmony of particular phases of reason and nature,"—that wherein " the interpenetration of reason and of nature is independently brought about, in so far as
this unity of reason and nature bears itself like the whole in an
organic manner.†—The doctrine of goods alone is fully developed, while the doctrine of virtue and of duties is treated
but very briefly and meagerly.

In the *doctrines of goods* Schleiermacher distinguishes a
twofold moral activity : (1) In so far as reason exerts itself
upon nature as external to it, it is *organizing*, in that it makes
nature an organ of reason ; (2) in so far as the interpretation
of reason and nature is already posited, the activity of reason
is of a *symbolizing* character, in that it makes itself recogniz-
able in its work. These two activities manifest themselves in
turn in two different manners. In as far, namely, as reason is
the same in all men, in so far also these two activities are alike
in all; but in as far as individual men are originally and in
their very idea different from each other, in so far also is the
activity of an individual character, shaping itself in a peculiar
manner in each individual. This notion of a legitimate personal peculiarity, Schleiermacher emphasizes very strongly,
without, however, really grounding it philosophically.—*Virtue*
expresses itself either as enlivening or as militant: as *enlivening*, it expresses the harmonious union of reason and nature ;
as *militant*, it overcomes the resistance of nature ; under another phase it is either *cognoscitive* or *representative ;* thus we arrive
at four cardinal virtues:—the enlivening virtue as cognoscitive
or representative is *wisdom* or soundness of judgment; as representative it is *love ;* the militant virtue as cognoscitive is *pru-*

* *System*, p. 54.   † Ibid., p. 72.

dence; as representative it is *persistence.* (In his academical Dissertation on the notion of virtue, Schleiermacher varies in form somewhat from his System of Ethics.)—The very unequal carrying out of the subject in detail presents, together with great acumen, also much unsound and fruitless sophistry; the brilliant thoughts shoot forth in every direction in sharp-cut crystal-gleams before the dazzled eye of the beholder, but often only to dissolve themselves suddenly again into a state of formless fluidity. The interrupted, incomplete, un-uniform presentation, as given in the hastily-edited edition, render the reading of this work very difficult, and the ethical results appear by no means so rich as, from the pretensions of the system, one might be led to expect; and it is often impossible to resist the impression that the work abounds in unprofitable sophistry. The academical Essays that belong here, though ably developed, present after all but mere fragments of the whole.

A wholly different picture is furnished by the *Theological* Ethics, which was edited by Jonas in 1843, from Schleiermacher's posthumous papers, and from notes written by his hearers, under the title: "Christian Ethics according to the Principles of the Evangelical Church." * The idea of the moral is developed from the Christianly-determined self-consciousness; hence ethics is the analysis and presentation of the Christian self-consciousness, in so far as the same tends to pass over into act. The moral subject is not considered as a mere isolated individual, but predominantly as being a member of the Church, and as influenced by the spirit of the Church. The state of the human self-consciousness as in communion with God through Christ, is salvation and blessedness. This salvation, however, is primarily merely an incomplete but progressive one, seeing that we are always still in need of redemption; hence our life is a constant alternation of pleasure and unpleasure, and therein lies an "impulse" to activities in view of arriving at true blessedness. In unpleasure lies the impulse to a manner of action whereby the momentarily-disturbed normal state is to be restored, that is, a *restorative* or *purifying* manner of action; in pleasure lies the impulse to a manner of action which subordinates a lower life-power (as willingly yielding itself to a higher one) directly and without any resistance to the higher

* *Die christliche Sitte,* etc.

one, thus educating the lower power, and, hence, deepening and extending the harmony of the two,—the *deepening* and *extending* manner of acting. Both manners of acting aim at effecting something, at bringing about a change, and, hence, constitute unitedly the *operative* form of action, whereby man is to pass from one condition into another. The *purifying* form of action relates primarily to Christian communion, and appears as Church-discipline and as Church-reform (reformatory action); and then again, in relation to civil society, as domestic discipline, as the administration of civil justice, as State-reformation, and as purifying action in the relation of one state to another.—The *extending* form of action, which is essentially the educating of the, as yet lower, but willing life through the higher, takes place primarily in the sphere of the *Church*, —aims to widen and intensify the efficaciousness of the Holy Spirit as dwelling in the Church, and of Christian sentiment. This presupposes the propagation of the human race, the production of human personalities. Hence the extending form of activity in the Church is primarily the communion of the sexes, and then the inner extending and heightening of the life of the Church. Then also the extending form of action relates to the *state*, and looks to the training of all human talents, and to the transforming of nature for the spirit,—in both cases as one common act of all the individuals belonging to the human race, and hence a maturing of all the citizens through spiritual and material commerce; (in this connection it is treated of property, of trade, of money, etc.). This is the first part of ethics, that which embraces the operative form of action.

Now, between the moments of pleasure and unpleasure there occur moments of satisfaction (and which are consequently distinguished from those of pleasure), that is, of relative blessedness, the fundamental feeling proper of the Christian, and which is at the same time also an impulse to acting. This acting, however, aims not at effecting a change, but only at revealing itself outwardly, at making known its condition of happiness to others, and hence is not an operative but a *representative* acting. The operative form of acting is only the way for attaining to the perfect dominion of the spirit over the flesh, that is, to the feeling of blessedness; and the active

expression of this feeling and of this dominion is the representative form of action, which manifests this inner self-consciousness by means of communion with others, and hence
from motives of love. The essence of love is the inner necessity of the constant intercommunion of self-consciousness as
separated by personality,—rests upon communion, and develops it to a higher degree. Although the representative form
of action takes its rise from the communion of the subject with
God, yet this communion is mediated by the Holy Spirit that
dwells in the Christian society. Hence the representative form
of action relates primarily to the evangelically-religious communion,—is *divine worship*, or the sum total of all actions
whereby we present ourselves as organs of God by means of
the Holy Spirit; it embraces, in the wider sense, also the virtues of chastity, patience, endurance, humility, in so far as in
them is manifested the dominion of the flesh over the spirit.
Then again, this form of action relates to general human
communion, which is the outer sphere of this action, as divine
worship is the inner, in other words, the sphere of *social* life,
the representative form of action in the intercourse of men, as
not immediately connected with Christian communion, not,
however, as an operative form of action, but predominantly
merely as beholding and enjoying. In this connection, Schleiermacher considers, first, the social life proper, and particularly social intercourse in eating and drinking under circumstances of luxury and decoration, and, then, art, and lastly
play.

However much we may admire the creative genius whereby
Schleiermacher endeavored to establish and carry out his
highly peculiar classification of ethics, still in reality we cannot but declare it as unadapted and unsuccessful; and, in
spite of the great and almost idolizing admiration shown by
the public for the skillful thought-artist, this piece of art has
not succeeded in calling forth any imitation. At the very first
glance one recognizes the utter unnaturalness of making Christian ethics begin with Church-discipline and Church-reforma-
tion, and close with the subject of play; while, in the second
part, is presented the widening form of action in Church-communion, and, in the third, the ecclesiastical worship of God,—
as also the unnaturalness of placing sexual communion along-

side of Church-communion as simply its presupposition, and
of treating it only subsequently to the discussion of Church-
discipline and domestic discipline,—and of treating of four
Christian virtues, in isolation from all the others, under the
head of divine worship, and among them that of chastity,
which of course falls under the head of sexual communion,
whereas in fact all and every other of the Christian virtues
might with just as good right be treated under the rubric of
divine worship. The chief subdivisions of Christian acting as
purifying, extending and representative acting, cannot by any
means be sharply separated from each other; on the contrary,
in each one of them also the other is necessarily involved; the
extending or distributive acting is not possible otherwise than
by a representing. At all events the purifying activity could
not be the first, for the obtaining and confirming of life-communion with God must, as moral activities, precede the purifying of the already-obtained communion. The feelings of
pleasure and displeasure are, as pure states of experience, not
by any means *per se* the bases of the Christianly-moral activity; both feelings may *per se* be just as readily immoral as
moral; and the first moral striving must be directed to the end
that the pleasure and displeasure themselves be moral, whereas
they are here presupposed unconditionally as " impulses " to the
moral; but this system of ethics is not written for saints (who
might indeed be regarded as determining themselves by the
simple feeling of pleasure or unpleasure *per se*), since it sets
out with a purifying form of action, relating to the subject
himself. It is true, Schleiermacher brings this pleasure and
displeasure into relation to communion with God; but the
apostle distinguishes, also in the saints, a pleasure and a displeasure in this God-communion (Rom. vii, 22 sqq.); hence if
there exists also in the Christian, before his final perfection, as
yet an unpious pleasure and an unpious displeasure, it follows
that the moral striving must in fact direct itself primarily upon
this pleasure and unpleasure. Furthermore, the entirely unusual separating of the pious pleasure-feeling and of the blessed-
ness-feeling (so fully that two chief-divisions of ethics are based
thereupon), is neither justifiable nor practical. The objective
goal of the moral activity, that is, the doctrine of moral good,
is rather presupposed than developed. Knowledge or Chris-

tian wisdom is thrown quite disproportionately in the background, behind the subjects of feeling, of disposition, and of acting. In general we find, notwithstanding the great dialectic art employed, especially in the analysis of ideas, still quite frequently an indefiniteness and unfruitfulness of the moral ideas in their practical significancy,—an excessive prominence of the subjective peculiarity and a corresponding unprominence of a simple Biblical spirit. The ecclesiastical element with which, from unecclesiastical quarters, Schleiermacher has been reproached, is in fact reduced in him to its merest minimum. "With the exception of the free activity of the Holy Ghost *nothing* is to be regarded as absolutely fixed by the Holy Scriptures, but every thing as accepted only *provisionally*, and to be regarded as remaining subject to a constant revision." All symbolical settlings of doctrine are Romanizing, and must be made revocable.* We cannot see, however, why precisely the activity of the Holy Ghost is to be regarded as an absolutely-established point, and not also subject to a constant revision,—why it is not "revocable"; and just as little can we see why this activity, if it is valid at all, should not lead to a real knowledge of the truth, and hence to a definitively-established knowledge.

Richard *Rothe*, standing in part upon Schleiermacher's stand-point, but also making use of Hegelian and Schellingian philosophy in combination with his own somewhat peculiar and daring form of speculation, furnishes, in his "Theological Ethics" (1845–'49, thoroughly revised, 1867) a system of theosophy embracing also a large portion of dogmatics and even some extra-theological topics, which, however much we may admire its erudition and earnest thought-labor, yet, in view of its wonderful commingling of Christian faith, extra-Christian philosophy and extra-philosophical fantasy, we cannot avoid regarding as a failure. Rothe manifests, in contrast to a large number of more recent speculative theologians, an estimable sense for scientific honesty; and where he deviates from the ecclesiastical and Biblical view (and this occurs in very essential and fundamental things) there he does not disguise the antithesis in fine-sounding words; not every one, however, could succeed

* *Christl. Sitte.*, etc., *Beil.*, p. 184.

so naïvely as Rothe in harmonizing with a pious faith in other respects, such questionable contradictions to the general Christian consciousness as are found, *e. g.*, in his doctrines of the omniscience of God (which he limits to the past, the present, and the necessary), and in his doctrine of the church (which he treats in the spirit of entire anti-ecclesiasticism). His merely-apparently profound and frequently very un-bridled speculations do not constitute a steadily progressive and regularly-developed line of thought, but are in many respects mere plays of thought and fantasy; and it is only after passing through these portions of the work (which, though treated with a certain amateur-fondness, are yet really very unfruitful of ethical results, and are presented in a not unfrequently sadly misused language), that we enter, in the third part, upon a frequently excellent, beautifully-presented, and really ethical current of thought, though not without also occasionally meeting with surprising eccentricities. Rothe's view of ethics as a science we have already men-tioned (§ 3, § 4).—The moral task of man is, by virtue of his free self-determination, to appropriate material nature to his own personality; hence the idea of the moral is: "the real unity of the personality and of material nature, a unity as im-pressed upon nature by the personality itself in virtue of its nature-determining functions, or, the unity of the personality and of material nature as the appropriatedness of the latter to the former." Morality is an independent something along-side of piety, and rests by no means upon piety,—is entirely co-ordinate to and independent of it. Ethics falls into three divisions: it considers (1) the moral as being a product, that is, the pure and full manifestation of the moral in the un-folded totality of its special moments and of their organiza-tion into unity, that is, the moral world in its completeness —the *doctrine of goods.* The good is the normal real unity of the personality and of material nature, the appropriatedness of the latter to the former. Here Rothe considers, first, the highest good as an abstract ideal, irrespective of sin; (in this connection are treated also of six forms of moral communion, of which the highest and most comprehensive is the State, which is ultimately destined to embrace all moral life, and to absorb the communion of piety, namely, the church, into

itself; the church has only a transitional significancy, but the state a higher, permanent one). Hereupon follows a complete treatment of eschatology. The other, next-following, phase is the highest good in its concrete reality; here it is treated, first, of sin, as something inhering in human nature, and hence necessary and originally co-posited in the divine world-plan; and, then, of redemption, where a complete doctrine of redemption is presented. (2) The causality or power bringing forth this product, that is, virtue, and hence the *doctrine of virtue*, is treated of in the second part, and, in connection therewith, also the corresponding un-virtues. (3) As this power is a self-determining one, hence there is need of a determined formula of the moral product, namely, a moral law, by the observing of which, on the part of the producing moral power, the real production of the moral world is conditioned, namely, the *doctrine of duties*, which in turn falls into the doctrine of self-duties and the doctrine of social duties.—In the two first and rather speculative parts of the work, Rothe treats of many things which one would not look for in a work on ethics, *e. g.*, of pure matter, of space and time, of extension and motion, of atomic attraction and repulsion, of gravity, of fluidity, of crystallization, of vegetation, of comets, and the like; these digressions into the sphere of natural philosophy belong among the oddities of the work. The excessively artificial schemata are repeated in constant and very strange application, the quadropartite division being throughout observed, even though the observing of it requires the invention of entirely new definitions and new words; and not unfrequently are found entirely useless and profitless splittings of ideas. The chief fault of this work, however, seems to us to lie in the fact, that it unhesitatingly lays at the foundation of Christian Ethics, theories which are utterly foreign to the Christian world-theory, such as that of the philosophical ethics of Schleiermacher, which, however, Schleiermacher himself declared to be inapplicable to Christian ethics. Rothe's notion of the moral is endurable only in a philosophical system such as Schleiermacher's; and, even there appearing only as an oddity, is not only *per se* entirely unsound, but also utterly in contradiction to the entire evangelico-ethical consciousness. This consciousness has as

its moral goal something utterly other than the appropriating of *material* nature to the personal nature; the kingdom of God has with this nature primarily and essentially nothing to do.

The other more recent writers on ethics keep themselves more independent of recent philosophy. The work of Harless: "Christian Ethics" (since 1842 in five almost similar editions; the sixth edition, 1864, greatly enlarged), is a brief, able and purely-Biblical treatise,—practical, purely-evangelical and well written; but the scientific form is faulty; the ideas are not sharply distinguished nor always held fast to; the clearness is more frequently appearance than reality; the development of thought is neither vigorous nor uninterrupted; the classification (salvation-good, salvation-possession, salvation-preservation) is not capable of being kept distinct; the second and third parts overlap each other, for there is no possession without preservation; and what appears here as preservation is in fact possession; the general introduction is insufficient, and Harless himself says of his book, that it contains "no trace of a system." *—The work of *Sartorius*: "The Doctrine of holy Love, or Elements of Evangelico-Ecclesiastical Moral Theology," (third edition, 1851–'56), is intended for the general public, and is not a scientific treatise, nor yet a book of edification; but it goes beyond the limits of mere ethics, and embraces love in the widest sense; hence it treats also of the love of God to himself, and of its realization in the Trinity, and to man,—also of creation and redemption, thus combining much dogmatical matter with ethics. The spirit of the work is purely evangelical, of ardent faith—enlivened and enlivening. The discussion, however, remains mostly in the sphere of the general; the individual moral phenomena are neither completely nor closely examined.—(W. Böhmer: "Theological Ethics," 1846–'53).—C. F. *Schmid's* "Christian Ethics," edited by Heller, 1861, is of a truly Biblical spirit,—earnest, judicious, and giving evidence of Christian life-experience; the scientific classification and form are not happy—are not derived from the subject-matter, but outwardly thrown upon it; many weighty points are omitted, and the manner of treatment is unequal.—*Palmer's* "Ethics of Christianity,"

* *Vorr. z. 6 Au. XV.*

1864, is an outline destined for wider, cultivated circles; the view taken is sound and evangelical, morally earnest and judicious, and the style pleasing, light, and untechnical.— T. *Culmann's* "Christian Ethics," first part, 1864, is based upon Baader's theosophy, and is in sharp antithesis to all rationalistic superficiality, although, notwithstanding its many ingenious and even profound thoughts, it strays away into many, and even anti-Scriptural, assumptions and dreamy brain-fancies.

SECTION XLIX.

The ethics of the *Roman Catholic* Church since the dissolution of the Order of the Jesuits has been becoming, even in the circles which stood in connection with this Order, considerably more cautious; in other respects it has been treated (when not casuistical) principally on the basis of Thomas Aquinas. The influence of recent philosophy has made itself in many respects apparent; in part, there has been also a noticeable approximation to the evangelical consciousness, without, however, rising beyond a hesitating half-way position. The ground-character of the Romish church as distinguished from the evangelical, namely, its tendency to conceive the moral predominantly under the form of *law*, whereas the latter conceives it more as *virtue*, remains the same even up to the present.

During the last two centuries the ethics of the Roman Catholic church has made decided advances toward the better. The growing indignation against the perversion of the same by the Jesuits rendered even the Jesuits themselves more cautious, although also the works of the earlier Jesuits have been very largely in use up to most recent times. Alphonzo de *Ligorio's Theologia moralis*, since 1757, (an enlargement of the work of Busenbaum), is yet to-day one of the most highly prized hand-books of ethics; (on it are

based the works of Waibel: "Moral Theology," 1841–'47, and of Scavini: "*Theologia Moralis*," ninth edition, 1863.) The Jesuit Stattler of Ingolstadt (*Ethica christiana communis*, 1791) taught, however, pretty boldly the old principles of the Order; whereas, on the other hand, the opposition thereto was growing more emphatic, and has resulted in bringing about a purer moral view. The moralists who based themselves on the Scholastics, especially on Thomas Aquinas, have been very numerous; (Besombes, from and after 1709; Amort, 1739, '58, who wrote also a system of "Casuistry," 1733, '62; Tournely, 1726 and subsequently; Concina, 1745; Patuzzi, 1770; and others); of the large number of ethical works, however, only a few have any thing original; the majority simply compile from their predecessors.—Under the influence of Kant, wrote Isenbiehl (1795), Muttschelle (1801, Schenkl (1803), and others; Riegler's "Christian Ethics," 1825, rests in part on Schenkl, and is much used, though scientifically unimportant. Braun, in his "System of Christian Catholic Ethics," (1834), and Vogelsang in his "Compendium" (1834), applied the philosophy of Hermes to ethics. *Sailer's* "Hand-Book of Christian Ethics," (1818, '34) is of a very mild and generally evangelical spirit; and the approximation to a purer evangelical view, though often somewhat infected with Rationalism, shows itself also in other more recent moralists. *Hirscher's* "Christian Ethics" (1835, fifth edition, 1851) is doubtless scientifically the most important, and its general view is largely based on essentially evangelical principles; distinctively Romish views are in many cases very much modified and, advocate-like, idealized and brought nearer to evangelical views; this, however, is not accomplished without some sophistry. Also Stapf ("Christian Ethics," 1841; *Theologia Moralis*, fourth edition 1836) endeavors to shape the older ethics more Biblically; Jocham's "Moral Theology," 1852, is simple and clear; Martin, 1850–'51; Werner, 1850.

These improvements of Romish ethics do not succeed, however, in changing its ground-character as in contrast to evangelical ethics; the notion of the meritoriousness of human works as co-working toward salvation is not yet overcome,—virtue is not mere thanks, but it establishes claims; the moral life is not

the spontaneously-out-streaming radiance of the faith-inspired
loving soul, but it is a something yet distinct from faith and relatively independent,—a laborious working upon salvation as only
associatedly conditioned by faith, but not yet really obtained.
The divine will has not as yet become an inner property of the
believing soul in spiritual regeneration, but simply still hovers
before it as a something other from and objective to it; hence
the largely predominant character of legality in Romish ethics,
even where, on the basis of Thomas Aquinas, the form of
the doctrine of virtue is chosen.　And here is manifestly the
reason why the Romish form of theology has produced a far
richer ethical literature than the Evangelical, seeing that in
the Romish Church not merely the scientific but also the practical need for moral instructions and rules, is much greater
than in the sphere of the Evangelican consciousness, which latter is no longer "under the law," and has consequently in ethics
less a practical than a purely scientific interest.　To the Catholic the Gospel is essentially also a new *law*,—simply a further-
development of the Old Testament law; and it is the task of
ethics to digest this new legislation and shape it more or less
into a statutory form; only to a Romish moralist is it possible
to take up into a treatise on ethics a civil criminal code, as
Stapf has done, in detailed thoroughness, with the Austrian.
The Christian never succeeds, here, in bearing in himself the
Divine will otherwise than in a law *learned* by study; the law
and the moral subject still continue exterior to each other, and
the former is objective to the latter; to act according to the
authority of an outward law appears as a special merit; the
law interpenetrates not the human soul, and the soul not the
law; there remains between the two an impassable gulf; hence
the law and the person content themselves, at last, with the
outward; obeying outweighs loving; and loving is never a
merit, as obeying, however, may be.　Because of the placing of
faith simply *along-side* of works, there lacks to the moral the
unitary center-point in the heart, and hence the good appears
predominantly as a *plurality* of virtues, and the moral life predominantly as a countless sum of single cases; hence in Romish
ethics the predominance of the casuistical treatment, which is
not yet thrown aside even in the most recent treatises; the
thought of ethics awakes at once in the Catholic's mind the

notion of a *Summa casuum;* also, in this respect, we see a manifestation of the predominant character of externality. The notion of a God-sonship manifesting itself in a new free life never comes to full appreciation in Romish ethics; the notion of a son of the Church is, in it, much more familiar; and here at once the ecclesiastical State, with its legal character, steps into the fore-ground of the moral life.

END OF HISTORY OF ETHICS.

Books for the Family,

PUBLISHED BY NELSON & PHILLIPS,

805 Broadway, New York.

BIOGRAPHY.

Abbott, Rev. Benjamin,
Life of. By Rev. J. FFIRTH. 18mo......................... $0 55

Anecdotes of the Wesleys.
By Rev. J. B. WAKELEY. Large 16mo 1 25

Asbury and his Coadjutors.
By WM. C. LARRABEE. 2 volumes........................ 2 25

Asbury, Francis, Life and Times of;
or, The Pioneer Bishop. By W. P. STRICKLAND, D.D. 12mo. 1 75

Bangs, Rev. Dr. Nathan,
Life and Times of. By Rev. ABEL STEVENS, LL.D.......... 1 75
Half morocco 2 25

Biographical Sketches of Methodist Ministers,
By J. M'CLINTOCK, D.D. 8vo. Imitation morocco........ 5 00

Boehm's Reminiscences,
Historical and Biographical. 12mo.................... 1 75

Bramwell, Life of William,
18mo.. 0 60

Cartwright, Peter, Autobiography of,
Edited by W. P. STRICKLAND, D.D. 12mo....... .... 1 75

Carvosso, Life of,
18mo.. 0 75

Celebrated Women, Biographies of,
With twenty-eight splendid Engravings on steel, executed
by the best American artists. Imperial 8vo. Printed on
beautifully tinted paper. Turkey morocco, gilt edge and bev-
eled boards.. 20 00

Chalmers, Thomas,
A Biographical Study. By JAMES DODDS. Large 16mo. ... 1 50

BOOKS FOR THE FAMILY—BIOGRAPHY.

Christianity Tested by Eminent Men,
Being Brief Sketches of Christian Biography. By MERRITT CALDWELL, A.M. 16mo.................................... $0 68

Clarke, Dr. A.,
Life of. 12mo.. 1 50

Clarke, Dr. Adam,
Life of. New. By J. W. ETHERIDGE, M.A. 12mo......... 1 10
Half calf.. 9 35

Clark, Rev. John,
Life of. By Rev. B. M. HALL. 12mo................... 1 25

Cromwell, Oliver,
Life of. By CHARLES ADAMS, D.D. 16mo................ 1 25

Dan Young,
Autobiography of. By WM. P. STRICKLAND, D.D. 12mo... 1 75

Early Crowned.
A Memoir of MARY E. North. 16mo.................... 1 25

Emory, Bishop,
Life of. By R. EMORY. 8vo.......................... 1 70

Episcopius,
Life of. By FREDERIC CALDER. 12mo.................. 1 20

Fletcher, John,
Life of. By Rev. JOSEPH BENSON. 12mo.............. 1 25

Fletcher, Mrs. Mary, Life of,
By Rev. H. MOORE. 12mo............................. 1 50

Garrettson, Rev. Freeborn,
Life of. By NATHAN BANGS, D.D. 12mo............... 1 95

Gatch, Rev. P.,
Sketch of. By JUDGE M'LEAN. 16mo................. 1 90

Gruber, Jacob,
Life of. By W. P. STRICKLAND, D.D. 12mo.......... 1 76

Hamline, Bishop,
Life and Letters of. 12mo......................... 2 25

Hedding, Bishop,
    Life and Times of. By D. W. CLARK, D.D. Large 12mo. . $2 25
    Gilt 2 75
    Half calf.. 3 00

Heroes of Methodism,
    By J. B. WAKELEY. 12mo........ . ... 1 75

Levi , Samuel,
    Biography of. 12mo. 1 25

Lives of the Popes.
    12mo...... .... 1 75

Maxwell, Lady,
    Life of. By Rev. JOHN LANCASTER. 12mo.......... ...... 1 25

Methodism, Women of,
    By Rev. ABEL STEVENS, LL.D. 12mo 1 50
    Gilt edge... 2 00

Moore, Rev. Henry,
    Life of. By Mrs. R. SMITH. 12mo........................ 0 90

Mother of the Wesleys, the.
    By Rev. JOHN KIRK. 12mo.............................. 2 00

Nelson, John,
    Journal of. 18mo.. 0 50

New England Divines,
    Sketches of. By Rev. D. SHERMAN. 12mo................. 1 75

Ouseley, Rev. Gideon,
    Memoir of. By Rev. W. REILLY. 18mo................... 0 65
    Gilt... 1 25

Pillars in the Temple;
    Or, Lives of Deceased Laymen of the M. E. Church Distin-
    guished for their Piety and Usefulness. By Rev. W. C.
    SMITH. With an Introduction by C. C. NORTH. Large
    16mo., pp. 366 .... 1 25

Pioneer, Autobiography of a,
    By JACOB YOUNG. 12mo ....· 1 75

Roberts, Bishop,
    Life of. By C. ELLIOTT, D.D. 12mo.................... 1 00

BOOKS FOR THE FAMILY—BIOGRAPHY.

Rogers, Hester Ann,
Life of. 18mo................................ .... $0 65

Smith, Rev. John,
Memoirs of. By Rev. R. TREFFRY. 18mo................' , 75

Successful Merchant, the.
By Rev. WILLIAM ARTHUR, A.M. 16mo..... .... 1 ×

Village Blacksmith, the.
18mo... .... 0 75

Wall's End Miner, the,
Or, A Brief Memoir of the Life of William Crister. By
Rev. J. EVERETT. 18mo..................................) 50

Walker, Rev. G. W.,
Recollections of. By M. P. GADDIS. 12mo................ 1 75

Watson, Rev. Richard,
Life of. By Rev. T. JACKSON. With Portrait. 8vo........ 2 75

Wesley and his Coadjutors.
By Rev. WM. C. LARRABEE. Two volumes. 16mo. 2 25

Wesley Family,
Memoirs of the. By Rev. A. CLARKE, LL.D. 12mo........ 1 75

Wesley, Rev. Charles,
Life of. By Rev. T. JACKSON. With Portrait. 8vo 2 70

Wesley, Rev. John,
Life of. By Rev. RICHARD WATSON. 12mo........ ... ... 1 25

DOCTRINAL.

Admonitory Counsels to a Methodist.
Illustrating the Peculiar Doctrines and Economy of Methodism. By Rev. JOHN BAKEWELL. 18mo................. 0 44

Analysis of Watson's Institutes,
By Rev. JOHN M'CLINTOCK, D.D. 18mo.. ... . 0 53

Angels,
Nature and Ministry of. By Rev. J. RAWSON. 18mo....... 0 35

BOOKS FOR THE FAMILY—DOCTRINAL.

Apology for the Bible.
> A Powerful Antidote to Infidelity. By BISHOP WATSON.
> 18mo.. .... $0 56

Apostolical Succession,
> An ESSAY on. By THOMAS POWELL. 12mo........... ....• 0 10

Appeal to Matter of Fact and Common Sense.
> By Rev. JOHN FLETCHER. 18mo....................... .... 0 55

Baptism,
> Its Subjects, Mode, Obligation, Import, and Relative Order.
> By Rev. F. G. HIBBARD. 12mo............................ 1 75

Baptism,
> Obligation, Subjects, and Mode. An Appeal to the Candid
> of all Denominations, in which the Obligations, Subjects,
> and Mode of Baptism are Discussed. By Rev. HENRY SLICER.
> 18mo.. 0 55

Baptism,
> Obligation, Subjects, and Mode. In two Parts. Part 1.
> Infant Baptism; Part II. The Mode. By H. M. SHAFFER.
> 18mo.. 0 55

Beatitudes,
> Lectures on the. By C. C. CRUM. 12mo.................. 1 00

Benson's Commentary.
> Five volumes., sheep. Imperial 8vo........................ 25 00
> Half calf... 28 00
> Plain calf.. 28 00

Bible Hand-Book,
> Theologically Arranged. By F. C. HOLLIDAY, D.D. 12mo. 1 50

Bible, Index and Dictionary of,
> A Complete Index and Concise Dictionary of the Holy Bible.
> By Rev. JOHN BARR. 12mo............................. 1 00

Butler's Analogy of Religion,
> Natural and Revealed. 12mo............................. 0 60

Calvinism as It Is.
> By RANDOLPH S. FOSTER, D.D. 12mo.............. ..... 1 25

Calvinistic Controversy.
> Embracing a Sermon on Predestination and Election. By
> WILBUR FISK, D.D. 12mo.............................. 1 00

BOOKS FOR THE FAMILY—DOCTRINAL.

Campbellism Exposed,
By WM. PHILLIPS. 18mo......................... ...... $0 70

Christ and Christianity.
A Vindication of the Divine Authority of the Christian Religion, Grounded on the Historical Verity of the Life of Christ.
By WM. L. ALEXANDER, D.D. 12mo...................... 1 50

Christ Crucified.
(Divinity of Christ.) By GEORGE W. CLARKE. 18mo....... 50

Christ of the Gospels, the,
By TULLOCH. 16mo....................................... 1 25

Christian Pastorate,
Its Character, Responsibilities, and Duties. By Rev. DANIEL P. KIDDER. 12mo..................................... 1 75

Christian Perfection,
By Rev. J. FLETCHER. 24mo............................. 0 40

Christian Perfection,
An Account of. By Rev. J. WESLEY. 24mo.............. 0 45

Christian Perfection,
Scripture Doctrine of. By GEO. PECK, D.D. 12mo......... 1 75
Abridged. 18mo.. 0 40

Christian Purity;
Or, The Heritage of Faith. Revised. By RANDOLPH S. FOSTER, D.D., LL.D. 12mo.................................. 1 75

Christian's Manual,
A Treatise on Christian Perfection. By Rev. TIMOTHY MERRITT. 24mo.. 0 49

Christian Theology,
By A. CLARKE, LL.D. 12mo................... ... 1 25

Church Polity,
By BISHOP MORRIS. 18mo 0 40

Church Polity,
Essay on. By Rev. ABEL STEVENS, LL.D. 12mo.......... 1 00

Clarke's Commentary.
Six vols., sheep. Imp. 8vo............................. 30 00
Half calf.. 34 00
Plain calf... 34 00
Turkey morocco, full gilt.............................. 46 00

BOOKS FOR THE FAMILY—DOCTRINAL.

Composition of a Sermon,
Essay on. By Rev. JOHN CLAUDE. 18mo.................. $0 55

Colenso Reviewed,
Fallacies of. By Rev. CHARLES H. FOWLER. 16mo 0 75

Commentary on the Lord's Prayer,
By Rev. W. DENTON, M.A. Large 16mo 1 00

Defense of Jesus,
From the French of Menard St. Martin. By PAUL COBDEN.
16mo 0 75

Defense of our Fathers,
By BISHOP EMORY. 8vo................................... 1 00

Discipline of the M. E. Church,
Changes in, made by the General Conference of 1868.
Pamphlet. 12mo....................................... 0 20

Discipline of the M. E. Church,
Guide in the Administration of the. By BISHOP BAKER.
New Edition. Edited by Rev. WILLIAM L. HARRIS. 16mo.. 1 25

Discipline of the M. E. Church,
History of the. By Rev. ROBERT EMORY. Revised and
brought down to 1864. 12mo............................ 1 50

Doctrines and Discipline of the M. E. Church,
New edition. 1872. 24mo.............................. 0 50
Morocco, tuck, gilt edges.............................. 1 00
12mo. Roan flexible. Red edge......................... 1 25
Morocco flexible. Gilt edge........................... 1 75

Emory, Bishop,
Life and Works of. 8vo................................ 8 00

Episcopal Controversy and Defense,
By BISHOP EMORY. In 1 vol. 8vo....................... 1 20

Episcopal Controversy Reviewed,
By BISHOP EMORY. In one volume. 8vo.................. 0 90

Evidences of Religion ;
The Scientific. By WILLIAM C. LARRABEE. 12mo......... 1 25

Evangelist, the True,
By J. PORTER, D.D. 16mo.............................. 0 66

BOOKS FOR THE FAMILY -DOCTRINAL.

Fairbairn on Prophecy.
Prophecy in respect to its Nature, Function, and Interpretation. 8vo... $3 00

Fletcher, Rev. J., Works of,
Four volumes, 8vo 12 00
Plain calf... 14 00
Half calf.. 4 00

Fletcher's Checks to Antinomianism,
Two volumes. 8vo.. 6 00

Hamline's Works, Bishop,
Vol. 1. Sermons... 2 00
Vol. 2. Miscellaneous 2 00

Harmony and Exposition of the Gospels,
By JAMES STRONG, S.T.D. Beautifully Illustrated by Maps
and Engravings. 8vo...................................... 5 00
Half calf or half morocco................................ 6 00

Harmony of the Divine Dispensations,
By G. SMITH, F.S.A. 8vo 2 00
Half calf or half morocco................................ 4 00

Heaven, Scripture Views of,
By Rev. J. EDMONDSON, A.M. 18mo....................... 0 55

Hibbard on the Psalms.
The Psalms Chronologically Arranged, with Historical Introductions, and a General Introduction to the whole Book. By
Rev. F. G. HIBBARD. 8vo................................ 8 50
Half morocco... 4 50

Historical Confirmation of Scripture,
By WM. BLATCH. 18mo.................................... 0 85

History of the M. E. Church.
Revised Edition. By NATHAN BANGS, D.D. 4 vols., 12mo.. 6 00

Homiletics, a Treatise on,
By DANIEL P. KIDDER, D.D. 12mo........................ 1 11

Homilist, the,
Sermons for Preachers and Laymen. By Rev. ERWIN HOUSE.
12mo 1 75

Horne's Introduction to the Bible.
Abridged edition. 12mo.................................. 1 50